THE ULTIMATE VIOLATION

THE
Ultimate Violation

JUDITH ROWLAND

1985
Doubleday & Company, Inc.
Garden City, New York

Grateful thanks to A. Nicholas Groth and the Plenum Press for kind permission to reprint from *Men Who Rape* by A. Nicholas Groth and H. Jean Birnbaum (New York, Plenum Press, 1979).

Library of Congress Cataloging in Publication Data
Rowland, Judith.
The ultimate violation.
Includes index.
1. Rape—United States. 2. Prosecution—United
States. 3. Rape victims—United States. I. Title.
KF9329.R69   1985   364.1'532   84–13606
ISBN: 0-385-18960-5

For my parents,
Marjorie and Alan Rowland,
who always believed in me

PREFACE

The subject of rape has received considerable attention during the last decade: professionals from many disciplines, and for a wide variety of purposes, have focused on its victims, offenders, causes, preventions, and treatments. As a practical matter, however, neither those who work within the criminal justice system nor the American people have a much better understanding of its complexities than they did before this awakening.

To attribute the lack of insight about rape to an absence of information concerning its victims, offenders, causes, preventions, and treatments is both unfair and inaccurate. There is an ever-growing body of knowledge addressing each of these issues. It is much more a case of, as they say, "the right hand not knowing what the left hand is doing."

My purpose in writing this book, and the need I would hope it fulfills, is to link together the knowledge that many have gathered in semi-isolation while working in their own little corners, so that the results may be shared both among themselves and with the American public. In addition to this primary goal, a reading of the book is intended to continue a process of education and enlightenment for men and women everywhere on a subject so long cloaked in myth and misunderstanding.

In an effort to reach the broadest possible audience—potential jurors, law enforcement personnel, the nation's prosecutors and judges, even mental health professionals, and, certainly, future and past victims —I have tried to write the book in a style similar to the manner in which I spoke to my juries: by eliminating the "wherefores," "hereinafters," "priors," and "subsequentlies" when "so that," "following," "before," and "after" would do far better. If I had been unable to pass along to my juries what I had learned about the dynamics of rape, it would have made little difference that I alone understood the significance of this knowledge. The fact is, I was able to pass it on. I have done my best here to accomplish through the written word what I succeeded in doing with the spoken one.

Another cliché, I suppose, but one which I have found to be more accurate than not, is that truth is often stranger than fiction. The stories of rape told in this book are true. The names of victims, offenders, and other related characters have been changed to protect their privacy. Generally speaking, their names are unimportant—only their stories have meaning. There are exceptions, however, for the names of those people who have pioneered in the field, those who are the experts and have the expertise to pass on to the rest of us. Some of these people include Dr. Ann Wolbert Burgess, Lynda Lytle Holmstrom, A. Nicholas Groth, Pauline Bart, and Drs. Joshua Golden and Marianne Felice. I have had the good fortune to know and to work with each of them during my years in the criminal justice system, as I came to discover that we all need to look beyond the confines of our own lives to find bigger answers. I want to thank these people, not only on my behalf but on behalf of all those who have benefited already, and those who will benefit in the future, from their efforts.

I have chronicled here, in story form, the histories of four rape trials, three of which I myself handled, between 1978 and 1980, while serving as an attorney in the felony division of the San Diego County District Attorney's office.

In combination, these four stories represent a broad selection of victims and offenders. Of equal importance, they encompass an even larger assortment of illustrative situational factors, coping and behavior patterns, personal and system reactions. In other words, the reader should come away with a much clearer understanding of what rape is and is not, of who rapes and why, of who become victims versus those who are able to avoid being victimized, of options for coping and strategies for prevention, and, finally, what should be happening in a rape trial—as opposed to what is happening—in our nation's courtrooms.

Each story is, of course, unique and touches profoundly the lives of those involved in many varied ways because each has brought a distinct set of life situations to the courtroom. On the other hand, each case is much like a variation on a theme: the psychological trauma suffered by victims is the common denominator.

It is primarily to the women who are victims of this most outrageous and humiliating crime that I address this book: to them and to the nation's criminal justice system, whose prosecutors and judges not only must deal with the mechanical and legal aspects of the aftermath of rape but must learn to understand better why rape occurs and what it does to its victims in order to do their own jobs better.

Long after the physical injuries have healed, and even more so when there are none in the first place, the emotional scars of rape linger on. It is this emotional aspect of rape, and the toll it exacts from its victims, which is by far the least understood by the public in general, by the criminal justice system and its prosecutors, and even by the victims themselves. I have often had women approach after hearing me speak, and for the first time confide that they were themselves victims of rape as long as thirty and forty years before; that they have lived with the confusion, the shame, the guilt, the helplessness, only now coming to understand the reasons.

In looking for answers to questions generated within the criminal justice system, I found a need to turn elsewhere, outside the system. It was as a result of this search that I discovered evidence of various oft-repeated coping strategies used by rape victims in the face of attack. I, too, had found this in my trial work. I also, and most significantly, found the results of research which describe what its discoverers came to call the rape trauma syndrome. This syndrome consists of what have been found to be clusters of symptoms, following certain patterns and phases, suffered, to a greater or lesser degree, by virtually all women who have been victims of rape.

With this knowledge came the dawn of my work with rape cases in the courtroom. Over a period of three years, from 1978 through 1980, I managed to fit the information found in this newly discovered research into a legal framework, and to make it available to juries in rape cases as a tool in helping them decide the credibility of a rape victim.

The basic premise is simple: the defendant claims consent, the victim reports force. If an expert can educate a jury about rape trauma syndrome and explain how this particular victim suffers from the symptoms, then should it not be beneficial to a jury when evaluating two versions—consent versus rape—in reaching a verdict? Indeed, that is exactly what happened. Jurors were quick to understand the concept and to evaluate credibility in light of the evidence when armed with this knowledge.

What I have accomplished in the courtroom can be learned by others. I call it the multidisciplinary approach to rape within the criminal justice system. It requires the cooperation of three integral component parts: (1) law enforcement (police officers, detectives, and their investigators); (2) criminal justice (prosecutors and judges); and (3) mental health (rape crisis counselors, doctors, nurses, psychologists, and psychiatrists). Each must have a thorough understanding of the responsibilities of its role and, in addition, have a working knowledge of the other two. All three parts must move together to make it work for the victim—whether or not she chooses the courtroom as her arena.

In fact, once all the parts are working together, it is likely that more women will report their rapes, more prosecutions will be initiated, and more offenders will be convicted. I have found this to be true, certainly in my case. The numbers in each of the above categories are, at present, abysmally low—unlike the projected numbers of victims: it is currently estimated that one in every three women in the United States will sometime during her life become the victim of a rape.

When I first began this book, I had recently left the District Attorney's office and writing about my experiences served as a much-needed catharsis. While the goals and purposes were even then as I have described them here, I felt frustrated and even betrayed by the criminal justice I had supported for eight long years. Once I had left the District Attorney's office, I was better able to view things from the vantage point afforded by the separation of both time and distance. I noticed a gradual, but significant change in my thinking. Now, some three and a half years down the road, I no longer embrace the "them against me" attitude which working as one of only four or five women in an office of over 150 men can understandably create. In some ways, it was a "them and me" situation, but not so black and white as I saw it at the time. Then, it was men fighting women trying to do the job of men in a still predominantly male profession. Again, while that was certainly a factor, the "bigger picture" must take into account the all-important "perspective" from which things were seen.

What I brought with me to the prosecutor's office in the early 1970s was a woman's perspective on life experiences; that and a singular failure to understand how the corporate game was played, I might add. It is only natural that the men—lawyers, judges, even male jurors—brought to the legal profession and the criminal justice system a whole set of life experiences of their own, based on the perspective of the male.

It is not now surprising that I failed to recognize during all those years that the problem was not just the *fact* that I was a woman, but that I truly saw, evaluated, understood, and then responded to life experiences from a completely different vantage point. I do not now mean that there wasn't also a lot of plain old-fashioned discrimination. But the failure of the legal system—from its lawyers, through all levels of its courts, right up to and including the United States Supreme Court—to understand what neither they nor I were aware of is forgivable. Through this book, I hope to give some insight into the phenomenon, in the hope that false assumptions will no longer cause the woman's perspective to remain invisible to legal analysis.

Historically and traditionally, the law and the legal profession have defined rights, responsibilities, duties, and privileges in terms of the needs of men. Only as they were the subjects or objects of the laws did women figure into the system; only as property did they attain any status of their own. Nowhere was this more evident than in the treatment of rape; women were victims only secondarily. It was the men who owned them who were considered the primary victims, and it was their rights the laws had been designed to protect; in order to discourage violations of these rights, punishments were meted out to the offenders.

Lest I be accused of being discriminatory, I will mention that I realize rape victimization is not confined to women. Men, too, fall prey to this trauma. In fact, because of our sociocultural heritage, male rape victims may be even more severely traumatized emotionally than women. More needs to be done, certainly, to understand this phenomenon. But my book is for the hundreds of thousands of women who, because of this same sociocultural heritage, have for centuries suffered unjustly a stigma of guilt and shame. From the perspective of a woman and the training of a lawyer, I have chosen to challenge this stigma.

When the time comes to thank the people who have helped along the way in an effort of this magnitude, one always fears somebody important will be left out. Hopefully I shall not be guilty of that.

First I would like to acknowledge the San Diego County District Attorney's office for providing me with a forum for our mutual learning experience. Without both of us, the end result could not have been this rich and rewarding. Further, the National District Attorneys' Association, of which Mr. Miller is the immediate past president, has been, and will continue to be, a strong voice for victims' rights. I am certain this book heralds only the beginning of our joint efforts to focus national attention on America's overlooked victims and to make the criminal justice system our chosen arena for victim advocacy.

To the victims with whom I worked, and who allowed me free rein with their lives for periods of months at a time, this book is offered as a tribute to their bravery. And to the Honorable Carlos Cazares, the late T. Bruce Iredale, and especially William Low, judges of the San Diego County Municipal Court and Superior Court, I offer my thanks for their courage to accept new and innovative concepts into an old and traditional system.

When I first thought this book ought to be written, it was not my intent to do the writing myself, but only to tell the story to a "real writer" and to have that someone else write the book. With the combined encouragement of a fellow writer, Elaine Mueller, and my editor, Lisa Drew, I finally gathered the courage to do it myself.

The book could not have been completed without the efficiency and good humor of my manuscript typist, Donna Araujo, my office assistant, Richard Fischer, and my secretary, Cynthia Molinar.

My "home editorial staff," as I have come to refer to them, consisted of my sister, Melanie Rowland, and my husband, Steven Golbus. I did not always like what they had to tell me, but listening to them usually paid off.

Finally, to my children, Kirsten and Justin, I want to acknowledge that it was not easy to hear Mom say for over three years, "Not now, I have to write!" I am hopeful that in the future both of them will find the results worthwhile.

*Rape is an act of violence and humiliation in which the victim experiences overwhelming fear for her very existence, as well as a profound sense of powerlessness which few other events in one's life can parallel. . . . Rape is best understood in the context of a crime against the person and not against the hymen. Short of homicide, rape is the "ultimate violation of the self." ***

—Elaine Hilberman, M.D.,
American Journal of Psychiatry,
April 1976

* The term "ultimate violation of self" first appeared in "Crisis Intervention: An Investigation of Forcible Rape," *Police Chief,* 1974, by Katherine White-Ellison, Ph.D., and Morton Bard, Ph.D.

THE ULTIMATE VIOLATION

1

IT WAS FIVE MINUTES to ten in the morning when the elevator doors opened and the large "Superior Court" sign hanging on the wall announced my arrival on the third floor. I turned down the long corridor and could see Department 14 some one and a half blocks away. How many times I had made this same journey before, the rape victim beside me, the jury selected, and with a scribbled opening statement on top of the stack of books and papers I carried.

Sandy was holding up well as she kept pace with me.

"Take a deep breath, try to relax, don't let the defense bait you, and give me time to object to his questions." All were last-minute reminders for her as we approached the courtroom where she would within minutes be sworn and take the witness stand for what I knew were to be many hours of anguish as she relived that August night of terror when she had been raped by a roommate's friend.

What am *I doing here?* My thoughts were always the same in these last moments before trial. My feet continued to carry me toward the courtroom, while my mind attempted to hustle them in the opposite direction.

Why do I keep doing this? I must be crazy! My answers, too, were always the same: *Because there's nowhere else you would rather be going than into that courtroom to face a jury on a rape case.*

Especially this one. I took a deep breath and held the door open for Sandy. She accepted my smile of encouragement. We were ready for the People.

At one o'clock on the afternoon following the attack on Sandy, I was shuffling through papers on my desk, fighting back post-lunch yawns and looking for the surge of energy that would take me through the afternoon. It had been a particularly sultry August, bringing not only the traditional hot, dry Santa Anas but also a mixture of heavy, moisture-laden tropical storms swirling up from Mexico.

Outside, downtown San Diego dawdled in the early-afternoon heat. Close to the breezy harbor, the weather was not quite oppressive, but only a few minutes inland, tempers and temperatures rose sharply. Nighttime in particular brought increased discontent as the humid air hung trapped inside houses unaccustomed to the becalmed cycle characteristic of this peculiar weather pattern after dark. Open windows invited both hope of relief from the windless air and fear of unwanted intrusion.

Violence leapt noticeably during weather like this. Confrontations between spouses, assaults upon children and against strangers—all requiring the attention of extra-duty police patrols, which were most evident along the boardwalks where beach communities swelled to overflow with those seeking comfort or entertainment.

My case load, too, reflected the trend. On this particular day I was hoping to find time to work on an infant homicide case due to come to trial in October—set up an interview with the victim's grandmother and his seven-year-old brother, who was my only witness; or perhaps get up to the rehab center along with my Philippine interpreter to speak with the victim of a domestic quarrel which had left her paralyzed from the neck down.

I knew, however, that my time could be cut into by any number of things: requests that I review reports or files, or issue a search warrant; calls from harried witnesses in future cases, and when court resumed within an hour several floors below me, last-minute calendars to scan before appearing as the District Attorney's representative at some probation or sentencing hearing.

My cubbyhole office, made to feel more so by the fact that I shared it from time to time with visiting deputies from the Attorney General's staff, looked across the hall into the one occupied by my boss, Daly Bell, chief of the Superior Court trial division. His two secretaries, who were seated at desks between our offices, represented the only other women in the vicinity of my world.

Thank God for Ruth and Carol. Although there was one other female deputy in the felony trial division, she was several corridors away and not readily available when I was suddenly overcome with the need to commiserate in a female fashion from time to time.

Because of its location, my office provided me with a good vantage point from which to keep track of things. It also, however, made me overly accessible to many potential interruptions. It was this very possibility I sat contemplating when Daly appeared in my doorway silhouetted against the light from the window behind the secretaries' desks. He leaned against the doorframe in that unhurried, but purposeful after-lunch way I recognized even before he spoke.

"I've got a case I want you to reject," he began. I knew immediately it was a rape case. Not unwisely, I had to admit, Daly had brought me several complaints during the past year with this introduction, and predictably his review of the facts had left someone—the police detective, the victim, her family, or some combination—less than satisfied with his stated intent not to prosecute.

My dissatisfaction with the District Attorney's attitude toward sexual assault cases and other crimes involving women and children victims was well known both within the office and at the Police Department. It was not unusual for a detective to just happen by my desk on his or her way to Daly's office and casually let the facts fall, wondering if I might be able to "help out" if Daly was looking for someone.

My interest had been first aroused when I was a relatively new prosecutor. As only one of four women attorneys in an office of over a hundred men, I seemed to get a disproportionate number of assignments involving crimes committed against females. At first resistant, I slowly came to see a real need for someone to give considerably more attention to what was—or, rather, was not—happening to these cases.

I would hear another deputy bemoaning the quality of both case and victim as he geared up for battle before a serious trial in a way only those who have ever faced a jury firsthand can truly understand. An atmosphere of tension emanated from his office and I would keep watch for the arrival of a "victim."

From descriptions I had heard of her—"flaky," "loose," "dingy"—I figured I'd probably recognize her right away. These and other designations were so consistent that surely, I thought, there was a particular look characteristic of this kind of victim. I wasn't sure what exactly, but somehow, with experience, I would acquire the ability to tell.

But it never happened, so I decided to see if listening to them testify would teach me how to identify these "types," and I would slip into the back of the courtroom.

Word seemed to get around when a rape victim was about to take the stand, and my heartbeat always quickened when I saw how many strangers she had to face. As she recounted the events of her ordeal, I would follow along, visualizing everything in my mind. Curiously, or so it seemed at the time, I had no trouble understanding why she did, or did not, behave in a particular way.

I would put myself in the place of the witness on the stand, and I would wonder what I would have done; try to talk *my* way out, to run, to scream?

How was she feeling *while this was going on?* I wondered. *What was she* thinking?

No one ever asked her things like that. Only *why* didn't she run, or scream, or fight? To these questions, the most common response was "I don't know."

"She was scared to death," I would whisper to myself. "I'd like to see what *you'd* do." But of course, he could have no idea, could he?

I made a special effort always to remind myself that I was a lawyer and that I must not lose my perspective. I was unsure for a long while whether my roles as advocate and woman were merged inappropriately. I certainly was told they were by both sides.

There is now no doubt that this conflict between my legal training and my gender was illusory. My dilemma was created by the very fact that I was a woman and was approaching problems from a new and different vantage point. Anything new is distrusted. It is clear to me that a woman's perspective in the criminal justice system is essential. At least now it is clear to me. Then it wasn't so easy.

As one of so few women in the San Diego District Attorney's office during the 1970s, I was frequently cast in the role of unwitting spokesperson about crimes affecting women and children. I became increasingly sensitive to community concerns and developed a close relationship with the law enforcement personnel assigned similar tasks. Together we grew to have a mutual respect and then understanding that naturally resulted from continued exposure to assault victims.

Throughout these years, I had many heated debates with the office hierarchy about ways to improve office policy both in and out of the courtroom on cases of sexual assault, domestic violence, and child abuse. By August 1978 everyone knew that if my assessment of a case agreed with Daly's, no further complaints were likely to arise. He had chosen the cases he handled in this manner with considerable care, and I had to admit that he had been accurate so far.

My blessing upon Daly's decision not to prosecute was always given with reluctance. In virtually every instance in which I had told a victim we could not pursue her case, I had believed her story, and had told her so. But my years as a prosecutor had taught me that the emotional damage that comes from losing in the courtroom, heaped upon that already caused by the rape itself, could result in emotional suicide. Because of the *way* many rape cases were handled in the courtroom, they were earmarked for defeat before they got going.

Most women who have been through the process of case evaluation and have been denied prosecution are left with a feeling that no one believes them. Ironically, this is often true even when the case is accepted for prosecution.

The difference between acceptance and rejection of a case rarely lies with the victim herself, but rather turns upon whether the facts she presents fall in such a way as to add up to a "triable case," using outdated and uninformed criteria designed to accommodate many standard crimes, but not rape.

As Daly stood at my door this particular day, I swelled with sudden anger as my afternoon's plans evaporated.

"The detective," he continued "is waiting at the reception desk— with the victim." He handed me the reports and ambled away.

I looked to see which sex crimes detective had been assigned the case. It was Sografo. I figured he did not agree with Daly, and I was right.

Jerry Sografo was every inch the Italian cop his name suggested. He was tall, with rugged good looks, and his earthy Latin qualities were softened by generous streaks of silver in his otherwise jet-black hair and just enough lines in his face to convey an overall appearance of authority and maturity. He spoke with his eyes—and, of course, his hands—in tones which were undeniably persistent but somehow stopped just short of challenge.

I had been both in the courtroom and on the speaker's platform with Sografo. He had seemed an unlikely candidate for the sex crimes detail. Early on I asked him if his arrival at detective status had been somewhat clouded by the nature of his assignment. He admitted he had gone with both feet dragging and with little compassion for or desire to understand the plight of the victim. In fact, he confessed, as a kid growing up, he had walked a fine line between the way of life he now protects and the one he fights daily to protect against. This, coupled with his traditional Italian background, had made the thought of duty as a sex crimes detective particularly distasteful.

He was amazed, he recalled, at how quickly he came not only to listen to but to hear the women whose stories came across his desk. He found it not at all difficult to believe them and was outraged at the attitudes of indifference toward them on the part of both policemen and lawyers.

As he strode into my office on this busy day, I could see Sografo's eyes blazing, although outwardly he appeared calm. He lowered himself into a chair facing my desk.

We usually followed a ritual in these case reviews. He would sit quietly while I read the reports, ready to answer any questions I might pose and speaking first only to bring me up to date on something learned too late to be reflected in the reports or to provide the human element that eludes form 515 in quadruplicate. This time, however, he began to speak before I had arranged the stack in front of me, and after several attempts to quiet him, I gave up.

"Daly asked you to reject this, didn't he?" He shot the words at me in a tone more of fact than of question. I did not reply but he knew the answer.

"Judy, this lady is class. She's credible, she wants to prosecute. I don't buy for a second she'd have anything to do with him."

He looked at me. "He told me one story, then changed it. She's been consistent all along and the witnesses corroborate her."

After reading the ten pages of reports, which included statements of both victim and suspect about what had happened, I gathered the papers and walked the few feet across the hall to Daly's office.

"Not this time, Daly. I don't agree with you."

"For God's sake," he sighed, "she lives and sleeps with a male room-mate, she parades around nude in the house for everyone to admire, she lives in Ocean Beach, she leaves her door unlocked—and she's got herpes."

"You realize," I began as I shook the papers in my hand at him across the desk, "that the facts which you have chosen to believe come

entirely from the statement made by the suspect or have nothing whatsoever to do with rape?"

I could feel my irritation growing and it had to be evident in my
voice.

"What about the *fact* that he also said, 'I told her to spread her legs
and I fucked her . . . I figured since Stan was having sex with her, I
would too. I had been drinking quite a bit and I don't really remember
everything'? How about the *fact* that she ran into the street naked from
the waist down directly into the headlights of an oncoming car? How
about the *fact* that she said she tried to scream and he put his hand
over her mouth? How about the *fact* that she says he forced her to
orally copulate him and he denies it? And how about the *fact* she says
the herpes line was used hoping it would discourage him?"

I shook my head. "She doesn't have herpes, Daly."

I realized as I checked off each item aloud that I was becoming even
more outraged at the thought of how summarily he had treated the
victim's immensely plausible story in contrast to the cavalier statements
made by the suspect. However, he was the boss. I decided to back off a
little.

"I'm going to talk to the victim. I'll be back after that."

While I waited for Sografo to bring the victim to my office, I angrily
shuffled papers around on my desk trying to figure out how today's
priorities could become tomorrow's: I knew the afternoon would be
long gone before this problem was resolved.

I was at that familiar crossroads which preceded every sexual assault,
domestic violence, or child abuse case that started out like this: not yet
dedicated to it, I knew I ran the very great risk of precisely that.
Simultaneously, I was plagued by the temptation to take advantage of
the easy out Daly had given me and by a compelling need to examine
the case beyond the point that was expected, or even wanted. This was
always the most difficult stage of a case for me. Fortunately, it came
first; mercifully, it was brief.

As Sografo introduced Sandra Adkins to me, I was immediately impressed by her poise. Her looks, her clothes, her speech, all indicated—
how had Jerry put it?—class, but her poise carried all the other qualities. She was tall, five feet eight inches, slim, with medium-length
natural strawberry-blond hair and soft blue eyes.

She was fashionably dressed in a mid-calf-length linen skirt and a flowered silk blouse. Her simple gold jewelry was clearly real, and over-all one could see that she gave considerable thought to her appearance. In French she would definitely be *la jeune fille bien élevée.* I liked her instantly. Sografo excused himself, since he knew I preferred to inter-view women alone, unless it appeared I would need a witness to some-thing during our conversation, and then I would send for him.

Despite her appearance of composure, it was clear that Sandra was nervous. She twirled the ropelike strap of her handbag between her fingers throughout our conversation, and displayed a classic and often misinterpreted sign of tension: a frequent and inappropriate laugh which reflected anything but gaiety. Many times I have heard com-ments by jurors, witnesses, and even those who should know better, such as other prosecutors and judges, that their final decisions against victim credibility turned on a giggle or a smile. As I got to know Sandra better, I noticed this characteristic whenever she was ill at ease. It was to be many months before I saw her true smile, which was relaxed and genuine and spread comfortably across her face along lines which ema-nated from the corners of her mouth and eyes.

At this point, I observed, the giggle definitely was a minus in the trial column. My assessment of her courtroom potential was already in overdrive. Her poise, too, might be a double-edged sword. She could be *too* composed for a jury. From my earliest recollections, prosecutors gave a big plus to a rape victim who could cry on the stand; of course, not too much, because it could then be argued she overreacts to every-thing and is therefore given to flights of emotional fantasy.

More than occasionally I've heard a deputy's post-trial lament that the lack of, or overabundance of, tears had signaled defeat for his case. I have seen the powerful impact on jurors of tears at just the right moment, but somehow there seemed something fundamentally wrong with this analysis. I just couldn't put my finger on what it was.

I had considered all these things in only the time it took for Sografo to introduce Sandra and for her to take the seat previously occupied by him.

As angry as I had been with Daly's interpretation of the facts and events in the police reports, I could not deny that the case, on the face of it, could be a defense attorney's delight. The issues virtually jumped off the pages: single girl, twenty-seven—the perfect age for lumping her in with the swinging singles generation—living in a part of town notorious for its freewheeling and drug-dealing way of life, sharing a house with a single male, and, the real clincher, sleeping with this unrelated male willingly and without benefit of marriage. All told, this was exceeded on the sensitivity scale only by race and abortion.

Suddenly concerned, I glanced at the reports again. Witnesses: "Stanley M. Pease, WMA, age 27, victim's roommate, employed at San Diego College Day Care Center."

I was relieved to see that race was indeed not an issue. I noticed, too, in this quick review, that the victim also was employed at the SDC Day Care Center.

Although the questions I wanted to ask Sandra Adkins were backing up in my head like rush-hour traffic, I always started an interview with a rape victim on a subject completely unrelated to the assault. I have found that the rapport established with the victim during this first interview sets the pace of the relationship forever, no exceptions. Trust, credibility, cooperation on both sides, all would be either defined or denied in this first stage. Not that there isn't plenty of room for pangs of doubt or futility during the months before the case is finally concluded. But I have never, to my recollection, encountered insurmountable credibility problems after a first interview which resulted in the filing of a rape case. And neither have my juries.

"Sandra, or do you like to be called Sandy . . . ?"

"Sandy," she replied softly.

"Sandy, what do you do at the day care center?"

"Actually, a little bit of everything." She was warming up. "The center was set up to . . . to take care of preschool-age kids of students at SDC, so they kind of wanted to teach them something. But it's a lot of babysitting, too."

"And Stan does the same thing?"

"Uh-hum. We both have our California teaching credentials, but you know . . . teachers can't get jobs, so to stay in a place like San Diego, we work at the center," she concluded in an almost apologetic tone.

I learned that she had originally moved to California from Iowa to take advantage of a free university education, had gotten her credentials, and, unable to find a teaching job, worked at various preschools. This way she earned enough to allow her to indulge in her real passion —travel, especially to Mexico and South America. Sandy spoke fluent

Spanish and made purchases each time she traveled in anticipation of someday opening her own import shop. When she returned from a trip in April, she found work at the day care center, where she met Stan.

She had been staying with a girlfriend while looking for a house. Then, in June, Stan mentioned that one of his roommates had just moved out, and he offered Sandy the room at a rent she could not find elsewhere. The third housemate was also a female and she lived in a converted garage behind the house.

It was time to discuss facts.

"Sandy, do you know this man, Nicholas Harter?"

"Only as a friend of Stan's. Actually, I didn't know his last name at all until Detective Sografo told me this morning."

I debated with myself, then asked, "Has anyone told you what he said happened?"

"No. What did he say? I assume from what's going on that he says it didn't happen, or something like that," she concluded in an even tone.

"Oh, no, he admits it happened, but he says it was consent."

"That's a lie," she replied without hesitation, but accompanied by the nervous laugh.

"And you hadn't been sleeping with Stan either?" My spirits were rising slightly.

She lowered her eyes and studied the purse strap.

"It was only a few times, when I first moved in, and, well, we just decided to be friends. I can't imagine why he ever told Nick about it." The nervous laugh.

My spirits, though dampened, were still intact. I asked her about Harter, and she said he didn't appear to have a job and as often as twice or three times a week would hang around the house all day with several other friends. They would drink and smoke dope late into the night. Neither she nor Linda, the other roommate, ever participated. Linda would testify to this, and so would Stan.

As for parading nude around the house? She could recall one occasion when she had taken a shower; afterwards, when she opened the bathroom door, she found that Stan had come home in the meantime in the company of some of his friends. They were all in his room, which happened to be between the bathroom and her bedroom. The door was slightly ajar. She made a dash for the bedroom. She didn't know if Harter was among the group in the bedroom or not.

I made another note to be sure to ask for the names of any regular visitors to show (hopefully) that none of them had ever seen Sandy behave as Harter proclaimed. I'd also try to jog Stan's memory. Maybe he could recall the incident.

Sandy went on to tell me that it had, in fact, been Harter who tried to strike up a friendship with her on several occasions, and she who had shown no interest. She thought him slovenly. Besides, he had a girl-friend, Kelly, who was often at the house with him.

I had grown increasingly puzzled as Sandy described this relationship and living arrangement with people who appeared to be so out of sync with her own way of life.

Stan, she explained, seemed to live in two different worlds. She knew him first at the day care center, where she and others observed him to be a sensitive, even gifted teacher who related marvelously well to small children. She had known him this way for two months before she became his housemate. Until then, she had not socialized with him and did not, therefore, know his friends.

Once living with him, she found that in his private life he chose to surround himself with people far less educated and with little or no ambition. He allowed them virtually free access to the house and even fed them on occasion. She confronted Stan at least twice about the caliber of the friends he cultivated, trying to convince him that he could, and should, do better. She expressed a particular dislike for Nicholas Harter.

I wondered if Stan had told Nick all this. Another note.

Why hadn't she left?

Making the minimum wage, working twenty-eight hours a week, owning a cat, it was not easy to find a place to live. But she had been planning to move.

Had she told anyone about these plans or about Stan?

Yes, she replied. In fact, two other teacher friends knew about her situation and one had promised to help her look for a new place over the next weekend. She was now staying with this friend temporarily. She had not returned to the house since the attack, and she never would.

I added her friends' names to my growing witness list. I already had an increasingly clear picture of how and why this rape had happened. Emerging was a woman who, limited by finances, found herself sharing a house with a man she thought she knew pretty well, but whose social life was so at variance with his professional one that it would have been impossible for her to foresee. She realized she wanted out of the situation, and had taken steps in that direction. But the stage had already been set. Among this roommate's circle of friends was one in particular whose personal advances she had spurned. He would, before it was over, become her tormentor.

On the evening of August 15, Sandy began, she had left work at 5 P.M. and had visited a friend's small clothing boutique in La Jolla to look at some imports from Mexico. After returning to the day care center at 7:30 for a teachers' meeting, she stopped at a store to pick up some cheese and was home by 10 P.M.

The light was on in the converted garage and Linda's car was there, so she assumed Linda was home, although she never actually saw her. Stan had called in sick that day, but she knew that he had gone to the mountains with Nick and two other men from his circle of friends and that they planned to camp overnight. Stan's door was locked when she arrived home and no one else was in the house.

The week before, Linda had reported losing her key to the back door for a second time in as many months, and since the only bathroom was in the house, Sandy left the back door unlocked. The front door was locked and bolted. After a light dinner of fruit, crackers, cheese, and a glass of rosé, Sandy prepared for bed. It was a hot, humid night, but rather than leave the windows open, she put on only the top portion of a pair of shorty pajamas which came to her hips. She set the alarm, turned out the lights, and went to bed. It was 11:15 P.M. Her next recollections were the hazy, sketchy sort which occur during that stage between sleep and consciousness when impressions, not pictures, are descriptive. They were of a man entering her bedroom. She could see it was a man silhouetted against the light shining through the window from the street. There was a vague familiarity about the man and she was not yet alarmed.

She looked at her clock and remembers the time being 12:45 A.M. She began to tell the man he was in the wrong place, thinking he had come to sleep on the living-room couch, as some of Stan's friends did occasionally. It was at this point that the intruder kneeled on her bed and she realized he was not wearing any clothes.

Instantly she was fully awake and trying to scramble out. But the bed was against the wall in a corner, with a large footlocker at the bottom. Not only was her attacker blocking her only avenue of escape but he had her pinned under a sheet. He threw her back down with force enough to cause her to bounce as she hit the mattress. She opened her mouth to scream, but before any sound could come out a hand pressed down tightly across her face.

"You'll do *exactly* as I tell you," he commanded in a voice that increased the wave of panic that began to build at his first touch. She could sense his strength and power in the way he threw her to the bed and prevented her scream. He was now on all fours, straddling her, his arms on either side of her head, his legs in a like manner across her chest.

I asked Sandy what was going through her mind at the moment she realized she was pinned with no apparent avenue of escape. It was in answering this question that she began to do something I had never seen before. She explained that she had seen at least one film about what to do if raped and had read several articles. As she teetered on the edge of hysteria, words from these articles suddenly began to flood her head, replacing panic with some strange order.

What was the advice? What was she to do? Stay calm, they all urged, try to stay calm, repeat it over and over to yourself. Although most women think they are going to be killed during the course of a rape attack, she recalled, the vast majority are not; but be calm.

So she began to repeat this over and over to herself, while at the same time assessing her situation.

Her mind raced. What else had the articles said? Don't scream unless you think it useful, because this might result in more force being used against you. She remembered that all the windows were closed— ironically, to keep out intruders. Better to be uncomfortable than raped, the article said. Screaming would do no good, for no one was home in the house next door. Her neighbor, a woman deputy sheriff, was on the night shift.

Stay calm. She could smell the alcohol on his breath, his face was so close. If she was right about the identity of her attacker, she had seen him after he'd had too much to drink on at least two other occasions. Alcohol made him loud, more aggressive, and violent. She had seen him hit his girlfriend once when they had argued and he had been drinking. She decided against any course of action which might provoke him.

Her remaining alternatives? She remembered advice about claiming to have a disease. She decided he would not believe that she had gonorrhea or syphilis, so she told him she had herpes.

His reply: "Then we'll give it to all the guys in the Navy." Now she knew he was drunk.

He ordered her to take off her top. After initially refusing, she complied rather than have him do it, all the while telling him he didn't want to do this.

He inserted two fingers into her vagina and shoved them up and down. She complained of pain and he mumbled something to the effect that she was really enjoying it.

He told her to spread her legs and she told him to spread them himself. He then commanded her: "Spread them!" Again the unfamiliar tone from the familiar face frightened her and she complied.

He told her to put his penis inside her, but it was not erect. He ordered her to put it in her mouth until it was hard. Stay calm, stay calm. The odor was terrible. Her heart pounded in her ears. She again complied and he completed intercourse.

She did not kiss him, hold him, or respond in any way. She remembers her arms were stiff at her sides. I noted this for cross-examination of the defendant, who claimed it had all been an act of love.

When he had ejaculated, he left the bed almost immediately and walked into the next room. Sandy knew she was going to report the rape to the police. The articles had all emphasized positive identification. She still only thought she recognized her attacker; she had to be sure. She followed, and watched him pick something up from the floor in the living room and disappear into the kitchen. She moved forward, and when she got to the doorway she could make out his form on the other side of the kitchen. She reached around the wall for the light switch. The light confirmed her identification and brought an instant command: "No light! No light!" She flipped the switch off and backed across the living room to her bedroom, quietly put on the pajama top, and eased toward the front door. As she unlatched the screen door and was reaching for the dead bolt, he appeared at the kitchen doorway.

"What are you doing?"

Up to this moment Sandy had done everything she could remember having read, she explained. Now the calm was slipping from her grasp along with the door latch. In an instant the door was open and she was on the front porch, tears spilling down her face. Almost immediately she was bathed in bright light as she raced down the steps, gulping for air. She ran straight toward the source of the light. A car was making a U-turn in front of the house. She blurted out to the startled occupants that she'd been raped and that she was afraid the man was still in the house.

I asked for their names. Sandy knew only where they lived and had already told this to the police.

At the exact moment that Sandy had emerged from the door, Jack and Barbara Pendleton were returning home from an evening of dancing. As Jack swung the car wide to make the U-turn, his headlights caught a sight both he and Barbara will long remember. A woman whom they knew lived in the house appeared on the front porch and ran down the stairs straight to the passenger's window. She was hysterical as she approached, and continued to glance back at the house.

How did she look? By the expression on her face, they thought she was going to tell them that someone inside had died, or that the house was on fire. She was clothed only in a pajama top. When she told them she had just been raped and she thought the person was still inside, they took her into their house.

What did they notice about her? Well, they first gave her a blanket to cover herself, and then watched her go around to all the windows and pull down the shades. She next checked the doors to make sure they were locked. They asked if she wanted to clean up in the bathroom, but she declined, saying she had to stay as she was until the police came, that it was important. She let Jack dial the police phone number, but she insisted on reporting the rape herself. They stayed with her until the police took her away.

Sandy mentioned to me during our first interview that she vaguely remembered that this house looked as if someone was preparing to move. I had her point out the place to Sografo as he took her home later that day.

Jack and Barbara Pendleton moved to Wisconsin forty-eight hours after being contacted by Sografo and I brought Barbara back for trial five months later.

2

I WAS SUDDENLY AWARE that the pace of activity flowing past my office door had quickened. I glanced at my watch. It was 4:20, and many of the deputies were drifting back from court as the judicial process concluded its day.

Par for the course, I told myself. I was hooked and knew my day was far from over. I jotted down a list of key words to remind me of questions not yet covered, while trying to make an accurate mental allocation of the time left. In less than forty-five minutes, as lemmings to the sea, the next flow of activity would be toward the elevators, taking in the process those with authority to approve a plan which was rapidly forming in my head.

I continued the questions mindful of these reflections.

"Sandy, were you going with someone in particular before you were attacked?" I realized I had posed this question in the past tense. She wouldn't catch it, I hoped. During the two years which lay ahead I would come to recognize some important dynamics in the effects of rape on relationships. On that particular day, however, the purpose of the question was far more pragmatic. Without a previous at least some-what steady relationship, a common accusation hurled at rape victims is the "post-pickup change of heart" allegation. On the other hand, the presence of a boyfriend requires that consideration be given to a possible defense approach proposing that the victim cried rape after an episode of unfaithfulness followed by overwhelming waves of guilt. Proclaiming rape, such reasoning continues, is her only way to save face, and the relationship. Sandy explained that she had been in a somewhat serious relationship with a man, a deputy city attorney in fact, but that she had been more committed than he. Although he had initially displayed outrage over the attack, there was an almost immediate air of tension between them that only grew in intensity during the coming weeks. Sandy reported that the relationship deteriorated rapidly and within two months of our first interview she and Jim had split. Although they still see each other from time to time on a friendly basis, there has been no further romantic involvement.

How typical, this deterioration of sexual and personal relationships following a rape attack. I could not recall a case in which an existing relationship had weathered the trauma. Once again I could not quite put my finger on the significance of this phenomenon and I simply noted that Sandy "fit the pattern." This was also true with other important telltale signs that I recognized to be repetitions of elements of cases I had handled over the past several years.

If I had not yet figured out, at this point, the precise significance of the information that I had been gathering during my years as a prosecutor, I had, however, realized the usefulness of some of my discoveries. I now asked Sandy if she had ever thought about what she would do if she were raped. I had noticed that women who had actually addressed the question, whether only as a mental exercise or in a discussion with others, seemed to be able to handle a rape attack with better control than those who had never given the subject any thought. I also had noticed that even if women had considered what they might do, as often as not they did exactly the opposite under the stress of the attack. Jurors responded well to hearing these thoughts presented in this context, for no matter what the outcome, something of considerable persuasive value was conveyed. It got jurors thinking, asking themselves the same questions. Suddenly it did not seem odd at all that the victim had followed one course of behavior rather than another.

In Sandy's case, there emerged an enormous bonus in the response to this question. "It's really interesting," she explained. "You remember I told you I visited a friend after work, before the meeting at the day care center? Well, I don't remember how it came up, but we . . . that is, my friend and I . . . discussed that very question while I was visiting her." Sandy's eyes registered clear surprise as she explained these last thoughts to me. As it turned out, the manager of the boutique, a man whom Sandy had met on several previous visits, had introduced the subject. So now there were two more witnesses whose names were added to my list. My strategy, as always, was to build as strong a foundation as I possibly could to support all the evidence that I could muster concerning victim credibility. There was never such a thing as too much evidence in a rape case. And there never will be.

Had her behavior during the rape conformed to what she thought she would do? Pretty much, she explained. She had, as a result of her reading, decided that the best course of action during a rape attack would be not to resist. She was not very strong, she had never had self-defense training, and she was unsure of what resistance on her part might cause a stranger to do. She had expressed these views to her friend at the boutique at the time the manager had brought up the subject. They had even spent some time discussing her conclusion and how it compared with that of her friend, who was nearly six feet tall and had decided as a result of their conversation that she would have done the opposite.

I don't remember now exactly how Sandy let me know that there was another reason she would never have consented to intercourse with her attacker on that night. She explained to me in low tones, and a lot of twisting on the purse strap, that she used a diaphragm as her form of birth control, inserting it only when she was going to have intercourse during that part of the month when conception was possible. As it happened, the night of the attack was a borderline day in her risk cycle and she would have used the diaphragm in any instance of consensual intercourse.

We had obviously established the needed trust during our first meeting, but Sandy's revelation was not exactly the kind of supportive evidence I could just drop on a jury. I knew how difficult it had been for Sandy to speak these words aloud, and for me personally, it was at this point that her case achieved the status of "dedicated." The use of this information in a trial, however, was a matter which required a great deal more consideration than I had time to give it at that point, but I knew that I was going to pursue this case with all of my energies.

Frankly, it occurred to me, even as she spoke, that the confidence Sandy had just revealed to me would probably be better accepted in front of a jury than it would by my boss. And I was right. This thought jolted me back to the problems of the moment, and as Sandy finished her recitation, I spent a few moments explaining to her the areas which weighed heavily in the District Attorney's mind when considering the possibility of issuing, and ultimately trying, a rape case. In addition to the issues that were unique to her case, there were the old standbys to consider. In virtually every rape case where consent is the defense, and there was no doubt that such would be the case with Sandy, the same questions come up over and over again. Why hadn't she struggled more? Why hadn't she screamed or cried rape? Why hadn't she bitten his penis?

The attacker also knew some pretty intimate things about Sandy. Certainly high on the list was the fact that she and Stan had slept together. This would certainly come out at trial. I knew that I would have to reveal this information in the prosecution's case to preclude suspicions of secrecy on the part of the jury, should it be left until the defense had an opportunity to bring it out. Of equal concern was the question of the herpes. If she did have herpes, a jury could easily take the next step, with some help from the defense, of course: that the rapist was telling the truth, that he really had taken Sandy's statement as a warning, and that he had proceeded at his own risk. Or possibly that she was really loose, and even if she had been raped, she had gotten what she deserved.

Sandy listened quietly and attentively as I spoke. Now, as I asked her if she had any questions of me, I noticed that the nervous smile was gone and that there was no twisting on her purse strap.

"What you seem to be telling me is that everything I did right to save my life, those things, you know, in the articles and films, all of that is exactly wrong in terms of proving I am telling the truth."

I am seldom at a loss for words. Both my profession and my upbringing have bestowed upon me, for better or for worse, the facility of quick thinking, and usually quick answers. Sandy's observation was one of those rare occasions when the pupil turns the table and understanding flows out of rhythm. She had scarcely completed the thought when I was fully aware of how devastating it could be if her prediction turned out to be accurate. It was so absurd that thinking about it made me feel much as I do when I try to understand the size of the universe or the theory of relativity—totally mind-boggling, leaving me somewhat agitated inside, relieved only by a conscious effort to push the thought aside completely.

I wondered aloud, "Do you still have any of those articles?" Surely she wouldn't.

"Yes, I do."

The next time we met, she gave me two articles torn from different issues of *Reader's Digest,* published two years apart. In retrospect, I should not have been surprised that Sandy had kept copies of these articles. I have observed that there is a direct relationship between the amount of thought that has previously been given to the possibility of rape in their own lives and the victims' ability to deal with both the subsequent rape and the trial. The greater their knowledge about rape, and therefore the more thought given to the question of their own possible responses to a sexual attack, the more composed they appear from first office interview to last trial question.

It seems clear to me that there is a growing populace of women nationwide—those reached by some form of rape prevention education —who are less and less likely to cry on the witness stand and more and more likely to be angry about what has happened to them. Sandy was certainly one of the stellar examples of this observation. I was jolted back into reality when I realized that my reverie had carried me through a revolving door and that I was now back where I had started: facing the chilling, but accurate reality of Sandy's statement. I could not have pushed the thought from my head. It did not even occur to me to try.

I asked Sandy to wait for me in the reception room. I called Sografo back and gave him a brief rundown.

"She's right, you know," he added.

"Thanks, pal. Listen, I have an idea, one I've been kicking around for a long time, but it wasn't until Sandy came along that I could put it into perspective, give it some focus. Somehow, I have to get all this new knowledge about rape, like how victims react and why, all this new information about what we're teaching women to do and why . . . somehow I've got to find a way to make it evidence." My words came slowly, as the thoughts were formed while I spoke. "Not just argument, Jerry, not just talk, but *evidence* the jury can consider."

Now, making new law at the trial court level had become a way of life in the sixties and early seventies, *if you were a defense attorney.* It was rare, no rarer than rare, for a prosecutor to do it. Incredibly, this did not cause me a moment's hesitation. I have been from the beginning, and still remain, completely confident of what I had set out to do.

It was 4:45 when I gathered all my notes, the police reports, and Jerry, and confronted Daly with my analysis and conclusions.

"Assuming I agreed to let you try, and I'm not saying that I will, just how do you propose to get from here to there?" He moved an ashtray symbolically from one corner of his desk diagonally to the farthest corner as he spoke these final three words.

"I've mentioned this before, Daly, but I was waiting for the right case to give me the answer. I'm convinced all this information about rape has made it a field of expertise and that the way into the court-room is through the use of an expert witness. I'll define the expert witness and then find the right way to make it conform to the rules of evidence." Fortunately, Daly did not ask me for a complete legal analy-sis of how I expected to carry off this coup using rules of the California Evidence Code and the San Diego County Superior Court judges. Had he asked me for such a plan, I would have sounded ridiculous telling him that, although I wasn't certain at that moment how I would do it, I'd know it when I saw it.

We argued back and forth as I outlined the premise of my theory and he played devil's advocate. Daly enjoyed complete autonomy in all matters concerning the Superior Court division and waged a subtle and ceaseless campaign against any and all efforts to fragment his empire. But he was loyal to his "troops" (as he liked to refer to them) and the rewards were evident. I was no exception. I wanted to do well for him and by him. I could always count on his support when under attack by either the court or the defense bar. As this issue fit neither category, he certainly could have ordered me out. But somehow I think the whole idea fascinated him. He was very bright, down to earth, could talk to a jury of "folks" or lecture to a jury of scholars. But he felt too commit-ted on this issue to risk personal compromise.

"I'll tell you what," he finally proposed. "We'll take it to the front office; you can tell your side, I'll tell mine. If Creelman agrees with me, you go away; if he agrees with you, you've got my blessing."

I accepted immediately. I had been hoping he would reach this point. Perhaps the hour helped me too. Once before he'd given me this type of an offer on a case we disagreed on, and I had prevailed. I felt I had a better shot with Ronald Creelman than with Daly. He had no personal stake and he was a dyed-in-the-wool trial lawyer who loved a challenge. As senior trial deputy, he could, and did, try the cream of the crop, one or two handpicked cases a year. He was known around the office as the "Trial Prince."

Ronald Creelman was just putting on his coat as we surged into his office at 5 P.M. In addition to being intrigued by the challenge, as I had predicted, he was also particularly outraged by the suspect's cavalier approach. Somehow it must have touched some sensitive chord born of years as a prosecutor. No matter what the reasoning, at that point I could feel only exhilaration at my victory.

"Oh, by the way," he said, almost as an afterthought, as he closed his office door and headed down the hall, "this expert—make sure it doesn't cost any money."

My heart sank. I sent Sografo and Sandy on their way, telling her the good news, and him the bad.

"God, no money! What kind of credibility does he think I can get with no money? I've never heard of such a restriction. You know, Jerry, I think they really want to see me fall flat on my face. But I'm telling you, I won't. I've got a few months to pull it together. I know it will work. I'm sure I can do it." I hoped I could.

"I'm sure you can too, tiger. Let me know if you need any help."

"Sure, you've really been a great help today already." The thought suddenly struck me that he had probably planned this whole thing—at least part of it. "Jerry, you didn't by any chance tell Daly that I would . . ." I looked up—but he was gone.

The next day I filed a two-count complaint charging Nicholas E. Harter with rape and oral copulation. Three weeks later I presented enough evidence before a Municipal Court judge to convince him that Harter should be held to answer for the crimes charged in the Superior Court. Trial was set for early January.

Two weeks later, on a rainy October day, Sandy called to tell me she was pregnant. During Thanksgiving break she had the abortion.

The weeks seemed to race by that fall. I finally found the time to talk to the seven-year-old sole witness to the beating death of his baby brother at the hands of the mother's pimp. The preliminary hearing lasted six and a half days and required eighteen witnesses to convince the court that I had a case.

It soon became evident that the victim of the domestic violence case was going to be a permanent quadriplegic. But convicting her husband of a felony would mean his dismissal from the Navy and subsequent loss of all medical benefits for the family. The victim's life depended on the care, which on the outside would have been cost-prohibitive. On into the winter months I groped with this dilemma, finally concluding it on a somewhat hopeful note, but not with resolution, as such a desperate situation is without resolution.

A heavy load of cases followed one upon the other as fall turned to winter, and with the approach of the holidays everyone wanted to be free from worrisome cases. Whenever I could find a moment I would try to decide which issue was the cart and which the horse in Sandy's case: the budget or the witness. President Eisenhower is best remembered, I am told, as an administrator who had the ability to delegate authority. I am of that same persuasion but was far less successful. I approached the District Attorney's appellate division for direction. This is the repository of scholarly research within the office, where those deputies assigned are supposedly given a schedule commensurate with their need to be thorough and accurate. I can remember going twice and calling three additional times between September and December. No help was forthcoming and only the final call just weeks before trial elicited a response of any sort: that there was no precedent to follow. I already knew that, damn it. I needed some guidance, or at the very least someone who understood enough about the subject matter to be able to tell me if I was headed in the right direction. I had formulated what I thought to be a fairly reasonable approach, but it seemed so simple that I feared to risk ridicule if I divulged it and were found to be totally in error.

I also needed a "rape expert," and a cheap one at that. In September I called the offices of a prominent psychiatrist, a woman in San Diego, whom I thought might be persuaded to help. I got only as far as her assistant and was put on hold. After the appropriate wait, she was back.

"Doctor is quite interested in your ideas. She will be happy to discuss ways in which she might be of assistance to you. You know, of course, her fee is fifteen hundred dollars, with a five-hundred-dollar retainer. I will call to schedule your appointment after she has received your retainer and when doctor completes a review of the case file."

I attempted to explain the problem and was told I would hear from the office. Two days later there was a message in my box when I returned from court: "Doctor regrets that prior commitments will not allow her the time to assist you. Good luck."

Luck was just about what my budget could afford.

I had one idea left. Actually, it was the one I realized would probably be my only hope from the moment that Creelman announced my budget. I would create my own expert. And I had someone in mind for the role.

Anne Kennedy had been on the San Diego police force a little longer than I had been with the District Attorney. We were contemporaries and that created a bond between us in and of itself. I had been in particular awe of Anne since 1974, when she had volunteered to be a decoy in an attempt to catch a rapist who had been attacking young women walking late at night in an area not far from where Sandy lived. He would spring from a hiding place in the shadows, put a knife to the victim's throat, drag her to some nearby bushes, slit her clothing off with the knife, and rape her. I first became aware of Anne shortly after the rapist had been captured as a result of attacking her in precisely the manner he had his other victims. Of course, she was wired with hidden microphones and was under surveillance, but there had to be an attack before an arrest could be made. I thought she was crazy, but courageous. She had mentioned, when we discussed the case earlier, that the incident had given her a whole new perspective on the emotional trauma suffered by rape victims.

There were other reasons, too, why I felt she was my best bet. She had been active in promoting rape awareness throughout the city. She taught self-defense to women in the community college system. She had spent the last six to eight years assigned to either the sex crimes or the juvenile division as a detective. She was bright, friendly, not hostile, appeared feminine, and could speak. Best of all, she had no fee scale, since she worked for the police.

In late October, I called her and invited her to meet with me to discuss my ideas. I told her from the outset that I could not be precise about what I wanted from her. I gave her a detailed background on everything about Sandy's case.

She was interested and enthusiastic from the first moment. I showed her the articles about rape from *Reader's Digest* which Sandy had given to me. Anne reached into her briefcase and withdrew a file overflowing with clippings of various sorts.

"Here," she said after searching through the stack for a few moments.

What I held was a reprint from yet another issue of *Reader's Digest,* predating the two Sandy had read by eighteen months. The author was Anne.

I felt a rush of energy (I found each breakthrough made me feel this way). "It's fantastic! What's in the rest of that file?"

Anne proceeded to hand me articles she had authored: *Parade* magazine, *Psychology Today*, a series in both morning and evening local newspapers, program notes from TV and radio shows she had participated in. I could already see how I would qualify her as an expert. We would begin with her education, her police background, her involvement in community programs dealing with rape, show she was up to date on publications and films in the area, discuss her self-defense class, reveal her lengthy and numerous contacts with rape victims—and rapists. There was the rush-hour-traffic syndrome again. I had to slow down. What kind of an expert *was* she anyway? I knew her goal would be to show the jury why Sandy acted as she had—that in fact rape prevention educators *were* teaching women the things Sandy had described.

But so what?

The time had come to link the expert to a legal purpose. I sat down with the jury instructions on rape. I concluded I had two possible avenues. In California, in 1979, one of the elements that the prosecution had to prove in order to convict a defendant of rape was that the victim had resisted her attacker, but only with as much effort and for as long as she perceived it to be of any use. Of course, history had taught us that the victim must really resist for as long as the *jurors* felt she should. Therefore, this arbitrary and archaic requirement, along with several others, had been basic to the lack of successful prosecutions of rape cases for decades. What other crime in the entire Anglo-American system of criminal justice required a *victim* to prove something? Perhaps I could turn the tables: I could show that the expert was relevant, necessary to the case, because the jury had to decide the issue of resistance before finding guilt, and I would offer Anne as an aid to them in reaching their decision about whether she resisted or why she had chosen not to.

By now I was flipping back and forth between the jury instructions, the California Evidence Code, which contains all the rules by which lawyers must play out this game in court, and the legal definitions of the words in the code. Leave it to lawyers to say it in forty words when ten will suffice. The code allows jurors to hear evidence by experts, which they can then use to help them decide some fact or facts in the case, if the issues they are being asked to give an opinion on involve things beyond the scope of usual, everyday life. Surely I had the ability to make a judge see the application here. The problem is, it was the blind leading the blind. I was going to ask a judge, who probably knew no more about rape realities than the jurors, to give his approval to . . .

As a matter of fact, that is exactly what I am going to do, I encouraged myself.

"You know, Judy . . ." I'd completely forgotten Anne was still in my office. "I can also discuss the whole program of rape awareness training to show that the course Sandy followed is indeed what we, the rape experts, are advocating nationwide."

"Easy, lady," I chided. "Let's not get too carried away by your new title yet, okay? Yeah, I've considered that approach. It's my second avenue—to use you to give Sandy more credibility. Can you explain why you 'experts' are advocating nonresistance over fighting back?"

"Sure. Studies show that the chance of injury goes sky high if a woman resists. There is controversy about this idea, but it is the prevailing one to date."

"Anne, do you realize, I mean really understand, the scope of the new information that I'm going to try to get some Caucasian, conservative, male San Diego County Superior Court judge to not only listen to but wave his magic gavel over and pronounce as evidence?"

Although I was to suffer pangs on a sliding scale ranging from anxiety to anguish at various times between our first meeting and the day Anne took the witness stand, I never doubted that I was right. That, of course, has nothing whatsoever to do with success.

I had managed over the years to cultivate some minimal communication with a couple of women District Attorneys who were fortunate enough to be working in cities where there were established sexual assault units within the office. Sometime after Anne and I had our first meeting I picked up the phone and on impulse called the head of the sexual assault unit in Los Angeles. I explained what I thought I wanted to do.

"Have you got anything that might help me, Fran?" I pleaded.

"Well, I do have some articles, or reprints, or something in a file that is headed 'Rape Trauma Syndrome' if that will help you." She was talking and rustling through drawers and files.

"The rape trauma syndrome?" I repeated. "What is that?"

"Listen, kiddo, I've got a meeting to get to. I'll send you everything in the file. I don't need it anymore anyway. I'm going to head child abuse."

"Then you've never tried to use anything that you've got in that file, I take it." I was trying to make the whole sentence one word so she'd get her answer in before the phone went dead. "No." And this time, only silence.

Some days later a moderately full eight-and-a-half-by-eleven-inch manila envelope arrived for me from Fran. When I opened it I realized she had meant it when she said she was sending the whole thing. The articles were contained loosely in a short manila file, with the words "Rape Trauma Syndrome, etc." typed on a label across the lip.

I began to go through the papers. Altogether there were approximately six to eight short articles, probably reprints. It appeared that four of them had been published in the same April 1976 issue of the *American Journal of Psychiatry* as a sort of tribute to the research being done in the area of rape crisis counseling. The remainder were in the same vein but from different publications. The title of one article in particular caught my attention: "Coping Behavior of the Rape Victim" by Ann Wolbert Burgess and Lynda Lytle Holmstrom. I had never heard of them. I found the small italicized print in the lower left-hand corner of the first page. Naturally, they were on the east coast. Both were at Boston University. The former was an associate professor of nursing, the latter an associate professor of sociology. I noticed the article entitled "Rape Trauma Syndrome" was also by them. I decided to read them first.

Things were never the same again. I cannot overstate the influence the information contained in these articles has had on the maturation and development of my legal theories and approaches to rape and rape victims as a member of the legal profession. By reading these articles I had taken the first step leading out of the cocoon so many professionals dwell within all their lives, never daring to venture beyond their own ken. Quite by accident I had traversed the continent my first time out. The work of Burgess and Holmstrom, along with that of several other women professionals whom I came to know through them, has served as the very foundation on which to build the necessary woman's perspective within the criminal justice system. Not only have I come to realize that this perspective is essential to the understanding of the rights of women when they become victims and must deal with the criminal justice system, but, in addition, the sharing of this information and knowledge with the rape victims themselves in the cases which I have handled has helped their emotional recovery immeasurably.

Back in 1979, however, I was just beginning, and the "coping behavior of the rape victim" sounded promising. I read the article about it and reread it. I knew I couldn't get all the information contained in the research into evidence through Anne, but I did have a title for her.

I dialed juvenile sex crimes and asked for her. "How does 'an expert in the areas of rape prevention strategies and coping behavior patterns of the rape victim' sound to you?"

"Like two mouthfuls" she replied. "Could you run that one by me again?"

I sent a copy of all the articles to her and we began to discuss the added possibility of her not only explaining rape prevention programs but also attempting to dispel some of the myths and misconceptions that jurors still were steeped in.

Although not mentioned directly in the article, several references were made to what has now come to be called the "casual acquaintance rape." In growing numbers the rape cases that we see coming through the courts deal with the situation in which a woman is attacked by a man she knows slightly, through such means as living in the same apartment building, attending the same class, or meeting as a result of introduction through a roommate.

Anne appeared to be quite knowledgeable in this area, and her opinion that 45 to 50 percent of all rapes occurred between casual acquaintances was backed by government statistics. Now all I had to do was qualify her to testify as a witness.

My excitement at the prospect of success in this project was growing throughout the holidays. But could I really do it?

I went over and over it in my mind. The concept was clearly just. I could see no flaws in the application of the appropriate Evidence Code sections. I truly felt it might, just might, be an idea whose time had come. Surely the rape victim had waited long enough for something to develop to help her through this most humiliating and traumatic of life's experiences. I could see much more potential in the future too: a multidisciplinary approach to rape. If what I had read could all be put before a jury, convictions would rise sharply. Of equal importance, this information could greatly aid the emotional healing process not only for women who would fall prey to rape in the future but for those women who had lived in silent agony for as long as forty years without revealing to anyone that they had been a rape victim and had never understood the many and varied emotional symptoms they had been suffering throughout their lives and could probably attribute to this experience.

"Boy, do I sound like I'm giving a final argument." I snapped back to the reality of my cubbyhole and realized the phone was ringing.

It was Monday morning, January 9, 1979. For me, the first full trial court day of the new year. As the phone continued to ring, I realized it was 9:45 and I had been waiting for Jerry Sografo. Jury selection was to begin for Sandy's trial in fifteen minutes. "Judy Rowland, Deputy District Attorney, may I help you?"

"I sure hope so, lady," the familiar voice boomed in my ear.

"Jesus, Jerry, where are you?" I hissed back at him.

"Las Vegas, snowed in. How about that for a blue Monday?"

I could tell it was going to be one of those years.

3

I HAVE ALWAYS EXPERIENCED an emotional surge when passing through the doors of the Superior Court criminal presiding department. Not always the same emotions, of course, sometimes excited anticipation, other times borderline panic, still others outright fear, but definitely emotions heightened by this unique combination of place and purpose. It is the very heart of the felony trial attorney's world, ruled absolutely, if not always benevolently, by a single black-robed dictator. Here one's wishes might be granted, one's hopes dashed, courage lost, futures won. It is at once news desk, clearing-house, market floor, even auction block.

As with all things subject to the human order, within the legal hierarchy such things as who one knows, how well the game is played, your race, sex, and religion, all jockey about to define status. Nothing, however, not even a direct line to the governor, can hold back the flood gates of eventual doom if you are not prepared. While experience, and the wealth of knowledge which it affords, can plug the occasional hole in the dam, there is always a direct correlation between one's state of mind and one's state of preparedness on the morning of trial.

As I stepped into presiding that first court day of 1979, experience was precisely what I planned to draw upon. I had a delicate balance to maintain in order to preserve Sandy's case until Sografo dug his way out of Las Vegas. I needed to let the court know I intended to claim priority for assignment to a trial department as is allowed in cases involving sexual assault, while at the same time avoiding an actual assignment. I had several things going for me. With the holidays behind us now, everyone was eager to be first in line for trial. I would try to be just gracious enough, perhaps, to let one (short, of course) case be assigned ahead of me. I quickly scanned the calendar and discovered that several criminal trial judges were still on vacation while others were already involved with cases started before the New Year's recess. A few words with the defense attorney revealed that he had to be in two other courtrooms at the very moment we were speaking. This would drop us to the bottom of the calendar for second call, a perfect way to assess the condition of the trial schedule for the week without taking any blame for delay myself.

By second call I would no doubt be safe from assignment for one more day. What I now had to consider was the possibility that by trailing I could end up waiting anywhere from two days to two weeks. Such a fate for Sandy and all my other witnesses, whose lives literally would be in limbo until this episode concluded, was precisely what I feared most. It would then be up to me during days or even weeks of delay to attend to their emotional needs. It is a fragility much as the spider's as it hurries to mend new tears in its web lest progressive damage gone unrepaired destroy the whole.

"All rise," the bailiff began as I continued to churn through the alternatives. "Before the flag of our country and the principles for which it stands, the criminal presiding department of the Superior Court is now in session, the Honorable Eric Kinsey presiding."

Following the judge's lead, and as directed again by the bailiff, a sea of lawyers rose and fell as the black-robed figure entered and took his chair. He wasted no time in running through the calendar.

"Good morning, ladies and gentlemen, and welcome to 1979." He continued: "While there are seventeen matters which you assure me are prepared for trial this morning, I know it will come as no surprise to you, except possibly those of you for whom first calendar call is an annual event reserved only for the first trial date of the new year, that there are far fewer courtrooms than that available to hear you. To be precise, I have three, possibly four judges to send you to. None usually sits on criminal cases, but have graciously agreed."

I could imagine how graciously. Judges accustomed to hearing civil cases felt criminal matters beneath them, while those normally assigned to the latter found the former to be almost fatally dull. Not to mention the fact that each had to dust off those far corners of the mind to which they had relegated the rules of their unchosen arena.

Scanning the room casually, Judge Kinsey leaned forward, his elbow on the surface in front of him, with his head resting on his hand. "I think, ladies and gentlemen, we have a problem. Any suggestions?"

I knew immediately *my* decision was made. There was no way I would let a rape case be tried before a judge whose familiarity with the penal code might consist of unwrapping it each year when his new edition arrived. If ever I needed experience, this was it. Fortunately, Judge Kinsey knew he would have mutiny on his hands if he assigned a case such as mine to a civil court. So began the wait.

It was our sixth day to answer ready when the news came.

"People v. *Harter* is assigned to Judge Manuelo Olmeda, Department 14 of the Municipal Court. Any objections, counsel?" Judge Kinsey looked from John Ashbury to me and back again.

Damn. I was in a real bind. Still no good criminal trial judges available, over a week of waiting. But a Muni judge, with little felony experience; would he be willing to make new law? Unlikely. And, my God, a Hispanic judge; on the issue of consent rape?

Judge Kinsey was addressing me directly now. "Madam Prosecutor, any objections?" I had seen John shake his head.

"Oh, well, at least this one's familiar with criminal cases," I thought to myself resignedly. And Sografo was back. I followed suit. "No objection, your honor," I replied.

I had gotten along well with Judge Manuelo Olmeda from the first time I had appeared before him. He was intelligent, kept control of his courtroom, and, more importantly, knew the law. I also thought he was extremely attractive, with handsome brown eyes and those long dark lashes which only men seem to get. His jet-black hair and trim, compact frame completed what was an altogether pleasing appearance. However, I had never sized him up as a potential for something as sensitive as a rape case and, stereotype or not, I was worried about the Latin view of women and their place that he surely brought to the Bench. He could be medieval at worst, conservative at best.

What little I knew about him did not give me any clues as to where he fell within this range. He was the first Hispanic attorney appointed by Governor Brown to the San Diego Bench. When I first met him some four years before, he had told me of his large family, ten brothers and sisters, all of whom were college graduates and professionals. His youngest brother was then in law school, and when Rose Bird, Chief Justice of the California Supreme Court, decided to allow designated municipal court judges to sit on felony cases in order to relieve a backlog in the courts, Judge Olmeda was among the first selected.

Still, I had not really kept track of Judge Olmeda's record on issues affecting women. With Superior Court judges, who might sometime hear one of my cases, I never missed an opportunity to do just that. I would gather tidbits of information to stash away about their feelings on anything concerning women—whether it was eavesdropping at a nearby table during lunch, over a cup of coffee at the local legal greasy spoon, or at a happy hour on the way home. But with Municipal Court judges, who handled only misdemeanor trials, I just hoped the odds would favor me and keep my contact with the worst of them to a minimum.

"I think he'll listen to my arguments," I said to myself as I handed my card to Olmeda's clerk. "But will he be willing to stick his neck out to make new law? God, Superior Court judges are paranoid about getting reversed; how can I expect a Municipal Court judge to risk it?" Like a seesaw, my hopes rose, then crashed.

"Could you please tell the judge I plan to bring a motion before the jury panel is called? It may take a day or so." I was addressing Tony Jones, the judge's clerk. With this last pronouncement he looked up at me, his face registering surprise. Before he could respond, I quickly handed him a two-page trial memo.

"I think this will explain what I have in mind. John, here's one for you." I turned and handed a copy to my opponent. "And, Tony, could I use your phone for a minute? I need to tell my witness where we are and that she's needed now."

With a nod of approval to my request, Tony disappeared through a door behind the courtroom, file and memo in hand. John sat reading on the edge of the conference table which would serve as home base to us for the next week or two. I called Anne at the police station and told her where we were.

"What the hell is a rape expert anyway?" John inquired when I hung up the phone. The question was asked in a bemused tone, followed by a curt laugh, both characteristic of his reaction to almost anything presented to him by a prosecutor. He was having more fun with this one, though. "Is that someone who's gotten it often enough to know, or the guy who can tell you how to do it right?"

I was used to this attitude. I had long since learned not to react—outwardly, that is. "Maybe you'll learn something new, John," I replied unemotionally.

Coincidentally John Ashbury and I had gone through law school together. As with so many of my classmates during the mid-sixties, law was his second career. He had completed his twenty years in the service, had a pension, was in his forties, and wanted something new. He was definitely old school when it came to views about dating, sex, and marriage. I could vaguely recall conversations from our law school days concerning his then teenage daughter and what he thought of modern social values.

As an adversary for my first foray into new legal territory, I could not have been more pleased. John was easygoing and not given to theatrics.

Tony reappeared, minus both file and memo, explaining that the judge would see us shortly.

"Good." I was heartened. *At least he's going to read it before he asks me to explain what I'm talking about.*

Or maybe . . . not so good. I had debated whether to commit my ideas to writing for fear that a judge might jump to a decision, if not in a formal ruling, at least in his mind, before I could even have a chance to put Anne on the stand and argue orally. Talking was my forte. I figured my chances of success increased proportionately to the length of time I could keep a judge from ruling against me, on the theory that the longer he listened, the more times I could repeat my idea and the more likely he would be to see I was right. But the previous afternoon, when I had finally ventured to mention casually what I was about to do, my trial colleagues, who I knew would do their best to find a hole in my approach, were unanimously in agreement that I should prepare a memo explaining my logic.

Although I knew exactly what I intended to say, I did not want the judge to be confused. So I wrote out that first trial memo on experts and the criminal prosecution of rape cases in perhaps fifteen minutes. I had one of the secretaries in the steno pool type it up early the morning of trial, made my corrections, and had a final draft only minutes before I handed it to Judge Olmeda's clerk and to John. I did it from memory, for it was really nothing different from what I intended to tell the judge anyway. As time went on, my memos progressed into briefs, which translates to longer. The longer they got, the more intimidating to my opposition and the greater my success. I really don't think there was a direct correlation, but I know I would now never go to trial without first putting my intentions in writing.

After what seemed like a very short time—or was it long?—Judge Olmeda emerged from the back hallway holding the case file in an arm already securely robed, while the other groped for an uncooperative sleeve which trailed over his shoulder.

"Good morning, counsel," he said as he settled into his chair, both arms now neatly covered with his authority of office. "Is the reporter present, Tony? I would like to be sure everything we discuss is on the record."

His tone was even, unhurried, with only a hint of accent. I might not even have guessed his origin had I not known Spanish was his native language.

"Ah, I see we do have a reporter. Fine. Are we ready, then?" He looked from John to me.

Ready for what? I wondered. He had not even mentioned the trial memo. I noticed Anne slip into a seat at the rear of the courtroom.

"Yes, your honor," John began. "The defendant is ready to begin jury selection, if the clerk would only be so kind as to send for a panel."

John was obviously not sure what the judge was "ready" for either, but he figured he might as well grab the offensive and hope my whole idea would go away.

"I believe there is a lengthy motion the people wish to have heard. Is that not the case, Ms. Rowland?" His even gaze matched his tone.

"Yes, your honor," I replied. Relief crossed my mind, but hopefully not my face. "You have read my memo, then? Is it clear? Do you wish some explanation before I continue?"

"Not I, counsel, but perhaps Mr. Ashbury has some comment to make along those lines."

"Well, your honor, I can't imagine what kind of a sex expert she thinks the jury needs. It's up to them to decide who's lying, not . . ."

"Mr. Ashbury"—it was the same even tone—"this is not the time to argue. You will have a chance later for that. If you have no questions about the people's memo, we will proceed."

Before I knew it Anne was on the stand, had sworn to tell the truth, and had launched into a detailed résumé of her background. As I listened to her review her years in the San Diego Police Department and how she had come to be so knowledgeable about her subject, I realized how similar our situations had been. I felt as strangers might who, unbeknownst to them, have shared a part of their long-ago past. Upon discovering this common experience, they draw closer than first meetings usually allow.

While Anne and I were not strangers, it was the first time she had been my witness in a case. As horse responds to rider, or orchestra to conductor, so do answers to questions project a flow only to the degree that the one is understood by the other. This recognition of our professional parallels seemed also to be shared by Anne as we progressed through the examination. Although we had never taken a test run through the questions, she knew what I was looking for with each one.

"Detective Kennedy, how many women were on the San Diego police force when you started?"

"Perhaps a dozen women police officers. None who walked a beat, or anything like that."

"When you came on the force, was there any policy for dealing with the problem of sexual assault, or its prevention?"

"No, there was not."

"Could you tell the Court what changes have occurred in the department over the years since you joined?"

"Well, shortly after I came to the sex crimes detail in about 1971, I began to get more and more calls directed to me by the department from the public concerning rape prevention, self-defense, and the like. I was also frequently asked to interview women who could not, or would not, talk to a male officer about their attacks. I was asked to set up a community health program to present lectures and seminars to the public, and for private institutions as well.

"I screened films to use in training seminars, I began teaching new officers about rape prevention, human sexuality, and incest. I have probably addressed a total of fifteen to twenty thousand people on these subjects over the last eight or nine years."

I was keeping an eye on Judge Olmeda, who, with his even gaze, was watching Anne closely. He appeared to be interested. I had no idea, of course, what he was really thinking, and hoped for a hint. Maybe a question: by its content or tone I could glean something. I hesitated to give him the opportunity. Only silence. I went on.

"Detective Kennedy, have you and your colleagues been advising women as to what they should do in the case of sexual attack, or how to prevent one?"

"Yes, to both questions, but I think it should be clear that this is not the case only in San Diego, but all across the country we are recognizing certain self-defense and prevention guidelines."

"Would you tell us what those guidelines are, please?"

"I teach self-defense in three stages. The first is prevention of an attack. Try to prevent an attack from happening, try to avoid becoming the target. I do this in all sorts of ways, home security, car security, and all types of personal security.

"Secondly, being able to recognize the danger when it's there, which a lot of women can't do. In other words, there are many times when there is a dangerous situation and the person doesn't know it. With women freer to move about in social situations these days, we have seen a dramatic rise in what we have come to call the 'casual acquaintance rape.' These start out in seemingly harmless situations, such as a blind date, or meeting as classmates, or apartment house neighbors, and without even realizing it, the woman ends up alone with a man, and in danger of attack. Of course, you know how hard that kind of situation is to prove in court. And, third, the use of physical self-defense."

I felt exhilarated. Just to hear all this from someone sitting on the witness stand!

I glanced at John Ashbury. He was looking for some sign from the judge's expression. He was having no better luck than I at figuring out which way the wind was blowing.

Panic hit again. Maybe Olmeda was not going to say anything until I had convinced him my theory was fact. I would have to keep going until I could see agreement or understanding, or some positive sign. If I ran out of proof before he reached that stage, I would lose.

"Detective Kennedy, when you say physical self-defense, is there another type of defense that you teach, other than physical?"

"Oh, yes, and it goes with the first two steps, and that is mental self-defense."

"Can you tell us what you mean, please?"

"Basically thinking ahead of time, what would I do if someone grabbed me right now, what would I do, how would I react? And try to, in a way, psych yourself out to think, what would happen, how would I react, me, personally, not a hundred other people, me. Would I panic, would I be able to scream?

"Take precautions every time you go out. When you park your car, will it be dark by the time you get back? Walk with your house or car key in your hand and ready to use when you get to the door. Can you see around obstacles ahead? If not, walk right down the middle of the street, or go way around hidden places. Walk as if you know where you are going."

"Do you actually advise women that there is only one right way in various situations?"

"Definitely not . . ."

Whoops. There's a word I had advised Anne to drop from her vocabulary when she was on the witness stand. It's like "always" and "never," injecting a hint of inflexibility or dogma into credibility. She had used it back during our discussion and planning sessions. This was her first slip. She had seen it too. Her eyes widened as soon as the word came out.

No harm, my look told her. *You are right.* She got the cue.

"I feel really strong about that. I'm not standing on a soap box and saying you have to do one thing. Use your head. Stay calm. Know that there are a lot of options available to you, because if you manage to get out of an attack and prevent the homicide team from investigating it, you're a winner."

How glorious the sound of these words! How good this felt! We were moving in unison as if we'd been partners in many tennis matches, or had together shared trump across the table. But it was time to move on to Sandy's case.

I had given careful thought to how I would actually present the facts to Anne. Although I knew I would get the same answers no matter which way I gave her the questions, I wanted to minimize the chances of having a conviction reversed on appeal because I got carried away. I had narrowed my choices down to two. I could go on asking questions in much the same way I had in covering Anne's background, calling for narrative-type answers crammed full of information about rape statistics, victim behavior, and situational analysis. Or I could put every fact I wanted her to take into consideration into one giant hypothetical question. This latter method is how experts are questioned for their opinions about children who appear to be victims of the battered child syndrome. The format of: "If you were told this, this, and this, what would your opinion be as to cause and why?"

While I really preferred to continue with the narrative question/answer style we had settled into so comfortably, my instincts told me to follow what little legal precedence there was and to at least introduce the unfamiliar in a familiar setting.

I'll have other chances to try different styles, I encouraged myself.

"Here we go," I mouthed to Anne, as I rose from the chair and counsel table, where I had been seated up to this point. I wanted both Anne and the Court to realize I was about to do something important; that a new movement in the symphony was about to begin.

"Were you acquainted with a young lady by the name of Sandra Adkins before you met her through me?" I stood leaning on the guard rail which separated the legal arena from the spectators.

"No, I was not."

"And you are not the investigating officer on this case, is that true?" This question was for Sografo's benefit. He had been slightly miffed when he heard I planned to use Anne on Sandy's case rather than himself. While I had prepared him as backup should Anne not have been available at the last minute, I felt bias was an important consideration and hoped to distance Sandy from the expert by using someone not connected with her case.

"That is correct," she replied.

"Now, I am going to give you a series of facts in what we call a hypothetical. When I have presented all the facts to you I shall ask you questions. The answers you give should be your opinions based on the facts in the hypothetical situation."

For the next ten minutes I laid out Sandy's case as one might in describing the plot of a story for a friend who had never read it and whom you really wanted to feel as if he or she had when you finished. Judge Olmeda listened, jotting notes occasionally. Not even his timing on note taking was helping me. He did not interrupt or question Anne himself.

"Now, assuming all those facts as I have given them to you in this situation, and based on your training and experience in the area of sexual assault, self-defense, and prevention, do you have an opinion as to whether the resistance of the victim in this case was in conformity with your, and your colleagues', instructions to women in similar situations?"

"Yes, I do."

"And further, do you have an opinion as to whether or not this victim under these circumstances had any other reasonable alternatives?"

"Yes, I do."

"What is that opinion, in each case?"

"Objection, your honor!" I had nearly forgotten that John was there. My heart skipped a beat. His words were precisely the ones I dreaded hearing. Somehow I sensed the equilibrium of the situation could be maintained as long as no objections were spoken: that an undecided state of mind, which I was certain Judge Olmeda held, was more likely to sustain an objection than one which clearly understood the logic of what was going on.

"That's a compound question," John continued. "And I ask Ms. Rowland to pose them one at a time."

"She did, counsel. Objection overruled," Judge Olmeda replied in his even tone. Turning toward Anne: "You may continue, Detective Kennedy."

I did not even notice the court's clue; I went on as if my opponent's objection had been sustained and I had lost the round.

"I will ask you to answer the first question. Do you have an opinion as to whether the victim conducted herself in conformity with what you and your colleagues teach?"

"Yes."

"And what is that opinion?"

"She did."

"Now would you tell the court, please, why."

Like bullets the reasons came.

"Number one, as the hypothetical situation has been presented to me, the victim in this case was on her home ground, but totally unprepared for any surprise or any type of attack. She was not walking along the street looking behind bushes. She felt she was in a place of security and had gone to bed.

"Secondly, when the person came into her room, she was in a half-asleep, half-awake state, which further reduced her level of awareness. At first, she did not sense danger, okay. She did not recognize it when it was there. She was home in her own bed awakening from a sound sleep.

"Thirdly, when she did wake up enough to see who was in the bedroom, she recognized the person. He was a casual acquaintance to her, someone she knew through her roommate. Had the face been that of a total stranger her immediate reaction in what few seconds she had might have given her an edge to escape. Though your facts seem to show that past contact between the victim and the defendant had not been particularly cordial, it certainly had not been threatening.

"The fourth point to consider is the question of intoxication. The victim felt her attacker was intoxicated. She is certainly the best person to make that decision. In Ms. Adkins' case she had seen Mr. Harter after he had been drinking before and felt that he tended to be violent. I think we all have seen alcohol amplify our actions. It removes some of our inhibitions and . . ."

"I ask the court to strike the last part of the answer as to actions of someone under the influence of alcohol." John was on his feet, but his tone was not convincing. "Whether or not they become whatever it was she was about . . ."

I broke back. "May I ask her another question at this point?"

"Very well," replied the judge. I missed this clue too. I was too caught up in the flow of things.

"Detective Kennedy; does the involvement of alcohol in a situation figure into the advice you and your colleagues give to women?"

"Yes, it does."

Good, my eyes spoke to her. *You know what I am after.* We had not specifically discussed this in Sandy's case, but we had in general several times.

"In your opinion, both through training and personal experience, have you found that alcohol does fit a pattern in these cases?"

"Yes, I have. At least fifty to sixty percent of the rape cases I have handled myself have involved at least the suspect and often the victim, too, having consumed alcohol just before the attack. Studies I have read seem to show an even higher percentage of cases involving alcohol or intoxication—up to seventy-five to eighty percent."

I looked at John. He was either satisfied or confused. Whichever it was, I decided to push harder.

"By the way, Detective Kennedy, while we're on the subject of cases with specific problems, if you were to give an estimate of the five hundred to seven hundred cases you have handled, could you tell us what percentage involved the casual acquaintance situation?"

"I would estimate that at least forty to fifty percent of the women had, at some previous time, seen or had something to do with the person who attacked them."

Just a little more, Anne, I said to myself. And to her: "What have the studies shown?"

"Unfortunately, few real studies have been done up to this point on victims of casual acquaintance rape because of the increased embarrassment in reporting this type of rape. But there seems to be a general consensus among the experts that as many as eighty percent of the rape cases in 1978 involved casual acquaintance situations."

"Detective Kennedy, you talked about embarrassment as a reason for fewer reports of casual acquaintance rape. What, if any, are some other reasons women who are victims of this type of rape fail to report it?"

"For one, the victim feels she could be in real danger. This person knows her, knows her habits, often knows where she lives or works—knows many things about her that a total stranger in the street wouldn't know. Embarrassment, of course, may range from not wanting to admit what happened even to herself, to feeling blame for letting it happen, to realizing that she might not be believed, such as when a family friend is involved."

Just another inch, perhaps.

"Finally, Detective Kennedy, how many rapes do occur in the United States as compared to those reported?"

"Objection!" John flew out of his seat. His voice still unemotional, the quick laugh, but exasperation showing clearly. "This is all speculation, and for the record I object to the whole thing, but I can't let it go on."

I knew that was it too. Even a strongly sympathetic judge would have been hard pressed to let Anne continue. I always like the last word, however.

"Your honor, we all know that far fewer cases of rape are reported than occur. Perhaps as much as one in ten."

"Ms. Rowland, I think we are getting too far afield here. 'We all know' is not good enough, as *we* all know. So please confine your questions to areas affecting the facts of this case."

"Very well, your honor." By late 1980 I would have the statistics I needed to support this argument. At that time, however, my information consisted mainly of conversations with those who had conducted the few big studies on stranger rape and people like Anne telling me how many women had confided in her after having heard her speak. They would come up to her and whisper that they had been rape victims perhaps years before but had never told anyone. Since I began to lecture, and particularly after word got out that I was writing this book, I too have experienced this phenomenon. From complete strangers and women I hardly know to close personal friends of many years' duration, my interest in the subject seems to unlock the innermost ranges of their trust which have been buried for up to half a lifetime.

"Okay, let's get back to the hypothetical, Detective Kennedy. You were telling us the reasons for your opinion concerning the conduct of the victim. You had described casual acquaintance rape and were about to tell us how alcohol fits in."

Anne was still right with me.

"Yes. I should point out that in this case alcohol was a double-edged sword. Because the victim had some previous knowledge about the defendant, she originally thought he was in her bedroom by mistake, because he had been drinking. In other words, recognizing him and his intoxication threw her off the track even more. Only when she realized he wasn't wearing any clothes did she sense danger. But then it was too late. He was on top of her."

"And what of the victim's ability to get away, with the defendant on top of her?"

"Yes. That particular position, with someone actually, physically putting his body on top of you, is the most difficult, even for someone who has been trained, and this girl was not trained. In simple terms, all her strength was spread out, pushing up against gravity, and all of his was gathered in the superior position, on top, going with gravity."

"Should she have bitten his penis when she got the chance?"

Anne's eyes did not flinch. Nor did she.

"I hear that frequently as something a victim should have done. All I can tell you is, she sure better have made it count—or she most likely would have been dead. And this victim had very little going for her as an escape route, even if she had broken away. She was in her bed, under the sheets; the bed was in the corner and her door was across the room. She also knew this man could be violent, and there certainly isn't anything I can think of that might make a man more violent than the suggestion that you've made in that question. My opinion would be to advise against such an avenue of self-defense in a closed setting. In the open, where people can be reached easily, perhaps. Ms. Adkins should not have attempted it."

"Go on, Detective Kennedy." The thought that someday it might be commonplace for juries to hear this kind of testimony nearly made me lose my concentration.

"Once her attacker had entered the bedroom, and the victim had attempted to physically resist as your facts outline, but her resistance was overcome by his force, it would be consistent that she felt her best move was to use mental self-defense; to talk to him, to give him excuses, as she did about having a disease. This lady was really using her head. She reasoned that he wouldn't buy syphilis, so she made it something more common. Unfortunately, he didn't care if she had herpes. When the rape seemed inevitable she decided to try to remember everything she could—and to be able to identify him."

"Do you talk to women about the importance of identifying their attacker?"

"Absolutely!"

I knew Anne meant to use that word.

"I can't remember how many times I've wished the victim would do just that very thing."

"Do what?" I asked innocently.

"Identify. Be able to identify the suspect for me. If there's one thing I've ground into their heads, it's that they must be able to make a positive identification. There is no half way. You have to know for sure that you have the right person."

I knew John would try to discredit Sandy's credibility by asking why she followed her attacker through a darkened house instead of making good her escape. By anticipating as many defense moves as possible, I tried to take the wind out of his sails—by being the first to cover the ground. I had just blown any speculation the defense was surely hoping to inject about Sandy's failure to run for the door at the first available moment. At trial, of course, Sandy would tell the jury of her determination that from the moment of attack she was not going to let this man get away with what he had done.

John, too, could see what I was doing.

"Your honor, I would object to this line of questioning. Ms. Rowland is asking this officer for her investigative procedures and what *she* deems important. The issue is what Sandy Adkins deemed important."

What a golden opportunity to argue: "Your honor, I'm asking this witness, as an expert in the area, whether or not the conduct of the victim is reasonable under the circumstances. And she is telling us why it was important for her to identify her attacker. Does the Court understand the relevance of these questions?"

Easy does it, be careful not to sound patronizing.

"You may proceed." Judge Olmeda was already looking back toward Anne. For the first time I felt a flicker of hope. If the judge likes Anne's style, wait till he hears this. My next sequence of questions had fallen into place during this last exchange with John.

"Detective Kennedy, is there an explanation for the victim's obvious calm behavior during the attack and immediately after, which deteriorated into hysteria once she was out on the street? In other words, within ten seconds, from the front door to the car window, this change had occurred."

Again, Anne was right with me.

"I see it frequently and I have also experienced it myself."

Innocently again: "Was that the occasion in which you were attacked?"

"Yes. And I would like to feel that maybe I'm a little more trained than the average victim in the street. I remained perfectly calm during the attack and never took my eyes off the guy as he tried to escape so that I could swear that the person who grabbed me was the same one the stakeout team caught. But the minute my partner touched me after they caught the guy, I dissolved into hysterics. I couldn't stop crying. I also realized then what I had done with the lit cigarette I had been carrying for the express purpose of scarring an attacker so he could be identified later if he had gotten away; when he grabbed me around the neck, I reached down and deliberately put it out in the ground. We found it sticking out of the dirt. It was then that I really believed I had been dragged forty feet from the place where he first grabbed me to where he finally dropped me. I have absolutely no recollection of having been moved. I thought the whole thing took place where the cigarette was found. Not only that, it wasn't until the guys played the tape recording for me that I knew I had screamed. I would swear to this day that that was not true if it wasn't loud and clear on the tape. And I knew I was a decoy. Most women don't. And I reacted like that."

No one in the courtroom was moving. The tension was fantastic. Later the jury was to feel it, too. I pretended I did not notice.

"Have you an explanation for this kind of behavior?"

"Well, it's obviously a very traumatic experience, as anyone who has been through one can understand. But studies seem to show, and in my experience I have to agree, that women let down their guard only after they see safety is at hand. Some internal strength, instinctive strength, keeps control until it's over—when this same internal instinct seems to say okay, now cry, or tell someone or let loose. By the way, it seems women report rape to another person at a time when they feel relatively safe. That does not mean the first person they see, or the earliest possible moment. It means when they *feel* somewhat safe. It could be hours or days later. It could be never."

"Well, I guess that brings me to the second question."

With these words I resumed my seat. Papers rustled, courtroom personnel breathed again. I felt good. I was in control. Unfortunately, I was not in charge.

"Detective Kennedy, do you have an opinion as to any reasonable alternatives that this victim had under the circumstances that I have given you in assuming those facts to be true?"

"Yes, I do."

"And what is that?"

Anne turned toward Judge Olmeda. "I don't believe, under the facts given, for her own protection, she had any other reasonable alternatives."

I was done. Anything more would be repetitive or inviting reversal.

"I have nothing further of this witness at this time, your honor."

Now, good cross-examination is an art of the highest form. Attorneys who are good at it go for the jugular. The results of good cross-examination can be a witness who is unable to complete a whole, coherent sentence by the time redirect comes around. Even less able attorneys can confuse a prepared witness into mistakes which come back to haunt during closing argument or in the jury room. It must be akin to finally becoming a contestant on that game show you've watched for years at home. You have always known the answers—until the day the cameras turn on you. While John was no Melvin Belli, cross-examination always made me nervous. Part of my pre-trial preparation was going over and over in my mind any possible weaknesses the defense could grab on to during cross-examination. I played devil's advocate, or sought out an expert in a particular area to do it for me. I am certain I would have suffered cardiac arrest if ever a whole subject had escaped my scrutiny until some defense attorney's cross-examination.

John did not surprise me. But he did harp on the inevitable—not only from the defense standpoint but also from simply being male.

"Detective Kennedy, is it in keeping with prevention strategy for a female alone to leave the back door unlocked where many people know about it, males included? And sleeping with an open bedroom door in a house where it is known that male visitors frequently come in and out whom the woman does not know, would that be consistent with how to prevent a sexual assault? And is it also consistent with your teachings that a woman live in a party house? Or at least where people get drunk and use drugs?"

Anne never lost control. And this was to be the first of many tests. Like that commercial, she only got better.

"Mr. Ashbury, it would depend as to how many or which of those things were under her control and how much was beyond her control."

"And your teachings—would they not suggest that she find a new place to reside?"

"That would depend on her financial situation. We can't lock up every drunk in the street."

"Have you ever talked to Sandy Adkins about her financial situation? Or has Ms. Rowland ever discussed it with you?"

"No, to both questions."

He moved on to another favorite subject.

"Do you, Detective Kennedy, teach a means by which a woman can communicate to a male that she doesn't want sexual intercourse and in such a way that he cannot misunderstand it?"

This sarcasm in the form of a question was pretty mild, but I decided I'd break it up before it got too far.

"Your honor, I would object on several grounds. First, it's argumentative. Secondly, it isn't relevant to the witness's area of expertise and is beyond the scope of direct examination. Thirdly, it calls for speculation as well as a conclusion. Fourth . . . well, those will do."

I wanted to add, "I suppose a clear no is too simple," but I did not. I had to watch out for those raw spots.

John knew where he was going. "Your honor, I simply asked if this expert advised women about how to say no clearly. We are going into her qualifications and teachings in this field, are we not?"

"If that is your question"—Judge Olmeda looked from John to the witness stand—"you may answer."

"Yes, I do speak of several ways that a woman can communicate to a male, not a particular male, but what she does would have to fit the circumstances."

"And how would you advise a woman to inform a casual acquaintance, as you have defined one, in a manner that he cannot misunderstand, that his sexual advances are not desired?"

I did not want John to get any further with this line. Experience has taught me that whenever questions begin drifting toward the absurd it is time to call a halt, if at all possible. I used to think that people listening would also see the ludicrous as I did. In some types of cases this is true—but not in rape.

"Your honor, such a question is too vague and calls for speculation."

"I think, Mr. Ashbury, you are sidestepping the main issue here and that would be to address what the victim in this case did or did not do —not some unknown hypothetical victim."

"I'll withdraw the last question. And I have no more questions of this witness."

I was startled. Nothing else? Finished?

"Any redirect, Ms. Rowland?" came the words I was fully expecting but not ready to hear.

"Does the Court want anything further?" I looked him squarely in those deep brown eyes.

"No, counsel."

I could feel my heartbeat quicken and my voice quaver slightly.

"Then no redirect, your honor. Does the Court wish to hear argument?"

"No, counsel. I think not."

It certainly was a good thing I had not eaten lunch.

"The people have met their burden and will be allowed to introduce evidence of an expert in the area of rape prevention as it is relevant to the degree of resistance the victim chose to use and why."

While speaking, Judge Olmeda had been gathering the papers which had accumulated in front of him. As he concluded, he glanced at John Ashbury as if to accept his acknowledgment of the obvious success of my efforts. While John appeared to find the whole episode amusing, he was clearly frustrated and did not intend to concede so readily.

"I beg the Court's pardon, your honor, but what has this witness added that a jury cannot do? It's their job to decide if this woman was raped or resisted enough or is telling the truth. It is not something beyond the scope of ordinary, everyday life that the average person, or juror in this case, would not know or understand. Ms. Rowland can urge the jurors to *interpret* meanings of Sandy Adkins' behavior any way she wishes, just as I can. That's all this is, your honor, one way of interpreting behavior, and the bottom line isn't even the jury's interpretation of her behavior, but actually—really—it's whether the defendant could be reasonably expected to have seen her actions and words as resistance, as saying no."

I was getting nervous. These were exactly the kinds of arguments that had always been used in these cases. And Judge Olmeda was listening. He did not interrupt or change his expression. I was scrambling through my memory—was he one of the judges who stuck with the ruling, or could he be persuaded by the last word? Damn! That was the problem with an unfamiliar judge in an important case.

"No, Mr. Ashbury, I do not think what I have heard in this courtroom today can be viewed as generally known by the public. In fact, while I was aware of police and women's groups' efforts to better understand rape victims' problems, I was not familiar with any of the specifics Detective Kennedy has given here today. This information is important, and relevant for jurors to understand. It puts a whole new perspective on the behavior of women in these situations. It amazes me that, with so much going on in this area, no one has tried to use the results in court until now."

Turning toward me, he continued: "Ms. Rowland, I have been enlightened here today, and this sounds like only the tip of the proverbial iceberg. Just remember, in front of the jury do not go beyond bounds that have been laid out here, and I think you follow me. I realize you want more, but you have not given me enough for more yet. I have no doubt that you will do so in the future. Court is in recess until ten A.M. tomorrow morning." Turning to his clerk, he concluded, "Tony, please have a jury panel ready then."

Judge Olmeda stood, as did we. He descended the stairs, smiled at me, and left through the same door from which he had entered years, or so it seemed, earlier.

On the surface I was calm as John and I packed up our papers, compared court conflicts which would require time out from trial during the next several days, and exchanged general information regarding the proposed witness schedules and the like. Inside I was ready to burst.

I scanned the spectator section looking for just one face which understood what I was on the threshold of doing. Among the small group were two or three regulars who always followed my cases. While their expressions seemed to indicate they had gotten their money's worth from my performance, the look I was searching for was not there.

I looked at my watch: 3:45 P.M. Time to share my jubilation with—with whom? Oh, well, it sure beat defeat.

4

ALL ATTORNEYS ARE CONVINCED that there is one crucial phase in any trial which means life or death to the case. Needless to say, they do not agree on which part that is. Probably more veterans will tell you that opening statement or closing argument is the key. In the type of cases I do, if you know *how* to do them, there is no doubt: jury selection is it. The case is won or lost when those twelve people are sworn in.

At a time when disagreement was on the rise about just how much license attorneys should have in questioning prospective jurors, many favoring the idea that judges alone should do it, I was envisioning an increasingly active role for the prosecutor in jury selection, or "voir dire," as we call it in legalese—at least for crimes involving sexual assault and domestic violence.

While deliberation on many types of offenses can be approached somewhat unemotionally, sex crimes and wife beatings are not among them. Theft and fraud can be rather neatly defined, allowing many prejudices to be checked at the door, so to speak, even if personal interpretations might vary. Jurors are relatively free of cultural or societal bias and are thereby left to make their decisions primarily on the facts of the cases involved. Exactly the opposite is true with cases in which women and children are most frequently the victims. Due to centuries of beliefs concerning morality—women's, of course—and truthfulness—add children here—it is absolutely essential to dig deeper into the backgrounds of those who are asked to judge the sexual behavior of others. Because the vast majority of those in authority have been male, it is often difficult to explain the need for breaking tradition in this area without coming across as a bra-burning man hater.

Had my efforts been directed toward the problems of consumer fraud it would have been a different story. But I was not talking about white-collar crime. The result of my intense interest in crimes whose victims were almost exclusively women and children was the identification of my work as primarily the pursuit of a feminist, not a legal, cause. Intellectually, I told myself, jury selection in Sandy's case was going to be easier—now that the expert testimony would be coming in. This was only intellectually, of course, since I still felt compelled to succeed. Everyone was watching, many with a feeling that I could use a "come-uppance." I would have settled for a shoulder to cry on, or someone to tell how scared I was. As usual, I got pep talks from my father. But he thought I could do anything; always had. Maybe he was right, but I sure didn't feel that way as the jury panel filled the courtroom.

Judge Olmeda was robed and seated. John Ashbury and Nicholas Harter were there, Sografo and I, all in our places. We had swiveled our chairs around to face the spectator section as the men and women who held Sandy's fate filed in. There were so many more young women these days—men, too, but particularly women. They didn't bring with them the ideas their mothers had in the past. These mothers had been insulated from the world and a lot of its reality. Retired people had represented the other large segment of jurors in the past. For either of these groups, it was only with great difficulty that they faced the idea of thinking about, much less talking about, sexual habits.

Since the governor had done away with most excuses to avoid jury service, and the legislature had required employers to grant fully paid and penalty-free leave to those called for duty, a much truer cross section was appearing in California courtrooms.

I had found the new breed of juror much more flexible, far less dogmatic. While they didn't necessarily approve of the "newer ways," they were able to let others live as they chose, especially those with children in their teens and older. There was, however, no less need to cleanse their minds of lifelong misconceptions, prejudices, and myths before they could accept the reality of sexual assault and abuse.

It took me a total of ten seconds from the time he came through the door to notice the unmistakable Roman collar with its little nick under the chin; another couple of seconds to match up the black jacket and pants. A Catholic priest! In my wildest dreams it had never crossed my mind: how to question a priest as a prospective juror for a rape case. Even with sixty-three names to draw from, I knew he would be one of the first twelve picked. And once he was up there I would have to have a damned good reason to excuse him.

It's not fair! I screamed to myself while smiling cordially at those filing in. Out of one corner of my eye I watched the priest. He was elderly, gray-haired, looked very wise and benevolent—just like you would expect a priest to look. It was clear he got along well with other members of the panel and they respected him. As promising a sign as this might ordinarily have been in sizing up good jurors, it spelled a gloomy prospect this time.

The spectators' gallery was now full and we all swung back around to listen as the usual remarks of welcome were delivered by the judge. I could hear what was going on somewhere in the distance, but my thoughts were trained on this new dilemma.

No doubt, I anticipated dejectedly, *he'll end up being elected foreman.* I resolved not to let this unpleasant possibility keep me from picking an otherwise acceptable jury.

My thoughts jumped back to the present and I realized the judge had instructed Tony to begin selection of names.

". . . pick the first twelve names from the box, Mr. Jones." And turning toward the audience, he continued: "Ladies and gentlemen, please walk to the end seat, filling the back row first. Tony." He looked at his clerk.

"Ronald Caukinson, Joyce Kelly . . ." With each name I looked over my shoulder to see if the priest had moved.

". . . Floyd Finch, Paul Beringer . . ."

At this name the priest rose from his seat, stepping politely over those between him and the end of the aisle. He looked just as priestly standing as he had seated. He thanked the bailiff for holding the swinging gate for him. Even the marshal acknowledged the priest's greeting with extra care. I watched as he walked past me, nodded cordially, and mounted the two steps to the back row and took the fourth seat. I knew I had to get a break to consult someone with more experience about these things before I would even know how to approach questioning this priest. I looked at my watch. It was only 10:15 in the morning and we certainly weren't due for a recess.

I realized I was three names behind. I glanced at John's chart, caught up, and tried to concentrate on the remaining names: eight men and four women for starters. After we had been introduced, definitions of the charges were read by Judge Olmeda: "Count one alleges that on or about August 11, 1978, Nicholas Eugene Harter did unlawfully accomplish an act of sexual intercourse with a female not the wife of the defendant, who resisted, but whose resistance was overcome by force and violence, and who was prevented from resisting by threats of great and immediate bodily harm, accompanied by apparent power of execution in violation of Penal Code Section 261, generally known as rape."

I was watching the twelve people in the jury box. How they sat, were dressed, moved—everything had to be checked. A missed cue could mean the difference between letting the crucial signal slip by unnoticed and the elimination of a potential candidate for hanging the jury. I particularly watched their faces. While no one flinched as the charge was read, an earlier inquiry from the judge had already revealed that several of the younger women, and a couple of the older men, felt they could not be fair to a defendant if selected to sit on a rape case.

The judge went on: "Count two alleges that on or about August 11, 1978, Nicholas Eugene Harter did unlawfully compel another person to participate in an act of oral copulation by force, violence, duress, menace, and threat of great bodily harm, in violation of Penal Code Section 288 (A) (c)."

This time there was considerable fidgeting. Rape was tough to prove, but oral copulation was even more difficult. The same jury, on identical facts from one trial, would often convict a defendant of rape—intercourse being a normal sex act under the right circumstances—while hanging up on or acquitting him of oral sex—an act considered abnormal by many. During deliberations juror reactions ranged from simple disbelief that such things happen, through various stages of rationalization used to disguise their inability to use the words necessary to really tackle the question, to plain disgust and a virtual psychological block which, even in the face of strong evidence, would not allow them to brand a man with such a stigma.

Paul Beringer was listening intently, but seemed relaxed.

There's almost a halo over him, I mused. *Surely he has a weakness. Let's see, abortion, extramarital sex, cohabitation, drugs—I ought to be able to find something he can't be impartial about. This must be one of those times they're talking about when they say you have to laugh be-*

cause if you don't you'll cry. I smiled at Father Beringer. He smiled back. Perhaps he knew what was on my mind.

The usual questioning by the judge began: name, marital status, children—in this case, ages and sex—employment, spouse's employment, participation in lawsuits, close friends or relatives involved in law enforcement or who were the victims of crimes similar to the one charged today.

Most was routine. Except for the priest.

"I'm a priest in the Benedictine order," he began. "I'm Prior of the monastery."

Prior. Prior. That's high up. I groped silently while scribbling the word on my yellow pad. *I'll have to find out upstairs. I'd be really embarrassed to ask him what it meant.*

"I have spoken with you over the telephone," Judge Olmeda acknowledged.

The priest nodded. "That's right. We have some good friends among the attorneys and judges. My work, as head of a monastery, is of course somewhat restricted in the sense of not being connected much with the political scene, but we have considerable experience with a cross section of the community that comes to us for counseling. Also we have a retreat house in which I take a prominent part."

So, Prior means you're head of the monastery. My eyes spoke to him. *And you do lots of counseling. Great; lots of forgiving, right, and second chances?* I had decided. *But I'll get a second opinion if I can.*

I had been listening with one ear. Small talk between the judge and the priest. I tuned back in as Olmeda asked him if he had ever sat on a jury before.

"I have not, your honor."

Questioning went on the rest of the morning and into the afternoon. There was a wide range of backgrounds up there: one housewife, one furniture store owner, one collection agency owner, a contractor, two retired military officers, a district manager for a newspaper, a widow who ran the family avocado ranch, a carpenter, and three teachers— one elementary, one high school, one college level; there was a bachelor and a single woman, and lots of children and grandchildren.

Several were less than enthusiastic at the prospect of spending the better part of the next two weeks sitting on a jury panel. The college teacher had an out-of-state lecture, and the widow lamented that it was the middle of the avocado harvest and she had to supervise it. Another had oral surgery scheduled, and the high school teacher had exams to correct. One needed, he insisted, to pick up his unemployment check. The court agreed to excuse only the widow. The professor calmed down when he discovered that on Fridays, the day his lecture was scheduled, the jury would not be sitting. After the "juicy" charges were read by the judge, our unemployed carpenter decided his check could wait—that he really *wanted* to sit on this jury after all. When I later questioned his quick turnaround, he explained he realized it was his "civic duty." I had almost decided to kick him when one of John's questions revealed that he was a reformed alcoholic—had been for fifteen years.

That's a different story, I thought as I reconsidered. *He won't like Harter's behavior as a drunk."*

More questioning proved me right. As a dry alcoholic, he had strong feelings about uncontrollable drinking. I was sure John would excuse him. I was later surprised when he did not.

We lost three of the young women to the over-broad cart-before-the-horse-type question which invariably causes my best potential jurors to be immediately pegged by the defense: "Is there anything about these particular charges, that is, rape and oral copulation, which makes any-one here feel that they could not sit as fair and impartial jurors?"

What kind of a question is that anyway? No one *likes* rape, and the closer you get to any trauma—friend, relative, victim—the more strongly the initial reactions are likely to be. And the women's move-ment had heightened the awareness among younger women of the shabby treatment often received by rape victims. How else were they expected to respond to such a question? Especially when it was the first question.

The real issue is not how closely their associations have been with a particular offense, but rather the ability to distinguish the association from their role as juror. Granted, this may not be easy. But when they are later asked the far fairer questions about putting aside personal feelings to follow the law, their responses that they could be impartial jurors and follow those rules go unheeded because the damage has already been done, and they find themselves on the way back to the jury lounge.

John surprised me with yet another choice: a middle-aged woman who had returned to college six months before after raising a son who was a clinical psychologist and worked with men who battered their wives, and a daughter, who had been molested as a child and was now a volunteer rape crisis counselor. He left her sitting. This kind of pattern unnerved me. I figured I must be missing some obvious reason he did what he did and I would notice all too late her Nazi armband or her John Birch button.

He asked one matronly panelist whose daughter had been raped, "Was that a particularly violent or horrendous kind of act?" There was no response—at least audibly.

But the best came from the priest.

"Father Beringer," John began, his voice revealing a certain uncertainty.

The priest interjected as John hesitated and looked at his notes, "People call me Father Paul, please do."

"Fine, then, Father Paul it shall be here too." John's relief at the priest's easy manner was apparent. I felt it too. No one knew quite what to expect.

"Now, Father·Paul, have you . . . you have never been on jury duty before?"

"No, I have not. My first experience."

John's voice tried to be light. "I'll be honest with you. With the turned-around collar up there, and the nature of this—what we are going to be talking about—makes me a little reluctant; is there anything about this . . . because of the kind of case . . . that you would rather not sit on this jury?"

This was one time I was glad the defense got to go first. John was having a tough time. Much tougher than Father Paul.

"Well, Mr. Ashbury, I have been a Catholic since 1934. And if you know anything about the Catholic religion, part of our way of belief is for each one to confess his sins, and I have heard confessions for thirty-four years. I am well aware of the workings of human nature, of mankind, and we are supposed to counsel and have understanding."

I hadn't thought about his role as father confessor. There probably wasn't much he hadn't heard. But those words "counsel" and "understanding." Did he always forgive too? My earlier resolve to kick this priest was slipping a bit.

"Is it a sin in the Catholic religion for two adults to have consensual intercourse when they are not married?" John was getting braver.

"If they are Catholic, we would consider that against one of the commandments."

I liked his choice of words. Not judgmental—his answers kept an arm's length between his opinions and himself. But still, a Catholic priest on a rape jury?

John went on. "Now, adultery is only if it is a married man with somebody other than his spouse?"

"It is considered adultery when either the man or the woman is married."

"So that would be, in your religion, considered a sin?"

"Yes" was the neutral response.

I supposed John was getting at the fact that Harter had been living in a common-law relationship at the time he attacked Sandy. My best recollection was that the Catholic religion didn't look very favorably on this sort of thing. Maybe I wouldn't have to kick Father Paul. John could do it and my decision would be made.

"There is no doubt in my mind"—John's voice was now tinged with a defensive ring—"that the testimony you are going to hear at this trial will show that there was a sexual relationship between the accused and the accuser. Are you only going to chastise the man sitting here?" John pointed at Harter, who smiled inappropriately.

"We don't chastise, Mr. Ashbury. We simply listen. And if they are contrite, we give absolution for their actions. We don't—there is no condemnation."

I was impressed. Still no identification of issues with the people involved here. Everything impersonal, yet sincere. The pendulum was swinging further. Was I, too, being swayed by the priest's unassuming, but well-practiced words?

John's bravery had returned. "But don't you go to hell if you violate the commandments?"

"No, not if they are contrite. If they have seen they have made a mistake, the Lord will certainly take that into consideration and have compassion and mercy on them."

"Then you will not confuse legal principles of law with the ethics and canons of your profession?"

"I will try"—Father Paul looked John squarely in the eyes—"to be objective to the laws of the state."

John met and returned the priest's gaze.

"The problem is, Father Paul, Mr. Harter's problem is, that he is going to tell you that he sinned and he is not going to tell you he is sorry. He is not going to tell you he is contrite. That does not necessarily amount to a violation of the law of the state of California. Now, are you still going to consider that he should be punished for sinning and not being contrite?"

The reply was immediate, without a hint of disdain.

"That is in a different court."

Touché! I was really in trouble. I wanted this priest on my jury— even if it was because this whole thing sounded like it had come right out of a movie script. I was also curious. I wanted to test his obviously strong commitments to religious faith in a court of law. Everything about him seemed to indicate that Father Paul could handle the task. Or maybe I was getting overconfident.

Then it was my turn to talk with the jury. My examinations were always lengthy in these cases. I had a lot to do. I spent considerable time familiarizing jurors with the basic concepts of law, such as "reasonable doubt" versus "beyond a shadow of a doubt," and "circumstantial evidence" versus "direct evidence." I discussed duties such as the need to actually make a decision at the end versus throwing up their hands and walking away. I advised them to be aware of the Perry Mason syndrome and to realize that the mere fact an accused took an oath to tell the truth does not necessarily mean he would. I encouraged them to look carefully at witnesses, to examine their reasons for saying what they did, how they said it, and then to decide if any inconsistencies were just that or in fact were falsehoods. For some reason we never use the words "lie" and "liar." We just talk all around them.

"In other words, ladies and gentlemen," I concluded this phase of the examination, "does everyone understand the difference between entering this courtroom with an unbiased mind but not an empty mind?"

While I did not expect any individual responses to the questions which I addressed to the entire panel, it was a way to get their minds working within the legal framework. Besides, I had to do all my pre-instruction in this question/answer style or I'd never get away with it.

I had to be even more subtle as I worked my way into the pre-education phase. I wanted to let the jury in on the issues, both factual and moral, before they were empaneled. I also had to go as far as my guile and the judge's mood would allow in clearing out those who could not at least state more than halfheartedly that their personal feelings about rape could be separated from their duties as jurors. To accomplish this I had to be extremely careful. If I went too far too soon, I ran the risk of being cut off by an irate defense attorney or an exasperated judge before I had learned enough to make a decision.

In questioning jurors for suitability to hear a case, answers are supposed to enlighten the attorneys only as to the general ability of the prospective panelists to be fair, or to find a cause to excuse them for demonstrated biases reflected by the answers. Ironically, I have rarely heard a question put to a prospective juror in a rape case which does not fit this description. That is, however, not how our criminal justice system sees things—yet. In reality, proper jury selection in a rape case is not possible within the present restraints placed on the scope of permissible questioning. I was pretty clever when it came to disguising what could have been considered pre-educating jurors' reactions to the specific case facts. I did this partly by being careful to use the right inflection at the end of the sentence, and partly by the Socratic method: I asked only enough in each question to make it a question—never throwing away too much at once.

Once I had spent enough time—enough varied depending on the response of the group—getting them familiar with the rhythm of legal thinking, I talked with individual jurors. I always knew what general areas I wanted to start with and what specific things I wanted to get to. The actual in-between process, however, was usually up for grabs. I worked from the larger concepts to the smaller concepts. I did this by using what I have come to call the "block method." It is a way of cramming several subjects into my head at once without having to remember each question in order. When I was a new prosecutor I was so busy making sure I had my next question ready that I never heard any answers. There are some attorneys who seem to suffer from this affliction throughout their careers. Others simply choose to ignore what they have heard.

There is only so much that can really be planned ahead of time in jury selection. The rest has to flow from the unique combination of people in that box. While, as in baking, all the essential ingredients may be predictable, how it will look when it comes out of the oven depends upon the cook.

This one reads like the outline for a law school exam, I mused as I blocked out the areas I wanted to remember. Inevitably a defense attorney will provide a good jumping-off point at some time during the course of the questioning. John had given me a good one and I had marked both the juror and the question with a large asterisk-like symbol so I could find it easily when my turn came.

"Mr. Clarian." I was addressing a middle-aged bespectacled man with thinning but neatly trimmed brown hair who immediately responded to the sound of his name as a candidate for a job opening might—by jumping in his seat. His name had been drawn as a replacement for one of the earlier vacancies created when John had excused a young female juror whose description so fit my perfect choice to judge a rape case.

"Mr. Clarian, I didn't mean to startle you, or to pick on you for that matter. But I have to start with someone and you said something back when Mr. Ashbury was talking with you that needs to be looked at by everyone here."

I glanced at my notes, more from force of habit than necessity.

"You are the father of five children, three of them daughters between the ages of twenty and thirty, I believe?"

"Yes, the boys are younger," he replied, still tense in his seat.

"Ah, I was right. You do have a family which covers any number of generation gaps, don't you?" I smiled broadly.

With this, his arms, which had been folded across his chest in the protective manner of one at bay, dropped to his knees and rested there. "Yes, ma'am, but between school and home I generally always know the top forty." He was settling into his interview well and had just relaxed the collective tension of the eleven other people around him, all of whom were waiting their turns. Smiles and whispers replaced concerned anticipation.

"What Mr. Ashbury asked you about was something like, have you and your children experienced any major conflicts of the generation-gap type. As I recall, you said that there had been no such problems for your family."

He was nodding his head in confirmation as I spoke.

Not surprisingly, none of the panel had acknowledged any serious differences with their children which threatened the family relationship. John had put the question to the panel as a whole, asking them to raise a hand if they had something to say. I could not afford to let them off so easily.

I looked up and down the two rows of panelists as I continued. "Most of you here have children who are in the age range of Mr. Clarian's children; I am sure you are aware, if not through personal experience, then from reading or talking to others, that the generation between the ages of twenty and thirty often have certain lifestyles that are quite different from their parents', and they tend to have some conflict with their parents about those lifestyles.

"This is not to suggest, Mr. Clarian, that you or any of the other jurors have run into this particular problem, but you all certainly have opinions about the subject.

"The evidence in this case is going to show that the victim, Sandra Adkins, was living in a house with a male roommate and that they were not married.

"My question of you, Mr. Clarian, and of each one of you"—I scanned the jury box as I finished the sentence—"is this: do you disapprove of that lifestyle, and if so, do you think this feeling would influence your ability to be objective? In other words, would your feelings about lifestyles spill over and affect the victim's credibility in your eyes? Let's take your answers one at a time, Mr. Clarian."

I could see that he was with me and understood what I was after by the expression on his face—like he knew the right answer on "Name That Tune." If it hadn't been clear, I would have started over, as many times as it took.

"Yes. First I have to say I do disapprove of this lifestyle, yes."

"Going from there, do you think knowing Ms. Adkins had chosen such a lifestyle would, by itself, make you less objective to her side of the story?"

"No." He spoke thoughtfully, in a manner suggesting he had not considered such a separation of ideas before. "I don't think it would." If everyone else had followed our dialogue my next question would get us rolling. My plans didn't always work, however. I always felt I understood what Johnny Carson goes through when no one laughs after the joke, when, after my setup, all I got were eleven sets of blank stares and uneasy fidgeting.

"Is there anyone else?" No one moved. I had just begun. "Mrs. Best?" I said her name softly and in my most caressing tone.

"If you are asking if I disapprove, I would have to say yes, I do disapprove."

"Then I ask you the same question I put to Mr. Clarian. Would Ms. Adkins' chosen lifestyle affect the credibility you give to her testimony?"

"No, they are two different things. Her lifestyle is her choice."

"Mr. Melchior?" I was moving down the row, eliminating at least one element of surprise for those to come.

"Yes, I can't say that I would approve of that either, but I don't think it would color my feelings toward the testimony."

I took each juror in turn and received the same response.

"Let me take it one step further, ladies and gentlemen." I had come from behind the lectern that held my notes securely on its lip to place my vulnerability on an equal basis with theirs. "We all know that in that same age range, between twenty and thirty, there are differences of opinion about sex between unmarried people. Mr. Ashbury has already discussed this matter with Father Paul in the context of his religious beliefs, which govern not only his moral but his professional life as well. How about the rest of you? Are there any among you who disapprove of extramarital relationships in the sense I have defined them?"

Hands went up everywhere. John smiled approvingly. While I wasn't overjoyed, I was at least assured of a responsive, if not easily selected, jury.

I counted: six. I jotted down the names.

"All right, ladies and gentlemen, the evidence will show that the victim engaged in a consensual sexual relationship with her male roommate. It's uncontroverted. Are there any among you who feel that this fact about Ms. Adkins will affect your ability to be fair and impartial jurors?" I started down the list of six.

"Mr. Melchior?"

"I think that knowing what you've said about the young lady would even out my feelings."

I wasn't quite following him, but his choice of words suggested his meaning.

"Mr. Melchior, are you saying that the fact Ms. Adkins had a consensual relationship with her male roommate gives the defendant more of a chance in your mind?" The question was accusatory, but my tone was not.

"It makes them more equal in eliminating my . . . what prejudices I might have had beforehand."

For a long time I had been dumbfounded by how easily jurors related credibility to sexual habits. By the time I stood before the prospective jury which was to hear Sandy's case, not only was I expecting to hear the same theme, I had learned how to turn it to my advantage. I identified and eliminated those who confused the two vastly different issues, and used it as a model for those who obviously did make the essential distinction but who could not hear often enough how careful they must be never to forget the lesson learned.

Here was a juror who had felt "prejudiced" in the victim's favor until he was told she had premarital sex. I looked at Judge Olmeda. I wanted to ask him if he was learning anything. His eyes suggested he might be, but only for a moment.

"Mrs. Best? Would you tend to let your personal feelings about extramarital or premarital sex or however you want to describe it— would your personal feelings tend to interfere with the credibility you would give to Ms. Adkins' testimony?"

"I think I would think that had she done this before, that is, slept with someone else, I would tend to . . . I would tend to maybe lean toward the accused."

I kept the benevolent look as I listened intently to her answer, which she obviously had dug for deep down inside. At the same time it was hard for me to refrain from shaking my head in pity or disgust or frustration at this invisible, intangible "thing" or "things" which had allowed such ignorance to breed and prosper for so long. Here I was exposing it! Didn't anyone care? Wouldn't someone help me do something about it?

Not now. I couldn't afford to drift into one of those philosophical states of mind no matter how good it made me feel. *Someday I'll write a book, but right now I'm picking a jury,* I reminded myself. I was ready for the next elimination round.

"Are there others among you who feel, as Mrs. Best does, that because the victim in this case had previous consensual intercourse with a man, she would be more likely to have consented in this case?"

This was only another way of approaching the same question about truthfulness versus sexual habits, but jurors often did not make the connection themselves. I would take all the time they needed.

"Mr. Melchior, is that your feeling also?"

"I think so, yes."

"Mr. Clarian?"

"I would base my judgment on the evidence that was presented."

So now I had a juror who, after advising me he did not approve of the relevant lifestyle, and after hearing the dilemmas, was telling me his decision would be based on the factual, not the moral issues. Maybe so—I still needed to know more.

"In other words, Mr. Clarian, it is not your feeling that because a woman voluntarily consents to sexual intercourse with a male at one time, she is more likely to do it again?"

"No."

I double-checked with Mrs. Best.

"Is that the way you understood my question, Mrs. Best? Do you feel that once a woman says yes she is more likely to say yes again?"

There was a nod in the affirmative.

"Mrs. Nichols?" She was the middle-aged lady who had returned to college now that her children were grown.

"I do disapprove of the young lady's lifestyle, which is the question to which I raised my hand. I would not want it for my lifestyle. However, after cultural shock, so to speak, my husband and I have come to accept many things with the changing times—as the way of young people whose age differs, as their lifestyles do. In answer to the rest of your question, I would not consider her giving consent once or ten times before as related to this case. The issue, as I understand it, is forcible intercourse."

"You are exactly right," I answered, feeling more emphatic than I allowed my response to convey. Unfortunately, this lady would probably not get to hear the case.

"Mr. Frank?"

"I think I could say the same thing. While I don't approve of these things, I can still be a judge of the facts as you present them at trial."

I had gotten to Father Paul.

"Well, I think I answered it pretty well in what I said previously. The question is not what has preceded, but the facts here in court. The defendant is being tried for the charges which were read to us."

I knew from that moment on that I would be unable to kick Father Paul off my jury even if I had tried. He would surely be chosen foreman, and mercifully, in this case, would not lose sight of his terrestrial duties. But what of Sandy's abortion? I'd think about it some more, and maybe it would be better not to mention it. Perhaps that really would be the proverbial straw. At least I'd leave it out of voir dire and see how the case unfolded at trial.

I now had the makings of two identifiable camps among the jury: the one unable to separate age-old misconceptions about rape and deep-seated moral stigmas from a woman's ability to tell the truth; the other, having explored the terrain with me, declaring themselves able to put aside these beliefs and just try the case.

But there was still more ground to cover which might yet affect the outcome of this expedition.

I moved on to blocks of questions about women liking to be raped, women as temptresses by what they wear, how they talk, where they go. I questioned them about alcohol and asked if they felt someone who was under its influence should be held less responsible for his behavior than a sober person. No one agreed with such an idea.

We recessed for the evening and I was finally able to ask Daly about Father Paul. We didn't see eye to eye on a lot of things, but no one could talk better to the "folks" in a jury box than Daly. I always sought his advice and usually found it helpful.

"Hell, I've known Father Paul for years. A real gentleman and one of the most respected priests around. He's worked with dopers, alkies, pimps, murderers, presidents, and popes. You name it. There isn't a cop in the county who's been around over two years and hasn't heard of him. He's right, there isn't a damn thing he hasn't heard at least once through those confessional curtains. He could probably teach me a thing or two. Keep him. I don't know about your middle-aged college coed. She sounds a might eager to please. But you're probably right. Ashbury will kick her and your problem will be solved."

Almost as an afterthought he added, "Kudos on your motion, by the way."

"Thanks, Daly," I replied with the same enthusiasm. "At least for your advice." I trudged toward the elevator with my mounds of paper. Since I couldn't discuss these important things in the men's room like my colleagues, we usually met in the hallway, on our way to or from the elevator.

The start of our second full day of jury selection dawned with a sense of camaraderie among the twelve in the box. They had already been through a lot of soul-searching together and appeared to be hitting it off well. The remaining pool of potential candidates was also noticeably more relaxed as they chatted across rows and with those in front or in back of them. In fact, this seemed an exceptionally congenial group. Or was it still my exhilaration with the early-round smell of success that colored my vision.

Here you go again, I cautioned myself, while the courtroom came to order and the judge took his place. *Don't look for problems. There are plenty without that.*

"Good morning, ladies and gentlemen." I was again standing in front of the lectern offering to meet them on their turf.

"I will not be long this morning. Thank you for your continued patience. You now know our reasons for doing this. Both the defendant and the victim are entitled to an unbiased jury of their peers."

God, I hated that speech. It was so hypocritical: we were no more looking for twelve unbiased people than we were going to the moon. What the defense, in particular, did not want, if at all possible, was anyone who had any real knowledge about the subject matter of the trial. No contractors on a construction site theft case, no nurses on a hospital liability case, no rape crisis counselors on a sexual assault case. No one who could lend true insight and experience to the decisive issues.

I always liken the defense position in a criminal case to that of someone who had a roomful of paintings from among which the best one had to be selected. The judges of this competition were to consist of the first twelve people who purchased a head of lettuce at the corner supermarket on a Monday morning. They would then be taken to the roomful of paintings and told to pick the one they "liked best." No previous experience needed. No art appreciation classes, no composition or color courses. Just what seemed prettiest. Naturally, the same group also would make an ideal jury for a rape case.

I would not allow my jury to be handed their assignment without giving them at least a basic course in their subject matter. The questioning eased into the final stage: connecting the law they would have to use with the facts of the case. This was a very touchy area. If too thinly disguised I would be accused of trying to argue my case before it had begun. Our rules call for linking law and fact after the evidence is heard, just before the jury adjourns to deliberate. I was careful to phrase the questions so that I could clearly claim, which was the truth, that I was looking for fundamental prejudice and therefore reason to excuse a juror for such a cause.

"Is there anyone who feels resistance means physical resistance only and does not include verbal resistance? Or that physical resistance means fighting until there is no strength, or life, left?"

There was a volunteer. She was one of the housewives from the original twelve.

"If the resistance is verbal only, I would sort of hesitate to say she absolutely said no."

Another common belief. It was particularly important in a case such as this where resistance appeared minimal because it was mental rather than physical.

"Mrs. Flynn, do you feel that you would have more trouble believing a victim if she were not beaten than if she had physically visible injuries?"

"Yes, I think it would help me understand better what had happened if she were hurt."

I backtracked and again went over some of what the evidence would show about Sandy's actions. We ended up with a split about the impact of emotional damage much like the one the previous day's discussions had produced in the lifestyle and extramarital sex areas.

I always wound down in a long voir dire by asking the whole panel if anything had occurred over the course of our discussions together which might now cause them to change an answer they had given me previously. Even here one hand went up.

"Yes, Mrs. Flynn."

"I have to ask you one question, if you don't mind. When you say, 'Will you be able to convict if you are convinced of the accused's guilt beyond a reasonable doubt?' I don't know what happens after conviction, but I feel very strongly that should it become evident that the accused is guilty, he will definitely need some sort of psychiatric treatment or something. Does that go with conviction?"

She was genuinely concerned.

"Mrs. Flynn, you and the rest of the jury panel will be instructed that you are not to take penalty or punishment into consideration when deliberating the facts. The question I have for you, then, is: Not knowing the answer to that question, will you be able, if you feel the evidence shows he is guilty beyond a reasonable doubt, to convict the defendant?"

"I think so." She was faltering, searching herself.

"Remember when I talked to you about the people's burden of proof? That it was not beyond any possible doubt, but only reasonable doubt? Do you feel that not knowing what could happen to Mr. Harter if you helped convict him might make you push me beyond that reasonable doubt to the point of any shadow of a doubt? Remember I used those expressions?"

"Yes, and I have been thinking about what you said since yesterday. I really have. I think honestly I might do that."

I believed her and assured her I did.

"But, Mrs. Flynn, the bottom line is this: I am telling you that when you go into the jury room, you will not know any more about the question you have asked than you do right now. If you have a hesitation about whether you can convict, I need to know now."

The answer was clear, if not direct.

"I could convict if I am a hundred percent sure."

She would make me run the extra mile that the law did not require. I checked with all the other jurors to see where they stood. I was humbled once again by how close I had come to missing an issue altogether. Damn. I'd never remember everything.

By midafternoon John and I had excused and replaced the jurors we each felt could least serve our respective cases and I had led the replacements, and their replacements, through the now familiar territory of questioning which took them to one of the two clearly identifiable positions I had established about the facts in Sandy's case.

It was 4:30 when John and I finally acknowledged our mutual satisfaction with our jury and one alternate. They were sworn in and excused until the next morning at ten o'clock. I felt I had already been in trial a month. And I hadn't even given my opening statement.

I sank into my office chair just as the lemmings headed for the elevators. I called Sandy. We had a long evening ahead of us.

5

I HAD SCARCELY BID the courtroom good night when I found myself back the following morning. Sografo arrived as I was giving Sandy's emotional and physical appearance a last-minute once-over.

"Be conservative with what you wear to court," I had said, "but don't be obvious about it. No trench coats, waders, scarfs, or sunglasses." Contrary to popular belief, I had noticed a tendency by rape victims to cover their bodies with long sleeves, high necklines, and baggy pants. It clearly represents a psychological protection to help shield that which has been so brutally taken by the attack. I have never had to tell a victim to be more discreet in front of the jury.

"Be yourself," I continued, "just not the after-five yourself." Sandy had followed my instructions exactly. She wore a mid-calf-length brown wool skirt with woven bands of pastel yellows and oranges. Her blouse was long-sleeved and unbuttoned only at the throat. Around her neck were two slim gold chains which fell along the outside folds of the blouse.

"Are the boots really leather?" I asked admiringly. They were a muted chocolate brown and disappeared under the hemline of her skirt. Only when she crossed her legs did I see the tops, which came to just under the knee.

"Yeah," she answered in the same controlled manner I had come to cherish more and more as trial approached. "I get one real pair each winter. These are last year's, so they won't look like I went out and bought them just for the trial." There was a hint of a real smile just under the nervous laugh, which had also not changed from the time of our first meeting.

"Well," I observed with a stamp of approval, "you couldn't have been more covered up in a nun's habit. Only the skin of your face and hands will see neon today."

I wondered if my reference to a nun had been inspired by Father Paul. I was still doing flip-flops over the decision to leave him on the jury. But Jerry Sografo knew of him as well, and was as certain as Daly had been that for all his otherworldly duties, Father Paul had both feet planted firmly on the ground. I simply didn't have time to think about Father Paul anymore. He was on the jury and that was that.

"Jerry, do you have the mug shot of Harter I wanted?" I always asked for a photo taken at the time a suspect was arrested and booked in a rape or child molest case. It was often the last time during the course of court proceedings that he would look exactly as he had on the day he had attacked a victim. Once a defense attorney got hold of him, the first things ordered frequently were haircuts, shaves, and suits. By the time a jury saw him sitting next to a lawyer on the first day of trial, it was often difficult to distinguish client from attorney. One victim in an earlier case had actually not recognized the defendant at trial because he had looked so different—and there had been no identity issue in the case at all.

Nothing burst the young business executive image quicker than a mug shot which the jurors could pass around revealing a bleary-eyed, unkempt, mustached face staring back at them. I would then ask the defendant why he felt it important to clean up so much for the nice folks on the jury but had apparently felt the victim would like to make love to him in his come-as-he-was attire. Trial rules allow the prosecutor to comment to the jury about the changes in a suspect's appearance and to offer any possible reasons for them. "What you see now is *not* what she got then," I would remind the jury in final argument.

"Yes, I have it right here," Jerry replied, opening the folder he had resting on his knee. He slid a small picture out from under a paper clip attached to the corner of the file. "I don't think he'll ever be nominated for Mr. All-American." He handed the print to me across the desk.

I had seen Nicholas Harter once, at the prelim, and then only for an hour or so. I looked at the photo Sografo had given me. It was pretty much as I had remembered him. Thin, almost gaunt face, with expressionless eyes, long stringy hair, and about a two-day five o'clock shadow on his chin. I thought about the classy lady sitting across from me voluntarily making love to him. I shuddered. "Ladies and gentlemen," I fantasized silently, slapping the picture down, "I rest my case."

Both Jerry and Sandy jumped as Harter's mug shot hit my desk.

"Sorry, just thinking." I looked at my watch. It was 9:50. "Sandy, we'd better go. Jerry, here's a list of the witnesses and the order I plan to use them. Would you please call the first two and tell them to be on standby? Then meet us downstairs."

Sandy and I headed for the elevator again. The only signs of her tension were two small dark spots on the underarms of her blouse. She couldn't hide the perspiration.

The only time I didn't mind having the elevator stop on every floor between seven and three was on opening day of trial. It gave me just a few more seconds to calm my inner hysteria. It got worse with every trial, especially incest and rape. It was much worse after I began using the expert testimony. I guess I felt an even heavier responsibility. If my mistakes should cause an appellate court to reverse a hard-fought conviction, I wouldn't know how to face the victim.

I felt as if the slightest excuse would dissuade me from going on with Sandy's case—even as we approached Department 14, with the jury selected. I repeated the now familiar script to myself. "It's simple, you know," I said as we drew closer to the courtroom door. "You're a masochist."

The first thing I saw once Sandy and I were inside the courtroom was a transformed Nicholas Harter. He was clean-shaven, and while his hair was still stringy, it was trimmed. The blue jacket of his leisure suit hung uncomfortably over his still thin shoulders. The brown loafers looked to be about six hours old and just as unhappy to have Harter's feet stuffed into them as he appeared to feel about the entire outfit.

Sandy saw him at the same instant I did. My eyes and nod let her know I would take care of that later.

I delivered my opening statement, which was brief and only partially specific. Things were always too uncertain to make lots of promises to a jury. Nothing is more disastrous to a woman or child victim than to tell the jury they are going to hear evidence which either you are unable to provide due to some eleventh-hour problem or is thwarted by a suddenly uncooperative witness. This departure is somehow felt to be a direct reflection on the credibility of the victim. The phenomenon is not nearly as prevalent, nor has as serious results, in traditional crimes. What can be forgiven as innocent or inadvertent in other types of cases is interpreted as a deliberate attempt to fool the jury on the part of the child or woman in a sex case.

Sandy took the stand at 10:25 A.M. on Wednesday, January 24, 1979. She was not excused until 4:45 that afternoon. Except for an hour, she was questioned continuously. By the time she left the courtroom the jury knew her well—no, actually they knew her much better than that.

At Disneyland there is an attraction in which, while riding in a car moving along a track, one experiences the sensation of becoming smaller and smaller, simulating first penetration by the rider into a snowflake, then a molecule of the snowflake, an atom of that molecule, et cetera, until finally the traveler is deep into the nucleus itself. Overall the effect is a feeling of intimate participation in inner space. I took the jury on such a journey with Sandy, only it was into her mind that they traveled.

We began with a diagram of the house Sandy lived in, detailing her bedroom. We placed the furniture, the doors, the windows. Then we repeated the process for other rooms and moved on to the neighborhood. We told the jury whom she knew, where they lived, and when they were home.

I guided her through a recital of her educational background in general and of her job at the day care center in particular. She explained her decision to move in with Stan, giving her reasons, and did the same for her decision—unfortunately not in time—to leave. She sketched her impressions of Harter and his girlfriend, Kelly, which later figured so prominently in her reactions to his attack. With particular care we retraced her steps on August 10, 1978, from the time she got up in the morning until the time she set her alarm and turned out the light that night.

We then chronicled the dark events which changed her life forever during the early-morning hours of August 11.

Sandy cried uncontrollably twice that day. The first time she was describing her effort to fight Harter off and, along with the realization of its futility, came her tears. Later, as she relived the moment he forced his penis into her mouth and ordered her to make it hard, it happened again. While not surprised, considering what I was making her do, I was a bit unprepared. It was the first and only time I ever saw her cry. It was entirely appropriate and I could see the jury was moved, so I left it at that. As my research went on in the years ahead, I found an answer for what had happened to Sandy that day in trial, but at that time it was one more thing that I understood but could not put in perspective.

It was part of my plan, as I guided the jury into Sandy's thoughts, to anticipate cross-examination by the defense. I wanted to head off possible inferences which might affect credibility because of an unasked or incomplete question on my part. I also needed to fully account for Sandy's behavior and her time by introducing through her testimony the supporting witnesses who would follow. Anything the jury was sure to learn anyway I wanted them to hear from me first. On the other hand, I had to guard against starting the fire and getting only smoke, while allowing Ashbury to fan it into flame.

To explain and confirm Sandy's reasonable responses to the attack, I would, of course, have Anne Kennedy follow her to the witness stand. But I wanted more than confirmation. Whether as beholders or observers, the idea was to make the jurors visualize, not just hear, what had happened to Sandy.

"How did you feel?" and "What did you say?" are questions often put to the recipients of sudden good fortune. Desire to know the answers to these types of questions is equally strong when the news or event is tragic. We just don't ask—at least not directly. But we want to know. Aside from sheer curiosity, such understanding of how others deal with trauma makes us thankful it wasn't us, helps us sympathize with the victim, or perhaps heightens our awareness of the strengths or weaknesses of the human mind and body. These things my jurors would feel.

"Ms. Adkins, what was going through your mind when you realized you were trapped?" I asked her following her description of Harter's initial attack as he straddled her body.

"A lot of things went racing through my mind; how I was going to get out of this alive, or without getting hurt, what I could do."

"So it occurred to you that you might be hurt or that he might even kill you?" I had not put this question to her before.

"It was the first thing that went through my mind—that he could kill me. But then I started trying to remember the things I'd read on rape—you know—what to do."

"Ms. Adkins," I pressed on, "what I want to know right now is what was going through your mind at that very moment about what you read."

"It was that you should only fight back if you felt you had a chance."

"Had you determined at that point that you didn't have a chance to get away?"

"Yes."

"Go on."

"It was that . . . if you felt like . . . you are in a situation where you aren't going to be able to get help, that the best thing to do is to do what he tells you and try to stay calm, not to provoke the attacker."

"Did you tell yourself to stay calm?" My voice was saying that the same thing applied to her present situation.

"Yes. I told myself I needed to stay . . . to try to stay calm, stay in control, because I knew if I couldn't stay in control that I'd have less of a chance."

"And did you stay in control?"

"I tried to, yes."

Just as she had done so clearly for me the day we first met, Sandy now recounted for the jury all the things that had made her decide not to resist her attacker—at least physically—after her initial attempts to flee and to scream were overcome: the odor of alcohol which brought to mind the violent streak she had seen before, the force with which he threw her down on the bed, escape routes considered and rejected.

". . . and then, there was his . . . voice." She looked at me as if now seeking approval for this revelation.

"What about his voice?" I encouraged, emphasizing the first word.

"It was different. He didn't yell or anything . . . he commanded me and I . . . like when he first told me to take off my top, I said no. Then he said, 'Take it off!' and I did. And when he told me to spread my legs, I said no to that too. Then he said, 'Spread 'em!' and I did. It was the tone that scared me, and I . . . obeyed."

Sandy had told me about her brief verbal exchanges with Harter, but not the effect his voice had on her. She appeared to have only just realized it herself. I had heard this thing about voice before. I wanted her to be more specific.

"Are you trying to say it was the difference between what you remembered his regular voice to be and the way he sounded the night of the attack that frightened you?"

"Yes, that but . . . something else too. Oh, I don't know." She breathed the words out with exasperation at her inability to explain. "Maybe it was that it *seemed* different because I was so afraid he might hurt me. I just know it scared me."

Maybe it was her terror which set the tone apart. But as Sandy had said, it was something else too. It stirred thoughts in that place where I kept things I couldn't quite pin down. I made a mental note to add it to my interviews of rape victims in the future.

I continually reminded myself that Ashbury would, when his turn came, plead consent. To ensure early juror rejection of such a defense, I was attentive to any detail which could help erode this claim. I decided to begin with the forced oral copulation. For those who disapproved of it under any circumstances, it could only repulse them. For the others, I had a feeling they would understand and empathize.

"You've told us, Ms. Adkins, that his penis wasn't hard and that it wouldn't go in."

"Yes," she replied softly, looking at her lap and feverishly twirling the purse strap between her fingers.

"What happened next?"

"He said, 'Put it in your mouth.'"

"What did you say?" I could hear the control slipping from her voice.

"I said, 'I don't want to,' and he said, 'Put it in your mouth and make it hard.' And he pushed it . . . he was over me and he pushed it up to my mouth."

"Did you do it?" I could see the despair in her face as the tears began to flow down her cheeks.

"Yes. I didn't want to do it. I can remember just the smell of it . . ." The last words trailed off in her efforts to gulp back the sobs, but they had already escaped.

"Just take a minute," I soothed. "Sit there and take a minute." I left my seat and quickly moved to her side, grabbing a Kleenex from the box the bailiff had earlier removed from his drawer. I touched her shoulder and handed it to her. I then moved quickly away. I dared not be too comforting.

Ashbury was nervous. "Your honor, might this be an appropriate spot to take another recess?" he suggested, referring to the first time Sandy had cried in front of the jury.

But I could see Sandy did not want to prolong these excruciating moments. She forced the words through the revulsion she felt as she spoke them.

". . . so it got hard and then he said . . . commanded that I put it inside of me and . . ."

"Did you?"

"Yes." She was holding on, but each word was painfully controlled.

"What happened next?"

"He just started going back and forth, and I didn't want his body to be on top of mine—to touch me—and I was holding it up with the palms of my hands so it wouldn't come down on top of me. And then all of a sudden he stopped . . ." She realized she had put her hands out in front of her, palms up, fingers toward me, when she was describing how she tried to keep Harter's body away from hers. Embarrassed, she put them back in her lap.

In my mind I could see all of this actually happening to Sandy as she was describing it. I glanced at the jury. I heard someone swallow. *She's not up there alone,* I said to myself.

"During this entire time, Ms. Adkins, did the defendant ever kiss you?"

"No."

"Did you kiss him?"

"No."

"Did you put your arms around him?"

"No."

"Any words of tenderness or love?"

"No. But when he had his finger inside me he said, 'It feels good, doesn't it?' or something like that."

"What did you say?"

"I told him he was hurting me. And to stop."

"And did he?"

"No. He put two fingers in and moved them harder after I told him he was hurting me."

Frame by frame we moved along, advancing to the next only after each one had been carefully viewed.

In preparation for the supporting evidence to follow her, I guided Sandy through areas about which I intended to call corroborating witnesses.

There was the problem of allowing the back door to remain unlocked.

"Had any efforts ever been made to keep the back door locked?"

"Yes. There had been a key when I first moved in, but there wasn't a key for each person, so we used to keep it under the flower pot on the back porch, but that wasn't working out too well because someone was always forgetting to put it back."

"So you had other keys made?"

"Yes. I took the key to a locksmith and had two keys made. I brought them back and they didn't fit."

"When was that?"

"That was in June."

"Were you away the entire month of July?"

"Yes."

"So on the night of August 10 you had been back for only ten days, living in the house?"

"Yes."

The next day Stan and Sandy's third roommate, Linda Sims, backed her up in every detail.

"Sandy was a little upset with me for not putting that key back," Linda admitted when I asked if Sandy had spoken to her about it. "She didn't like the idea of leaving the door unlocked, but while she was away on vacation someone lost the only key."

We talked about Sandy's decision to move into the house.

"I was looking for a place I could afford. We didn't know if the day care center would be staying open. It was supposed to close in June, so I needed a place I could live in even if I lost my job. And I wanted to live in a house. I'd been living in apartments for a long time. I also had a kitty and it's really hard to find a place that will accept pets."

"How much was the rent?"

"My share was a hundred twenty-five dollars a month, including utilities."

And had she been making plans to move out of the house before the assault?

"Yes. In June I told two of my girlfriends I wanted them to help me find a new place as soon as I got back from my trip."

"Did you look when you got back?"

"Caroline and I were planning to look the next weekend but then . . ."

Caroline Jacobs not only corroborated everything Sandy had said; she told the jury they had all gotten their preliminary notices of job termination from the day care center—and she brought hers to court.

I asked Sandy if she had any previous friendship with Harter.

"No. As a matter of fact, I even talked to Stan a couple of times about him."

"What did you tell him?"

"I remember wondering why he had a friend like, who was . . . well, you know, like a bum. He came over with his girlfriend and all they did was smoke pot and get drunk—along with some other of his friends who were just like him."

"Did you ever socialize with this group?"

"No, I didn't."

We needed to be first to let the jury know of Sandy's earlier intimacies with Stan.

Had she slept with Stan during the time that she lived in the house?

"Yes, three times, right after I moved in."

"Was it consensual?"

"Yes."

"Are you still friends?"

"Yes. We decided we were better friends than lovers."

"Were you aware that Mr. Pease had told the defendant you had slept with him?"

"No."

When Stan testified he admitted he had told Harter that he had slept with Sandy.

"Why did you do that, Mr. Pease?"

"Well, Nick thought Sandy was a looker, but uptight. So that he wouldn't waste his time, I told him she didn't think much of him."

"What was his reaction to that?"

"It was something to the effect that 'she needs a good stiff dick to make her a little more pleasant.' "

"So it was then you told him that you had, in fact, slept with Ms. Adkins?"

"Yes."

Stan also confirmed Harter's volatile temper when drinking and his belligerence toward his girlfriend and said that Sandy never flaunted herself in front of Harter, or anyone else, to his knowledge.

I still had not decided if I would tell the jury about Sandy's abortion. It was a subject of such great controversy and strong convictions. Could those jurors who, in particular, had promised to put aside personal biases for the sake of duty be expected to go that far? If Sandy's credibility hung in the balance in any of their minds, her birth control practices could quickly blur the last bounds of justice, perhaps already stretched to the limit.

I felt things were going well enough, though, to at least test the waters, if not take the plunge.

"Ms. Adkins, do you practice any form of birth control?" My heart was already shifting gears.

"Yes, I do. I use a diaphragm." She was looking directly at me.

"When do you use it?" I was looking directly at her.

"You put it inside of you before intercourse."

"Do you ever have intercourse without using it?"

"Only right at my period when I know I can't get pregnant."

"Do you keep track of your menstrual cycle?"

"Yes."

"Where were you in your cycle at the time of the incident on August 11?"

"It was at a fertile time." I was having difficulty looking anywhere but at Sandy. I could see the same was true with her.

"Did you have a diaphragm in that night?"

"No."

"Did you consent to this intercourse?"

"No."

"If you had consented would you have put the diaphragm in before engaging in sexual intercourse during the fertile time of the month?"

"Yes." I decided to look at the jury, cautiously.

I was watching Father Paul in particular now, and nothing in his manner or on his face revealed that this information affected him. But just saying the words necessary to have gotten through this bit of testimony had been scary for me. I decided not to mention the abortion. It was just too risky.

I felt an urgency to put some distance between this last sequence and the jury. I stood, stepped around behind my chair, and faced the witness stand. Only at the sound of my chair did heads turn away from Sandy, where they had appeared to have been waiting for a secret not yet revealed. My next questions would make it clear that they were to hear nothing more. Silent clues, however, might be more conspicuous to some by their very absence. I would find out after the trial.

"Ms. Adkins, on the evening of August 10, did you have a conversation in which you talked about what you would do if you were raped?"

"Yes, I did. I had a couple of hours after work and before I had to go back to a staff meeting at the school. So I went to visit a friend who owns a shop in La Jolla. The woman who works with him mentioned a mutual friend of theirs had been raped. I told them about an article I had read the Sunday before in the newspaper which had really disturbed me. About a woman who was raped and shot and they think she'll be a quadriplegic. This sort of led to Christine—that's the lady who works for my friend—and I talking."

"Did you tell her what you thought you would do if you were attacked?"

"Yes."

Again, as she had once done for me, she outlined for the jury all the things which had contributed to her awareness of rape over the past several years. There were magazine series from major publications such as *Cosmopolitan* and *Reader's Digest,* a pamphlet from one of the community clinics, some newspaper articles, and two lectures, plus a film at the college where the day care center was located. She wanted, she explained, to be able to help herself as best she could under whatever the circumstances might be.

"Tell me, Ms. Adkins, do you carry anything with you for protection against attack?"

"Yes, I carry a police whistle." She reached into her purse and pulled out a key chain with several keys on one end and a slender whistle on the other. She held it up where the jury could see. Two of the women nodded in apparent recognition.

"Do you recall how long you have had that whistle?"

"Approximately three years."

"How did you come by it?"

"A girlfriend of mine had bought one for each of us because, where I work, lots of times I get off late and it's dark outside, and I have to go from where I work to my car."

"Do you carry it in your hand when you are walking to your car?"

"Yes. You're supposed to hold it so that one key sticks out from between each finger, sort of like spikes. This way if someone grabs you, you can jab hard and fast, or blow the whistle if you have more time." She held the police whistle up again, this time with a key protruding out from between the fingers of her clenched hand.

It was hard to imagine that the jury, priest and all, could not see how carefully this victim had considered the threat of rape and what to do about it. But just in case . . .

"As a result of all the things you've told us, had you decided on a course of action before August 11?"

"Yes, I had."

"Were you relying on information from all the sources you have described when you decided what to do as the defendant's body held you pinned to your bed?"

"Yes."

I looked at my notes. I had only one item left on my list of three pages—and it had been a real last-minute scribble.

"Ms. Adkins, does Mr. Harter's appearance here in court today match your recollection of how he looked when he would visit Mr. Pease?"

"No, he looks very different here."

Only her eyes moved to where Harter sat at the table. And only for a second.

"Have you *ever* seen Mr. Harter look as he does here in court to-day?"

"No, never."

I had the mug shot of Harter marked as evidence. I placed it on the table in front of the witness stand where Sandy sat.

"Do you recognize the person in this photo?" I asked her while tapping my finger on it.

"Yes. It is Nicholas Harter."

"Does he appear in this photo as you remember him?"

"Yes. He does."

With the permission of the judge, I handed the photograph to a juror with the directive to pass it on. As it went from one to the next, there were varied reactions. From none at all to shaking heads, slight grimaces, and one or two long stares, first at the photo, then at Harter and back.

I had finished. Everything was ready for Anne Kennedy to take up where Sandy left off. I still worried that I might be leaving something out. But I could think of nothing.

"Your honor"—I looked at Judge Olmeda—"I have no further questions of this witness at this time."

The judge nodded his acknowledgment and looked to my opponent.

"Mr. Ashbury," he queried, "do you wish to cross-examine the witness?"

What followed was typically distasteful for me. I accept without hesitation our system of justice which grants to those accused of a crime protections guaranteed by the Constitution and its amendments. What I reject with a conviction grown strong through years as a victim's advocate are the extremes to which the interpretation of these rights has been taken, leaving in its wake the fragmented lives of a far more innocent segment of our society than those it purports to protect. Born of a century of excessive abuses practiced against the poor and the weak, vigorous Supreme Court action in the 1960s sought to balance the scale.

As a vast majority of our laws had originally been designed with "free men" the intended beneficiaries, it is not surprising that corrections in the system did little to help women on either side of the legal fence, I might add, but that is a separate story. In fact, by spreading ever wider the protective umbrella over the accused, victims of crimes which are primarily committed against women and children faced a new and even more insidious vulnerability.

Under the guise of denying defendants the exercise of their rights, it became more difficult to curb, and consequently easier to abuse, some offensive trial practices which allowed indiscriminate testing of a female complainant's truthfulness both inside and outside the courtroom. Among these were psychological examinations to search out possible reasons why a woman, or a child, might be fabricating an account of sexual assault, and, for the same purpose, the right of a defense attorney during cross-examination to dissect the past, usually unrelated, sexual history of women and girls. Even in states such as California where recognition of certain injustices along these lines has resulted in corrective measures, trial by inference, innuendo, or suspicion, guarded against scrupulously on behalf of the accused, all too often is the accepted goal in attacking victim credibility.

Ashbury did not prove to be as fierce at using the ammunition Sandy's case provided as I had feared. As time passed it became obvious, too, that my strategy had taken the wind out of his sails. I had left no surprise for him to spring on the jury making me—or Sandy—look like the "bad guy." Of course, there was still room for a rich assortment of inferences.

"Now, Ms. Adkins, did you *finally* move away from the house after August 11?" he asked, placing emphasis on the word "finally."

"Yes, I did."

I could see the next question coming.

"With whom did you move . . . ?"

"Objection!" I broke in, already sensing the goal. "Irrelevant, your honor."

"Your honor, they opened the door," Ashbury countered righteously.

"To what?" I asked, having already weighed the harm to Sandy's case between allowing the jury to know the answer and letting them infer what they might by not hearing it.

"To this line of questioning." He looked over to me as if the logic of his reasoning could not be escaped. "You asked if she had moved away and discussed it with others, and I am pursuing that area."

At one time I might have treated this apples-to-oranges type of thinking with a flip response. Experience has taught me that all too often judges find my opponent's analytical processes more to their liking than my own—particularly in this kind of case. I had learned to take it all very seriously. I also had no intention of arguing with Ashbury in front of the jury and, perhaps, letting him do indirectly what he could not do directly.

"It's irrelevant" came the decision from Olmeda before I had quite replied.

But Ashbury did not intend to let it go. He requested to be heard outside the jury's presence. We were to repeat this process several more times before he had finished questioning Sandy.

"All right, your honor," he began once we had settled into chairs behind the closed doors of the judge's chambers. "It is my understanding, and strictly from hearsay information—I have no positive evidence of it except perhaps through this witness on the stand—that, in fact, number one, she has a boyfriend. Number two, that for some time prior to leaving she had been wanting to move in with him. Number three, he declined to let that happen. Number four, as soon as she reports a rape, I think she moved in with him. Now, I am saying that there may be a cause, in effect a motive for her to fabricate her testimony simply to provide a way out of a living situation she made sure other people knew she did not like, and into one she wanted very much."

I found it hard to know where to start! Should it be with the eight or nine "maybes" sprinkled among the things which perhaps were true, or with a string of speculations which perhaps equaled motive? I considered the absurdity of the proposition and had to smile: that a woman—in order to get to move in with her boyfriend—would run naked into the street, endure endless interviews, be subjected to an embarrassing physical examination, and spend long hours answering detailed questions on a witness stand about intimate personal facts in front of twelve strangers; and just for insurance, during the fertile time in her menstrual cycle, not take any precautions, planning to use a resulting pregnancy as her ace; an abortion is simple enough and its threat would bring round any but the most callous, certainly a boyfriend, to take her in during her time of need.

A new variation on an old theme: usually, the argument goes, she has been unfaithful to husband or boyfriend, discovers she is pregnant, and cries rape to cover herself, or, having become pregnant by a lover who refuses to acknowledge or reneges on his responsibility, she cries rape to get even.

As absurd as any of these combinations appeared to me in light of the facts of this case, the theories which I brought into the courtroom on such matters were, and are, far from the accepted views. Deeply rooted in men's historical and cultural portrayal of the female and her role, these views were, like it or not, the norm. I had to realize that my success now depended to a great extent on how seriously I treated this and similar situations. There were rules, protocol to follow. By treating them as less than legitimate factual interpretations by tossing out sarcastic retorts and snide comments, I could drive the judge and jury farther from my control. After all, men predominated among the judges, and my women jurors had been raised in the same society from which all jurors were selected.

This analysis of what I had to contend with was far from gratifying, but it did make sense and kept me from making a foolish mistake at some important time during the trial. It would be another year and a half to two years before I was to realize that it was my perspective as a woman within the system itself which caused this inevitable conflict. It was not for another two years after that, having left the District Attorney's office and having put some time and distance between us, that I realized this barrier of men against women which consumed so much energy is really a communication gap which exists because of the very different perspectives we each bring to a problem.

As I prepared a reply to Ashbury's comments, I tried to remember where Sandy *had* moved after she left the house. My impression was that it had not been to her boyfriend's place, but I couldn't recall. I wasn't sure I asked directly, but I must have been satisfied enough with whatever impressions I had concerning her new living situation to be sure it wouldn't present a trial problem. Now my concern was, I could not, and would not, represent to the judge that she had *not* moved in with her boyfriend merely on the basis of impressions.

"It is totally irrelevant where she moved afterward, your honor." I'd stick with the broad approach first, and narrow it down. "She planned to move before the rape. The only motives here are self-serving to Mr. Ashbury. They are attempts to influence the jury and to discredit the victim by inference, both condemned as methods of proof by our courts. Further, it is a fishing expedition by defense counsel. Mr. Ashbury had six months to find anyone who could provide him with a motive for Ms. Adkins to have fabricated her claim of rape. He is obviously aware that a boyfriend existed and that he lives in town. He could have found him."

"No one will talk to us." Ashbury pouted helplessly.

"Come now, counsel." I looked at Judge Olmeda as I continued. "He never complained to me of any inability to reach witnesses, never. Mr. Ashbury knows I would have cooperated with him."

And now for the law. "Finally, your honor, even if there is a possible inference of motive from what Mr. Ashbury describes, the prejudicial effect far outweighs substantive value, and I ask that its use as evidence be denied under Section 352 of the California Evidence Code." This section allows a judge to keep out even valid evidence if its real purpose is to discredit a witness on a side issue rather than to help the jury get to a truth.

"Are you prepared to say that she did not move in with a male?" Ashbury went on before Olmeda could reply.

Damn, I didn't want to answer that, but the judge seemed content to let this continue.

"I am not prepared to say that."

"But I am." Ashbury looked smug. If I only knew for sure whether to let him do this. I decided to try to end it again.

"Well, it's irrelevant." Without warning Olmeda had ruled. His expression had not changed and we were both a bit surprised.

Prepared and patient, I decided. *That's what it takes with this judge. And to keep talking until he is ready to make up his mind.*

As we returned to the courtroom I wondered if the defense would now bring up the abortion. It was a double-edged sword, to be sure. Ashbury had to consider how the jurors might treat Harter during deliberations if they tended to believe Sandy and thought he had put her through the added trauma of pregnancy and abortion. Such evidence could be sufficient to swing otherwise undecided votes against his client, if only from outrage.

Well, if he did go into the abortion, at least the decision would be out of my hands.

But he did not.

He went on to the relationship with Stan, asking Sandy if she had been his supervisor, if she liked him more than he liked her, and if she had told him she was moving—to all of which she answered no.

He wondered aloud if she disliked his client because of his manners, which she described as vulgar and crass, and went on to inquire if it was also because of his appearance—his facial hair and clothing. She replied, "Yes," to the first question, and to the second, "No, I don't think so. I try not to make opinions of people by the way they look."

"How about the fact that he drank and got drunk? Would this have a bearing on your feelings toward him?"

"Yes."

What a question! Was she playing into his hands for some Perry Masonish finale or was this groping in the dark? The nagging feeling just wouldn't go away.

"How about the fact that he smoked pot, did this have a bearing on your feelings?"

"I think probably because of the excess of it."

"Now, Ms. Adkins, did Stan drink?"

"Yes. He did."

Sandy glanced at me between blinks. She must have been following my thoughts.

"Did Stan get high on pot?"

"Yes."

He was getting ready.

"So that Mr. Harter and Mr. Pease were no different?"

"Objection," I challenged quickly. "The question is argumentative and calls for a conclusion."

The court sustained me.

So that was it. If both men were so much alike and she had slept with one, she probably chose to sleep with the other and consequently the jury should not believe the claim of rape. While not strong enough to have allowed Sandy to go into so much detail about her actions, this theory had to be dealt with.

But Ashbury didn't know when to let well enough alone. By the time he left the subject he had given Sandy the opportunity to describe the gifted teacher, loyal friend, and considerate roommate, all characteristics which, in her assessment of the two, set Stan apart from Harter.

Ashbury next moved on to the knowledge Sandy had about rape before the attack.

"The articles about rape you read, Ms. Adkins, did they tell you means of self-defense a woman could use to protect herself?"

"Yes."

"What were those means?"

"To scream or yell."

"Okay, what else?"

"To poke someone in the eye or throat, or jam the palm of your hand up into the nose, or to kick them."

"Kick them where?"

"In the groin. But in the article it said when . . . if you decide to do that, that you . . . you have to make the decision at the time that you think it will work, because if you miss or don't do it right, he could really hurt you."

I couldn't believe Ashbury had thought this was going to happen. Or maybe he had just made a mistake by asking too many questions and it had gotten out of control.

"Anything else that we missed with respect to the articles?" He seemed to have something in mind.

Sandy hesitated but only for a moment. "To say you have a venereal disease," she answered.

"You read that too?" He tried to make his tone disbelieving. Either he was taking these jurors for fools or he knew something I didn't.

"I read that too, yes."

"Incidentally, did you have a venereal disease on August 11?"

"No." She returned his accusation in a steady but tense tone.

"Let me ask you this: in those articles that you read about rape, did they indicate that you should keep the doors locked to avoid such an incident?"

"Yes."

"But you left your back door unlocked?"

"Yes, but I've explained . . ."

"Thank you, Ms. Adkins, you've answered the question." Ashbury said this in his most defense attorney voice.

"Now, was your bedroom door open the night of August 11 when you went to sleep?"

"It was ajar . . . yes, slightly opened."

I noticed that the twisting on her purse handle accelerated.

Easy, easy. Barely lifting my fingers off the table in front of me, I made a subtle motion with my hand as one might in confrontation with someone grown irate in an attempt to calm him down.

"And isn't it true, Ms. Adkins, that people you didn't know slept in the house at Stan's invitation?"

"Only if Stan was with them or had been with them." She was searching to remember.

"Wasn't that place, in fact, what is known as a crash pad?"

"No, it wasn't."

"But you didn't approve of what was going on in the house, did you?"

"No."

"You didn't have a chance to get out of there for six months?"

"Objection, argumentative."

"Sustained."

He had made his point, I suppose. That, while insisting she practiced the advice she found in the articles about rape, she actually followed some unsafe ones as well. There was no denying this observation, and I would not try. Instead, in my argument to the jury I would reiterate the reasons as first Sandy, and later Stan, described them.

Stan Pease came across as the young, clean-cut, attractive professional Sandy had first seen at work. Only because they had been filled in by us did the jury already know what it had taken Sandy several months' observation to discover. This, too, would be my approach in arguing the case to them. Stan also revealed that he had known Nick Harter since grade school days in New Jersey. When Nick showed up in San Diego after several years with no contact, Stan wanted to help him out. He recognized the drinking problem and the irresponsible lifestyle.

"But we were friends. We go way back," he expressed to me as I probed their disparate personalities for the common bonds. "That counts for a lot. If I'd known he could do this, though . . ."

While Sandy had done admirably on the questions concerning her choices of resistance, the subject of injuries—actually, the lack of injuries—was more tenuous. A favored theme of the defense, and often a yardstick used by jurors to measure the strength of the prosecution's case, victim injuries rate second only to sexual history as a test of credibility.

By injuries, of course, I am referring to physical injuries which can be seen on the body, such as wounds, bruises, cuts, bumps, and lumps. Terror, fear, anguish, humiliation, anger, isolation, frustration, loneliness, loss—all flood the mind and sap the spirit, but cannot be seen by the eye alone. What of these injuries? In 1979 I had not yet figured out how to show the jury what I knew. I could *tell* them, but this was not evidence they could consider when deciding the case. Nothing the attorneys say during the trial is evidence. Evidence comes only from the witnesses who testify.

I could ask Sandy on redirect about the nightmares she began getting right after the rape. Always the same one: someone was after her, trying to kill her, and just as he was about to get her she would wake up. Sometimes she'd wake up crying, other times shaking, occasionally screaming. At first it was almost every night, then a couple of times a week. Now it happened at least monthly.

Even if I told the jury about the nightmares, it would benefit Sandy's case only if they already believed her, perhaps enraging some into quicker votes of guilty. I wanted to show the jury that nightmares and other similar telltale signs are the stuff from which credibility flows. For the time being, at least, I'd have to settle for an explanation of Sandy's coping strategies by Anne Kennedy. I counted on this to minimize the absence of physical injuries.

"Ms. Adkins, you claim Mr. Harter grabbed you roughly about the mouth, is that correct?" Ashbury was referring to Sandy's description of Harter's reaction as she attempted to scream.

"He shoved my head back down on the bed with his hand over my mouth."

"Was it hard enough to bruise you?"

"No, it wasn't." I detected a hint of anger.

"What other force was used?"

"When he grabbed me, I tried to get out of bed. He grabbed my arm and threw me back down on the bed."

"Hard enough to leave any bruises?"

"No. The bed was soft."

"In fact, Ms. Adkins, you had no bruises or contusions or lacerations of any kind anywhere on your body after this incident, did you?"

"I was very sore, very, very sore, around my vagina. It hurt me a lot."

"Just there?" He emphasized the first word.

"Yes," she replied.

How humiliating! She couldn't even get mad at this outrage—because I wouldn't let her! For that matter, neither could I. It was part of the game for both of us. But I could hurt for her.

It was nearly 3:30 in the afternoon as Ashbury eased into the final phase of his interrogation. At the time it did not seem more significant than or even as significant as any number of other problem areas. At least not in a case as clear-cut as Sandy's.

"Weren't you incensed that he seemed so unconcerned about what had happened?" Ashbury asked of Sandy, following her description of Harter's actions after he left her bed.

"Not that he seemed unconcerned, that he thought, you know, that he could rape someone and get away with it."

"Didn't it appear to you that he thought what he had done was all right?"

"When I said all right, I meant that he could do it and not get caught, or reported."

I could see where Ashbury was headed. I made a note to ask for a jury instruction explaining that intoxication and its resulting behavior was not a defense to rape.

"Isn't it true"—his tone becoming increasingly accusatory—"that it seemed to you that he felt what he had done was all right . . . that nothing was wrong?"

Ashbury had produced a transcript of the preliminary hearing and had Sandy read her earlier testimony. The last question summed up what he felt she had said.

Sandy held firm to her earlier intent. "He seemed to act as if I wouldn't do anything about it."

"He didn't run, did he?"

"No, he didn't."

"Or chase you out of the house?"

"No."

"Or order you not to tell anyone?"

"No."

"Then everything he said or did would lead you to believe he didn't think he'd done anything wrong?"

I objected before Sandy could answer. It was a conclusion Ashbury wanted the jury to buy, but he wouldn't get the victim's help.

The nagging feeling was coming in louder. Maybe Ashbury had something else in mind. A jury instruction, unique in the United States to California, gives every man a defense to a charge of rape which could only be the product of a male perspective on the act. It declares it a complete defense to the charge of rape if the defendant *thinks* he has consent. There is language which warns jurors that the belief must be reasonable and in good faith, but once the legalese is sifted out, what is left is the part about whether or not the defendant *thinks* he had consent. This is what the jury really hears.

At the time of Sandy's trial I had not considered what impact this defense might have on my expert testimony. I thought of the whole problem as a balancing act: whoever came up with more credibility weight on their side would win. I had the toughest job. I needed enough for all twelve jurors to slide in next to Sandy on her side. The scale needed to look like a teeter-totter when we were finished and my feet had to be the ones on the ground—not just my toes, but my feet. Ashbury, on the other hand, needed only to make this scale look slightly unbalanced in his favor and I would lose.

Anyway, I thought with guarded assurance, *the way things are shaping up, no one will believe him if he tries to make it look like he thought he had her consent.* At least I certainly hoped they wouldn't.

I could hear Ashbury's words as I considered how best to stack my side of the scale.

"Your honor, I have nothing further of this witness, but I would ask that she remain available." He looked at Sandy. "Thank you, Ms. Adkins, for your patience."

Sandy managed a nod as the bailiff held the gate for her to exit. I stood as she passed me and whispered that I would call her later, and that she had done wonderfully—and she had.

When the jury had been excused for the evening and everyone was gone, I sat for a few minutes in the empty courtroom letting fatigue flow through me, replacing the tension which had occupied the same space all day. It always felt good, this time to relax.

I wondered if what I was going to do the next morning—call an expert witness in a state criminal prosecution to explain for the jury the coping behaviors of rape victims—would be a first. It was exciting to contemplate.

6

THE FOLLOWING DAY Anne Kennedy gave our first guided tour through the maze of new knowledge that has resulted from the interest and perspective which women's involvement in the professions has brought to the subject of rape. We stuck to the path dictated earlier by Judge Olmeda, stopping frequently to be sure we left no one behind. It was better than the first time through, I assumed, at least partly because we'd done it once before. But of more significance to our feeling of accomplishment was the fact that we were reaching our first audience, our first class; men, women, the public, our peers, someone's parents, brothers, sisters.

I was thrilled to see that no one looked sleepy, pulled out any knitting, or even yawned. As expected, Anne's account of her troll for a rapist had the jury's undivided attention, which she kept from that point on.

Ashbury did no more with Anne's cross-examination than he had at our pre-trial hearing. I wanted to believe it was because there was no way to discredit the premise upon which her testimony was based, but I knew better. If this approach to rape cases caught on, some pretty ingenious minds would soon be at work looking for holes and flaws.

Even while I felt exhilarated with my case as Anne left the courtroom, I kept reminding myself not to slack off.

There is no such thing as too much evidence in a rape case, I repeated silently. *Never, never too much evidence.*

The jury heard from everyone I had promised them, and they heard *what* I had promised them. Even some of the more elusive witnesses managed to find their way to the courtroom: the not so responsible friend with whom Harter had spent the day of the rape, accompanied by Stan and a visitor from Ireland on what had started out as an overnight trip to the mountains; Harter's strangely loyal girlfriend,

Kelly; and the emergency room physician who had examined Sandy that night when the police interviews were over.

Ah yes, the medical exam. Sandy's case was typical of a long tradition of disinterest by the medical profession in the treatment of rape victims. In 1979, while the exams themselves no longer took place on a table in a room off the detectives' lounge in the police station, it had become an annual pursuit to convince one or two hospitals to renew their agreement with the Police Department to conduct necessary medical examinations of reported rapes.

Feeling lucky to have their cooperation in the first place, no one was willing to risk losing it by requesting an elaborate protocol or reporting system by hospital or doctor. Even today, by the time court rolls around and subpoenas go out a few times, disgruntled physicians are of little help on the witness stand. Not infrequently their notes are such that their testimony does more harm than good to the victim's case.

I called the doctor to corroborate Sandy's initial complaints about soreness and tenderness around the vaginal area. I also knew if I didn't call him Ashbury would do one of two things: not call him and then wonder aloud to the jury in closing argument why they hadn't heard any medical evidence of Sandy's complaint; or he would call the doctor to tell the jury there were no physical injuries. I figured, once again, that the best defense was a good offense—well, at least *some* offense. But Ashbury did have a good time with the report.

"Dr. Wiley, this is a copy of the report you made on Sandra Adkins, is it not?" Ashbury handed him the paper I had marked as an exhibit.

"Yes," he replied, taking the document and turning it over.

"And at the time you prepared this examination report, did you find anything—any physical injuries?"

"There were no signs of the usual physical injuries. No redness or signs of any bruising or lacerations." His tone was so sterile and empty.

What the hell does he mean by no "usual" signs? I looked at my copy for these words. They weren't there. *The least he can do is not ad-lib,* I thought to myself angrily.

Ashbury continued, satisfied. "In this report I see you have Roman numerals one, two, and three. What does Roman numeral one say?"

He knew damn well, of course, since he'd asked me the same question when I had given him the report some months before. My father was a doctor and everything around our house written by him had always looked like Wiley's report—postcards from Europe, letters at camp, even notes to school excusing me for this or that. Absolutely unintelligible to the untrained eye with less than fifteen years' experience. But I had told Ashbury what Roman numerals one, two, and three said. I hadn't wanted to, but I did. He mused as how that certainly didn't look like a report on a recently raped and ravaged woman.

"Roman numeral one says 'mental state stable,' meaning 'normal.' "

"And Roman numeral two?"

" 'Overall appearance, normal.' "

He didn't ask for Roman numeral three—it was the observation about physical injuries.

How could these doctors spend ten minutes looking up a woman's vagina and asking a few questions, and then, for all time, memorialize the essence of her most intimate being as "stable" and "normal"?

Another stirring in that I've-seen-this-so-often-before place in my head, but no time to do—not during trial, certainly, and well, after trial I could write a memo or talk to someone. No—the problem was bigger than a memo or just talking to someone. It would be a full-time job overhauling these reporting methods—maybe someday.

But now Wiley was walking out the door and I needed another witness.

"The people call Kelly Stack," I announced hurriedly.

It has always been such a puzzlement to me why women like Kelly stay with men like Nick Harter. A few of the reasons are easily recognized: cultural indoctrination that a woman needs a man to be fulfilled, the so-called natural instinct of the woman to be a mother, the fear of loneliness. But some of the reasons, no doubt, are quite complex and require more than simple observation even over time will allow.

This is not the place to offer any real expertise on the motives of women like Kelly in hooking up with men like Harter, but it is the place to offer some insight into what happens to the relationship when these men rape. While it is quite common for a victim's ongoing sexual relationship with a man to disintegrate following a rape attack, this is not true of the attacker's relationship. These women often stick by the men, attending court proceedings, testifying for them, and even lying to protect them.

Kelly Stack was probably not as extreme an example of this phenomenon as my mental film clips conjure up. Even today the first image I have of her is physical: like from the song "Tall and tan and lean and lovely"; long, straight corn-silk hair, model-slim figure, neat, clean, articulate, and educated. While Harter barely finished high school, Kelly was a college graduate—and more.

"I received my B.A. in 1975 from Denton College in New Jersey. I majored in sociology and urban studies. My undergraduate internship was with the Bradford, New Jersey, Police Department from January through June 1975. I worked with them two days per week. That was a requirement for my urban studies program.

"I am currently a full-time graduate student at State University doing social work, hoping to complete the Master of Social Work degree this coming May 1979. Specializing in geriatrics, or aging, and mental health.

"I just completed my year internship in January through December 1978 with the city of San Diego, where I served as a social worker. I am also working part-time as a social worker for a local psychiatric board and care home for mentally disordered adults ranging in age from eighteen to sixty-four."

From the testimony of various witnesses it was learned that Harter had not really worked steadily before he came to California, or after, at his supposed trade as a carpenter.

Kelly had worked and gone to school.

"I worked for four or five years back in New Jersey as a bank teller part-time while I was going through undergraduate school. And when I came out to California I obtained a bank teller's position also."

She had, she explained, followed Nick when he decided to seek his fortune out West.

Kelly and I had only one conversation before we traded questions for answers in court. The rest of what I knew of her probable testimony I learned from Ashbury, Stan, and other associates. What I recall so well is her parting comment as she was about to hang up the phone the one time we did speak.

"I mean, why in the world would he have to rape a woman anyway? He knows he could just come home and I'd be there."

It never failed. In every case I tried someone for the defense—twice a girlfriend, once a brother, once a mother, among others—observed that the defendant need not have resorted to rape for sexual pleasure. Indeed, they were right. These men had, in fact, not raped for sex, but rather for power and out of anger. It was far more an act of violence than of sexual gratification.

Although she was evasive in court, Kelly had confided her concern about Harter's drinking, and what he did when he drank, to several witnesses. The same was true of his treatment of her when he drank.

"Ms. Stack," I asked carefully, "does the defendant become more aggressive when he drinks?"

"Aggressive?" She repeated the word, but did not deny it. "Well, not aggressive exactly, just argumentative, possibly."

"Does he become louder, more offensive?"

"Maybe, when I argue back."

"Do many of these arguments happen when the defendant has been drinking?"

"No," she replied with a sincere voice. "We don't argue often."

I pressed her harder. "Ms. Stack, does the defendant strike you?"

"No." This time emphatically.

I came back just as emphatically. "Did you tell Mr. Pease that you worried about the defendant after he'd been drinking?"

"Maybe—yes, but not because he hit people."

"But because he does get angry and into arguments more easily when he drinks?"

"Sometimes, but mainly when I argue back."

"You and the defendant had quite an angry confrontation the night of this incident, didn't you?"

"Yes, I suppose we did."

"And it was in a bar and he was quite drunk at the time, wasn't he?"

"Yes. He was." She looked helplessly at Ashbury.

"Were you angry with Mr. Harter too, Ms. Stack?"

"Yes, I was quite angry."

"Why were you angry?"

"Well, because Nick had told me he would be home at eight P.M. I fixed dinner and waited until ten. When he didn't come home I decided to go look for him."

"Has he done that before?"

"Maybe, once before."

Stan testified that Harter often told Kelly he would be home at a certain time, knowing he would not, but wanting her to stay home. In fact, Stan knew that the night of Sandy's rape, Harter had really planned to stay over in the mountains with their friends and had re-turned to San Diego only when the car he was in became separated from Stan and his group. He had informed Kelly he would be home early, he laughingly told Stan, so that she would not go out and have a good time, maybe with other guys.

Kelly had finally figured it out, she told Stan, and was furious that night as she stormed around searching for him. Only by chance was he even in town.

"What happened when you found him at the bar?"

"Well, I mean, it was a brief exchange. He was just so intoxicated. And I just didn't like his attitude. He just said, 'Stop following me around like my mother. Why are you looking for me?' "

Suddenly it was crystal clear.

"Had the defendant ever told you before to stop acting like his mother?" I asked.

"Maybe, once before."

"Just once, Ms. Stack?"

"I don't remember exactly, but at least once."

So he was drunk, had fought with his girlfriend, who really was the one to be justifiably furious, and on top of that she reminded him of a mother who had followed him around when he was younger. Shortly after Kelly stormed out, Harter decided to try the action at yet another bar. Angry, drunk and stranded, he passed by Stan's on the way and Sandy's fate was sealed. She had not treated him with the respect he felt due him either, I reminded the jury in closing argument. I urged them to put it all together.

Finally it was Harter's turn. His story was as incredible on the stand as I had felt it would be from my first angry reading of Sografo's report five months before. Again I was bewildered by how easily Daly had accepted this fantasy on first glance.

After walking into the house through the unlocked kitchen door to see if Stan was back, Harter discovered Stan's bedroom door was locked and decided to sleep on the couch, he said. He stripped in the living room and then noticed Sandy's door ajar. Not knowing she was there, he claimed, he decided to sleep in her room.

"Then what did you do?" Ashbury inquired.

"I proceeded from the sofa into Ms. Adkins' bedroom, approached her bed, which was a mattress on the floor, and as I stepped on the bed I stepped on her foot and she said, 'Ouch.' "

"Then what did she do?"

"She really didn't do anything. After I stepped on her foot, I laid down on the bed, and Sandy told me if I wanted to sleep to go out into the next room."

"Did you go?"

"No, I did not."

"Why not?"

"At that time is when I reached over and inserted my two fingers into her vagina."

"What did she do or say then?"

"She told me to stop because it hurt."

"So did you stop?"

"Yes, I did."

Oh, so close and yet so far, I thought.

"What did you do next?"

"As I pulled my hand out from between her legs, I climbed over in between her legs, because at this time her legs were spread already from my two fingers being in there."

"Was there any conversation?"

"There was none. I was just fiddling around trying to get it in."

I was trying to picture this in my head. I looked at the jury. Three men had assumed the "show me" position, arms folded defiantly on their chests. Many of the women were glaring fixedly at him. I was startled at the strength of their hostility.

"Okay, what happened next?" Ashbury was doing this like he was talking about a bad check or a stolen battery.

"I was having a problem getting it inside of her. So I advanced my body up toward her chest and had my penis in my hand and asked her if she would give me some head. She shook her head and said no."

So now he was admitting he'd asked her to orally copulate him. But then what happened when she said she would not?

"I then went back down in between her legs and asked her to help me get it in."

He had denied anything about oral copulation to Sografo.

"Did she help you?"

"Yes, she did."

"Was it erect?"

"It was in the middle."

"Okay, then what happened?"

"After she had inserted it inside of her, I proceeded to go through the motions of sexual intercourse, and after I came inside of her, I was through. I was finished and I got up."

He was finished all right. I was writing words to help me remember for my cross-examination.

"Now, during this time did you threaten her in any way?"

"No, I did not."

"Did she tell you anything which you could interpret as a sign that she didn't want to have sexual intercourse?"

"The only other thing I can recall is that she told me that she had herpes, but my penis was already inside her and it was too late." He shrugged his shoulders.

"Okay. So you were through. What did you do then?"

"I got up and left her room."

I wondered when his fatigue had fled. When I asked him in cross-examination, he explained that the episode had given him renewed energy. As I recall, it's the opposite for a man—especially after drinking. I wondered about that to the jurors—looking at the women—during closing argument. Their expressions, and some nods, made it clear that they knew what I meant.

"By the way," Ashbury inquired as an afterthought, "when you walked into the room and when the sexual activities were going on, were you able to recognize Sandy Adkins?"

"Oh, yes," came the confirmation.

"So it was light enough for you to see her?"

"Oh, yes. The light comes right through the window."

"And it was light enough for her to see you?"

I could have objected, since it was speculation on his part whether Sandy could see him. But this was one of those times I wanted the answer—especially when I could anticipate it from the previous two questions.

"Oh, yes," he answered for the third time. "She knew who I was."

But it had been too dark for him to see anyone asleep in the bed until he stepped on her? I asked him this when my turn came.

"Well, the light was behind me and, you know, my body blocked it, so I couldn't see her until I was real close."

"I see" was my only response.

I asked him about, and he denied, each and every act or word of force Sandy had said had been used against her. With these exceptions, the stories were very similar.

"Now, Mr. Harter," I probed, "what was it exactly that you were thinking of when you lay down on the bed and put your fingers in Ms. Adkins' vagina, that made you think that it was going to be all right with her?"

"Because at one time Stan had offered me the services of his other roommate, Linda Sims. He had indicated that if I wanted a good blow job or a good lay to see Linda. And at that time, probably, since Sandy had been, supposedly from Stan's mouth, screwing him, you know, on a daily basis, plus having a boyfriend and other men coming around, then I figured that, you know, that he offered me one roommate, you know, I figured that it was the same for the other."

It took all my effort not to change my tone of voice.

"I see. And Stan told you that he was screwing Sandy on a daily basis?"

"Told who?"

"You."

"Told me?"

"Yes."

"Not directly. I mean, he told me that he was screwing her. Anytime he wanted her, he could have her."

"And other men did it too?"

"Yes."

"And do you know who these other men were?"

"Well, I know one that was her boyfriend at the time that she supposedly had."

"I see. This is something you saw happen?"

"What? Watch them have sexual intercourse?"

"Yes."

"No, I'm not—I don't go for that. I don't watch people."

"So you figured since one roommate had been offered to you by Stan that the other roommate was fair game?"

"To my knowledge, yes. The way he was."

"Did Stan tell you that Ms. Adkins didn't like you and didn't approve of you?"

"I don't think Stan ever really said that to me. And I don't see how he could, because there was no reason why she would not like me other than I was not working."

"Was this something also that was told to you?"

"This was something that was told to Kelly. That Sandy thought that all of the people that came over to that house were sleazies."

"This is not something Stan told you?"

"Stan didn't tell me anything."

"Did you discuss this fairly often whenever you saw Sandy, that she thought she was too high and mighty?"

"I never discussed anything with Sandy."

"I am asking, did this come up when discussing Sandy, that you thought she was too high and mighty?"

"Did I think she was too high and mighty?"

"Yes."

"Well, Ms. Adkins did seem to think she was above us all."

"Did you tell Mr. Pease that Ms. Adkins needed a good stiff dick?"

"Did I say that to Mr. Pease?"

"Yes."

"That's quite possible."

I smiled sardonically to myself while thinking that when the time came he really couldn't even give her that.

"Now, referring again to that conversation that you had with Detective Sografo, do you recall telling Sografo that you had seen Ms. Adkins walk around the house nude and flaunt herself in front of you?"

"That's correct."

"Could you tell us, please, what that was about?"

"Well, one day me and Mr. Pease and my girlfriend, Kelly, were sitting in his room listening to music and getting stoned. And Sandy came walking out of the bathroom, and walked by Mr. Pease's door, as you can see on the diagram. She had to go to her room and she had a towel.

"And as she walked by the door, she did not have the towel draped around her like she says. She had the towel just in front of her, and, as she passed by, she looked and seen everybody in there. And she more or less lifted it up in front of her and giggled and trotted off."

"And that's what you meant when you said you saw her walking around nude and flaunting herself nude around Mr. Pease and his friends?"

"To one of my recollections. I don't know of any other occasions that that might have happened."

"Did you, when describing this incident to Detective Sografo, say that you had 'fucked' Sandy?"

"I might have put it that way, yes."

"Is that how you refer to the act of sexual intercourse?"

"Objection!" I had expected that from Ashbury. If he hadn't objected, I would have thought he was sleeping. I had clearly asked that question out of anger.

The entire cross-examination required great concentration on my part so that I didn't sound sarcastic, or worse. But I was *thoroughly* enjoying myself. I figured it was the least I could do for Sandy.

Sografo had slipped me a note while I had been going over the diagrams with Harter and talking about how he got to the house that night. I turned it over but did not look at it until late into my examination.

"Ask him," it read, "if there were any cars in the driveway. When I got there Sandy's car was parked in the driveway, right next to the house, only a foot or so from the kitchen door."

God, I'd never even thought about her car. I stared at Sografo. Of course, it had to be there!

I asked for a two-minute break and sent Sografo to call Sandy. He was back in less than the two minutes, jubilance etched in his face.

He leaned close as he slipped into his chair next to mine. "Bingo. She was parked where I told you. She's ready to come back whenever we call."

"You're wonderful," I whispered excitedly. "Tell her to be in my office at one-fifteen."

I was nearly delirious with my latter-day Dr. Watson. Here was the Achilles' heel, the fatal flaw we all loved to see.

From the diagram it appeared that the driveway area extended to a depth which would allow only a compact car to be clear of the sidewalk, and into which perhaps two cars could fit side by side.

"If there are cars parked in the driveway," I asked casually, "do you have to go around them to get to the kitchen door?"

"Yeah, unless you walk right along the wall of the house," he replied unsuspectingly.

"Well, Mr. Harter, it would be hard to miss a car that was parked in the driveway if you walked along the wall to get to the door, would it not?"

"What do you mean, hard to miss?"

"I mean, you'd see a car there?"

"Oh, yeah."

"And you've seen Ms. Adkins' car in the past, haven't you?"

"Yes, I have."

"What kind of car is it?"

"I think it's a yellow Gremlin."

"Is it your testimony, Mr. Harter, that you did not see Ms. Adkins' car parked in the driveway on the night of August 10?"

"I did not see her car there."

"Is it your testimony it wasn't there?"

"I said I did not see her car there."

"It is also your testimony that if a car was there you would see it walking through the driveway toward the door?"

"If I was looking for a car, I would see it, I imagine so."

"And Mr. Pease's car, was it there?"

"Definitely not. But he loans his car out a lot, so just because his car isn't there doesn't mean he isn't home."

I thought to myself, *You may not have known whether or not Stan was home that night, but you certainly knew someone else was.*

Both Sandy and Sografo took the stand during rebuttal and placed her car in a spot where Harter would have had to crawl over it if he'd walked a straight line from the sidewalk to the kitchen door.

After that I quit. There was no more. If it wasn't enough by now, it never would be—even in a rape case.

It was the third day of the second week of trial when we argued our cases to the jury. I always liked pulling it all together and putting it into the law. I have practiced over the years to keep it clean, clear, straightforward, to speak in people language, not lawyer language. I wasn't trying to impress them, just convince them, and if they couldn't understand what I was telling them, they certainly weren't going to convict.

I am used to being frustrated when I listen to the defense argue its version of a case. Sometimes because it's so bizarre that I'm afraid a jury might actually believe it, other times because it's downright embarrassing and foolish.

But rape cases, along with child molesting, wife beating, and perhaps paternity, always have room for new lows.

Ashbury caught me off guard. He had been defining the elements, or legal parts, of the crime of rape, each of which the prosecution must prove beyond a reasonable doubt, and he'd come to the element of resistance.

"Now, the next thing is 'where she resists, but her resistance is overcome by force or violence.'

"There has got to be someplace you draw the line between rape and sexual intercourse, normal sexual intercourse as tradition tells us.

"The male is the dominant—the chaser. In other words, when you wanted to have intercourse with a woman, if you walked up and said, 'Let's go to bed,' if she said yes, you'd probably drop her because you would assume she was a prostitute of some kind.

"So that there is a requirement, I mean, a traditional requirement, traditional expectation, that the woman say no.

"I don't know, I think all of you are married, I am. And if I had to have sexual intercourse only when my wife said yes the first time, I think I'd join the church, because that's the way it would be. So it is expected, and a man expects that there is going to be a no, at least before things even get going.

"And I think the law is written in such a way as to take that into consideration.

"In other words, there has to be resistance. Now, it doesn't mean you have to fight, kick, and bite. But it is, what the instruction says, there has to be enough resistance. Resistance has to be sufficient that it is reasonably apparent to the male that she is resisting. Now, that's the purpose of resistance, to make it apparent that this is not consensual so that some degree of resistance is necessary.

"It's right here in front of me, 'the conduct of the female person be only such that to make the absence of consent in the actual resistance reasonably apparent.' Now, that's very clear-cut, and I don't think it requires any additional comment."

I was dumbfounded. Had he actually said that part about his wife? To a jury?

There was embarrassment, outrage, shock—all on jurors' faces. I was disappointed. He was taking the challenge out of this. But if they followed the instructions, they were not to let their feelings about the attorney influence them. I wondered how they could after that.

The rest of his argument was predictably unimpressive. He talked a lot about the defense of consent and what was reasonable in coming to this determination.

"So to me, it only goes to show that maybe there is a question as to whether or not, you know, he was that violent, or she was that scared. I don't know. She said that she remained calm because she read the things she read, but that works two ways. If she remained calm and didn't tell him, you know, doesn't struggle somewhat, he's got a legal right to rely on that."

Could anyone believe that? What was scary, though, was that any *one* person believing it ever so slightly was all it would take for me to lose.

Ashbury pretty much summed up my feeling about the defense case, if not with great literary verve, certainly with clarity, as he described his general view of the prosecution's case. He was referring at the time to the last-minute revelation about the location of Sandy's car.

"Whether or not Nicholas Harter saw that automobile, I don't know. It would appear that if that drawing is to scale, and the car is really as big as it is indicated on the diagram, and the car was parked in front of the gate, he would probably have to move the car to get through the gate. But remember, this is five and six months ago. I don't know where that car was.

"I don't know whether Mr. Harter knew where the car was. I don't know what to tell you about the car. I really don't. And frankly I don't think that's significant.

"The significance is what happened in those few moments when he walked into that room. And the rest of it, as far as I am concerned, is garbage. Thank you."

It remained to be seen if the jury agreed with him, or whether the so-called "garbage" was what made what went on in "those few moments when he walked into that room" perfectly clear.

7

WAITING FOR A JURY'S VERDICT is something like waiting for the results of an audition or a job interview. Second-guessing what you should not have done—or should have done—second-guessing what the jury in its ignorance will not do—or will do; second-guessing why they've come back to ask the questions they did, or why they don't ask others; or why they haven't come back at all. It is a torturous continuum of self-analysis and inadequacy which can go completely unnoticed by the uninitiated, but is glaringly evident to anyone who has been through the process.

One of the most obvious symptoms is frequent and inappropriate readings of the wristwatch, followed by calls for verbal confirmation from anyone close enough to comply that, indeed, the time is correct and only minutes have passed since the last request. A more subtle sign, yet detectable even among those feigning the nonchalance expected of veterans, is the immediate and startled response to the telephone's ring —anyone's telephone. Trial attorneys whose fondest game is to be several hallways, if not floors, away from the sound of their ringing phone, can be seen leaning against doorways close to theirs, one ear listening to the conversation within, the other straining to identify a sound from that small instrument which can herald the desired announcement.

After several months the ring of one's office phone really is distinguishable from everyone else's, and can usually be singled out from others even at some distance—except when a jury is out. While working at my desk, when I hear frequent cries of "Is that my phone ringing?" from the same voice, it is a sure sign a jury is deliberating.

I looked at the time.

I had now been waiting two hours and eight minutes since watching Father Paul and the other eleven jurors head out the back door of the courtroom on their way to deliberate Sandy's fate.

It was 12:10. No doubt they had gone to lunch. John and I had agreed that Judge Olmeda could excuse the jury for such things as lunch and to go home in the evening without our presence.

"At least I can stop wondering what they're doing for the next hour and a half," I said aloud while I continued to create different piles out of the large one which had accumulated during the past weeks of trial and preparation for trial. Fortunately I could apply myself to such paper shuffling or phone calling while I was waiting. Concentration on anything more significant than the grocery list or a dinner menu is extremely painful to the expectant trial attorney awaiting a jury's verdict.

My heart was caught particularly unprepared when the phone interrupted my labors. I dug it out from under the files I had only intended to prop alongside it. In the process they melted back into the center of the desk.

"Judy Rowland," I responded, heart pounding.

"This is Department Fourteen. The jury has a verdict." It was Tony's familiar voice. "I've notified Mr. Ashbury and the defendant. They'll be here in fifteen minutes."

I looked at my watch: 2:10.

"Thanks, Tony. I'll be right there. Oh, by the way, do you know who the foreman is?"

"No, I didn't see." He hung up quickly before I could ask any more questions, all ridiculous, of course, in light of what he had told me.

So they've got a verdict! That meant I wouldn't have to worry about trying the case again. They had all agreed. And so fast! Inside I was dancing, ecstatic. Incredible! No, not incredible, predictable. But I wouldn't act that way.

What if they found him not guilty? What if they really felt she was *probably* raped but had some doubt on something which they felt was reasonable?

There was no way the verdict could be "not guilty." I *knew* I had at least three or four of those jurors convinced before they had left the courtroom. But I could still be scared to death about it.

I picked up a legal note pad and my jury seating chart. I would mark the verdicts on it and note the foreman with a large "F." Not that I was likely to forget in this case, but it was force of habit.

I looked into Daly's office as I walked down the hall. Naturally, he, along with almost everyone else, was back in court.

I'd tell my parents at dinner. They were coming that night. My father would be proud as always, and ask me everything. He'd done the same two years before, when I had convicted a woman of murdering her son two years before that, making new law in the process. Everyone had been at lunch that time.

We were, once again, all in our places as the jury filed into the courtroom, this time from a different door and for the finale rather than the overture.

So much hinged on this! People have always told me I look so composed at these times. Thank God it appears that way. Inside I was a wreck. I could see my pen shaking in my hand. I didn't dare try to raise it. Longingly I eyed the paper cup filled with water on the table in front of me. My lips were so dry that they stuck together as I smiled at the somber jurors. I just knew if I tried to pick it up I would spill it.

As each jury member came through the door, I looked for the verdict forms which would identify the bearer as foreman. It was not Father Paul. As my gaze moved from his empty hands to his eyes, he met my surprise with a look of understanding. Even after the rest were seated, my repeated stares asked him for an explanation.

He turned it down! I suddenly realized. *He wouldn't do it.*

Am I right? was the question in my eyes this time. An almost imperceptible nod of his head gave me the answer.

I had noticed the verdict forms enter while the priest and I carried on our visual dialogue. The fellow with five children, the elementary school principal. It figured. He was an administrator.

Things looked good. But you could never be certain. I wondered if they could hear my heart.

"Mr. Clarian," Judge Olmeda began. "I see you are the foreman of this jury."

"That's right," he replied.

"Has the jury reached a verdict as to count one?"

"Yes, your honor." His tone fit the seriousness of his task.

"Has the jury reached a verdict as to count two?"

"Yes, your honor," he repeated.

"Will you hand the verdicts to the bailiff, please."

I watched the two sheets of paper as they changed hands. Without looking at them himself, the uniformed carrier strode the few steps from jury box to judge's bench and handed them up to Olmeda.

It had been too fast. I hadn't been able to detect any writing on them, let alone any specific writing.

Quickly the judge scanned the forms. My eyes never left his face. Try as I might, in all my years of trial I have never been able to read a verdict from the judge's face, even judges whose faces could be read for other purposes.

They must teach them at judge's college, I thought once again.

In the usual rites of passage, Tony stood to accept the forms from below as the judge extended his arm to him.

I breathed deeply. I dared not move or the silent screaming inside would burst out. Things seemed to be happening in slow motion.

"Mr. Clerk," said the judge, "would you please read the verdicts."

"The Superior Court of the state of California in and for the county of San Diego; the people of the state of California against Nicholas Eugene Harter, defendant. Verdict: we the jury in the above-entitled cause find the defendant, Nicholas Eugene Harter, guilty of the crime of forcible rape in violation of Penal Code Section 261 as charged in count one of the information."

Now it was my turn not to show emotion. Shakily I recorded the verdict on my form, adding an "F" to Clarian's square on the juror seating chart. I took some deep breaths. I am not certain, but I think I stop breathing while verdicts are being read. At least it always feels that way afterwards.

They found him guilty of oral copulation too, and Olmeda had the bailiff take him into custody, there to wait the three weeks while the probation department readied its report with a sentence recommendation.

Behind me I could hear Kelly gasp and then sob as the verdicts were read. I noticed the reporters from the two local papers were taking notes. My usual followers seemed pleased.

As I turned to walk out, I realized the audience filled all but one or two seats. Not a prosecutor among them. Nor had there been during the trial.

If only they had come. Perhaps they would have recognized my "cause" as a legal one first—one made no less legitimate because the issues could also be interpreted as being feminist. I was to find a definite pattern in the years ahead in this inability of men in many fields to see past the so-called feminist focus of a woman's career direction and to give to it the same credibility as any other substantive work in that same field. It is a part of what Betty Friedan has identified in her book *The Second Stage* as one of our nemeses. Women professors seeking tenure, women attorneys seeking appointment to the Bench, women sociologists seeking validation of their research—all have obtained a toehold in their respective fields which for so long had been denied them. But they are stuck. They are jamming up together at the top of the entry ladder and just below the bottom of the executive one. And those women whose work is most obviously identifiable with issues exclusively—or nearly so—affecting women are finding it difficult, if not impossible, to go on. What happens next?

In 1979, as I left Department 14 with that first victory in tow, I had not yet recognized the phenomenon I have just described. Frankly, I wasn't even thinking about it. After two hours with the members of the jury who had agreed to meet with me, picking their brains and exploring everything I could learn from them, I was more convinced than ever that I had been right about my theory on the expert witness. And I was floating.

It was 4:30 as I set out to track Daly down in the maze of corridors on the seventh floor.

"Daly, I got the conviction!" I told him in a tone clearly unable to hide the excitement I felt. "We did it!"

"No, you did it, kid. And it was a nice piece of work. You deserve the conviction." He put out his hand to me.

"Daly, I mean we—the prosecution—finally got a break—*we* got something in for a change. It wasn't the defense this time!"

"Oh," he replied as my words sunk in. "You're right, that's true, we don't often get a break."

Football conversation continued all around us. Some were listening with one ear and wanted to know what was going on. Two or three were vaguely aware from hearing along the line that I had been experimenting with something in a rape case.

I slipped out and headed for Creelman's office.

I don't think I made it sound like "I told you so," I thought of my exchange with Daly. *I'll thank Ron for sticking by me. He'll appreciate a good battle won.* He'd already gone for the day.

I went back to my office. The piles were still there in their embry-onic divisions. I called Sandy with the news.

"We won! The jury believed you from the beginning. They let every-one go around and talk about the case and then they voted. It was unanimous, Sandy."

"Wow." It was all she could come up with for the first few moments. Then: "Even the priest? Was he the foreman? Did they believe it all?"

"Yes, even the priest. No, he wasn't the foreman. They asked him right off, but he told them it would look like his 'higher court' was running the show." I thought again how much I respected this man.

"And you know what else?" I had almost forgotten. "They asked me if you had gotten pregnant. They suspected as much from the testi-mony about the diaphragm. I told Father Paul why I had decided against telling the jury. You know, he apologized! He apologized for being the reason that I left out such important information. I don't think there's an old rape myth around that would have made them believe Harter."

A little later I met Sandy and some of her friends at a local lounge, and we hugged and toasted our mutual victory. She wanted to hear everything the jury said. We laughed and had some wine. I was ex-hausted physically and emotionally. I knew the feeling from other ver-dict nights. It was the reason I loved trial so much—for that feeling. This time, though, it was particularly intoxicating.

The next afternoon a huge floral arrangement arrived at my office with a card which read: "Thank you for giving your all and even more. The best attorney the D.A.'s office ever had!"

When I later thanked Sandy, she said it was not from her.

Three years later when I was going through the file in preparation to write this book, I turned the card over and got, for the first time, a hint about who might have sent the flowers. It was signed: "The women of San Diego."

Life for me went on as usual after Sandy's case. While I hoped what I had done was getting around to the right places, I acted as if it was no big deal, was part of my job. As I look back, it is now obvious that no one was talking about it, but I just didn't notice. Although things were not what I had hoped, I was able to keep afloat on the wave of my victory alone. I really believed in the validity of what I had done and it gave me immense satisfaction. Given time, perhaps, others might agree.

The newspapers carried articles about the case. Ashbury vowed to appeal, I vowed to do it again. Ashbury told the press that it was irrelevant whether the jury believed the victim resisted what she thought was a rape—that the issue was whether the defendant believed, as a result of her having resisted "so little," that he had consent. I was chilled by the realization that the law in California might just be interpreted like this. It was a real possibility. I wouldn't think about it.

Three days after the newspaper accounts about the case appeared, I received a letter from one of the jurors. It was the middle-aged lady whose children had grown and who had returned to college. She had seen the news articles and felt compelled to respond to Ashbury's claim that the expert was irrelevant.

She felt, among other things, that this testimony enhanced Sandy's credibility in a juror's view when she described how her behavior during the attack was much influenced by the articles she had read giving advice for women in rape situations. More importantly, she made an observation which assured me that the jurors, at least, understood the difference between what I used the expert for and what the defense claimed was the *real* issue: whether Harter reasonably believed he had consent. She wrote:

"Secondly, and equally important, the expert's testimony established the state of mind that induced Adkins' behavior after Harter climbed into her bed. Such testimony is just as legitimate as Harter's testimony regarding Adkins' lifestyle and alleged 'flaunting' of her naked body . . . which was admitted to establish Harter's state of mind and, according to the defense, to justify his behavior.

"Mr. Ashbury said, according to the *Union:* 'It's just not a proper subject for expert testimony.' He is wrong! It is every bit as important to establish a victim's . . . state of mind as it is the rapist's state of mind to justify or not justify conduct.

"From the legal standpoint, according to instructions we, the jurors, received, the alleged victim need only resist enough to make it clear to the alleged rapist that she does not want to have intercourse with him. How much is enough?

"Expert testimony helps to clarify that point. Why must a woman jeopardize her physical well-being or life on top of suffering the emotional trauma of experiencing infuriating, demeaning treatment, just to satisfy a jury that she has resisted a man's advances?"

She closed by saying she would be available to me if judges in future cases were reluctant to admit similar testimony. I showed it to Daly and Creelman. Neither could remember any letter like it before.

I was to take her up on her offer sooner than I realized at the time.

While there was little official interest in my courtroom success following Sandy's case, there began the first signs of a phenomenon which continued up to the time I left the District Attorney's office. In what at first was a trickle, later almost a steady stream, other D.A.s would happen by my office, plop down in a chair across the desk from me, and ask if I had "a minute" for them to "run something by me." The "something" was invariably a rape case and the "minute" almost always turned into hours. I was never able to resist the temptation, even with those who had barely spoken to me, much less asked my opinion, before that time. No one was willing to attempt the use of the expert, but several found my victim interview style useful and many beefed up their victim's credibility by adding witnesses to their skimpy lineup. Witnesses who could talk about the changes in the victims since the rape, or who could corroborate the victim's story in useful particulars: constant fears and nightmares described by roommates, parents, or spouses; vague and distant episodes at work described by longtime colleagues; emotional reactions to the sight, sound, or smell of something reminiscent of the attack.

At the end of three weeks following Harter's conviction, he was sentenced by Judge Olmeda. Over my strong objections and after lengthy discussions, his punishment was to be a year in the county jail, minus the time he had served, less what is known as "good time" (meaning you do what you are supposed to do anyway while not trying to escape): in all, a little over seven months for forcibly raping a woman.

Harter had gotten into an alcohol treatment program and had brought the entire group to the sentencing to speak in his behalf. Kelly testified for him, and he said he wouldn't ever disappoint her again. Even the probation officer assigned to the case was having difficulty in recommending a prison sentence.

"After all, she wasn't hurt," he told me over the phone one day after a distraught Sandy had called to pass on her exchange with him.

I was incensed by his failure to at least feign compassion, but not surprised at this distinction. There is rape—and then there is rape. One was real, the other only sort-of real. Sandy's case fell into the latter group: no physical injuries, no torn clothes, not between strangers, no hardened criminal with a violent record.

In 1979 many judges in California were choosing local jail sentences for jury-convicted rapists over sending them to prison for the felony they had committed. A movement was afoot to take that choice from them and to require that a prison sentence be imposed in all cases concerning convicted rapists, but it was too soon to predict its outcome. Since that time such a law has been passed and a judge's choice of sentence in the case of a convicted rapist is not whether he will go to prison but rather for how long.

I left the courtroom that day frustrated at my failure to have had a lasting effect on Olmeda's ideas about rape. Out of sight, out of mind, I supposed.

As expected, Ashbury filed an appeal. That same day I received a call from a lawyer on the Attorney General's staff.

"Hi, I'm Grant Soames, Deputy Attorney General. I've been reading about your expert testimony in the paper and I told my boss I wanted to handle it if there was an appeal. Well, we got it today, and I'm it. I'd like to talk to you about the opening brief."

We set a time for him to come over for an initial meeting.

When we hung up, I immediately dialed another number at the AG's office.

"Pamela Belkin, please." She was one of several women attorneys in the appellate department whom I had gotten to know. I related the conversation I had just had with Grant Soames.

"Pam, I'd hoped you'd take this appeal. You do the most scholarly work up there, and this issue needs the views a woman brings to it," I lamented.

"Don't prejudge Grant," she advised. "He's very excited about this issue. He started talking about it the first time he read about it in the paper. Besides, he's asked for the case and it would be real sticky if I took it away."

My concerns were only partially appeased when I said goodbye to Pam. I'd just have to hope she was right about this fellow. It certainly was the first time any A.G. had ever personally requested to handle the appeal on a case. It was also the first time anyone had shown this much interest in my idea; and how ironic, I thought, it was a man.

From the first time I met Grant Soames it was obvious his interest in Sandy's case was genuine. He thought it was an idea whose time had come and he wanted to be there. It was strange, hearing someone else talk about *my* case the way he did. Fleetingly, just for a moment, I was jealous, protective. He would get to argue the case before the appellate court, not I; maybe even the state Supreme Court. These feelings passed quickly and, as it turned out, we worked well together from the beginning. He was to prove an invaluable ally.

During the following couple of months, I was mired in the new year's quota of burglaries, auto thefts, and drugs, with a liberal sprinkling of search warrants, case reviews, and psycho calendars. With this last I was always tempted to use someone else's name in court, like my seventh-grade gym teacher's (the one who made us shower in front of everyone), in case one ever really escaped and came around to do some of the things they often promised me they would if ever given the chance.

Grant finished the appeal on the Harter case and now we just had to wait—at least a couple of months more. As with time spent after the end of a serious relationship, I had almost forgotten about it when the subject of the expert testimony was back to light my fire—but with a new twist.

"Remember the Albert Drake case?"

At the question I swiveled my chair away from the wall on which hung the calendar of Sun Valley I had bought the year before when I'd gone skiing with my husband. It was now mid-April and I knew that gazing at the graceful figure gliding along a downy-soft slope was as close as I would come to a ski trip this season.

"Sure, I remember it," I said, now facing the chair across from my desk into which Susan Christianson had settled. Susan and I were the only women assigned to the Superior Court trial division and often looked to each other to share anything from the trials and tribulations of our male-dominated world to the noon exercise class offered a block from the courthouse.

"Why?" I asked when she did not go on once I had acknowledged her question. "You make a decision about it, or is that why you're here?"

The pensive look she gave me made her Brooke Shields eyebrows almost touch at a furrow above her nose. As usual, she wore no makeup and I couldn't tell if she was extra tired or extra serious.

"Well, a little of both, maybe," she answered slowly. "No, really . . . I think I've made a decision. I'm going to retry it—with some important changes. That's what I want to talk to you about."

The case Susan was referring to was a rape case she had tried the previous fall, which had ended with the jury hung six-six, just about as indecisive as it can get. These kind of stats do not usually lead the DA's office to retrial.

"You're going to try the rape expert." I said it as a statement, not a question. She had toyed with the idea several times, always mentioning it whenever I went to her for reassurance with my own impending trial. Even after the Harter case we had spent time mulling it over. I knew the facts of the Drake case almost as well as she did.

"Yes, I am," she answered firmly. "Will you help me?"

"Of course I'll help you." The words came out before I could stop them. I looked around my office with its piles of files. "I don't suppose you're here to tell me I've been taken off my other cases and assigned to help you win Drake, that it's top priority and nothing is to interfere?" I smiled my Walter Mitty best.

"No, I wish I could tell you that," she apologized. "But I've cleared it with the front office and they've given their blessings. It's not much, but neither is this case's track record. And," she encouraged, "it shows their faith in your theory."

Great. Why not let me do my work and hers too? Two for the price of one. No skin off their noses.

"Okay, Susan, let's run through it." I gave the picture on the calendar a last wistful look and dropped my eyes to the numbers below. "How about tomorrow afternoon—two-thirty? By the way, is Stacy willing?"

"Yes, but it's going to be touchy. She's having trouble with her fiancé."

Stacy Billings was no Sandy. Although in the Navy and trained as a radio operator, she was just holding on. She cried a lot and "almost" changed her mind a lot. I was somewhat surprised she had agreed to go through with the case again.

As it turned out, she had *not* yet decided to go through with it again. The next day I discovered it was my job to convince her—and with her fiancé present!

From the moment I walked into Susan's office I could feel the tension. It wasn't just all around me, it cut right through me. I knew Ken Westin, Stacy's fiancé, and I would never be the best of friends. I also knew I wasn't going to have Susan conduct her interview in that atmosphere.

"Listen, Susan, I'm expecting a long-distance collect call from a witness, so I need to do this in my office." Turning to Ken, I continued. "I've only got room for two chairs in my office. Would you mind waiting in the reception room, please, Ken? Sorry for the inconvenience." I guided Stacy out the door as I finished the second-to-last sentence, and by the end of the apology was almost out of hearing range. When Susan joined us a couple of minutes later, she had managed to convince Ken, temporarily at least, that he wasn't missing anything.

"Stacy," I began once we were settled in the far more relaxed, and disorganized, confines of my office. "We want you to know that we understand how hard this is for you. No one is going to force you to do anything. Getting your life back together is the most important thing for you to consider. You're about to be married and I know Ken isn't happy with your decision to cooperate. How do you feel about all of this?"

"Well, Susan told me you had something brand-new to make the case much better, so I told her I'd listen . . . and . . . here I am."

She sat rigid, dressed in her uniform, hat in her lap. She looked so much more in control than she really was. It was definitely the uniform.

"Uh"—I shot Susan a look laced with arsenic—"so you haven't agreed to do the case again?"

"I'm not sure I could stand to lose again." Her eyes filled with tears. "It wouldn't be good for Ken or me either. But a part of me wants to win." She looked at me. "I think it's the strongest part of me, but I'm not certain."

"You don't have to be certain," I said gently. "Nothing about your life can be certain right now, Stacy. But many women find themselves able to get back a whole lot of the control over their lives that someone took away in a rape if they follow through with the trial." I was telling her something I'd read, not something I'd experienced, and I felt I was on shaky ground. It turned out to be true, but I didn't know it then.

"But I *did* go through with the trial—and look what happened!" Her silent tears were dropping on top of the hat on her lap.

So that's it. Now I'm supposed to tell Stacy how it's going to be different the second time. On the other hand, she didn't have to come, I considered. The fact that she's here means she wants to hear how things would be different this time. She is willing, it seems, to risk her future marriage. Maybe she *really* wanted this for herself, but didn't know how to say it—or maybe she was too confused to know why she'd come.

We spent the next three hours talking. We went through the facts from beginning to end. When we had finished it was obvious how it would be different this time. I encouraged her to think about it and to talk the situation over very carefully with Ken. She said she'd let us know.

When Stacy and Ken had gone, and after I'd told Susan what a conniver she could be, we sat down in her office and choreographed the case. The next day I called Anne Kennedy and Grant Soames. I had an idea. I also had a child abuse murder case about to go to trial against one of the best-known, and most often successful defense attorneys in town. I knew I'd need help for Susan that I would not be free to give. I never could figure out what deputy AGs did anyway. Grant *had* to have more time than I did for Stacy's case.

Grant brought his lunch over a few days later and I laid it out to him.

Stacy Billings was a nineteen-year-old girl from Oregon who, like many girls her age, had done something to get away from the stifling home life in a small town. She chose the Navy, and found herself stationed in a large city, very much alone and lonely. At a YMCA party she had met Ken, about a year before the rape. He was a civilian volunteer at the Y and had never expected to meet his future bride at a military dance. After dating for a couple of months they got an apartment together. Their romance had been uncertain almost from the beginning. While Stacy was young and naïve, she had ambitions to be independent and successful. Ken saw a girl who needed someone to take care of her and he wanted to be the one. She liked Ken's role as protector, but it often reminded her of the home life she had just escaped. It was her inability to integrate these confusing goals that led to their frequent disagreements—not arguments or fights, just doubts on her part which could be felt by and reacted to on Ken's part. It was a result of this miscommunication between them that had led to Stacy's rape.

Stacy wanted some time for herself; some evenings to shop alone or go to the movies with girlfriends. Ken mistrusted her motives for these outings, which he thought were excuses to go out behind his back. So one evening in May 1978 he made a date with a mutual friend of theirs to "talk"—only he didn't tell that part to Stacy. He let her think it was a real date. Her response was anger and she reacted in a very predictable way: she decided to go alone to the dance at the downtown YMCA—the same Y where she'd met Ken almost a year before. It would be the first time since they had met that she'd be going there without him. Within a few minutes of arriving she knew it had been a mistake. The anger she had felt toward Ken quickly turned into a strange lump in her stomach and she thought she would be sick. She made up her mind to go home, but knew the other girls would not want to leave. She decided to take the bus and found the bench in front of the Y a peaceful refuge for her thoughts—and her stomach.

Stacy heard the car stop in front of her by the curb, but did not look up. She was deep in conversation with herself about Ken, about their future, about her future.

"Need a cab?" the voice was gentle and deep. Stacy looked up to see the familiar words "Limelight Cab Company" written in blue letters across a green background. The front passenger door was open and a uniformed driver, young and clean-cut, was leaning toward her from behind the wheel.

"No, thank you," she replied hastily. "I'm waiting for the bus. I'm sure it will be here any minute." She looked anxiously up and down the street but saw nothing.

"I can get you there a whole lot faster than a bus—and with no wait." He was still behind the wheel, smiling reassuringly.

"Well, I can't afford a cab anyway," she answered with finality. "I came with friends and didn't bring much money."

"How much is that?" He slid over to the passenger seat, only a few feet from where Stacy sat on the bus bench. He was nice-looking she thought, and friendly.

"About thirty-five cents." She smiled weakly, thinking he'd surely be gone with that information. Actually she had enough for a cab but didn't like to take them.

"That," he replied without hesitation, "is exactly what this cab rents for. Where do you want to go?" He was now holding the rear passenger door open for her, standing on the sidewalk, chauffeur style. Seeming to sense her hesitation, he added, "It's really slow tonight. I might as well get something. It's better than nothing."

Stacy thought about her choices: wait hours for a ride back from a girlfriend, take a bus which was nowhere in sight, or go right away in a cab—for thirty-five cents. In seconds she was sitting behind her uniformed escort. *Better than a bus bench,* she thought, *to sort out one's future.*

She told him where she wanted to go, and he asked if she knew how to get there. She gave him directions and then continued to answer questions he asked about how she was, where she came from—small talk, it seemed at the time.

His name was Albert. What was hers? Without looking she gave him her first name. She seemed sad. What was wrong? Nothing, really. Man problems? How did he know? Good guess.

She turned back toward the window. She thought about home for the first time in weeks, then pushed it out of her mind. *No, I'll work this out myself,* she thought silently.

When the cab got to the intersection nearest Stacy's apartment, the driver turned in the direction leading away from, not toward, her block. She quickly told him, and although he nodded as if he understood, he continued to drive, getting farther and farther away from the area. He drove on a freeway for a while, exiting into a residential neighborhood. Stacy had no idea where she was. She was nervous, but not yet scared. Why?

Well, he had told her he had nothing else to do that night and his questions had led her to tell him something about her problems with Ken, so she figured he was prolonging the trip to keep up the conversation.

Within a minute or two of leaving the freeway, he pulled to the curb in front of a stucco house with a large porch and a small lawn. He told her it was his house.

Stacy was suddenly aware that she had not heard any calls on the radio, as one usually does in taxis. She asked him if he was really on duty and it was then he said for the first time that he was not. Now she was getting scared.

Before she could decide what to do he was out of the cab and came around to the passenger door. He held it open. She got out, realizing she stood a better chance of escape outside. As they walked toward the house she looked up and down the street, but could see no street name. Then, for reasons due most likely to her background in a small town, she took out a five-dollar bill from her purse and handed it to the man.

"This is for as far as you've taken me, thank you. I'll just call another cab." With that she turned away from the house and headed back toward the street. He hesitated only a moment and then she could see him move toward her from behind. Instead of grabbing her as she suspected he might, he told her he was sorry and did not know what he had done that had made her mad.

"Then he said he would take me home. I mean, I was really confused, and I felt sort of stupid too, you know, for thinking all the bad things about him. After all, he *was* a cabdriver and worked for a company I'd heard of and, well, was just being friendly."

So she got back in the cab.

Now they were off through more neighborhoods like the one they had just left. This time her mind did not wander. He began talking to her again, asking more questions, offering an ear. Some of the questions she answered. Some she did not. While she did not trust him, she also did not want to make him angry. Some of the questions were getting personal. She watched for the bright lights of the city ahead. San Diego gave off a glow from miles away. That's how she always knew where downtown was.

Suddenly they were on a freeway. But which one? Panic crept in. She wheeled her head around. At first it was only the headlights of the cars behind . . . but above them . . . there it was, the glow of the city. They were speeding *away* from it.

The cab left the freeway and continued into the dark, distances between houses and lights growing farther apart. No more stoplights now, just signs and two-lane roads. She could smell country—like home. She thought about jumping out the next time he stopped. But where would she run? What would she say? Would anyone let her in? What if he caught her? She decided she'd try anyway the next time he stopped.

Without warning he pulled the cab to the side of the road. Almost before the engine was off, he slid over the seat and had grabbed Stacy's left arm. She was leaning against the right-hand door, attempting to open it. She struggled to free herself, fumbling awkwardly for the handle with her right hand.

Now he grabbed her right arm too. As she struggled, the thoughts and emotions pulsing through her head changed from fear to anger and back. She called him "a son of a bitch." This was strong language for Stacy, as she *never* swore. She begged him to let her go. She threatened him, saying her boyfriend would kill him if he touched her.

In between she struggled.

During this time her attacker had not spoken. Now he began to ask her what was wrong, what had he done to make her fight him? He said he did not want to hurt her, only to "love" her.

What was wrong? What had he done? Certainly it was obvious! He'd asked the same thing before and then made her a false promise. He knew what he was doing, she thought. But maybe she could get him back to civilization if she played her cards right.

Now he was on top of her. If he wanted to love her as he said, she pleaded, they should go to his house; if he really cared.

It wasn't working . . . the struggle, both with words and with strength, was futile. It would, she decided, be best to just give in and not cause any trouble.

"I felt that I'd have a better chance of surviving if I cooperated. At least that's what I'd heard was true. I even saw a movie that suggested a victim should submit when resistance seems useless. And I tried *everything* to get loose or to get him to take me home."

She allowed him to undress her and he placed his mouth on her vagina. She was so scared but told him it felt good so he would not hurt her. Then he had sexual intercourse with her and told her to orally copulate him.

As they drove back to the city she dressed herself and studied his face. She planned to turn him in. When the car stopped in front of the house which he had earlier identified as his, Stacy sprang from the seat and bolted out the door. She ran several blocks until she found a phone booth. She called her fiancé's best friend because she and Ken didn't have a phone. The friend took her home and she called the police.

"And this," I summed up for Grant, "is how the jury will hear the facts the second time around. And Anne Kennedy; with your help, they'll hear from the expert."

I suggested to Grant that Susan could ask the Court's permission to put my juror from Sandy's case on the stand, that he could introduce the transcript of the testimony Anne gave and offer at least two ways to hear the evidence: the hypothetical I'd used already or the narrative I was leaning toward in the future.

"Next you'll probably suggest I ask for a transfer over here," Grant said, laughing, when I stopped for air. When he saw I was considering the idea, he quickly shook his head. "Oh, no, you don't. I'll help Susan. But I never liked courtrooms much. Too much like a fishbowl. I like to wax eloquent to the higher authorities."

I thought of Father Paul, and smiled.

A week later Anne Kennedy read the transcript of the first trial and I filled her in on what I'd learned from the new interview. Could she shed some light on anything for the jury?

Yes, she said, she would be able to talk about several things not covered in Sandy's case.

Why hadn't Stacy been suspicious of an offer by a cabdriver to forgo a fare? Because she had trusted the appearance of his position. People often are fooled by uniforms. Many people, not only women, are fooled by what they think a uniform, or a title, or even a position represents. Because of this, women climb into cabs or undress for examination by doctors, or pull over at the sight of a flashing red light on a dark, rainy night.

Stacy's guard was down.

Why hadn't she jumped out on one of the many occasions the car had slowed down or even stopped? Because she was headed away from the only familiar thing about her surroundings—the city itself. Such an escape was, in her mind, illusory. Although no weapon was ever seen, the thought of one was always in her mind.

Why did the defendant know so many personal details about her? Because he'd asked so many questions which she unsuspectingly had answered, thinking he was lending a sympathetic ear.

And once again, while no direct threats had been made against Stacy's life, it was on the thought of death that she dwelled throughout the ordeal.

Anne's testimony appeared to be needed even more in the Drake case than it had been in the Harter case.

While the foundation upon which the defense had been built in both cases was clearly that of consent, Albert Drake ran, as they say, a much tighter ship. Absent here was the distance between victim claim and suspect denial, differences the jury could use to apportion out credibility.

According to Drake, he had picked up a distraught Stacy, who told him of her fiancé and their problems. He knew many details about her, some of which she herself could not even remember telling him—like the date on which they planned to marry.

He claimed that when he got to the intersection nearest Stacy's apartment building and turned the wrong way (on purpose), she said nothing, so he kept driving. Since she was talking to him about her problems, he hoped to get to know her better. After they drove around a while, he went to his house. When they were walking toward the door, he was surprised when she gave him the five dollars, and they simply got back in the cab.

Eventually, he reported, they got out to the country and he put his arms around her. She screamed and threatened him, but he didn't know why she was scared. He told her he didn't want to hurt her, just to make love. He was able to calm her down and finally she said she liked him and they had sexual relations. After talking and holding each other they left, but on the trip back to town she got colder and colder, and ran away when he stopped in front of his house.

While I had no trouble seeing through this story, I was not going to be on the jury, and it was clear that the victim and suspect versions of what had happened were closer in this case than they had been (at least by trial time) in Sandy's. Twelve people had already split right down the middle on this one.

The differences between what Stacy Billings said took place that night and what Albert Drake claimed happened would only become important in proportion to the degree of credibility given the claimant by a jury. To help them, we would offer the expert witness, addressing the issue of resistance. Jurors would be given a clear understanding of

Stacy's thoughts about resistance, and the reasons for her actions, every step of the way. Susan would "visualize" the facts for them, and Anne Kennedy would interpret the coping behaviors. Together they would close the credibility gap in the victim's favor.

But there was an even more compelling reason for my interest in Albert Drake: strong circumstantial evidence suggested that Stacy had not been the first woman he had attacked.

The Limelight Cab Company had provided the police with some odd information during the investigation of the Billings case. The night before Stacy was raped, a man had called a dispatcher to report having seen a company cab on an east county road. He had been on his way home from a party at about 1 A.M. As he drove along a lonely stretch of back-county road, he noticed a Limelight cab parked toward the side of the road but not completely off the lane of traffic.

For some reason, he decided to go back and look again and he made a U-turn. Just as his headlights illuminated the rear of the cab, its lights went on and it began to move away from him. He followed behind and could see the outline of two heads, a male behind the wheel and a female in the front passenger seat. Then he saw the female turn toward the door and he was certain the door began to open. By this time the cab was picking up speed. He watched as the driver leaned across toward the passenger and appeared to pull the woman toward him with a sudden jerk, while at the same moment the door shut. There seemed to be a struggle going on between the two, but by now the cab was on a fairly well-traveled road heading for a freeway entrance. The witness pulled close enough to read the license number as the cab sped onto the freeway, where, after several minutes of attempting to follow, he abandoned the effort. Early the following morning he reported to the company what had happened. The license on the cab was the one assigned to Drake. But no one had made a report of a sexual assault that night in that area or fitting the description provided by the witness. And he was unable to identify the defendant in a photo lineup. He had only seen the driver from the back. Drake denied the entire incident.

The prosecution had chosen to use information provided by this witness at Drake's first trial. It was used as a "prior similar act," meaning it resembles the manner in which the crime charged was carried out in so many ways that a jury may infer that if the defendant committed one, he probably committed the other. Even with this circumstantial evidence to enhance Stacy's case, the jury hung six-six.

The decision to use prior similar act evidence is always risky. Appellate courts often reverse convictions which they feel are obtained primarily because a trial judge has allowed a jury to hear testimony about another, similar criminal act which then weighs heavily in its decision to convict—by association rather than on the basis of the events of the charged offense, so the argument goes. While I felt this evidence was the strongest reason to assume Drake's guilt, I did not want to provide an appellate court with a way to skirt the expert testimony issue altogether and possibly reverse a conviction for the improper use of a similar act. We decided that Susan would not use this evidence in the second trial. I wondered, though, how many women Drake had terrorized in this manner. The detectives kept looking, but even up to the time of the second trial, no one had come forward.

After my initial flurry of activity with Stacy's case, I had to leave Susan, Grant, and Anne to carry on. I was immersed for the next weeks in the preparations, negotiations, and presentations of cases ranging from child abuse to forgery to robbery to escape from a county honor camp. I caught glimpses of Grant as he came to see Susan. He became completely engrossed in his efforts to get the expert testimony accepted. When the time came for trial, this proved no easy task.

The first thing to happen was the assignment of a visiting judge from Orange County to preside over the case. Now, Orange County is not well known for its liberal thinkers. In addition, visiting judges do not like to step on toes out of their backyard. They want to fit in and "do like the natives do," so to speak.

I slipped into the courtroom the day Susan began the hearing to have the expert evidence admitted. Later that day I was back to hear Grant offer the letter from my juror, a transcript of Anne's testimony from Sandy's case, and suggestions of alternative methods by which to introduce the expert testimony. When the judge left the bench for the evening, it was clear that he was having trouble with the decision but he appeared to understand the theory. He agreed to make a ruling the following morning. We were not hopeful.

To everyone's surprise, the judge allowed the prosecution use of the expert, but imposed even stricter guidelines than Olmeda had for me. The trial lasted six days and the jury was out less than two hours. The verdict was "guilty," and when Susan and I spoke with members of the jury, there was no room for doubt: without the expert it would have been a different story. As a matter of fact, without the expert it *had* been a different story.

Drake was sentenced to prison, but he never went. The case went on appeal and during this time the sentence was put off. Stacy went on her honeymoon, but I was not surprised to learn later that the marriage had lasted less than a year.

Once again the trial was well covered by the local press. I was interviewed by a couple of radio stations, appeared on a TV program, and was asked to speak at a number of conferences. The stream of advice seekers began to pick up. I felt a growing frustration with my heavy case load and my inability to devote my energies to a subject which held such an abiding sense of urgency for me. If only I could get a handle on all the rape cases filed and apply some uniformity to the way decisions to prosecute were made. I knew I could not try them all, but at least if they all came across my desk I could give them an experienced review. Later, if asked to advise on some, I would recognize them. Most importantly, I was sure this system could provide me with the scope I needed to identify what I sensed to be the threads of patterns and profiles among all cases.

I wrote a memo to the District Attorney himself, outlining my ideas. I asked Daly to give me a list of his objections to the establishment of a sexual assault unit. Then I asked if I could go on a fact-finding trip around the state to see if his criticisms held water in cities where the District Attorney's office had a sexual assault unit. He said I could go but would have to work it around my case load. I was still trying to fit it in somehow when I left the office almost two years later.

8

MAY AND OCTOBER have always been my favorite times. They are tolerant months, absorbing the old and the new—when what needs to be done and what should have been finished blend indulgently together. No one ever expects you to start or complete anything in these months. It is this lack of urgency which attracts me so wholeheartedly to them.

Unfortunately, May and October are closely embraced by the immediacy of June and September. What could mark time in May becomes insistent by June. What was compelling in September can linger through October.

During my years in the District Attorney's office, most months resembled Junes and Septembers. What kept me moving forward were the certain sanctuaries of my Mays and Octobers—that is, until I had been two years in the Superior Court division.

It was sometime during the last week of April 1979 that I noticed there were more case files lying around my office in various stages of reconstruction than were upright and ready in the two metal organizers framing my desk.

"It would be nice," I mused, threading my way carefully around the desk, "if this mess could be handled like my checking account; when it doesn't balance, I close it and open a new one."

I told myself to look at the bright side, the fact that I still saw humor in all of this. But it was the glimpse of a feeling I had not experienced before darting across my thoughts, like a figure caught just out of the corner of one's eye—when you turn around to look it isn't there, or maybe never was—that left me with an uneasiness I could not completely shake.

"Judy, may I come in, or is it a bad time?"

The sound of a male voice sliced through my reverie. I had neither felt nor seen anyone enter the room.

"No, no," I replied, recovering quickly. "I'm just trying to decide whether to burn the place or just abandon it. Have a seat, Jim. I've got at least"—I looked at my watch—"at least six and a half minutes before calendar call. Unless it's about taking over that rape case of yours; then yes, it's a bad time."

My smile blunted the words, but their sincerity could not be overlooked.

"I understand," he answered. "I just wanted to be sure you hadn't changed your mind."

Jim Cross was one of the best-looking men I had ever known. Medium in build, Ivy League in dress, he looked as if he had just stepped from the pages of some collegiate magazine. But his best feature by far was his eyes. They were Robert Mitchum's minus the macho. Just having him there to look at snapped me out of the doldrums. But he was also an exception to the great-looking-man syndrome: he was considerate, quiet, and caring. I had found him to be a private person who did not spend time discussing women or sports. I had wondered on a number of occasions if he would stay with the District Attorney or, if he did, whether he would be happy.

It did not come as a great surprise when, in February, Jim confided to me that he was leaving the office at the end of May. He had a rape case which was bothering him, he had said, and wanted to recommend to Daly that I take it over for trial—if it made it that far. I had told him no, emphatically, not to do that. He'd respected my wishes, but had returned several times to voice his lack of confidence in, and rapport with, the victim.

The first time had been right after the preliminary hearing. He had been waiting for me one day when I returned from a calendar appearance. He did not move as I slid past him and released my armload of files on an almost empty patch of tabletop behind my desk.

"Well, how'd it go?" I asked, turning my eyes toward his while guiding my load to rest before it could set off a paper avalanche. Gone were those gentle, friendly eyes. It was evident that something was very wrong. I was startled by the fury his expression delivered from an otherwise motionless face.

"What in the world happened?" I demanded, searching for the source of his anger.

Without shifting positions, moving only his mouth, his words were forcibly controlled.

"You know," he started slowly, "how you always hear that someday the worst thing you can think of will happen when you're in court? Today it happened to me, only it was even worse than they said it would be."

I no longer had to guess what Jim was like when he was angry. To a yeller like me, it was the scariest kind, this quiet wrath.

"It took me ten minutes to ask her the questions I needed for bind-over. I didn't know how long the defense would cross-examine, but, you know, nothing ever comes of it."

I could now detect a hint of desperation just under the surface.

"I objected when the defense asked how long she'd known her attacker," he went on. "I was overruled. I *really* objected when he asked what she was wearing the first time they met. What, I thought to myself, was with this guy anyway? Maybe he thinks she was nude? I was overruled again. So I decided not to let it go and voiced that thought to the judge, to show how ridiculous the question was unless, of course, she had been nude."

Jim looked at me for the first time, drawing his stare from his knees, with which he appeared to have been conversing up to this point.

"The judge caught the sarcasm I intended and asked the defense if he was trying to infer she hadn't been wearing anything or if he really needed to know what she was wearing. 'I was trying,' replied the defense attorney, 'to imply that she wasn't wearing anything, your honor. I am certain the evidence will show she was totally naked at the time.'

"I knew the second I looked at her that it was true."

Now the level of Jim's voice was rising, as was he. He went on as he paced my office with his hands thrust deep into his pockets.

"By the time cross was over, he'd gotten Terri to admit she had been posing at a damned nudist modeling session for amateur photographers or something, that she was being paid to do it, and that her roommate does this all the time."

He stopped pacing and looked at me with blazing eyes. "Then he asked if she had posed at the defendant's request and if she had seen a picture he had taken of her. I had been watching him open his briefcase during these interminable questions and then he whipped out a photo. Of course, he asked for it to be marked for identification and showed it to me. I almost shit. It was my darling victim standing ankle deep in water, absolutely nude, smiling sensuously in what was obviously a pose."

He fell back into the chair. "I actually pretended to know that all of this was coming and managed to keep the picture out on relevancy grounds. But Jesus Christ! I wanted to kill her—and she knew it. Somehow I got the thing bound over for trial, although God knows why. I got her back in my office and screamed at her. She said she was afraid to tell me, can you imagine, because she didn't think I'd believe her! What the hell did she think I'd do finding out *this* way?"

As I listened to Jim, I had to admit my limits of credibility were being stretched. But something still made sense about everything Jim was relating to me—only I certainly wasn't going to tell him that.

"Jim, hadn't you ever asked her how she first met this guy . . . ?" I fumbled for a name.

"Dickenson O'Conner," he supplied quickly. "And I thought I had, but I suppose I just *assumed* she had started at the beginning. I must not have said, 'Was that the *very* first time you met him?' or whatever. She said she met him through her roommate, who knew O'Conner had an employment service. I just assumed, I guess . . ." His expression was apologetic and forlorn at the same time.

The next time Jim had come to see me about the O'Conner case had been several weeks later. I again found him waiting for me when I came back from court.

"Remember I told you about Terri's roommate, and how she introduced her to O'Conner and that she was shocked by what he did and was so supportive of Terri's story?"

Jim was speaking so fast I hardly had time to remember what case he was talking about, much less to answer any of the several questions he shot at me one right after the other.

"Well," he went on, barely taking a breath, "yesterday Christie, that's the roommate's name, called and went on and on about how Terri took pills the day she met the defendant and how she didn't pay her share of the rent, etc., etc. Without her testimony this case stinks. So I've got Terri in my office right now. I asked her about the pills and she admitted she had taken something that day. I also asked her if she or her roommate paid the bills and she said her roommate had been for the last couple of months because she'd been out of work, but she had promised to pay her back."

He threw his hands up in exasperation. "Every time I see her something else pops up. She's promised I've heard the whole story now—no more surprises. But somehow I don't know . . . she seems flakier than a few weeks ago."

"Have you explained to her that you are *her* attorney, and how important it is for you to know everything?" I asked, understanding how each felt.

"Of course I've told her. Every time we go through this, I've told her."

"Look, Jim," I counseled, glancing at my watch, "you have to understand that we represent as much of a threat to Terri's feeling of security as her attacker did. Why should she think you want to make things better? The movies on TV, the horror stories about what happens to rape victims, about what prosecutors try to do, what defense attorneys try to do, all this is what most women think about during the time we're busy mapping out our evidence. I'll bet that's what's going through Terri's mind every time you sit down and face each other."

"I *do* want to believe her." I could see he really did. But I just didn't have time to hear everything I needed to know in order for me to tell him what was happening to Terri and to explain why they appeared to be on a collision course.

"Jim, catch me at some time closer to the trial date and I'll help you out if I can." I was on my way back to the elevator again. "But don't, I repeat don't, volunteer *me*," I cautioned over my shoulder.

What I really didn't need was another case—of any kind. I had just finished an emotionally draining felony child abuse trial in which the judge's unfamiliarity with the field had only added to my other difficulties. In order to ensure my availability for that case, one involving child witnesses whose memories had to be tapped as quickly as possible, I had continued a rape trial and a complicated rape prelim involving a sixteen-year-old girl who had been under a commitment to a county mental facility at the time she reported being attacked by an orderly. I was in the midst of a series of radio appearances, had given two of three promised lectures to local high school classes on the legal aspects of rape, and was finishing my term on the board of a local child abuse council.

Coming up within the next few weeks was the sentencing of a defendant who had committed a brutal rape of a six-year-old girl and whose attorney planned to mount a vigorous bid to keep his client from imprisonment in the state facility for mentally disordered sex offenders. I needed time to orchestrate my own presentation for maximum commitment.

Simultaneously, I had to move swiftly, but cautiously, to lay the groundwork for a case involving employees of another county agency. The sixteen-year-old victim's story had already caused a division of loyalties and was beginning to ripple toward the top rungs of my office. The press was sniffing scandal (they were right) and my daily quota of inquiries from them was escalating.

In addition to the previously postponed rape case I was heading to court on as I left Jim with his problems, I had eight other trials set for three weeks in May—during the fourth, hopefully, I could take the week off I had scheduled some months before.

"No," I concluded convincingly, "I don't need another case."

When Jim was, for a third time, waiting for me one day about a week later, I knew there was a message someplace that I had been missing.

"Terri's case came up on a defense motion last week." He was looking at me very tenuously. "A *Ballard* motion and for substitution of attorneys. Both were granted, and now it's been continued until June, after I'll be gone."

I stopped what I had been doing and looked at him.

"She's seen the psych and come out fine," Jim continued enthusiastically. "No fantasizing tendencies he says, so the *Ballard* isn't going to hurt us at all."

What did he mean by "us"? I continued to stare at him, saying nothing.

"Now don't get angry with me, but I made a decision to do something you won't like—but it's okay, if you'll just hear me out before you say anything. I told Daly what happened and proposed that you be assigned the case—but only, *only* on the condition you have complete control and absolute authority to dismiss or settle it if and when you think, in your sole judgment, it should be done."

There. The hook was set. That strange anxiety was back. I could feel May slipping into June before its time.

Jim sat studying my face for reaction.

I wanted to tell him to forget it, to race back to Daly and cancel the deal (which I knew he had already written on the chart he kept for all of us under the blotter on his desk). I wanted to rush into Daly's office myself and tell him I'd do all these cases if he'd just stop assigning me the other stuff. I really wanted to do that most of all. Looking back, I wish I had. But I wasn't sure how to pull it off, so I didn't try.

I took a deep breath and let it out with a grunt.

"You're certain I have complete control, absolute authority, no ifs, ands, or buts?" I asked, somewhat intrigued with this unusual condition.

While Daly normally followed our recommendations, it was rare to have him grant a carte blanche on so serious a felony. The logic of this move on his part did not escape me for a moment. I recognized it for exactly what it was—a compromise, without which Daly could not have rationalized giving this mess to me with the state of my case load. And as always, he knew a dismissal from me would sit a whole lot better than one from him. He was a star negotiator; he knew how to sweeten a deal. How could he lose?

Stupid question. No, my quandary was really: how could I turn it down?

"Do you know anything more about what happened than you did right after the prelim?" I asked with resignation.

"Well, I know a little more, or rather she told me some things, but there's no way I can talk to her about this now. But what she said was . . ."

"No, Jim," I broke in abruptly. "Why don't you get me the file and Terri's phone number." I sighed again. "Tell Daly I'll accept under the conditions he gave me—*all* of them."

"Okay, I will." Jim breathed with relief. "And I really appreciate your doing this." He stopped at the door and turned toward me. "You know, even after all this, I still do think the guy did it . . . and you're the only one who's got a shot at proving it."

I could tell he meant it, although his clear satisfaction with the outcome over our meeting was apparent.

"Thanks for the vote of confidence, Jim," I said with equally mixed emotions. The next day I made sure Daly had meant what he'd said about my powers of life and death over the O'Conner case. He had. So much for fraud as a way out.

Just maybe, I reasoned, the facts might turn out to be as impossible as Jim thought they were and my job would be a sure, if not simple, one: to explain to the victim the untenable position she had put us in for trial and to dismiss the case.

I would not take pleasure in the dismissal if it turned out that way. Such a result is often due as much to the way a case is handled as to the facts themselves. Inexperience, ignorance, insensitivity, priorities, all play varying roles in what not infrequently can be a disaster for both victim and prosecutor. During my years in the office I was sure the fault lay exclusively with the prosecutors, for treating the whole area of sexual assault in such a patronizing fashion. Now I understand that there were several conflicting dynamics at work which played a constant game of Catch-22 with these cases—and with me. But I'm getting ahead of myself. Writing, much like trial work, presents such a discipline challenge to lawyers!

The first thing that struck me when I sat down to review the file in Terri's case was how long it had been dragging on. The attack had occurred during the first week of October and the preliminary had followed about a month later. The trial date, however, had not been set until early March of this year. I had always noticed a direct ratio between the quality of a rape case at trial and the length of time which had elapsed getting it there: the longer it took, the worse it looked.

While California law gives trial priority to rape, child abuse and molest, homicide, and a few other odious offenses, there is a clear tendency to procrastinate if the case looks wobbly—and so many of them do—hoping for a plea, a break, or even a miracle. Of the three, a plea to a reduced charge is usually the outcome.

I flipped to the case notes Jim had kept. Indeed, in February he had offered the defense a 245a felony Nolt, nine-month lid, to be reduced to a misdemeanor after successful completion of three years' probation. Translated, that means plead to an assault with a deadly weapon as a felony, District Attorney not oppose local time (Nolt), and recommend a nine-month maximum in jail rather than a prison sentence if the judge decided to lock him up for a while. The most jail time he could serve under this arrangement, then, would be six months, due to the formula that is used.

The entire charge would become a misdemeanor after three years and eventually could be dismissed from his record. No one would know O'Conner had ever been charged with a rape, and he would be able to truthfully deny having been arrested or having a felony record for employment and other positions of trust.

I also looked over the witness list. It contained standard names: police officers (2), detectives (2), victim (1), witness (1), examining physician (1).

Next came the work sheet, or factual brief of the case. It is the private evaluation each deputy is responsible for preparing after prelim so that the senior prosecutors have some idea of the worth of a case at review. This evaluation has five sections: (1) charges; (2) proof; (3) deputy's evaluation; (4) defendant's record; and (5) negotiations to date.

I smiled understandingly as I scanned Jim's conclusion under number three, deputy's evaluation: "Terrible!" No wonder he had been coming to see me for so long. Since November of last year he had been trying to rally a case for trial which he initially had little faith in, and for which every subsequent turn of events seemed to result in a further erosion of his confidence.

"Saving grace," a second paragraph went on under evaluation. I certainly hoped so. "Defendant calls victim's roommate shortly after the attack and states something to the effect: 'I just fucked your roommate and wanted you to be the first to know. She resisted at first but gave up after it appeared useless.' Victim is nineteen, white; defendant is thirty-five, black."

I was reaching for the phone before I'd finished the last sentence. "My God, Jim, did you just *forget* to tell me about the race and age difference between Terri and O'Conner, or were you saving it to make my day? And how about that phone call to Christie Sheppard, the roommate? Has she changed her story about that now or what?" I was steaming.

"Okay, okay," the pleasant voice came back. "Hold on. No, she has not changed her story, and no, I didn't forget. I said I still believed he did it, remember? I thought the things I told you were more important, though—to the decision of settling, or dismissing, or whatever."

There was a pause. "But I hope what you think is so important did make your day. Did it?" His tone was hopeful.

"Let's say it's improving, Jim, it's improving. Is there anything else I might run into that maybe you should tell me about? You know, like . . ."

"I know what you mean, Judy. No, nothing else. Damn, I'm sorry. Really."

I hung up and settled back with the investigator's reports. Coincidentally, Sografo was the detective assigned to the case. In ten minutes I'd read the file, and in those ten minutes I was sure that Terri Richardson was telling the truth. Proving it, of course, was an entirely different proposition.

Once again I wondered, as I reread the parts of Sografo's case summary which made me so sure of O'Conner's guilt, why I saw so much more to these reports than anyone else. No, actually I knew I saw these things because I was approaching the problem from a woman's perspective; the question really was: how do I establish the credibility to make others see beyond the words, to understand what I saw, and why?

"So let's see, Mr. Dickenson O'Conner," I mused as I returned my attention to the reports in front of me. "All I have to do now is figure out how to convict you."

I made appointments for interviews with Terri, Christie, and Sografo, who was obviously not displeased to hear of my acquisition.

"Déjà vu, as they say, or something like that, huh, Jude? Have you called Anne Kennedy yet? Or do I get to try my hand this time?"

"Not yet, Jerry, not yet, and no, you don't get to try your hand—remember, you're the investigator—bias, prejudice, remember Harter? Now there's your déjà vu. And, Jerry, don't go to Las Vegas the first weekend in June, okay?"

That afternoon I slipped the still new-looking "Expert Testimony—Rape" file into my briefcase. It had been a while since I'd read the Burgess and Holmstrom articles on victim coping behaviors and rape trauma syndrome. Maybe I could come up with something new—or even a repeat performance would do. That evening I reviewed the articles, and my options.

If only we'd get some direction from the appellate court, I thought nervously. *Am I setting up reversible error and more agony for these women if I have to try their cases again?*

I inquired regularly of my sources at the appellate court to see if there was anything they could tell me about when a decision on the cases might be made. But they were closed-mouthed and I could not glean even a hint from them.

On the other hand, I deliberated, *if I don't win, there won't be any convictions to reverse, now will there?*

"Well, then it's settled," I concluded aloud as I pulled into my parking space the next morning. I phoned Anne.

By the time Terri Richardson sat down with me for our first meeting, I had some loose ideas about my approach to her case which several readings of the Burgess and Holmstrom articles had sparked: when *they* had interviewed rape victims for their studies, the primary purpose had been to discover the best track to effective treatment. Why couldn't I, knowing what I was looking for and armed with their results, interview a victim in such a way as to analyze her for these same patterns—but with the purpose of using the results in court as evidence of rape and absence of consent?

This approach certainly made sense. All the studies so far had agreed with Burgess and Holmstrom that, for instance, there are distinct stages to rape trauma.

The first stage is an immediate or acute phase, which disrupts much, if not all, of a victim's normal life patterns, and which continues for days or even several weeks following an attack. Victims exhibit a cluster of symptoms such as flashbacks, nightmares, and the inability to eat, sleep, or work. They may have strong reactions to sights, sounds, or smells which remind them of the ordeal, among a variety of other symptoms.

The one element held in common by all who are classified as suffering from this syndrome is the feeling that they have been confronted suddenly, and imminently, with death. A resulting fear pervades the lives of these women, which may express itself in numerous ways: as a general jumpy feeling about anything from the ring of a telephone to the touch of a friend; or in a wide range of mood swings from humiliation, shame, and guilt to self-blame, anger, and revenge; or in the overcautious approach they take to anyone or anything.

In the immediate aftermath and for several days following the assault, rape victims may experience physical pain in areas of the body abused during the attack long after any visible injuries have disappeared: tenderness of the breasts if bitten, discomfort in swallowing if forced to orally copulate, a stinging sensation in the vagina following forced intercourse. Sometimes there are symptoms of this sort without injuries ever having been present.

When I read this, I could not help but think of Sandy Adkins in particular, and all the others I had seen in general, during my years in the District Attorney's office. And the ones I'd seen were a mere drop in the bucket. How many hundreds of thousands of superficial medical exams by uninformed physicians, for instance, had resulted in reports which reflected females "in no apparent distress" and whose complaints of physical (not to mention mental) symptoms could not be documented? In court came the double whammy when these complaints became smoke for the fires of credibility that could be fanned into raging infernos of doubt by defense attorneys. After all, if the doctor, regarded so much above mere mortals, could not find any "injuries," then who to believe? It didn't take long to figure out.

While symptoms such as fear, nightmares, and phobias specific to the rape are characteristic of both phases of rape trauma syndrome, Burgess and Holmstrom describe the second stage of this syndrome as the long-term process, or reorganizational phase, which may affect the victim's life for anywhere from several weeks to many months or even years following an attack.

"Rape," they said, "represents the disruption of the lifestyle of the victim, not only during the immediate days and weeks following the incident, but well beyond that to many weeks and months. Various factors seem to influence how the victim copes with the rape crisis, such as the victim's personality style, the people available to her who respond to her distress in a serious and concerned manner, and the way in which she is treated by the people with whom she comes into contact after the rape."

Moving, sometimes frequently, rearranging furniture, inability to concentrate or complete work (or work at all), going "back home for a visit," all are common to victims during this second phase. But one symptom in particular caught my attention this time: their reaction to sex and their interaction with the men in their lives following an attack. It is often shattering, with divorce, the breaking off of long-standing relationships, fear of and/or abstention from intercourse, sleeping in separate beds, or even rooms, from mates, being among the more common responses.

There was Sandy again, and Stacy, and in fact almost every victim I had ever met. How clear the picture. Back from the recesses where I had sent them came the images of the unanswered questions—the ones I for so long could not quite put my finger on. In addition to providing meaning for the sexual patterns I had observed but did not know what to do with, there were other explanations. Like the effect that the long-term process and reorganizational symptoms obviously had on the uninformed prosecutor's perspective of his victim; while she was suffering through predictable patterns of recovery, he was seeing a "flakier than ever" case, and the resulting frustrations on the part of each was making the success of either less and less possible.

In actuality, it was certain that, with the passage of time, the "flakier" a case looked to a prosecutor's traditional approach, the stronger it really got if recognized in the context of rape trauma syndrome: with the passage of time a clearer pattern of symptoms emerged.

I had to keep reminding myself of the limitations placed on me not only by my budget but by the court. While all this information about rape trauma would prove exceedingly useful to my interviewing, to my case preparation, and even to clearing up scores of previously shadowy and even unformed questions, the real focus of my efforts in 1979 was still on coping behaviors and their relevance to the element of resistance. I knew, with careful planning, I could expand Anne Kennedy's ability to pass on some of the rape trauma information hidden among her answers to coping behavior questions. There was a clear overlap between coping behaviors and rape trauma. What Anne couldn't do, or when she'd gone as far as she could, I'd use the victim herself to carry on.

So with Terri I would look for lots of the same kind of detail that I had with Sandy, step-by-step probing, motivations for reactions, how she felt and why.

I had seen a reference to a forty-five-minute shower in the preliminary hearing transcript. I would ask Terri about it. And her clothes—I could see someone had thought to pick them up, but there was no mention anywhere about how, or where they had been found, or what Terri had intended to do with them. The Burgess and Holmstrom articles had many examples of women washing themselves and the clothes worn during the attack over and over. Or of getting rid of the clothes in various ways.

Another piece in the puzzle: every victim I had ever interviewed wanted to or had gotten rid of the clothes she had been wearing during the terror of attack.

There were so many details, which up to this point had only served to confirm my personal faith in a particular woman's story, that could now be used to form the basis for a jury to test a victim's credibility.

My excitement was running high as Sografo introduced me to Terri Richardson. But what if this didn't happen the way it was supposed to? I'd have to be calm, expect the worst, be delighted and surprised with success.

Like Sandy, Terri was fair-skinned, with blue eyes and blond hair. These were, however, their only common traits. Terri, at nineteen, lacked the sophistication of dress or personality which had so impressed me on my first meeting with Sandy. Actually, it was a sophistication derived not so much from maturity as from upbringing, and after I had spent some time with her, I could see that Terri at twenty-nine would be much as she was at nineteen.

She had lived in a small midwestern town until age thirteen, when she moved to San Ysidro, a comparably sized community in San Diego County adjacent to the Mexican border. Her education had been completed with high school graduation, and for the past two years she had worked mostly as a waitress and dental hygienist. She had actually taken a course to become a dental hygienist but had found the work dull and quit her job at a local dentist's office shortly before the rape had occurred. It was when her savings were getting low, after four months of unemployment, that the chain of events leading her to Dickenson O'Conner were set in motion.

Terri was shy with those she did not know, but made friends quickly. She reminded me of a Botticelli, the fifteenth-century Italian painter who always depicted his women as fair-skinned, blue-eyed maidens, tending to be short and more padded than lean. This gave her a hint of sensuousness, yet baby fat also came to mind. She was to tell me later that she had gained considerable weight from nervous eating in the weeks after the attack.

Another check on my list: Burgess and Holmstrom considered immediate weight loss, as much as 10 percent of body weight, to be a symptom in the acute phase of the rape trauma pattern. Why not weight gain? It seemed reasonable that the gain or loss of weight as a symptom of trauma might depend on the individual's usual eating responses to crisis. Many stopped eating, others stuffed food in anxiety-ridden times. Several years later I was to consult with an attorney trying a civil suit on behalf of a rape victim who had gained over a hundred pounds since she had been gang-raped some eleven months before.

I would be sure we discussed this weight problem when Terri testified, for the benefit of the jury of course—particularly women jurors.

Unlike Sandy, Terri had read no articles on rape, had seen no films, and had not attended any lectures dealing with the subject. Once, recently and in passing, she had thought about what she might do if she were ever attacked. She had even talked about it on that occasion.

"With whom?" I asked.

"It was with my father and I don't even remember how it came up. I told him I would fight to the death, that no one would ever rape me."

"But you didn't, did you? Why, do you suppose?" I wondered aloud.

"No, I sure didn't. I froze, I guess I was petrified . . . I couldn't do anything. I mean, he only grabbed my arm . . . and held it . . ."

"How did he look, and sound?" I ventured cautiously.

"You know"—she looked a bit surprised as if I had hit on something she had been thinking about—"his eyes changed so much, and his voice . . . I mean, his eyes got hard, glassy, unreal-looking, and instead of talking sort of higher and fast his voice got real slow and deep. Almost like I didn't recognize it. That was what really scared me. He held my arm and with those eyes he commanded me to go into the bedroom. And I let him lead me in. He commanded me to take off my clothes. Well, I didn't, but I remember letting him do it. I felt so helpless." Tears came to her eyes. "And I still do."

So Terri had reacted, in the face of the real-life situation, exactly the opposite from what she had intended to do. How truthful this sounded. I guessed a jury would agree.

Terri cried during our first interview and was often near tears when we discussed the case. It was still to be that way at trial. Her ability to cope even after six months was clearly marginal. I seemed to be on the right track, and could see that, given six months to work with, I would know by the time she left my office that first day if she suffered from the rape trauma syndrome.

I asked Terri to describe her eating and sleeping patterns right after the rape.

"At first I had no appetite. I didn't eat anything for three whole days. It hurt to swallow for some reason. Then I began to eat a lot, you know, and gained weight. I don't think I slept for the same three days that I didn't eat. I remember not even going to bed the first two nights. After that I couldn't sleep more than a couple of hours at a time for a week or so, and that still happens two or three times a week.

"I've had nightmares, but I can't remember what they are. Only that I wake up feeling like I'm about to be hurt. Very scary, afraid."

I asked her if she felt safe and, if so, when and where.

"I never feel safe. I couldn't stand the apartment where I lived, but I'm so afraid to be alone anywhere. I never was like that before. I carry things with me, like kitchen knives and sticks, when I go out. I wouldn't go out at night for a long time, even with friends."

"What about boyfriends? Do you have one?" I asked. "I mean, did you at the time, or do you now?"

"I'd been dating Cory for about six months before, but we broke up last December."

"Were you sleeping with Cory before you were raped?" I inquired gently.

"Yes . . . but do they have to know that? We never slept together after that day." She looked frightened. "I couldn't," she said in almost a whisper.

So no intercourse, a broken relationship. I felt as if this interview was the answer sheet on a multiple-choice test.

"I felt," she went on, not in response to any question from me, "that it was taken from me, stolen, I didn't give it. I'm so sad all the time. My friends say it's like someone died or something, the way I act. Do you understand?"

"I think I do," I answered her honestly. Grief, loss, death—it was making so much sense.

It was a shame the jury would never hear most of what we had covered so far—at least not a jury in this case. Anne couldn't talk about study results and syndromes—at least she couldn't call them that. She had to stick to what she'd done and seen. But I was already reflecting on what I might need in a case in order to test out what was taking shape in my head. And that meant someone who *could* talk about all of these things in front of a jury.

Now that I had satisfied myself that I believed her, there was still a lot of ground to cover with Terri and the need for a bunch of good answers to some pretty dismal questions.

"Okay, Terri." I began by looking her in the eye. "I believe you, and I believe that you were raped. I want to try this case. But we—you and I—must have no doubts about our trust for each other. You have to tell me everything. I don't want to be surprised, ever—especially in the courtroom. I will always be truthful with you. Nothing you can tell me would be worse than *not* telling me. Nothing you tell me will hurt us more than if you don't tell me and I can't be the one to decide if the jury should hear it or not. If I know what's coming, or just how to recognize it, then I'm in complete control of where the case is going. Now, why in the world didn't you tell poor Jim Cross how you met Dickenson O'Conner?"

She had been listening intently to me the whole time I had been speaking, but at the question she closed her eyes and blinked back tears.

"Because I didn't think he believed me anyway, and I was sure he wouldn't if I told him that I was . . . nude. It . . . it doesn't look good, you have to admit."

I certainly had to agree with her there. But I could also see in Terri's reasoning the plight of most rape victims entering the criminal justice process along with their first-stage rape trauma syndrome symptoms of self-blame, guilt, and shame. They run head on into people like Jim, who read the reports with little understanding of how "this" could have happened, how she could have been so dumb. With victims asking these same questions of themselves, it is not surprising they reveal only what an interviewer asks and sometimes only what they think the prosecutor wants to hear.

Moreover, victims often have no idea of the importance attached to certain information. It doesn't appear to have anything to do with what has happened to them. Sometimes they are right. Other times, however, when prosecutors come by this knowledge through the grapevine, it directly affects the always fragile credibility between the two.

Prosecutors, I reasoned, suffered from some of this same ignorance:

they didn't know the importance which *should* be attached to certain information.

I had come by some of this information as a result of my curiosity, simply because, as a woman, I wanted to compare my ideas about what I'd have done first, or thought to do next, with the victim's reaction. The rest seemed to flow naturally from the first: a need to know what it all meant. Once I knew there was more significance to the first group of questions than mere curiosity, and that proven patterns gave meaning to the latter, logic told me it then became the prosecutor's *obligation* to ask the right questions in order to be properly prepared to try a rape case. It also seemed logical that if I kept winning, sooner or later I would get my point across.

"Well, let's begin with how you met Dickenson O'Conner," I said, breaking into my own thoughts.

Terri explained that he had been a friend of her roommate, Christie Sheppard, for several years before she and Christie had gotten an apartment together in May 1978. She had heard about Dickens—that was what Christie, and everyone else, called him—often. Christie had lunch with him two or three times a month and would tell her about their conversations. They traded tales of their sexual adventures and ideas about many personal aspects of their lives.

To the best of Terri's knowledge, Christie had not ever been to bed with Dickens. Fortunately, when I asked her, Christie confirmed this. It eliminated one motive for the defense to fling at a jury—revenge by a jilted lover.

"But I never actually met him until the day of the shoot."

"Ah, yes, the nude photography shoot." How did she happen to do that? I wondered. Did she do it often?

"No . . . no . . . I'd never done anything like that before. Really. You can ask Christie."

I intended to.

"I know I'll never do it again." She looked so defeated. "It had been four months since I had had a job and Christie was getting pretty antsy about my not being able to pay, you know, my share of the bills. She has a good regular job and has been doing this modeling stuff for a long time—she's real cute."

"Did she ever try to get you interested in nude modeling before?" I asked. I could hardly wait to meet Christie.

"We talked about it way back, even before we were roommates. I told her no way could I do that! My father would have killed me."

A look of panic suddenly crossed her face. "You aren't going to tell my parents, are you?"

"You don't even want them to know about the rape?"

"No, I couldn't . . . it would hurt them too much. It was so stupid . . ." She trailed off.

"Have you seen your parents since the rape?"

"Oh, yes. I just don't want them to know, that's all."

"Tell me, Terri, do you think you see them more, less, or about as often as you did before you were raped?" I asked, recalling what Burgess and Holmstrom had found about a victim's need for support and increased family contact.

"Maybe . . . maybe," she answered slowly, "a little more often than before. Yeah, I don't do as much as before, and I see them more often.

"Anyway," Terri said, remembering what we had been talking about before my distraction, "Christie said maybe I should give some thought to doing a couple of jobs with her, like the amateur nude photography shoot coming up. Her agent was looking for models, no experience necessary, and we'd each get paid forty dollars take-home for six hours' work. That's a *lot* of money."

Agent, huh? So Christie had an agent. Important. The credibility of anyone who had modeled nude had to be carefully reviewed for a jury. An agent in the picture would have the effect of blunting the risqué undertones associated with this whole subject and would lend an air of respectability, not to mention credibility.

When I interviewed Christie, she gave me the agent's name. He ran a very reputable business, and while Christie only did nude assignments, the majority of his clients did not. He also made a fine witness and did for the jury precisely what I had predicted. He provided corroboration for Terri's story.

". . . So I finally said okay, I'd do it, but I was so nervous I almost didn't go. Christie finally got me in the car that morning—it was a Saturday, I think—but halfway there I really started to panic and told her to take me home.

"Well, we stopped the car and Christie gave me a Valium to see if that would help. I guess it did, because we got there okay. This guy told us all the rules, like no touching, no suggestive poses, no exchange of names and phone numbers between photographers and models—like, it was real strict.

"Then he gave us a map and our assigned places. Every hour or so we'd move on to a new spot. We got to take breaks and had lunch too."

"Were you nude during your breaks and lunch?"

"No, only when we were actually posing. Otherwise we had robes to put on during breaks and in between places."

"When did you meet Dickens?" I wondered why we tended to refer to someone by a nickname, when otherwise, if he didn't have one, we surely would use his last name.

"It was at lunch break. Christie was already talking to him and she introduced us."

"When did you find out he had an employment agency?"

"Then. At lunch. I think Christie had told him I was looking for a job, because almost right away he started telling me he could help me."

"Did you know he took a picture of you? And by the way, did he have anything besides a Polaroid?"

"Yes, I knew he took a picture of me. And all he had was a Polaroid. It seemed sort of strange for a photographer to only have an instant camera. But I thought maybe he was going to use it to paint a picture from. Some of the other girls had said they thought there were artists taking pictures to use like that."

"Did you see him anymore that day after lunch?"

"Oh, yes, the rest of the day he sort of followed me around when I changed places, and talked to me during breaks. He told me Christie would bring me to fill out an employment form in a few days."

I later asked Christie if she remembered Dickens trailing around after Terri. She had noticed, but figured he was getting some pre-employment-type information.

"And did you go in to see him a few days later?"

"No, it was almost a month later. I really didn't look hard in September," she confessed. "Christie and I went to his office one evening, on a Tuesday. I filled out this form and we talked about the kinds of jobs I was looking for."

"Waitress or dental assistant?" I asked, remembering her previous experience.

"Yeah, and he thought he might be able to find me a job as a secretary too."

"Terri, practice always saying 'yes' instead of 'yeah' when you answer a question, okay?" I gently instructed. "It makes a much better impression on a jury. Did he have you take any skills tests for a secretarial job?"

"No, he didn't. But I'd never been a secretary, so I wasn't sure if he was supposed to. I wondered, but thought, hey, he had an office that said he was in the employment business and he made a file and put the form I filled out in it. I figured he was okay."

"So did he say he'd call you, or what?"

"Yeah, I mean yes, he said he'd call in a few days when he had some interviews lined up. But when he hadn't called by Friday, I called him. That's when he said to come down between eleven-thirty and noon and he'd have something for me by then."

He sure did have something for her, I thought, grimacing.

When Terri arrived at the employment agency, O'Conner met her at the door, telling her he had to make some phone calls from his "other office" and would she mind going with him? He explained it had something to do with message-unit charges which didn't apply to the "other office." He volunteered to drive, and she agreed.

The first pangs of anxiety hit Terri when O'Conner pulled into the parking lot of a large, well-known apartment complex. Why, she wondered, was he bringing her here? As he parked the car, he explained that his "other office" was in his apartment and message units didn't apply to residential phones. He tried to make as many calls as possible from this "office." Since the calls were for more interviews for her, he hoped she wouldn't mind.

How had she felt then?

Silly to be worried, she concluded. The explanation certainly made sense. And Christie had known him for so long. It was broad daylight . . .

And did the apartment look like an office?

"The first thing I saw when he opened the door was this big desk with papers all over it and one of those stacking things on top. And there was a phone right there on one end."

Any remaining hesitation vanished as soon as she saw that desk. It certainly had been silly to worry.

"I mean, Christie had known Dickens for two years."

O'Conner went immediately to the phone and appeared to dial two or three numbers one right after the other, although he spoke to no one. Busy, or no answer, he informed her as he sat down next to her on the couch.

Was she concerned yet?

"He said he'd try again in a few minutes, and the explanation he gave didn't make me worry. Then he asked me more questions about myself, like I told you he'd done in the car. So he could tell employers more about me, he said."

"Wait a minute, Terri," I said. "You didn't tell me what you talked about in the car."

"I'm sorry, I've talked about this so many times sometimes I forget what I've said and sometimes I think I've already said it. Well, anyway, the kind of questions he asked me in the car and kept asking me about when we were sitting on the couch were like about dating, and did I have a boyfriend, and then they got even more personal. At first I answered them, like how old was I when I'd first had sex, and was I comfortable having sex? That, he said, would give him an idea about how quickly I got to know people. God, how dumb could I be!" She shook her head and looked at me. "Then he asked if I'd ever done anything unusual in sex—I don't remember the word he used and he just real fast kept on asking them because I didn't answer."

"At this point he was talking fast, really fast? Was that the way he usually talked?"

"Yes, real fast."

"What was going through your mind at that point?"

"I . . . that's when I started getting nervous, and I was just . . . I was thinking that I just wanted to go."

"Now, when you had come in, had you noticed if the door had been locked?"

"I'm not sure; it's hard to remember. But when . . ."

"Let me put it this way: in your mind at that time, did you think about the door?"

"Yes."

"And did you think it was locked or unlocked?"

"It was locked."

"Are you sure?"

"Well, I didn't hear it, and I don't remember seeing him lock it. But I remember looking at the door and knowing that it was locked."

"Okay, Terri." I realized I was getting off our subject. "You said that you were getting nervous when he was asking you these personal questions while you were sitting on the couch. What happened next?"

"Then I sat up on the couch, and he told me to turn around, and then he put his hands on my shoulder and started to rub my shoulder."

All the earlier anxiety was instantly back, Terri related, as her voice now clearly reflected even in the telling. She immediately got up from the couch and told O'Conner she thought it best that she leave.

She had taken only a step or two toward the door when she felt the vise-like grip of his hand clamp down on the upper part of her right arm. The floodgates of fear, terror, and panic opened with a thunderous roar, rushing together through her body. She tried to pull free and kept telling him she had to go, not to do this, that she didn't want him to touch her. But she could not shake free.

What was she thinking at that moment? Did she contemplate escape, or talking him out of whatever he was thinking of doing, or trying to hurt him?

"No, nothing like that," she almost whispered. "I was practically paralyzed. I thought he might kill me. Everything seemed like, like when you're dreaming and you try to run away but you don't seem to move. That's how the whole thing felt."

So Terri had virtually no coping strategies to come to her rescue. But she did see the whole experience as if from a dream, using this way of protecting her emotions from the reality of her terror; putting distance between herself and her mental brush with death. Burgess and Holmstrom had described this as a coping strategy too. Victims who pretended to be somewhere else, or thought about something else, far away, during the attack.

In addition to what she had already told me about his voice and eyes, Terri remembered the way he had smelled.

"He was sweating so much he got me all wet when he was on top of me. It smelled so bad. Afterwards, when he let me go in the bathroom, I just wanted to get that smell off of me. I kept washing my face and washing but it wouldn't go away."

Terri was crying uncontrollably now and would each time she had to talk about the events of the sexual attack itself. We stopped for a while and I told her not to worry, that many women have this same reaction, among others. She was visibly reassured each time I did this with her between our first interview and the day of trial. I think it's much like having an operation: if the doctor explains the procedure, and what to look for, say, one day after surgery, then three days later, then a week or a month after that, it is not nearly as frightening when the unpleasant symptoms do, in fact, appear.

For Terri, this inability to get rid of her attacker's smell caused her tremendous anguish. After her forty-five-minute shower when first getting home, she showered twice more that day, and at least two or three times every day for almost three weeks. She still took multiple showers, though not every day. Christie would verify this. So would Francesca.

"Who's Francesca?" I asked at the mention of this name for the first time.

"She's my best friend. I've known her since seventh grade when I first moved to San Diego."

"How long after the rape did you see Francesca?"

"Maybe two hours."

"Was she the first person you saw?"

"Yes, the first. But I didn't tell her."

"Terri, before I forget, what did you do with the clothes you were wearing at the time of the rape? I know the police took them from you, but I mean, what were *you* planning to do with them?"

"I put them in a paper sack and threw them away."

"You mean in the trash?" I asked in a surprised tone as I reviewed the report filed by the police officer who took Terri's statement that first night. No, not a hint of where the officer had found the clothes.

"Yes, in the trash. The cop who came that night had to take the bag out himself. I wouldn't."

I called this officer later and his recollection agreed with Terri's.

I realized law enforcement knew no more than criminal justice about what I was discovering. It still was hard to believe such a fact was of so little consequence to this officer.

I explained to Terri the reason for my surprise, and tried to use this example as a way to further cement our mutual trust, and gave her a brief summary of how she seemed to fit the pattern of rape trauma syndrome. The showers, fears, clothes.

I took it one step further and asked if she had had any unusual reactions to black men since the rape.

"Till the last month or so, I couldn't be near a black man. Just seeing one was awful. I'd get this feeling like I'd burst and I'd run, actually run away. If there was a black cashier at the grocery store, I'd be sure not to get in his line."

How about her reaction to black women?

"No, not black women, just black men."

Had she ever been fearful of black men before the rape?

"No, as a matter of fact I worked for a black manager at the last waitressing job I had before I was . . . attacked. There were no problems. Francesca can tell you too. We worked there together."

Francesca. I'd nearly forgotten about Francesca, although sooner or later I'm sure I'd have gotten back to her, even without Terri's reminder.

"You know"—Terri spoke as if she'd just realized something—"maybe . . . well, I'd never thought about it before you asked . . . you know . . . how I feel about black men since the rape. When I went to pick Francesca up from work that day, something happened on our way back home."

"What happened?"

"I was driving and Fran was sitting beside me in the passenger seat. We were just driving along and she says, 'Would you look at that guy staring at us?' I looked out my window and there was this car driving next to us with two black guys in it. The one, the passenger, was smiling and waving at us. Well, I freaked and started screaming and crying. Fran got us over to the side of the road and at first I wouldn't tell her what was wrong, but then I did tell her . . . about the rape."

My excitement was equal to Terri's distress as she described her freeway encounter. I could picture it. I could see a jury picturing it too.

"Do you know where Francesca is now?" I was almost shaking with anticipation.

"She's at work. Do you want me to call her and ask her what she remembers?"

"No!" I nearly yelled. "Terri, I don't want you to discuss *anything* about the rape, or this incident, with Francesca, or anyone else, unless I give you the go-ahead. Okay? Not until after the trial. It's very important the defense not be able to claim conspiracy, or fabrication. It's crucial. Do you understand?"

"Yes, I do." She seemed chastised.

"I don't want you to feel badly for offering to help this way, Terri. But *the* best thing is for you to tell me like you just did and I'll talk to the witnesses."

I was reaching for the phone.

"If it won't get her in trouble I want to call her now."

"It's okay," Terri assured me.

Within minutes I had Francesca on the line and explained who I was and why I was calling. I then listened to her account of what had happened that day. Her story was as chilling as anything I'd ever run across in any of my cases. I expected to hear cameras whirring and a close-up of her face to appear on the screen as she recited this frightening experience. But this was no movie.

". . . after I pointed out these two guys Terri kind of looked over at them to see what I was talking about. When she did it, she like started to cry and scream and she let go of the steering wheel. She put her hands over her face, and I mean we were going fifty miles an hour. Well, I grabbed the wheel and between us we got the car over to the side of the road. All Terri would do is keep her hands over her face and cry."

"Did she tell you about the rape?"

"Not at first, but finally, yes. I told her to call the cops, but she said she wanted to think about it some more. She didn't know if the police would believe her. Well, I told her I believed her and she *had* to report it. We were still talking about it when she finally got me home."

"Had you ever seen Terri react like that before? About anything?"

"No, never. She used to be real easygoing. Now she's so moody; always unhappy."

"You've known her for seven years, Francesca. Has she ever shown any bad feelings toward black men, or any fear?"

"She never dated a black man or anything, but she never made comments about black people or anything either. Not until after that day. After that she has been terrified of black men. She cried just seeing one once. But she's much better now. We both work at Rick's restaurant and the manager is black, like the manager was at the restaurant we worked at together before. When I first told Terri about the job opening a couple of months ago, I also told her she had to interview with a black man. It was hard for her, but I was there and she did it. Now they talk all the time."

Terri agreed that things were getting better with black men now. But her manager had put his hand on her shoulder a couple of weeks before and she'd pulled away violently.

This was dynamite stuff! Wait till Anne heard. We'd spend plenty of time on victim reactions and similar things this time—assuming, of course, I got the expert in. My insides were dancing. I'd get the expert in.

I finished the interview with Terri, covering in detail what was done and said every step of the way. I knew, for instance, that after the rape, but before she and O'Conner left his apartment, there was a knock on the door, and O'Conner let a man in who stayed for five minutes or so, then left. What I needed to know was why she hadn't told him what had happened.

"Because they seemed to know each other . . . and he was black too. I didn't think he'd help me."

How logical. Anne had said women often don't report until they feel safe. This not only made sense, but here it was in action. I'd let the jury hear this reasoning in direct examination of my victim—before the defense could be the first to ask about it with an accusatory flair.

I also noticed that the defendant tried to get her to go on an interview at a local restaurant as he was driving her back to her car. Of course, she refused, but he did leave her alone in the car for a few minutes while he went into the restaurant to get an application form. Why hadn't she run then?

"Why?" She looked blank, then puzzled. "I don't know. Where would I have run? Who would I tell? I couldn't do anything. I just sat there."

Her expression alone would convince a jury, but there was more I could do with that: feelings of hopelessness and loss of control of one's life were first-stage rape trauma syndrome symptoms. While I couldn't tell the jury in these exact words, I could weave the thread of this behavior or lack of coping ability through the whole case.

By the time Terri left my office after our first interview, we had spent three hours together and I had doubled the number of names on my witness list—and I used every one of them at trial.

When Anne Kennedy and I got together she sized up our approach with enthusiasm.

"This is a classic casual acquaintance rape, you know," she observed as she tossed the file down on my desk. "A longtime friend of a roommate who trusts him and whom she trusts. The appearance of legitimacy—that home office—and a series of events which catch her with her guard down. Who knows how she might have coped or reacted if she had been suspicious all along. It could have been different. Her complete surprise makes it harder for her not to blame herself for what happened and makes her recovery even more difficult."

"Okay, Madam Expert, I'll open the door and you keep going until they stop you. I'm willing to take the chance." And we did.

By mid-May 1979, I felt like June was nearly over. Between my other trials, speeches, and sundry assignments, I interviewed all the witnesses in the O'Conner case. Since I knew I wanted a plea to the charge of forcible rape, I did not bother with negotiations, but did telephone the defense attorney's office to leave that generous offer.

By far the most important testimony in the case, other than the victim's, was Christie Sheppard's. I admit to falling prey to certain old stereotypes. Until I met her, I kept picturing something between a harlot and a Medusa. What I saw was anything but.

Christie was not quite five feet tall and weighed just about ninety pounds. She had chestnut-brown hair and emerald eyes. She was cute, adorable, with a body to match. Sexy, however, she was not. She liked to model nude because of the money—and, I could tell, she knew her body was appealing. And while she did confide many details of her sexual life to O'Conner, he was the only male friend to whom she did so.

It would have been very hard for Christie to believe Dickenson O'Conner capable of this terrible act but for a couple of things.

"He's always telling me his preference for white women—particularly blond-haired, blue-eyed white women. He'll see one on the street and comment about her. He also lives with a white woman who is blond and blue-eyed. I met her a couple of times."

But the second reason Christie believed Terri was far more compelling; a phone call she received at work the day of the rape.

"It was about three-thirty in the afternoon. He just said, 'Hi,' and I said, 'Hi.' Then he said he wanted me to know that he'd just fucked my roommate, that at first she resisted, but that no one can resist for forty-five minutes and she'd given up. He said he wanted me to hear it from him first before she told me. I said, 'Oh,' or something equally stupid, and we hung up."

"And what did you do then?"

"I tried calling Terri, but there was no answer at the apartment. The next time I tried was from my boyfriend's house at about seven-thirty that evening. Terri sounded real upset and asked me to come home. My boyfriend came too. He's a San Diego police officer. I told him about the phone call from Dickens on our way to the apartment. When we got there he talked to her for a while and then she told us what happened."

I spent a lot of time asking Christie if the defense would be able to come up with anything, no matter how farfetched it might seem, to suggest that she was lying. I didn't tell her that at trial O'Conner likely would deny having made this statement—or at least would back-pedal considerably, as he had with Sografo. I noticed in his report that during his interview of O'Conner, when he'd asked him about that phone call to Christie, he had admitted the part about intercourse but denied anything about resistance.

As the time for trial grew closer, and I compared the evidence I had mustered with the inherent weaknesses which this case certainly had, I felt we had more than an even chance of coming out a winner. Conditioned, of course, on Anne Kennedy being allowed to testify.

9

I T   T O O K   M E almost a week to get a courtroom to try the O'Conner case, and even then we had to accept another Municipal Court judge who had been empowered to hear felony cases.

Jonathan Billingsley was as different from Manuelo Olmeda as tequila is from tea. While Olmeda had a Latin background, Billingsley had been born in England. He had moved to the United States as a child, but the proper Englishman in him had already taken. He rarely swore, and reserved the occasional "bloody" for those situations which clearly fit the dictates of protocol.

When I first met Judge Billingsley he had struck me as a somewhat pompous stuffed shirt. As I got to know him better, I realized this was primarily because the hint of an English accent he retained made him sound affected. I had no difficulty imagining him as the brave white knight riding upon his trusty steed to rescue the fair maiden in distress.

It was this image of chivalry and fair maidens which concerned me most when deciding if I could trust him with Terri's case. He also had a certain stubborn streak, triggered most easily by rudeness in his courtroom, and I had on more than one occasion been the lucky beneficiary of someone else's momentary lapse with this particular social grace. On the other hand, he was not rigid, and could be persuaded to bend with a certain gallant flair, if nudged in the proper gentlemanly or ladylike, as the case might be, way.

What really tipped the scales in Billingsley's favor, however, was the fact that he could usually recognize a good legal argument when he heard it. Sometimes I had the impression that he felt he carried the traditions of the entire Anglo-American legal system on his shoulders, and had an obligation born of his heritage to reason through even the smallest problem. At times, as when he was trying a traffic case, this could border on the absurd, but in a rape case it was more than welcome. I would be certain to let him know that it was precisely this quality which made me feel he would rise to the occasion.

By signaling my faith in his ability to handle this most difficult of cases, I was trying to do more than just butter him up. Because Muni Court judges had more at risk, they tended to be even less anxious to do new things in the courtroom than their Superior Court brethren. Judges kept track of appellate court reversals in cases they had tried, the way many of the rest of us keep track of our traffic record. And Municipal Court judges, who are rather low on the legal totem pole, do not want reversals to threaten their privilege of handling felonies.

So when I sat down with Judge Billingsley in his chambers to go over the case, I made sure that both he and the defense attorney had been given a copy of my trial memorandum the day before and that I had a definite plan to follow.

Grant Soames and I had held several strategy meetings during trial preparation, and we had decided that the best thing to do was to give the judge the transcripts of Anne Kennedy's testimony in the Harter case and the Drake case, let him read them, and then see where we stood.

My confidence is at the lowest point just before a judge is about to breathe life into my ideas, or to administer the last rites. It is a time of utter helplessness and frustration precisely because not knowing leaves one with no direction. Should I have stopped sooner, should I have said more, should I try again? Some judges are kind enough to give you clues by the questions they ask; others, like Billingsley, are simply thinking out loud.

When he and the defense attorney had finished both transcripts and we were all back in court, my immediate impressions of his impressions were all negative. "How can this 'expert,'" Judge Billingsley began, "give her opinion on the ultimate issue to be decided by the jury, that of whether or not a rape occurred? How can the 'expert' get inside a victim's head and tell about someone else's state of mind? And how can an 'expert' get away with answering a series of hypothetical questions which are really no more than the facts of *this* case thinly disguised?"

I answered each question in turn. I carefully explained that, as the Court well knew, California provided in its Evidence Code for both an expert and the jury to give opinions on the ultimate question to be decided in the case: the expert on the witness stand, the jury after deliberation. And that the expert is *not* getting into the victim's head to tell us what she's thinking, but rather the expert is interpreting information and passing on knowledge which have met certain legal standards; finally, the purpose of a hypothetical is to package a certain set of facts for an expert to interpret. Each side, both prosecution and defense, has the same privilege. The jury must believe both the facts and the expert on one side or the other before it can reach the ultimate issue. Thus to the jury alone is left the determination of overall credibility.

Judge Billingsley readily understood my reasoning in the answer to his middle question. But he was having considerable difficulty with the first and last. I guessed he had handled few child abuse cases, so I explained that I had chosen the hypothetical because it was the accepted way the medical expert related an opinion to a jury about the nature of injuries suffered by children, and, after all, only the facts of the case the jury has to decide can possibly be of interest to them.

As for the expert's opinion addressing the same question that the jury is supposed to answer . . . well, my feeling has always been that if this wasn't okay, the rule allowing it would not be in the Evidence Code. Judges, however, have never seemed to like this answer to that question. It's so simple that it's scary.

"Well, Ms. Rowland"—I recognized the resolution in his tone— "what I will allow you to do is to put on your witness to go into factors to be considered by the jury when they are deciding what action a victim should be taking. You can ask her, for instance, to explain the three areas she teaches about rape prevention, but don't go into any hypothetical on the facts of this case."

"So, your honor"—I was trying to be sure I understood him—"you want me to question her so that she answers in a narrative, like a story?"

"Well, yes. The jury can be educated as to what this whole field of rape is about, and how one can prevent it. There are things, like the number of rapes between people who know each other, that most people don't know, including me."

"I understand, your honor." I nodded.

I was delighted. It was a reverse of the old adage "Give them an inch and they'll take a mile." I really only asked for an inch and was *given* the mile. This way the appellate court would decide which style they liked best, a hypothetical or the narrative. Assuming I won, of course.

I wondered what the appellate court would have to say, if anything, about how I was "educating" my juries? Probably not much, since I was giving them such a gold mine of other issues to deal with. But as far as I was concerned, it was the key to everything that followed.

I used the same approach to jury selection for the O'Conner case as I had with Harter's. But I decided to be even more bold: I chose seven women to sit on the case along with five men. The cardinal rule has always been to get as many men and as few women as possible on a rape jury. Women, everyone agreed, spelled trouble for rape convictions.

I remember when I used to hear other prosecutors talk about their rape cases. The first question was "How is it going?" and the second was "How many women do you have?" At first I didn't believe them. It was just one more example of the insensitive male perspective. But as I continued to hear the votes on hung rape cases, there was no mistake about it: more men than women were ready to believe a victim's story.

I became a true believer after a nine-three split in a rape case I had watched for nearly a week. Guilt had been so obvious to me that I had not even done my usual amount of worrying for the trial deputy. I happened to walk down the hallway right after a mistrial had been declared by the judge. Among the people gathered there, I recognized several of the men to be jurors from the case. They appeared angry and frustrated as they spoke heatedly with the trial attorney. Standing a short distance away was a small cluster of women whom I also recognized to have been on the jury.

When I inquired of the men, they assured me I had heard correctly: all three "not guilty" votes were from women. Since this jury had consisted of nine men and only three women, I could understand their ire. I could not understand, however, what combination of forces was at work here. I was determined to find out.

Three years later as I was selecting the O'Conner jury, I figured I understood the dynamics of women jurors in rape cases about as well as I ever would. I also thought I knew how to turn the lion into a lamb, so to speak.

Historically, women had not participated in the jury process at all. They had little to do with anything outside the realm of the family and the home. In other words, they remained isolated from the "real world" and what people did with, and to, each other. Men, on the other hand, suffered from no illusions about how it was "out there." They knew what they were capable of doing and how far they would go to get what they wanted.

As I always tell my juries, common sense and life experiences are not checked at the courtroom door. They go right along to the jury box with them. Because much of life's experiences for women were limited to those of the housewife, what they brought along to the jury room was a yardstick of judgment which did not quite measure up to the task. It was impossible for them to comprehend, sometimes even in the face of overwhelming evidence, that a man could sexually molest his child, or that a woman could be made to have intercourse if she didn't want to. Men knew better.

Compounding the dilemma for women were the same myths and stereotypes about rape which pervaded male thinking. Unlike the men, however, who could draw upon their life experiences to help them out, women could not. So even when women heard a victim's tale which rang true, being unable to understand how this nice-looking boy sitting here in court could have done this terrible thing, they looked back to the victim herself: well, if she was raped, she must have asked for it; enter the myths and stereotypes to support their conclusion.

While the scenario I've outlined is certainly oversimplified, it is by no means simplistic. Generalizations can be dangerous, but they can be helpful too. My point here is not to prove the way things used to be, but to explain my understanding of a problem and how to change it.

It made sense that once women were in the mainstream and they became part of the survival game, they too would be equipped with the tools life's many twists and turns provided. Speeding up their integration into society were the increase in divorce and the new phenomenon of single women going it alone, both socially and professionally.

During this same time, the law in California affecting who would, and would not, be subject to jury duty was revised. No longer would anyone holding a job, having small children, or any of a select number of upper-class professionals be summarily excused. The voting age, and consequently juror age, was dropped from twenty-one to eighteen. Slowly the compositions of juries began to shift away from mostly white, middle- to lower-middle-class dispensable workers, the retired, and housewives. With more frequency the young, minorities, the highly educated, and, finally, women of all ages and from all walks of life began to appear when I swung my chair around to look over a new panel.

Still, the verdicts in rape cases did not seem to be reflecting much in the way of changed attitudes. I'm getting ahead of myself again, but suffice it to say at this point that attitudes alone are not enough. Changes in the law are essential.

By 1979, California law had undergone major evidentiary and legal reforms in the area of rape. I'm referring specifically to the elimination or repeal of several antiquated concepts used primarily by defense attorneys to attack the credibility of victims in rape cases. But the relevant observation at this point is that the subtraction of negative influences alone is not sufficient to even the scales for rape victims.

What I had in mind on the day that I began jury selection in the O'Conner case was to find out if, with the addition of the rape expert, women might not only be passable jurors but could become my strongest allies. I had already seen that I could personalize the experience for jurors. Would I now be able to raise their consciousness by bringing to their attention, through the expert, how their daily lives as women are constantly affected by the threat of rape. Men don't often consider where to park their cars if it will be dark by the time they return, or plan ahead a safe route to the front door, keys in hand, or walk with an air of assurance because this has been found to discourage would-be rapists (they tend to look for the lost, frail, uncertain woman).

It was with this in mind that I left seven women, representing the full range of ages and professional and social backgrounds, on my jury in the O'Conner case.

I could tell from the outset that Judge Billingsley thought very little of my victim, of her roommate, and of my philosophy about rape. What was so satisfying to me was watching his old attitudes slip away a little more each day.

It had begun when he realized an expert just might have something of value to say to the jury. It got better during the jury selection. There was no Father Paul this time, but it did not take me long to isolate the two different camps: those who could separate lifestyle, even if they didn't approve, from credibility and those who probably could not.

"You know, Ms. Rowland," Billingsley volunteered one morning as we sat waiting for things to get under way, "I tried to answer those questions you put to the prospective jurors. I must say, it wasn't quite so easy as I had thought."

My credibility was given another healthy boost the next day when I had Terri in court for the first time. It was her turn to take the stand when we went into session, and I wanted to be sure we got into the courtroom before O'Conner arrived. I thought this would help her calm down. She'd been extremely emotional for the past hour in my office.

Terri had not seen O'Conner since the day of the preliminary hearing the previous November, and I was not sure how she would handle this encounter. She wasn't sure either.

Things did not start out on a promising note.

When O'Conner entered the courtroom she began to shake visibly. Even the judge was concerned. We got through the swearing-in and her promise to tell the truth, but no further. She could not stop crying long enough to answer any questions.

"Your honor," I suggested, "may we have a few minutes?"

"Of course, Ms. Rowland," replied my gentleman judge. "Perhaps the young lady would feel more comfortable waiting in the corridor behind the courtroom, since the defendant and the members of the jury panel will no doubt be occupying the hall."

"Thank you," I replied, "we shall do that."

We had ten minutes. The first five were spent just calming Terri down enough to start over. I was beginning to wonder if she would be able to testify at all.

With the judge now standing in the doorway to his chambers, robed and ready, I could see my time was almost up. What happened next was obviously so real, so unrehearsed, that it could not have been anyone's idea. Judge Billingsley was still talking about it a year later.

Now, in the summer of 1979 the San Diego Municipal Court had one black judge among its number. As it happened, he was assigned the courtroom next to Judge Billingsley, which meant his chambers were also next door. As Terri and I stood with Billingsley and while his bailiff scurried out to reassemble the jury, this lone black judge was also preparing to take the bench. I was aware of him standing in his doorway, wearing his ankle-length black robes. It was only when his bailiff held the courtroom door open for him and he was striding toward it that

Terri saw him. In less than the time it took him to get through the door, Terri had bolted from the corridor, through the courtroom, and into the main hallway. By the time I got to the outside corridor, I found only a group of startled jurors.

I located Terri in a nearby ladies' room, locked in a stall, crying. With a bit more comforting, she was able to regain her composure and get through both my direct and the defense's cross-examination with only minor bouts of tears, particularly while describing the attack itself.

The judge's greatest vote of confidence came after hearing Anne Kennedy's testimony. His logic and her credibility were just an unbeatable combination. Anne told me a few weeks after the trial that she happened to see Billingsley in the courthouse corridor one day. He asked her if she had time to chat over a cup of tea in his chambers. Of course she accepted, and spent the next forty-five minutes listening to his exclamations and answering questions about coping behavior and rape trauma syndrome. The process of educating the judiciary one by one was clearly an impossible task. If I ever got the time, I thought to myself after hearing Anne's story, I might see if I could persuade the various national and state judge's colleges to have me, or someone who understood what I was doing, on their agenda. Well, someday.

My evidence went as I had planned and I could think of nothing more as I waited for the defense case to begin early during our second week of trial.

I had been watching Dickenson O'Conner as carefully during the trial as I had observed the jurors before. Every day he was neatly pressed, in suit and tie. Whereas Harter's clothes had looked better on a hanger than on him, O'Conner's sturdy but somewhat short frame accepted his wardrobe well.

In court he was polite, prompt, and attentive. What, then, did I find so disagreeable about him (aside from the fact that I believed he had raped Terri)?

By the end of the second day, I had it. It was the way he moved. His whole body announced conceit, pretension, haughtiness—and he was always tugging on the cuffs of his starched white shirt with a flick of first one, then the other wrist. He had an air of contrived superiority.

I was sure he'd be a good talker, probably smooth. When it came my turn to examine him, what I found was a fair to middling con artist whose Achilles' heel turned out to be that he just didn't know when to quit. As an example:

Q. "And where is your residence, Mr. O'Conner?" I inquired early during my questioning.

The answers usually started out simple enough:

A. "1748 Ellsworth, in San Diego."

Q. "And what type of residence is that?" I would follow in logical sequence. That's when it would get pretentious.

A. "Adult living facilities."

Q. "It's an apartment complex?"

A. "Yes."

Adult living facilities? Come on. I soon found that simplicity was *not* a part of Mr. O'Conner's m.o.: "correct" not "yes," "individual" not "person," "vehicle" not "car," "proceeded in" not "went in" were typical examples.

I also discovered, however, that if his answers were more than a couple of sentences long, he began to trip over his tongue.

Q. "What was the subject matter of that conversation?"

A. "One conversation was in particular to the point that she asked me, or rather, she told me that Christie had stated that I had given her a massage, if that's what you're inclining."

And modesty—this was also not a trait that the defendant could be accused of possessing.

Q. "And what," I began my lengthy inquiry into O'Conner's considerable enterprises, "is International Car Doctor?"

A. "It's a business in which we act as a broker between the shop and the customer."

What it turned out to be was sticking handouts under windshields of dented cars in parking lots, hoping to send the owners to one of several repair shops which had promised O'Conner a kickback of $75 to $150 on each car he sent in. This, of course, was added to the customers' bills unbeknownst to them.

Q. "And what is International Personnel Services?" I inquired while examining a business card O'Conner had extracted from a small holder. He had a business card for each of his ventures, all of which began with the word "International."

A. "It's a personnel agency that specializes in minority recruitment," he answered, only slightly obscurely.

Q. "You mean you find people jobs?"

A. "That's correct."

Q. "And how do you do that?"

A. "Well, I have a staff who knows the ins and outs of affirmative action, so, therefore, I provide you with that service."

Q. "Who is your staff?"

A. "I have several people who already work for other companies that have already done affirmative action programs, and I get them to work for me, through me, for another company."

So he really had no staff; he just found companies who needed to fill their affirmative action programs and matched anyone up he could find. Actually, this was rather clever, but when I sent my investigator around to the address on the card, the place had long been vacant and the phone had been disconnected. This was true of all the businesses. When I questioned him about this, O'Conner said each business was being run from his apartment—this, even though each card carried a separate address and phone number.

And we were only just starting.

Q. "And do you have any other sources of income?"

I was beginning to see the con artist in him.

A. "Yes, I do."

Q. "And what is that?"

A. "We have a cleaning company."

Q. "Oh, and what is the name of the cleaning company?"

A. "International Cleaning Service, ICS for short."

Out came another card.

Q. "Who is the 'we' you keep referring to, Mr. O'Conner?"

A. "My partner and I."

Q. "And where can I find this partner?"

A. "We've split now and I don't know."

When my investigator tracked down the person named by O'Conner as his partner, he vaguely remembered a man by the name of O'Conner having once been involved with him in something. I had planned to have the "partner" testify, but ended up deciding it was not necessary by the time cross-examination had concluded.

Q. "What type of work does the cleaning company do?"

A. "We . . . I . . . do construction cleaning."

Q. "What is 'construction cleaning'?"

A. "When a contractor is putting up a condominium, or an apartment complex unit, upon the final stages, before people move in, they need it cleaned. I bid on the job, then I sub it out to a cleaning firm, who will do it for less than I bid."

Hmm, very neat.

With some more questioning, O'Conner humbly admitted to having been a master baker in the military, to teaching tennis as a pro, to typing fifty words a minute (thus his ability to get along in so many businesses without aid of a secretary); and I was sure I would find some more.

I wondered if the jury was becoming as skeptical about O'Conner's accomplishments as I was. I knew this initial skepticism could be quickly turned to hard-core disbelief if my suspicions about the extent of O'Conner's immodesty were accurate.

"Oh, you also have a modeling business?" I inquired, in response to a previous question in which he had alluded to such an enterprise.

"Not really. I tell anyone that is interested I can send them to a referral service. I simply don't have the time."

"I can understand that," I replied with as straight a face as I could.

I kept waiting for that one opportunity. Like watching the puffer fish swell to fearsome proportions, barbs menacingly reaching out, and then, with the swiftness of a pinprick, collapse to a size so trifling that it would scarcely draw more than pitiable notice from unconcerned schoolchildren. That was what I wanted to do.

And it came. It was O'Conner's boast of proficiency at yet another calling that proved to be his undoing, and afforded me what I considered to be my "finest hour" as a trial lawyer during cross-examination.

It began during direct exam by the defense, with O'Conner's version of what happened in his apartment just after he tried to make several calls while Terri sat on the couch.

He explained that the lines were busy and that he then joined "Miss Richardson" on the sofa. At first they discussed job qualifications, for about ten minutes. Then, he claimed, she changed the subject, mentioning that her neck was stiff.

Q. "Did she indicate in any way that she wanted you to do something about that?"

A. "I asked her."

Q. "What did you ask her?"

A. "I asked her if she'd like me to rub it for her."

Q. "And then what did she say or do?"

A. "She turned around."

Q. "When you say she turned around, what do you mean by 'She turned around'?"

A. "Well, she was sitting with her back toward the wall, by the back of the couch, and when she shifted, she shifted with her back towards me."

Q. "Was it at this time that you placed your hands on Miss Richardson's shoulders?"

A. "Yes."

Q. "All right. And then what happened?"

A. "Then I began to massage her neck and shoulders."

Q. "Did she indicate that she did not wish that to happen?"

A. "No, she did not."

Q. "Did she object to your touching her?"

A. "No, she did not."

Q. "Did she tell you to stop?"

A. "No."

I was prepared for the part about the neck and shoulder rub, because of questions asked of Terri by O'Conner's attorney during her earlier cross-examination. He had inquired in various ways if there had been any discussion between his client and herself about a massage, or how good a massage he had once given her roommate, Christie, or did she tell him she knew he gave a good massage? It had never been exactly clear. In any case, I could tell from the direction these questions were taking that the defense would use it as a lead-in to sex in some way. I was, however, totally unprepared for what followed.

Q. "Well, then what happened after that?" O'Conner's attorney went on.

A. "After a period of doing it for a while, I just simply asked her did she wish for me to give her a massage?"

Q. "All right. Now, Mr. O'Conner, are you qualified to give someone a massage?"

A. "I have a license."

Q. "And where are you licensed?"

A. "In Boston, Massachusetts."

Q. "And did you in fact give massages to people in Boston, Massachusetts?"

A. "Yes, I did."

Q. "And where was that?"

A. "Massachusetts General Hospital."

Q. "For how long a period of time did you give such massages?"

A. "For approximately three months."

A licensed masseur too? Unbelievable! Was there anything this man couldn't do? We'd see. This time he had picked a profession about which I stood a fair chance of calling his bluff.

My college roommate at Berkeley was a physical therapist. For two years I had listened to her and her friends prepare for exams. And then after I had graduated and was working in San Francisco, and they had transferred to the medical center for their third year, I often served as a willing subject during wonderful massage therapy practices. I would be on the bed and they would hover over me on their knees arguing about muscle names and proper versus improper massage techniques. We always held these training classes at my apartment because I would be too limp to move when they had finished. On the way out they'd turn out the lights and lock the door. It was wonderful. After graduation, and since, they have refused to this day to give me a massage again.

Now, as direct examination went on, I dug back and tried to recall everything I'd heard during those memorable evenings. I made some notes of what I could come up with, and kept listening to the questions. Soon I abandoned my note taking altogether as the tale unfolding on the witness stand commanded my full attention.

Q. "Now, where did you commence massaging Miss Richardson, in what portion of her body?"

A. "Well, we both were sitting on the couch, and when she had turned around and I began to massage her neck, I asked her did she want me to give her a massage? Then she said, 'Yes.'

"Then she stood up and laid full body length on the couch, at which time I began to massage her shoulder again, and I told her that it was very—that it was a discomfort to me to give her a massage in this position, and I said, 'Plus, it's difficult with clothes on.'

"So she proceeded in getting up, and took off her trousers, and she took off her anklets and sandals right there."

What? Just like that? No questions asked? No discussion?

I looked at the jury. Most of the women looked at me and fidgeted in their chairs. My surprise and shock was evident, but was not the kind that I had warned Terri about. There was no way she could have told me to expect this testimony. The jury seemed to concur: folded arms, drumming fingers, muffled coughs—I recognized the signs.

Q. ". . . and at this time how were you dressed?"

A. "At this time, I still had on my jacket, my shirt, my tie, my pants, and other attire."

Q. "All right. Now, after Miss Richardson removed her slacks, anklets, and shoes, what did she do?"

A. "Well, I made the suggestion why don't we go into the bedroom where she'd be more comfortable."

How friendly.

Q. "And what was her response to that?"

A. "She said, 'Okay. Fine.' "

Q. "Did you hold her or grab her in any way at this time?"

A. "No, because I was walking toward the bedroom, and in the process I was taking off my jacket."

Q. "Did she follow you into the bedroom?"

A. "She followed me to the entrance of the bedroom, at which time I turned around, because she still had on her blouse, and I told her that she would have to remove her blouse if she wanted me to give her a full-body massage."

Q. "And did she remove it there?"

A. "Yes, she did."

Q. "And what did she do with her blouse?"

A. "She tossed it over on the couch . . ."

I could see it now: the burlesque queen bumping and grinding sensuously toward the bedroom door, blouse twirling, licking her lips, and with one last longing glance, she exited, giving the blouse a careless flick over her shoulder before disappearing off stage.

A. ". . . then she went on into the bedroom."

I was watching his face intently. He was avoiding mine.

I was aware of Sografo leaning close to my ear, mumbling something about never having heard any of this before. I waved him off.

Q. ". . . and what did you do?"

A. "I was behind her. She went in. She plopped down on the bed in a sitting position, and I informed her that she had to lie down on the bed on her stomach."

Q. "What did you do then?"

A. "I went over to the bed and I asked her to move over, which she did, and I began to massage her from the base of the neck."

Q. "How were you dressed this time?"

A. "I still had my shirt, my tie, my pants, my shoes, my full attire except for my jacket."

Q. "All right. Now please basically describe the massage you gave while Miss Richardson was lying on her stomach."

A. "I massaged her neck, and I came down to her shoulder blades, and then I came down to the back, or to the rear—rib cage, and then to the small of the back, and then into the hips or the buttocks, and then into the thighs, the back calf, and the ankle and feet."

I made a note to find out on cross-examination if Mr. O'Conner happened to know the proper names for any of the muscles which lay in the general areas of the human body which he had just described, or if his experience was limited solely to naming that which he could touch.

Q. "When you were giving that massage, did Miss Richardson object at all?"

A. "No, sir. No way possible."

Q. "When you say 'No way possible,' what do you mean?"

A. "Because it was almost like I was half putting her to sleep."

Q. "After you massaged the back of Miss Richardson, what did you do then?"

A. "Then I asked her to roll over."

Q. "And did she?"

A. "Yes, sir. She rolled over."

Q. "At this time, you were still fully clothed?"

A. "At this time, I was still fully dressed."

Q. "Then what did you do?"

A. "Then I started giving her a massage again from underneath the chin, down to her chest, to her breast area and her stomach. Again, her inner thighs and her thighs, and her calves and her feet."

Q. "All right. Now, when you were massaging Miss Richardson in her chest area, was there any indication of sexual arousal on her part?"

A. "Yes, sir, there was. In the process of massaging her breasts, her nipples did become erect."

I would be sure to ask him if breast massage was part of the training he'd received, and more precisely, exactly how one does it and for what purpose.

Q. "Now, did she still remain in this position on the bed?"

A. "Yes, sir. She was still laying on the bed, but she began to breathe rather heavily."

I was breathing rather heavily too, at that point, but it certainly wasn't because I was sexually aroused.

Q. "Was she conscious?"

A. "Very much so."

Q. "Was she apparently aware of you?"

A. "Very much so."

Q. "Now, when you massaged Miss Richardson in the hip area, did you massage her in the vicinity of her vagina?"

A. "Yes, I did."

Q. "Did she respond?"

A. "Yes, sir. She opened her legs wide."

Q. "At this time did Miss Richardson appear to be sexually aroused?"

A. "Very much so."

Q. "At this time, Mr. O'Conner, how were you dressed?"

A. "I was still fully dressed in a shirt, tie, my pants, my shoes, and my socks."

Amazing! He has a woman lying before him completely in the nude, and fully sexually aroused, and yet he is still "in his full attire." And, ladies and gentlemen, if you believe this, I have a piece of land that you might be interested in . . .

Q. "Now, did Miss Richardson make any effort to leave the bed?"

A. "No, she did not."

Q. "What did you do then?"

A. "Upon repeating the same, where I had originally started, and I hesitated at her vagina area, I stood up from the bed and I began to take off my tie and my shirt and my undershirt and . . ."

Well, it's about time.

Q. "Did Miss Richardson see you start to remove your clothing?"

A. "Yes, she did."

Q. "And did you subsequently, Mr. O'Conner, remove all your clothing?"

A. "Yes, I did."

Q. "Did Miss Richardson indicate to you that she objected to what was taking place at this time?"

A. "No, she did not."

Q. "Up until this point, Mr. O'Conner, had you in any way threatened Miss Richardson or done anything to overcome a resistance that she had made to what was taking place?"

A. "No, sir, not at all."

Q. "And what happened after you removed all your clothing?"

A. "I asked her to move over and she did."

Q. "Did you have intercourse with Miss Richardson?"

A. "Yes, I did."

Q. "Did it appear to you that Miss Richardson was at that time fully sexually aroused and desired intercourse?"

A. "Yes, sir. If she wasn't, then she had lubrication, a tremendous amount of lubrication in her vagina area, for no reason."

I could see that O'Conner's understanding of physiology was on the same level as his knowledge of human anatomy: that erect nipples could be the result of contact with cold air alone, and vaginal secretions the result of involuntary responses completely uninduced by sexual stimulus, had probably never occurred to him. I made another note to chat about it with him when it got to be my turn.

Q. "After this incident was over, Mr. O'Conner, did Miss Richardson indicate to you that you had offended her in any way while you were there in the apartment?"

A. "No, sir."

"Incident"? Is that how one described consensual intercourse? I was bursting through every pore to get at this man. *Patience, patience,* I chided myself. *Your turn will come.*

Q. "After the incident was over, what did Miss Richardson do?"

It seemed, in addition to his many other talents, Dickenson O'Conner was also quite fastidious. He described how, while Terri showered, he folded her clothes and placed them on the bed, which he also "tidied up." When Terri finished, he then showered.

Next O'Conner was asked to relate the episode concerning the entrance of a second black man into the apartment, and his account pretty much coincided with the one given by Terri. We learned that the man was a custodian at the apartment complex, and that his reason for coming into the apartment was to fill a bucket with water.

Within a minute or two of the custodian's departure, O'Conner and Terri also left.

What, I wanted to know, did they say to each other all during this time? Who suggested they leave? What happened to the phone calls he was supposed to be making? I jotted reminders to myself on the yellow pad, taking care to write them clearly enough so I would recognize what I'd written when I got back to them.

From the apartment, O'Conner explained, with Terri's consent, they went to look for jobs at nearby restaurants, and when he happened on an interview for her, he was rather perturbed because she refused to go in.

Since both Terri and O'Conner gave similar accounts of this episode, I had to assume it had happened pretty much as they described. God, what gall this man had! He rapes the woman and then goes on with life as if nothing out of the ordinary had taken place. He wants her to go for a job interview less than an hour after the attack.

This attitude was not a new one for me, but seldom had I seen such a blatant display. Not a drop of remorse, not a hint of concern, not so much as an "I could have read her wrong," which would have made my job, and the jury's, much more difficult: then I would have been forced to deal more directly with victim credibility and to rely more heavily on the expert's.

How did he explain her sudden change of heart? I mean, she'd been tagging after him the better part of the day, bugging him to help her find work, but here they were, with an interview only a few steps away —and she refused!

His answer when I asked?

A. "The young lady said her makeup was not right for an interview."

I certainly didn't doubt for a second that her makeup was not right for an interview. I've yet to see a rape victim with eye shadow, mascara, or lipstick applied just so, or who would care to go for a job interview anytime soon.

It really was scary to consider the centuries of victims who had left the criminal justice system no better off than when they had entered it because of twisted meanings supplied by defendants for behaviors and events so easily understood if explained from the right perspective. I was determined to supply that meaning.

After she refused to go for the interview, O'Conner recounted, he then took Terri back to her car and he went about his usual business, and except for the phone call to Christie later that day (he told her only that he'd made love to her roommate, according to him), he had given the "incident" little thought until Sografo's unexpected visit two days later.

In speaking of Sografo's visit, with an "I've been meaning to tell you" tone, O'Conner informed us all that he had not been given his constitutional rights to remain silent, to have an attorney, etc., until after he had been interviewed and had been arrested. I could feel Sografo come forward in his seat even before his hand touched my arm. I nodded without looking, scribbled a few words on the back of an old phone message, and passed it to him. I was glad that Sografo always followed department policy and took another detective with him when he interviewed a rape suspect. Hopefully Rex Norman would not be hard for Sografo to track down. I would definitely need him for rebuttal.

Five minutes later Sografo slid back into the chair beside me. One look and I was reassured.

How did the man think he'd get away with it? Who did he think he was fooling?

Not you, I trust. My eyes spoke to the jury as I scanned the rows.

When had he decided to do it? Although his attorney never gave me a straight answer in so many words, I think he was hearing a lot of it for the first time himself from his client on the stand. He would openly admit only to recent discovery of his client's claim of failure to receive *Miranda* warnings before interrogation.

"If you want my two cents' worth, I don't believe him for a minute" was my reaction to this development as defense counsel laid it out to the judge in chambers. "No, let me revise that," I corrected myself. "I don't believe him for one second."

"Nor half a second?" Judge Billingsley smiled.

Not until well after the case was over did it occur to me that O'Conner, at some point, may have panicked at the realization that he had been found out, and that he just might be convicted of rape. In such a state of emergency, rescuing the drowning man is made more difficult because fear blunts reason. When O'Conner saw himself going under, he began to flail.

10

BY THE TIME I begin cross-examination of a defendant, I almost always know where I'm going and what I want to accomplish. Order is maintained in my mind by grouping the questions in large blocks, so that I never really have to follow a script and run the risk of losing my place, but rather have the freedom within each block to move around, taking care only to be sure I've asked all the questions in that block before I move on to the next.

If, by the time I begin cross-examination, this fairly thorough outline is not pretty clearly set in my mind, I know I am going to have trouble. I don't think I have ever been further from this danger, or closer to a complete mental guide of where I was going in a cross-examination, than I was in the Dickenson O'Conner case.

First, why had he been at that nude photography session?

A. "Well, it's the third one in which I had been at, and there's another gentleman who used to work for me that is a cousin of the ranch owner, and so he invited me."

Q. "So you were not a photographer?"

A. "I fool around with Polaroids and miniature cameras."

Q. "I see. But you didn't read about this meet in a photography magazine, or by going into photography stores, and you weren't doing it for a class assignment or to try to sell any pictures?"

A. "No."

Q. "And what was your purpose in going there?"

A. "I was an invited guest."

Q. "And you said it was your third one. You had been to two others at the same place?"

A. "That is correct."

Q. "Also as an invited guest?"

A. "That is correct."

Q. "And the owner of the ranch knew that you were not a photographer when you were there?"

A. "I do not know what he knew."

We also learned that O'Conner knew he could not get onto the premises where the shoot was being held without a camera, and the only photograph he had of the entire shoot was the one of Terri Richardson that he had given to his attorney.

We went into detail about how he ran his "businesses," particularly his employment agency.

Q. "You said you had a secretary, Mr. O'Conner."

A. "That is correct."

Q. "And what was her name?"

A. "I would have to go back and look at the records, because I had all my secretaries from either Kelly Girl or Western Girl, which is a temporary employment agency."

Q. "Yes. But you never had a regular secretary?"

A. "No. I had all my temporary help."

Q. "As of October of 1978, Mr. O'Conner, how long had you had this business of International Personnel Services?"

A. "I had been in the business roughly about a year and a half."

Q. "And in all that time you didn't have a secretary, you just used temporary ones all the time?"

A. "No, ma'am. The secretaries which I had basically stayed maybe three or four months, and either left to pregnancy, marriage, many other reasons. So, therefore, since I was out of the office quite a bit . . . then we wouldn't need a secretary, or if I was going to be there, we wouldn't need a secretary, or if we had let the typing pile up to a degree, then we would get temporary help, because I also type fifty words a minute. So, therefore, I did quite a bit of the typing."

He wasn't going to make me forget the question I had originally asked.

Q. "So you don't know the name of the person who was your regular secretary?"

A. "No. I'm sorry."

Was that as confusing to you as it was to me? I said to myself as I eyed the jury.

Q. "Now, Mr. O'Conner, you indicated you'd been in the employment business for about a year and a half at the time Miss Richardson came looking for a job, is that right?"

A. "Approximately that."

Q. "If I were to come in looking for a job, as Miss Richardson did, what would you do for me?"

A. "Have you fill out an application."

Q. "What kind of an application?"

A. "Standard employment application."

Q. "Would you ask me what kind of job I was looking for?"

A. "That is on the application."

Q. "And do you have Miss Richardson's application, the one that she filled out?"

A. "Yes, I think I do."

Q. "Do you have it with you?"

A. "No, I do not."

And he was unable to find it at any time after that.

Q. "Now, on that application, did she put on there what kind of job she was looking for?"

A. "Yes, she did."

Q. "And what were those jobs?"

A. "Hygienist, secretary, waitress."

Secretary. Ah, yes. Now that was the one for which Terri had no skills.

Q. "I believe on your direct examination you also said modeling."

A. "Correct."

Q. "Is that also on there?"

A. "No. She did not put that on there. I wrote it in."

Q. "And why did you write it in?"

A. "Because that's another field that she was interested in."

Q. "Did she tell you that?"

A. "Yes, she did."

Q. "What kind of modeling did she tell you she was interested in doing?"

A. "When I asked her as to what type of modeling she was interested in, I told her she did not have the background in regards to clothing modeling and so forth. She stated to me, 'Any modeling that I can get.' "

I wondered what modeling was left if she couldn't do clothing "and so forth." Especially with the way she felt about modeling without clothes.

Q. "All right. Now, let's assume that I want to be a secretary. What tests and other information would you have from me?"

A. "Upon completion of the application, then I would have to tell you that I would get back to you."

Q. "Well, is there nothing that you would do to ascertain what my skills were as a secretary?"

A. "One, I would require, if you had previous experience, which your application would show me, and one main thing in which I would be interested in is in regards to whether or not you had a typing test."

Q. "Well, did you ask Miss Richardson any of those questions?"

A. "Yes, I did."

Q. "And is there a place on the application for them to reflect what their skills are?"

A. "Yes, there are."

Q. "And is that all filled in too?"

A. "No, because she did not have a certificate, and she did not take any exam, a typing exam."

Q. "And you don't give a typing exam there?"

A. "No. We don't give a typing examination there."

Q. "No kind of examination to see what kind of skills a person has in the areas of secretarial training?"

A. "We recommend that they go out and take an exam at a school, because the school will give a typing exam to you and a certificate so stating so."

Q. "I can remember applying many years ago for a secretarial job, and, as I recall, when I went in and filled out my application I seem to recall taking a typing test. Is that not the way it's done in the business anymore?"

A. "You may take a typing exam from the employer, your potential employer, not there at the employment agency, no."

Q. "Isn't it one of the things that you want to tell a potential employer about someone you are trying to get a job for, that is, what their skills are, and to your satisfaction know what these skills actually are?"

A. "Your basic employer will run the exam himself, or have his personnel department run the exam."

Well, one's "basic employer" had certainly changed a lot since my days of looking for a secretarial job, I guessed.

Q. "So you were then planning to look for a job for Miss Richardson as a model, hygienist, secretary, and waitress?"

A. "Whatever I could come up with."

Q. "Now, how do you go about lining up possible interviews, or let me ask this way: what did you do in Miss Richardson's case?"

A. "The thing which you basically do in regard for interviews is you contact various companies, various restaurants, various people in the field to see whether there are possible openings, or a possibility of an opening."

Q. "And did you do this in Miss Richardson's case?"

A. "Yes, I did."

Q. "Do you remember what you did?"

A. "In regards to?"

Q. "In attempting to find her a job after the interview."

A. "I made contact with the various—well, I won't say various, I'll say with quite a few restaurants, and I called a few businesses. We get a brochure that has a job listing on them requiring certain qualifications. I went through those to see if there was an availability in her situation. I contacted other agencies, as such, yes."

Q. "And you found nothing?"

A. "Not with the requirements which she had. I mean, their experience level was higher than what Miss Richardson had."

Q. "Had she told you her experience level in all the areas that you've mentioned?"

A. "Yes. She gave me a number of years and experience in which she had it."

Q. "Did you put all these things down in the application?"

A. "That is written on the back of the form that states 'comments.'"

Q. "And you will bring that application with you tomorrow?"

A. "That is correct."

Of course, he didn't.

Q. "Had she prior experience as a waitress?"

A. "Yes. She had a limited amount as a waitress."

Q. "Had she any prior experience as a model?"

A. "No, except for the shoot."

So O'Conner either had searched for or was considering searching for employment in three fields—as secretary, model, or waitress—for which the prospective employee had either very limited or no experience. The job for which Terri had actually received training, as a dental hygienist, never came up. Nor did I bring it up, since it was from omission that it drew its greatest strength.

O'Conner not only had difficulty remaining consistent with testimony from direct examination, but frequently had difficulty remembering what he had said only several sentences before during cross-examination.

Q. "When Miss Richardson came to your office and filled out the job application, her roommate, Christie, was with her, is that correct?"

A. "Yes."

Q. "And had you seen or spoken on the phone to Christie between that evening and the day of the 'incident' with Miss Richardson?"

A. "No, I had not."

Q. "So the last time before the day of the 'incident' that you spoke to her was in person that evening in your office?"

A. "That is correct."

A few minutes later, however, in trying to answer a question I had asked about when he had learned certain information from Christie, he apparently had forgotten his recent answer.

Q. "When did you find that out?"

A. "Well, I had found that out from speaking with Christie on a prior phone call that was made to her home, from my home."

Q. "And when had that phone call taken place?"

A. "That had taken place, I believe, sometime after I had seen her in my office that evening with Miss Richardson."

Q. "Well, Mr. O'Conner, I believe you just testified that from the evening when both of them were in your office, when you had last seen Christie, you had had no contact with her until the morning of the 'incident.' Now, is that not so?"

A. "That is correct. I did not have any contact with her. That's why I stated to her in person."

Q. "I believe I also asked you about the phone. But I take it your testimony is that you did speak to her on the phone between those two dates?"

A. "Yes, we had spoke."

At different times he had, then had not, told Terri that the phone calls at his "other office" were for her. When describing who went into the bedroom first, at one point it was himself, at another he was following her. Now she had not assisted him in taking off any of his clothes, then later she had unzipped his pants.

He did not allow factual inconsistencies alone to compromise his credibility: frequent variations in the manner he chose to answer the questions gave him a big boost in that direction as well. Frequently vague, often evasive, sometimes flippant, and once incredibly patronizing.

Q. "Did you order Miss Richardson to the bedroom?"

A. "No. I did not order Miss Richardson, because, basically, I don't feel that anyone should be ordered to do anything. I've always asked people, and if people do not consent with the asking, then I just simply drop it."

But Dickenson O'Conner went down for the final count when he deserved it most: during that massage in his apartment. We had just finished talking about the conversation that had taken place while he and Terri were sitting on the couch.

Q. "What happened next?"

A. "It was after this discussion, the fact is she mentioned that she had had—her neck was stiff."

Q. "Did you ask her where it was stiff?"

A. "She had pointed it out."

Q. "What happened next?"

A. "Then I asked her to turn around."

Q. "What happened next?"

A. "I began to massage her—her neck and her shoulder."

Q. "Now, you've testified, I believe, that you had been a masseur. Is that correct?"

A. "That's correct."

Q. "What kind of training did you have?"

A. "I had to take a course in Massachusetts General Hospital."

Q. "And how long a course was that?"

A. "Basically, two months of schooling, and I had to do three months in the hospital."

Q. "And what kind of massage work did you do?"

A. "Just simply worked with the rehabilitation of muscles. Well, basically, all you did is primarily run machines in the hospital."

Q. "You worked in the rehabilitation section of therapy?"

A. "Correct."

Q. "Running the machines?"

A. "Correct."

Q. "Now, you didn't actually give massages or administer the therapy yourself?"

A. "Let us say it was limited . . . because they did not want any of the personnel actually to unnecessarily touch the patients."

Let *us* say that O'Conner was describing the work of an orderly, an aide at best.

Q. "Mr. O'Conner, did you ask Miss Richardson how she'd come to have a stiff neck?"

A. "No, I did not."

Q. "And would it be correct and fair to say that one of the things you should know before you start to massage someone's neck when they have complained of a stiffness in it, is how it might have happened?"

A. "Could be for many reasons."

Q. "Well, that's my question of you. Is it not important to know how an injury may have occurred, such as why the neck was stiff, before you begin to massage it, given your background and training? Is it something you didn't think to ask her, or . . ."

A. "No, I didn't think of asking her."

Q. "You didn't think it was important to know how she may have come by this stiff neck?"

A. "It may have been important, but I did not ask."

Q. "Would it make a difference in what you might have done, knowing how she had gotten the stiff neck?"

A. "It may have."

Q. "I see. In any case, when she told you she had a stiff neck and pointed it out, you asked her to turn around?"

A. "Correct, and I immediately began to massage her neck."

Q. "When you say you began to massage, what is it exactly you began to do?"

A. "To take and use my hand on her neck."

Q. "Are you familiar with the muscles in the neck?"

A. "To some degree."

I was going to find out to an exact degree.

Q. "And in your course, did you learn what the names of the muscles are?"

A. "Yes. That's one of the requirements."

Q. "And you did know those names at the time?"

A. "At which time?"

Q. "At the time that you massaged Miss Richardson's neck."

A. "I didn't give it any consideration."

Q. "Could you name the muscles that you massaged, please, Mr. O'Conner?"

A. "Well, it's been a long time . . ."

And he couldn't name any.

Q. "How long did you continue to massage Miss Richardson's neck?"

A. "Five to six minutes."

Q. "And during this time you were both seated on the couch?"

A. "That is correct."

Q. "And what, if any, conversation took place between you during these five to six minutes?"

A. "There wasn't."

Q. "None at all?"

A. "No."

Q. "Did you think anything, Mr. O'Conner, of the fact that this woman had wanted to come to your office when you told her you had other things to do, wanted to get in your car and come over to your apartment, knowing that it was your apartment, and was sitting on your couch having a massage? Was anything going through your mind at that time?"

A. "In regards to what?"

Q. "I'm asking you."

A. "My primary interest was to make the phone calls."

Q. "Nothing else had occurred to you by that point in time?"

A. "No."

Q. "All right, what happened next?"

A. "I asked her if she would like me to massage her back."

Q. "Just her back?"

A. "Her neck and her back."

Q. "What did she say?"

A. "She said, 'Yes.' "

Q. "What happened then?"

A. "She stood up, and she went down to one end of the couch, and she laid out on the couch."

Q. "Did you ask her to lie down on the couch?"

A. "No."

Q. "Did you need her to lie down on the couch to rub her back?"

A. "It is a more comfortable position in which to do it in."

Q. "Meanwhile, Mr. O'Conner, do I understand you have your coat on all this time?"

A. "That is correct."

Q. "Were you not warm?"

A. "I may have been."

Q. "What happened next?"

A. "I asked Miss Richardson if she would remove her blouse."

Q. "What happened next?"

A. "She got up and she removed her pants."

Maybe she was hard of hearing.

Q. "Okay. She got up and removed her pants, and you had requested that she remove her blouse, is that your testimony?"

A. "Yes."

Q. "What happened next?"

A. "I asked her if she wanted a full-body massage."

Q. "And this was after you had asked her to remove her blouse and she had gotten up and removed her pants?"

A. "Yes."

Q. "And there was no conversation between you other than what you have told us?"

A. "No."

Q. "What happened next?"

A. "She said she did want a full-body massage, and therefore she took off her shoes and her anklets."

I was trying to watch this happen in my mind's eye as O'Conner was describing the scene. Frankly, it looked rather ridiculous. I could picture Terri now standing there in O'Conner's living room being directed to take off her blouse and first removing her pants, then her shoes, and finally her socks.

Q. "So she took off her shoes and her anklets. Was that in response to a direction from you or was that on her own?"

A. "She did that on her own."

Q. "I take it she's still wearing a blouse?"

A. "Correct."

Q. "And you were still wearing your coat?"

A. "Correct."

Q. "Now, up to this point, were you thinking of anything other than the phone calls for her interviews, or just giving her a body massage?"

A. "I wasn't thinking of anything in particular."

Just to be sure, I'd ask him the obvious.

Q. "All right. In other words, the idea of having sexual intercourse with her had not occurred to you yet?"

A. "No."

Q. "What happened next?"

A. "I started walking toward the bedroom and she was following me."

Q. "And there was no conversation between you about going to the bedroom?"

A. "No."

That isn't how I remembered it from direct examination. I wondered how the jury was following this.

Q. "Do you recall on direct examination testifying that you said it would be more comfortable in the bedroom?"

A. "That I had already stated."

Q. "And when had you stated that?"

A. "At the time when she took off her pants, and I asked her did she want a full-body massage?"

Q. "All right. So your testimony is that you began walking to the bedroom and she began to follow, is that correct?"

A. "Correct."

Q. "What happened then?"

A. "I stopped and took off my jacket."

Hallelujah. He finally took off the jacket.

Q. "What happened then?"

A. "Then, at that time, I made mention that she still had on her blouse."

Q. "And what happened then?"

A. "She removed her blouse and tossed it over on the couch."

The burlesque show again.

Q. "And during this time, from the time she first began to allow you to massage her neck to the time that she was completely nude walking into the bedroom, how much time had elapsed?"

A. "I'm sorry. I don't know. I'd say minutes."

Q. "And there was never any sign of embarrassment or modesty of any sort from Miss Richardson during this time, or any comments that would make you feel that she was uncomfortable?"

A. "No."

Q. "All right. What happened next?"

A. "We proceeded into the bedroom."

Q. "And what happened next?"

A. "She sat down on the bed."

Q. "Did she sit down on the end of the bed?"

A. "In approximately the center of the bed."

Q. "And what did you do?"

A. "I informed her that she would have to lay on her stomach in order for me to give her a massage."

Q. "Were you still wearing all your clothing except for the coat?"

A. "That is correct."

Q. "And what did she do when you told her she needed to lie on her stomach on the bed?"

A. "She got on her stomach on the bed."

Q. "What happened then?"

A. "I went over to her, to where she was, and I asked her if she could move over some so that I could sit on the side of the bed."

Q. "What happened then?"

A. "Then I began to give her a massage from the base of her neck."

Q. "Is this the same kind of massage that you had been taught to give?"

A. "Relatively, yes."

He was probably being accurate there.

Q. "Maybe I'm assuming. Were you taught how to give a massage?"

A. "Yes, I was."

Q. "And when you were taught how to give a massage, were you ever told to give a massage without using any kind of lubricant on the body?"

I was reaching as far back as I could to remember any scrap about proper massage technique.

A. "Yes, I was."

Q. "And you don't use a lubricant on the body to give a full-body massage?"

A. "It's not necessary."

It certainly had been necessary for my roommate to pass her exams.

Q. "So you weren't taught that is one of the things you should do?"

A. "I was taught that's one of the things you could do, not a necessity."

Q. "And did you use any lubricant on the body?"

A. "No, I did not."

Q. "And then you gave her a full-body massage, as you've described to us in direct examination, is that correct?"

A. "Correct."

Q. "Okay. Now, during the time that you were giving her the full-body massage, was there any conversation between you?"

A. "No."

Q. "And after you had her roll over, and began to massage the front, the chest area and down the front, was there any conversation during that part of the massage?"

A. "No."

Q. "How long a time did this massage go on?"

A. "Complete?"

Q. "Yes."

A. "I would say about fifteen minutes to a half hour."

Q. "And during this entire period of time, there was absolutely no conversation between you?"

A. "None that I recall."

Like watching soft porn with the volume turned off.

Q. "I believe you testified on direct, in response to a question by your attorney, that Miss Richardson became sexually aroused during the course of this massage because her nipples became erect, is that correct?"

A. "That is correct."

Q. "Do you associate an erect nipple with sexual arousal in a woman?"

A. "Could you clarify that?"

Q. "I don't think so. Do you associate in your mind sexual arousal with an erect nipple on a woman's breast?"

A. "Not necessarily."

Q. "But you said in this case that you associated an erect nipple with sexual arousal, is that correct?"

A. "That is correct."

Q. "Fine. Why is it in this case that you thought of sexual arousal?"

A. "This is part of what may take place in the arousement of a female sexually."

You're avoiding me.

Q. "Yes, Mr. O'Conner, I understand that that is what may happen, but my question of you is: why in this case did you think it was due to sexual arousal? Did she say anything?"

A. "No. She did not say anything, except I also mentioned that her breathing became heavy."

Q. "At the same time?"

A. "While I was in the area of her chest."

Q. "I see. All right. And you also testified that you massaged her vaginal area, is that correct?"

A. "That is correct."

Q. "Is that part of a full-body massage?"

A. "That is."

He certainly had attended a different school than my roommate from Berkeley.

Q. "What exactly do you do?"

A. "I use my hand on the outer lips of the vagina, and also on the inner thighs, because that, likewise, as other parts of the body, is a muscle."

Q. "So you were taught that, as part of a full-body massage, you massage the outer portion of the vaginal area, in other words, the labia?"

A. "Correct."

I was proud of myself. I had kept an absolutely straight face, and had tried not to notice the massive movement in the jury box.

Q. "And I believe you also testified, in response to a question by your attorney, at this point in the massage you felt there was sexual arousal because of some other reason?"

A. "Correct."

Q. "And what was that?"

A. "That was fluids that were coming from the vagina."

Q. "And you had done nothing but the body massage itself at this point?"

A. "That is correct."

I had managed to produce a mental image of Terri standing nude except for her blouse in the living room, ridiculous as that appeared, but I was having trouble just visualizing what O'Conner had described: this river of vaginal fluid flowing out across the bed.

Q. "And you were still fully dressed?"

A. "Correct."

Q. "Now, at this point, were you still concerned with just giving the body massage?"

A. "Yes, I was."

Self-control above and beyond the call of duty.

Q. "Having intercourse with Miss Richardson had not occurred to you?"

A. "Not at that particular time."

I wondered how long it would take.

Q. "What happened next?"

A. "I proceeded in giving her the remainder of the body massage."

Q. "Which consisted of what at that point?"

A. "Which was her thighs, her shins, and her feet and ankles."

Q. "I don't believe I heard mention of the arms at all in this massage. Did you give her a massage . . . ?"

A. "I include that in the shoulders."

Q. "I see. All right. What happened next?"

A. "Upon completion, I went over and gave her a brief massage again, starting again from the neck and coming down."

Q. "How was she lying then?"

A. "She was still lying on her back."

Q. "All right. What happened then?"

A. "Then upon completion of giving her a massage the second time, it's at that point that I began to remove my clothes."

Q. "So somewhere between the time you gave her the massage down in the vaginal area, at which point you had not even thought of having intercourse with her throughout the massage, and the second time you gave her the massage, which sounds as if it were done much quicker—correct me if I'm wrong—something had changed, am I correct?"

A. "The response in which I had gotten from Terri Richardson from her body."

Q. "She had said nothing, though? I mean, there had been no conversation between you at all about how she felt, is that correct?"

A. "No. But when somebody's body begins to come up and to meet your hand, and their legs begin to widen for your touch, and so forth—no, she did not say anything."

This is getting better by the second.

Q. "That's what I'm asking. She did these things—in other words, her body came up to meet your hands, and her legs spread?"

A. "Yes."

Q. "Okay. Was she looking at you?"

A. "Yes, she was."

Q. "Smiling at you?"

A. "She did not have anger in her face. She did not have displeasure in her face. I'd say content."

Q. "Where were her arms and her hands?"

A. "Down by her side."

Q. "So you gave her a second massage?"

A. "That's correct."

Q. "And then you began to remove your clothing, is that right?"

A. "That's right."

Q. "I take it up to this point in time during the second massage, you had not become sexually aroused at all?"

A. "No."

Q. "Okay. What happened next?"

A. "I began to take off my shirt, my tie, and so forth, and fold them and put them on the bed, and my socks, and it's at that point that Miss Richardson got up and she undid my belt and the top of my pants."

There he was, with this woman practically lunging at him for sex, and he was folding his clothes as he took them off.

Q. "Now, when you say she undid your belt and the top of your pants, where was she when she did this?"

A. "Sitting up in the bed."

Q. "Any conversation between you then?"

A. "No."

Q. "Okay. And it's your testimony that you had all of your clothes off?"

A. "That's correct."

Q. "Was it warm in the bedroom?"

A. "I really didn't pay that much attention."

It certainly was warm in this courtroom.

Q. "Was the room closed up?"

A. "Yes. The apartment was closed up."

Q. "When you say 'undid' your pants, what do you mean?"

A. "I mean to the degree that she undid the belt, undid the top snap, and unzippered it."

Q. "What happened next?"

A. "I removed my pants."

Q. "Well, is that all she did? She unbuttoned the pants, unzipped them, and then what?"

A. "Then she began to pull them down, but I took over."

Q. "And what did she do?"

A. "She just laid back down on the bed."

Q. "All right. What happened next?"

A. "Then we had sexual intercourse."

Q. "Without a word?"

A. "Yes."

Q. "Was there any kissing?"

A. "Brief."

Q. "When did that occur?"

A. "At the beginning of the intercourse."

Q. "Was there any foreplay?"

A. "The foreplay was more or less like in the massage."

I'd thought he'd said he wasn't sexually aroused, that he was only interested in giving a massage.

Q. "Well, did she participate in any foreplay with you?"

A. "No, she did not."

Q. "Did she caress you?"

A. "My shoulders. I mean, she put her arms around me, if that's what you are relating to."

Q. "Did you caress her?"

A. "Yes, I did."

Q. "And how did you do that?"

A. "By putting my hands under her shoulders."

Q. "Anything else?"

A. "No. I mean, like what?"

Q. "I'm asking what took place."

A. "A sexual act."

Q. "Period?"

A. "Correct."

Q. "Okay. And during this time, how long was this, this sexual act?"

A. "I'd say approximately fifteen, twenty minutes. I don't know how long."

Q. "And at no time during this fifteen or twenty minutes was there any conversation between you?"

A. "None that I can think of offhand."

Q. "So at this point there had really been no conversation between you whatsoever from basically the time you entered the bedroom, perhaps before, right through the intercourse, is that correct?"

A. "As close as I recall."

Q. "All right. After this fifteen or twenty minutes of the sexual act, what happened next?"

A. "The sexual act was completed. I got up, asked her if she'd like to take a shower."

Q. "Okay. And what happened then?"

A. "I went into the bathroom, got her a towel and a washrag, and gave them to her."

Q. "And what did you do?"

A. "She went into the bathroom, I went into the living room."

Q. "All right. And while she was in the bathroom, what did you do?"

A. "I collected her clothes, I folded them, and I put them on the bed."

Q. "What else did you do?"

A. "I tidied up the bed."

Q. "What did you tidy up?"

A. "I straightened up the spread on the bed."

Q. "What else did you do?"

A. "That was basically it."

Q. "You were still nude?"

A. "Correct."

Q. "Okay. You didn't take a shower with her?"

A. "No, I did not."

Q. "Did you ask her if she would like to have a shower together?"

A. "No, I did not."

Q. "All right. And you said it was about ten or fifteen minutes that she was in the bathroom?"

A. "Correct."

Q. "Did you go in there during that time?"

A. "No, I did not."

Terri had told me that she did not take a shower while she was in the bathroom, but had instead tried to wash the smell and feel of her attacker from her body.

O'Conner went on to relate that after Terri had come out of the bathroom he had gone in, taken a shower, and gotten dressed. He then found Terri fully clothed and sitting on the couch in the living room.

Q. "What happened then?"

A. "I got—I joined her in the living room."

Q. "And up to this moment, there still had been no conversation at all between you, other than do you want to take a shower or are you through with the bathroom? Is that right?"

A. "Nothing that I can recall. I mean, to any great extent."

Q. "Now, after you joined Miss Richardson in the living room, what was your intention?"

A. "At this time, I was going to take her out and I was going to see what's at the restaurants in the area, at least to fill out some applications."

Q. "You never tried to finish those phone calls?"

A. "No, I didn't, they were busy."

Q. "So you tried again?"

A. "No, I did not try again."

Q. "How did you know they were still busy?"

A. "Because, if you stop and think, the noon hour, up until two, is the main hour for any restaurant."

Q. "Are you saying, Mr. O'Conner, that you just figured that if you called these restaurants the line would be busy?"

A. "I made an assumption that they would be busy."

Q. "All four of them?"

A. "Correct."

Q. "So you were just going to go out and canvass and see what you could find?"

A. "Correct."

Q. "Is that the way you usually help people find a job?"

A. "On the normal, no, I normally don't have clients who are willing to follow me around."

And Terri Richardson had been no exception to this rule.

By the time I got to the phone call to Christie's office, which both Terri and Christie had described, O'Conner's denial of the statement which each claimed he had made was anticlimactic.

Q. "When you got her on the phone, what is the first thing you said to her?"

A. "I said—I said to her—I says, 'Christie,' I says—I asked how she was doing, and she said, 'Fine.' She said, 'I don't have much time,' and I says, 'Okay,' I said, 'I've made love to your roommate.' She said, 'So?' "

Q. "Okay. This was right after she said, 'I don't have much time,' and you said, 'Okay, I made love to your roommate'?"

A. "Correct."

Q. "And you didn't tell her you just spent forty-five minutes fucking her roommate?"

A. "One, I don't use that type of terminology over the phone, no."

Q. "You don't use it over the phone? Do you use it otherwise?"

A. "No."

Q. "And her response was 'So?' Is that correct?"

A. "That is correct."

Q. "Okay. And I take it it's your testimony that you didn't tell Christie that Miss Richardson had resisted at first, but that you overcame it, or that a person can't resist for forty-five minutes?"

A. "No, I did not."

Q. "Nothing even resembling that?"

A. "Nothing even resembling it."

And of his preference for blond white women?

A. "I had made mention to Miss Richardson that a lot of the females that I date were blond. That was the extent of my comment."

I never even asked him why he was dating and at the same time living with a woman, or if she knew. But I did make this observation in argument to the jury.

Finally, we talked about that conversation with Sografo, the one in which such an experienced detective had "forgotten" to inform O'Conner of his rights.

Q. "Did you know why Detective Sografo was there?"

A. "Detective Sografo stated at the door, when I opened the door, that he was investigating an alleged rape."

Q. "Did he also tell you that you were a suspect in that rape?"

A. "Yes, he did."

Q. "And that you had been accused as the person who had committed the rape?"

A. "Yes. I was aware of it."

Q. "Okay. Did you feel that it was a very serious charge at the time?"

A. "Yes, I did."

Q. "You took it seriously at the time?"

A. "At first, I thought it was a joke."

This attitude did give me some insight into what O'Conner thought about women and sex.

Q. "I see. Did you become aware that it was not a joke?"

A. "Yes, I did."

Q. "And that it was a serious charge, and that it had serious implications?"

A. "Yes."

Q. "Now, do you remember reading the report that Detective Sografo gave you which contained the allegation against you?"

A. "I glanced at it. I cannot say that I read it, no."

Q. "Knowing that you were being charged or accused of a rape, you only glanced at the report?"

A. "I only glanced at it."

Q. "You did not read it over?"

A. "I did not read it thoroughly, no."

Q. "And you did not read it along with Detective Sografo?"

A. "No, I did not. I only glanced at it."

Q. "Do you recall Detective Sografo asking you if there was anything in it that you disagreed with?"

A. "I remember him stating that, but I do not remember the answer in which I gave him."

Q. "You mean you remember Detective Sografo asking you that question after giving you the report?"

A. "Correct."

Q. "But you don't remember whether there was anything in the report with which you differed?"

A. "Because, as I stated to him, I only glanced through it."

Q. "You stated to him that you had only glanced through it?"

A. "That is correct."

Q. "Now, was it not after you had told Detective Sografo twice that there was no resistance that he then confronted you with the statement by Miss Richardson's roommate, Christie, to the contrary?"

A. "I think it would be about that time. I'm not absolutely sure."

Q. "And did he also bring to your attention a statement in the report that Miss Richardson had made relating that she turned so you could rub her neck because you asked her to? Do you remember that?"

A. "No. I . . . as I stated, I really didn't read the report."

Q. "But you did at no time, I believe your testimony is, tell Detective Sografo about a full-body massage, or for that matter about a body massage at all?"

A. "No, I did not."

Q. "Do you think that wasn't important that Miss Richardson was naked, in the nude in your apartment, before this incident took place because she wanted a full-body massage? You did not think that was important to tell the detective?"

A. "At that particular time, I think that I was rather shocked that the police officer was in my apartment, okay? And I being a suspect of rape, I think that was mostly what I was concerned with, and that everything else was almost like . . . I mean, I couldn't believe that this was taking place."

Q. "I see. But, yet, you didn't read that report of the actual allegations against you?"

A. "No, I didn't, because it was just a discussion anyway."

Q. "All right, Mr. O'Conner, I believe you testified a couple of minutes ago that you think that it was, in fact, after you had emphasized to Detective Sografo on two occasions that there was no resistance that he then confronted you with Miss Richardson's roommate's statement to the contrary, is that correct? Is that where we are?"

A. "That is a possibility."

Q. "And did you admit to Detective Sografo that you had made a phone call to Christie?"

A. "Yes."

Q. "And what did you tell Detective Sografo about the statement you made to Christie?"

A. "My statement to the police officer was that I had told Christie that I did have a sexual relationship with Miss Richardson."

Q. "Did the detective not ask you, also, if you had told Christie that she had resisted but that you can't resist for forty-five minutes?"

A. "I believe he stated that."

Q. "And what did you tell him?"

A. "I told him that was not true."

Q. "And yet, at this point in time, knowing what you did and what you were accused of doing, you still didn't tell Detective Sografo about the full-body massage?"

A. "I did not."

Q. "Well, Mr. O'Conner, I have here in my notes, which I took yesterday morning at about ten-thirty, answers to the following questions: 'Did you ever tell Detective Sografo anything about a massage that you gave to Miss Richardson?' Your answer was 'Yes, I did.' My next question was 'Did you describe to Detective Sografo the massage, as you are doing here today?' And your answer to that was 'Not in detail.' My question of you then was 'What did you tell him?' And your answer was 'I simply stated that I had given the young lady a massage.' My next question: 'And did he ask you what kind of massage?' And your answer: 'No.' My last question was 'Did you tell him what kind of massage?' And your answer to that question was 'No.'

"Now, Mr. O'Conner, I can show you that testimony since I've asked the reporter to transcribe it. Do you remember that testimony?"

A. "No, I do not."

And I left it all at that.

One other thing gave me some insight into what may have been going on in O'Conner's mind that day in his apartment when he claimed he and Terri had had consensual intercourse.

Q. "Is it your testimony that you didn't tell Detective Sografo that Miss Richardson offered some resistance but that she was just playing around with you?"

A. "That was—that was the question which the police put to me."

Q. "Detective Sografo asked you that?"

A. "Correct."

Q. "In those words?"

A. "In relatively close to that. He says, 'Are you sure that just in the midst of playing around she didn't say no and mean yes? You know how women are.' And I says, 'No. There was not any resistance.' "

Q. "Detective Sografo said, 'You know how women are'? That was part of it?"

A. "Correct."

My guess is that a conversation very similar to this had taken place between Sografo and O'Conner but that the meaning had been twisted by the storyteller on the stand.

How many other women had this man convinced himself wanted sex with him?

That evening I called Terri and asked her if she had heard of any other occasion involving O'Conner with a white woman. She told me she had heard of none.

Five minutes later Christie called me back to tell me, in strictest confidence, that there was another woman who had been raped by O'Conner, but she would never agree to testify. She was, Christie confided, afraid that he would come after her again. It had happened in the laundry room of her apartment complex while her husband was at sea. Even though I couldn't use it, this knowledge was important for me and my own inner peace. I knew I was not going to convict an innocent man.

I had to remember that I actually had not yet convicted Dickenson O'Conner of anything, although I felt quite high. It was different from the exhilaration of victory itself—more a personal satisfaction in knowing that I had probably just completed the best cross-examination of my career. I'd felt almost that way once about a final argument in a robbery case. You just know when you've done it. The problem is, once this happens you always feel the obligation to do it again, and are often disappointed when you can't.

It took the jury only an hour and a half to convict O'Conner of forcible rape. I again spent several hours with the jurors, probing for opinions, strengths, weaknesses.

"We all voted to give him the title of International Con Man," one of the jurors related angrily.

One of the five men had been elected foreman and the ballot had been unanimous for "guilty" the first time a vote was taken. The seven women had been tuned in with the expert and had shared this common bond with each other. They explained to the men how true it was that women spend a great deal of time and energy coping with the potential threat of rape or other physical assault.

"Could we ask you something about the sentencing?" one of the young women jurors ventured as I prepared to leave. "We know we aren't supposed to consider sentencing *before* the verdict, but now we want to write a letter to the judge telling him we think this man should go to prison for the longest time the law will allow."

"You know," said another, "this man is a real danger to women in this city. Why, he doesn't even think what he did was wrong. He's probably done it before . . . and since too; do you know anything about that?"

I knew better than to get involved in that conversation, and advised them that they were perfectly free to prepare such a letter and send it to the judge.

In fact, three weeks later, when I walked into court for sentencing, the foreman of the jury was there.

"We composed a letter explaining how O'Conner's attitude about women—that women say no and mean yes—is the scariest kind."

He and all seven women jurors had signed it. But they had sent him because they were afraid that if they came in and asked for a long prison sentence, O'Conner might try to exact revenge.

"They're really frightened," he explained.

Judge Billingsley told us that he had read the letter and that in all his years on the Bench he had never received one from jurors in a case before; nor had a foreman attended a sentencing. He asked the foreman if he would take the witness stand and explain about the letter and his presence at the sentencing.

I felt reassured that O'Conner was facing a prison term.

I was mistaken.

Billingsley sentenced O'Conner to county jail for less than one year. I was distraught, dismayed, dejected, frustrated, thwarted, and angry. What was he thinking? But I knew. While he'd been impressed by the expert on one level, he was still disgusted by the lifestyle of the participants on another. All rape was not equal, just as all victims were not. The knight in shining armor could see no fair maiden to be rescued here.

I'd had a foreboding at one point during trial when, while arguing over admission of some evidence for the defense, O'Conner's attorney had suggested that it was relevant because "she used sex as a way to get ahead."

Almost as an aside, and with a jovial yet sarcastic tone, the judge had quipped, "Most women do."

I had refrained from comment at the time, realizing it would have done no good and hoping it had been, while inappropriate under any circumstances, at least more joke than serious.

My frustration was exceeded only by my determination to persevere. Of three jury-convicted rapists in one year's time, two had gone to county jail, only one to prison; and he had gone, not for the seriousness of the rape, but because he was a repeat felony offender.

It was an epidemic in California, this tendency of the judiciary to sentence rapists to jail terms rather than to prison. So much so that new legislation had just been enacted as I finished trying the O'Conner case, taking from judges the authority to choose between a year in county jail and a prison term for convicted rapists. As of January 1, 1980, all convictions of rape would *require* a prison sentence. The judge's only decision would be to determine how many years within, a low-to-high range.

Except for the sentence O'Conner received, I was well pleased with my second foray into the arena with the expert. For Terri the trial helped close off a period of her life that had needed resolution. She had been believed by twelve people who had never met her before. Her confidence began to return and her social life began to pick up. She called me a few weeks before I left the District Attorney's office in late 1980 to tell me she was getting married and to invite me to the wedding.

11

By the time Terri's case was over, interest in what I was doing was beginning to mount. Unfortunately, I did not realize it for what it was worth, or I would have jumped higher and pushed harder.

In late June 1979, I was asked if I would speak to the California District Attorneys' Association Mid-Winter Conference being held in San Diego. Of course, I accepted, and addressed the several hundred prosecutors hot on the heels of O'Conner's conviction. I was keeping very good company, and followed the late California Supreme Court Justice Wiley Manuel to the podium, the first black California Supreme Court justice and one of the "earlier" women prosecutors on the same agenda. Things seemed to be looking up.

About the same time, I was asked to write an article for the California District Attorneys' Association's journal about my new courtroom strategies. It appeared in the Fall 1979 issue.

Now, I had heard about California's long arm of influence on the law across the United States, and after the publication of that article, I saw just how far it reached. Slowly at first, and then with more frequency, the calls and letters came. From Kansas, Washington, Oklahoma, Colorado, Michigan. They had read my article and asked if I would send anything I had to help them do the same thing. There were conference calls with chief prosecutors and trial deputies, conversations on specific cases, requests for ways to develop experts, and once, a trip to see me by an attorney and her investigator from a city in Oklahoma whose office wanted to see how San Diego was set up to handle rape cases. They were dismayed, and not a little surprised, to find that I was it—there was no sexual assault unit or specially trained investigators to work up the cases.

Then in September 1979 I spoke at the annual State Bar Conference, held that year in Los Angeles, to a combined group of prosecutors and curious defense attorneys. It was there that I first suggested that this kind of evidence might be significant in civil cases on behalf of women who sue their attackers for money damages. By the spring of 1980 there were so many requests for copies of my materials that we kept a complete set unstapled at all times ready to duplicate. By then my file on expert testimony was bulging and I emptied an entire file drawer to accommodate it.

I was asked by counties all over the state of California to appear for training programs and seminars. I designed and taught a course for one of the local law schools.

I was not the only one whose life was exceedingly busy. Anne Kennedy found herself with more requests for her testimony than her supervisors at the Police Department could handle, since every one was at best out of town, at worst out of state.

The cases were intriguing, and each time she came home Anne and I tried to evaluate what she'd done and how it had worked. The most difficult case involved an attack by two deputy sheriffs on a hitchhiker from a small mountain town in northern California, but the most exciting by far was a pre-dawn flight to testify in a rural desert community in Nevada. Because Anne had injured her knee, she could not sit for any length of time in a car, so the prosecutor chartered a plane and pilot to fly her round-trip.

I had been waiting for the appellate court decision in the Harter case for so long that by February 1980 I was no longer holding my breath for the few seconds it took me to shuffle through the mail each day. Such is the time, of course, when one should most expect the unexpected. I found it not in the mail but on my desk one afternoon, blending into the paper landscape so well that only a lucky glimpse of the name caught my eye. For an instant I had trouble remembering why my heart was pounding. It was all such a blur I couldn't focus long enough on the words to read the ruling. I forced myself to start at the beginning.

"Appeal from an order of the Superior Court of San Diego," it began. "Manuelo Olmeda, judge. Affirmed."

Affirmed! Affirmed! My God, we'd won! I flipped to the last page:

"Judgment affirmed," it agreed.

All three justices had concurred. No dissent, and the case was certified for publication.

"This means every other court in the state will look to Harter as precedent." I was trembling.

I fell into my chair and let out a screech of delight, then a cheer and another screech. By now I had attracted a small crowd of curious onlookers, which I chased away with assurances I was reacting to the receipt of good news. I shut my office door and forced myself to read each word, one at a time.

I read the names of all the parties, the recitation of issues on appeal (I hadn't realized there were so many), and the chronicle of the facts of the case, which I already knew so well. Finally I made it to "Discussion, Section I."

"Harter contends," it began, "the trial court erred by allowing an expert on rape to testify to the effect that the degree of resistance displayed by Sandra was entirely reasonable under the circumstances.

"Harter testified Sandra consented to intercourse; the issue at trial focused on whether the victim's resistance was such as to make 'reasonably manifest' the refusal to engage in the acts in question . . .

" 'While generally the woman has the power to determine for herself the extent to which she feels she can safely resist [citation], her conduct must always be measured against the degree of force manifested and each case must be resolved on all of the circumstances present [citations].'

"Thus, the issue was not whether in some abstract sense the victim's resistance was reasonable. The critical inquiry is whether resistance was sufficient to *'reasonably manifest'* her refusal to Harter."

Something didn't fit. I reread the first four paragraphs again. What did they mean, "the issue was not whether in some abstract sense the victim's resistance was reasonable"? There was nothing "abstract" about it. Was it someone's contorted interpretation of the case citation? Anne Kennedy had carefully laid out criteria to which Sandy's behavior was compared. And what was this *"reasonably manifest"* contrivance, underlined and in quotation marks?

I was puzzled. Somehow I wasn't feeling like I'd won this appeal.

I reread it a third time and then kept going. Anxiety turned to anger and raced on to disbelief.

"If the defendant," the court concluded, "had a bona fide reasonable *belief,* based upon 'all of the circumstances present,' that the prosecutrix voluntarily consented, the defendant must be acquitted of forcible rape irrespective of how reasonable an expert views the victim's resistance under the circumstances. . . . Evidence that an expert was of the opinion the prosecutrix's resistance was reasonable under the circumstances is irrelevant to the issue of *Harter's bona fide belief."*

Not since Philosophy Ia in college had I seen such a good example of Socratic trickery.

This logic was simply not valid. Virtually *all* relevant evidence is admissible in a case. Nowhere is it written that it has to be relevant only to the end or ultimate question, which in this case the appellate court had apparently decided was Harter's reasonable belief as to Sandy's consent. It need only be relevant to proving or disproving something which naturally or logically would aid the trier of fact, the jury, in answering that ultimate question.

In Sandy's case I had used the expert to help prove an element of the offense—that the victim resisted in a particular way and ceased resisting for specific reasons. Proof of this, and every element of the crime, was absolutely essential before the burden ever shifted, or any defense, consent or otherwise, need be raised. The appellate court didn't acknowledge a distinction between the two—resistance and consent—but there was one, and the jury had seen it.

Jurors had first been asked to examine the question of resistance in light of certain realistic standards (Anne's testimony), not by applying misconceptions so long associated with the stigma of rape. Failure to provide these standards weighed heavily against a rape victim, and in favor of a defendant, when next the jury turned to assess what made him think she had consented. If jurors first examined victim resistance from the proper perspective, the prosecution's burden would be met, the victim's credibility given a fair hearing (no matter what the jury's conclusion about this credibility might ultimately be), and they could then move on to determine consent based solely on *his* credibility and uninfluenced by the carryover effect of faulty conclusions about hers.

I was totally perplexed by this time. Affirmed? Was I reading this all wrong in my excitement?

"Okay, so read the whole thing before you jump to conclusions," I ordered myself nervously. I could see only two more paragraphs before a large "II" announced the next question on appeal and I could see by scanning it between sentences that it had something to do with jury instructions.

"Although the admitted evidence was irrelevant," the opinion continued, "this reviewing court must next inquire whether 'after an examination of the entire cause, including the evidence, it is of the opinion that it is reasonably probable that a result more favorable to the appealing party would have been reached in the absence of the error . . .' "

Error? God, it struck with the same force as hearing words like "audit" and "taxes."

So all my work, all the effort, all I knew so surely was right had been reduced here to "irrelevant error" and with such haste, so unceremoniously. But they were not finished.

The discussion concluded with the opinion that the expert's testimony had no "probative value" nor did it "disturb the jury's evaluation process." By implication this meant the testimony was so worthless that its overall effect was nonexistent and therefore, the court concluded, any "error" was harmless. This alone saved the case from being reversed.

It came as no surprise, of course, when a month later the Albert Drake case *was* reversed. I knew it to be inevitable from the moment I finished reading the court's opinion in *Harter*. How much clearer could it be that the expert alone turned the tables for Stacy when the first trial had ended in a dead heat and the second had resulted in a swift conviction?

I was sickened, too angry to cry, too numb to move. I finished reading, every word, all twelve pages. Ironically, and under other circumstances I would have been more appreciative, the opinion's final paragraph exonerated me from any lingering doubts anyone may have still harbored about my faith in Sandy.

". . . on this factual record of manifest guilt, error of such dimension [referring to something other than the expert testimony] does not warrant reversal."

So the appellate court had seen the case as being so strong, showing Harter's "manifest guilt" so clearly, that just about nothing would have resulted in reversible error—just about nothing could have altered the jury's decision to convict.

What the appellate court would never know is that I had made the case strong because of the *way* I had "packaged" and "marketed" it. I had read the reports and put them together in such a way that the facts now seemed to point, as the court described it, to "manifest guilt."

In reading the "package" I had given to them and finding my expert evidence "irrelevant error," the appellate court was simply repeating the same mistake that the jury would have made without that very evidence. I had injected a new perspective which, because of centuries of law designed by and for men, was invisible to legal analysis.

Six months later the opinion in the O'Conner case came down. The holding was identical to *Harter*, as was the reasoning, as were the three deciding justices.

In part it read:

> How these interesting observations and experiences of the officer would tend to prove or disprove there was forcible rape of Terri R. is not clear. The rape of Terri is not to be determined by statistics or by a popular survey of what victims in other rape scenes do or do not do. . . .
>
> The conclusion that the "educational" testimony admitted is not relevant to any issue in the case determines its inadmissibility but not whether it caused reversible error.
>
> After an examination of the entire cause, including the improperly admitted evidence, this reviewing court concludes it is not reasonably probable that a result more favorable to O'Conner would have been reached in the absence of the erroneously admitted evidence [citations]. Implicit in this determination is not only the strong evidence of a forcible rape, including O'Conner's admissions to witness Sheppard and Officer Sografo, but also that the erroneously admitted testimony has no credible value. It is not of such nature that its admission would cause an unfavorable tilt in the jury's evaluative processes.
>
> Because of its inherent weaknesses as probative testimony on any issue in this case, it is difficult to find prejudice or a misleading of the jury.

Well, they had again bought my package: so well, in fact, that the opinion was written as if there had never been any doubt that Terri had been a rape victim:

> The prosecution underestimates the perceptive abilities, the depth of knowledge and just the plain common sense understanding of human nature that is to be found in 12 jurors.
>
> There is no need for an "expert" opinion as to why a rape victim would seek to cleanse her offended body and soul. The belief in psychological, physical cleansing power of water is deeply embedded in both the Eastern

and Western psyche. To require an "expert" to explain to 12 adult jurors that a rape victim is humiliated, confused, in perhaps mortal fear and for these or other equally valid reasons that appear factually in evidence of rape, might not immediately flee into the street crying rape, demonstrates a profound mistrust of jurors.

How I wanted to rejoice in the knowledge I had handled the case so convincingly! But my distress with the court's inability to exhibit even a fundamental understanding of my approach was sufficient to make this victory a hollow one at best. I had indeed won the battle and lost the war.

Inside, I felt drained, fatigued. Outwardly, I was still hosting a full round of activities as a result of the considerable interest my controversial cases had generated. And for reasons I will never be able to explain, I kept looking for a new way to make my idea work.

Quite aside from my setbacks with the court of appeals, I knew that the next time I found a case ripe for an expert's testimony, I would need a new theory: a movement was afoot in California to delete the requirement of resistance from the definition of rape. Inside sources felt that the success of the movement was only a matter of time, and indeed, following a long and exhausting battle by women in the mental health, legal, and political arenas, the legislature did, in fact, make this change, which became effective on January 1, 1981. The new law made consent, or the lack of consent, the only issue for the jury to determine concerning victim behavior, shifting the focus from victim to defendant, where it properly belonged.

At least on paper the burden would shift. It would be a good step forward, but experience cautioned against too much optimism.

As never before, I was plagued by thoughts about that jury instruction which had haunted me so persistently since the first time I had read it in 1976:

CALJIC 10.23

RAPE—BELIEF AS TO CONSENT

It is a defense to a charge of forcible rape that the defendant entertained a reasonable and good faith belief that the female person voluntarily consented to engage in sexual intercourse. If from all the evidence you have a reasonable doubt whether the defendant reasonably and in good faith believed she voluntarily consented to engage in sexual intercourse, you must give the defendant the benefit of that doubt and acquit him of said charge.

This instruction had created a new, and complete, defense to the charge of rape in the state of California. It had slipped into acceptance so quietly, and now I was beginning to understand why. Like reasons for the use of an expert, the insidious implications of this required directive are invisible to analysis by a legal system so infused with the principles of the equality of *men*. Laudable are the built-in protections designed to give the individually accused parity with the powers of enforcement. Unseen and vulnerable, however, are the women and children in this scheme of things when legal principles crash head on into social and cultural biases. Nowhere is this more evident than during the trial of a rape case.

It had already happened to Stacy, and had come dangerously close to Terri and Sandy. And I was only one prosecutor in one city.

The appellate court rulings in *Harter* and *O'Conner* made it clear that this 10.23 Consent Defense had to be reckoned with. Short of getting it repealed, a task to which I fully intended to devote great quantities of my time in the future, I needed to find out where it had come from, just what kind of a case had warranted such a finding, and how it had risen to the status of an instruction without which a jury's verdict of guilt would automatically be reversed.

Back I went to my "Expert Testimony—Rape" file. By now it held reprints, clippings, case notes, and other assorted information, only a part of which I had been able to find the time to read. I was looking for an article I remembered getting from a professor at the University of Minnesota who was doing research on evidence problems in rape cases. We had been talking about 10.23 in one of our phone conversations when he had mentioned something about its having come from an English case decided the same year that California's new instruction 10.23 was introduced.

It was a long article and took three full readings before I was able to understand everything it said. Once I did, I was dumbstruck. It was a bigger monster than I had realized, not only because of specific abuse in its application to the California case, but because of total misuse at its origin.

I discovered that California, alone in the fifty states, has taken the position that among a defendant's rights to a fair trial when accused of rape is an absolute defense to the charge that he held a reasonable but *mistaken* belief as to consent. A jury must specifically reject this defense before convicting. In other words, guilt does not rest on the convincing force of the evidence to support a jury finding that a victim had clearly not *given* her consent. Rather, guilt turns upon an examination of the evidence a defendant claims made him think, be it mistakenly, that he had been given consent.

If a doubt is raised in the minds of the jurors (it only takes one to hang it) that the defendant thought, although mistakenly, he had consent, a jury must acquit him. Granted, his belief and the doubt raised must be reasonable ones by certain legal standards. But this requires the victim to *prove* lack of consent beyond a reasonable doubt in the face of overwhelming stereotypes and myths surrounding her behavior, while leaving the defendant to merely *raise* a reasonable mistaken doubt.

I do not contend that the prosecution should be relieved of its burden to prove the defendant guilty of a crime beyond a reasonable doubt. What I am against is a situation which requires acquittal even after this burden has been met, and this proof has been made, because the ultimate decision is based on the defendant's mistake. Such is the law, and the rape victim's plight, in California.

That the mistake must be reasonable, not unreasonable, and in this protection justice shall prevail, is an argument born of the same system before which distinctions of far less fine a line remain invisible to understanding. If the courts and juries confuse consent and resistance, how can they possibly be expected to discern the differences, if any really exist, between "reasonable" and "unreasonable" mistakes about consent? The answer is, simply, they cannot.

To know what happened in *People* v. *Mayberry,* the California case which created this defense, and in *Morgan,* the English case decision upon which *Mayberry* was no doubt based, is to be convinced that they cannot.

The summary of the facts of *Mayberry* that I use here are contained in the Memorandum of Points and Authorities in Opposition to Defendant's Motion to Dismiss which was prepared at the time the case was tried.

On July 8, 1971, at 4:00 P.M. the victim, Nancy B., was stopped by the Defendant, Franklin Mayberry, as she walked to the store. The Defendant grabbed her arm, and she struggled to be released. The Defendant swore at her, tried to hit her in the face with his fist, kicked her, and struck her in the stomach with a bottle.

The victim told the Defendant to leave her alone and continued to the store. She bought a newspaper at a liquor store and then entered the Safeway store. The Defendant suddenly accosted her again in one of the back aisles of the Safeway store. The Defendant told her to come outside and, seeing no security guard, the victim followed his directive. Once outside the Defendant verbally abused her and struck her with his fist in the neck region. The blow knocked Miss B. to the pavement. The Defendant then told her he wanted to have intercourse and she had no choice but to comply or there would be great violence. The victim tried to dissuade the Defendant but was unsuccessful. She decided to accompany him, feeling that perhaps a police car would pass or in some other manner she might prevent the Defendant's assault. The Defendant walked her to his residence on 7th Avenue. Once in the home, the Defendant removed his and the victim's clothing. The Defendant grabbed the victim by the hair and forced her mouth over his penis. He made her orally copulate him for about 30 minutes. The Defendant then engaged her in sexual intercourse. This lasted for a protracted period of time. While engaged in the act, the Defendant struck the victim. He banged her head against the wall and forced her head under her body, almost dislocating her neck.

The co-defendant, Booker Mayberry, began to pound on the door about this time. When the Defendant, Franklin Mayberry, did not open the door, his brother Booker broke it down. The victim was able to dress while Franklin was distracted. The brothers engaged in an argument, during which period of time Booker kept repeating that he also wanted intercourse with the victim. Booker struck the victim in the face with his fist. He also kicked her in the legs. He threw her on the bed numerous times. He choked her and when she tried to kick him he started to beat her in the face. She fell to the floor but was able to escape when the brothers began to fight . . .

There was no evidence to suggest the victim had ever known the defendant before the day of the attack, and considerable evidence to support physical injuries, including a medical exam and three witnesses.

The victim reported the attack immediately after her escape and admitted she had not tried to tell anyone of what was happening, either while in the store or on the walk to the defendant's apartment before the attack, for the reasons she had given.

The defendant claimed consent and denied both the victim's unwillingness to go with him and the use of threats of force.

While admitting that the jury had not found consent in this particular case, a unanimous California Supreme Court declared that not to be enough; additionally, the accused must be afforded the opportunity to offer, and the jury the chance to specifically reject, a defense based on a mistaken belief in consent. Among other things, the court stated:

> We by no means intimate that such is the only reasonable interpretation of the conduct, but we do conclude that there was some evidence "deserving of . . . consideration" which supported his contention that he acted under a mistake of fact as to her consent both to the movement and the intercourse.

From the decision in the *Mayberry* case, a committee of attorneys from the California State Bar fashioned a jury instruction on their reading of the case, and the new legal directive they saw in it. And that was the beginning of California Jury Instruction (known as CALJIC) 10.23.

I'd found the author of this marvelous article, Leigh Bienen, a master of understatement when he observed that "the court expanded the consent defense in rape on a set of facts which seemed to preclude the finding of consent." The court then reversed the conviction, and now in California, Bienen concluded, "even when force, injury, and the relationship of the parties established there was no consent, the prosecution must anticipate a defense based upon a reasonable but mistaken belief in consent. Such a defense focuses the trial upon interpretations of the behavior of the victim instead of the accused."

Bienen went on to observe that *Mayberry* had attracted very little public commentary in spite of its potentially alarming impact. I was gratified to know that I had not been the only one to see the danger; nor the only one to wonder if this was perhaps the system's way of attempting to "rebalance the equities," since the very same court earlier in the very same year had overturned the use of the age-old cautionary instruction.

The cautionary instruction had long put the testimony of a rape victim to a special test by telling the jury that the charge of rape was easy to make and, once made, difficult to defend against, so that they should view the story of the prosecutrix with caution.

The California Supreme Court had also recently removed from the defense arsenal the right to wave evidence of a victim's prior sexual history in front of a jury to support the unfounded assumption that once a woman has engaged in consensual intercourse the probabilities favored consensual intercourse ever after.

Since some form or combination of the cautionary instruction and prior sexual history evidence are allowed in the majority of states, an assumption can be made that the California Supreme Court felt compelled to give something "back" to the defense in return for what it had taken away. What they gave back was Caljic 10.23.

It is sad to realize that such reasoning as used by the California Supreme Court, and others as well, belies the legal system's true motives for much of what appears to be rape reform. It is a reluctance reserved only for crimes whose primary victims are women and girls, since the only other mistake-of-fact defenses allowed anywhere in the American criminal justice system are to charges of bigamy or statutory rape.

The English case from which *Mayberry* seemed to have been cut had gone a step further than the California Supreme Court. The *Morgan* case made it a defense to rape if the accused held a mistaken and *un*reasonable belief that the woman had consented! In *Morgan* a husband told three strangers he met in a pub that his wife enjoyed sex with men she did not know who broke into their house. He then encouraged them to find out, telling them his wife would feign non-consent, but liked this game as a prelude to lovemaking. When the three followed through and were convicted of rape, they appealed on the claim they had relied on a mistaken, albeit unreasonable, belief as to consent which should have constituted a defense. The highest court of appeal in Britain agreed. This was in April 1975, just a decade ago—and the same year in which *Mayberry* was decided.

Unlike the *Mayberry* decision, which went virtually unnoticed in the United States, even after the jury instruction was created, *Morgan* prompted such an outcry from the British people that major reform legislation was quickly passed, including the repeal of this defense, the guarantee of victim anonymity, the use of prior felony convictions suffered by a defendant if his chief defensive tool was an attack on victim credibility, and severe limitations on the use of a victim's prior sexual history. Rape is now defined in England as "unlawful sexual intercourse with a woman who at the time of intercourse does not consent, the man knowing she does not consent or being reckless as to whether she does. The presence or absence of reasonable grounds for this belief that the woman was consenting may be taken into account in considering whether he so believed." Thus, the unreasonableness of the belief will go to the honest, bona fide, and genuine nature of the belief, that is, to the defendant's credibility.

It is truly ironic, as Bienen notes, that while *Morgan* had been found so offensive and had occasioned far-reaching reform at home, it served as precedent for a case which was hardly noticed in California. Further, he suggests, *Mayberry* concealed the substantial harm it harbors by including the word "reasonable" as a qualifier, thereby lulling us into a false sense of security.

Not even from a first reading had I been fooled. I felt better knowing I was on the right track. And understanding *Mayberry*'s origins gave me the focal point in the search for a new approach to expert testimony.

Victim credibility is even more critical, if that is possible, to the prosecution of a rape case in the face of a defense of mistaken belief as to consent, because on the difference between what is a reasonable and an unreasonable mistake—that razor-thin, subjectively drawn line—may lie the pivotal key to a conviction or an acquittal. The jury most likely will have to make its decision based on credibility, that is, on which differences of fact to believe. Under such circumstances, expert testimony to support the victim cannot be irrelevant and without probative value.

My skills of legal analysis had matured by leaps and bounds from the days I had first conceived of resistance-relevant testimony and crafted Anne Kennedy into my expert to deliver the message to the jury. This was no simple sport I had taken up. There were rules and regulations to follow. If I broke the rules, I'd be out, but if I used them properly and they allowed me room to run, I just might make it. I couldn't mow down the baseman on my way to second, but I could sure steal the base if I did it at the right time. No more psychological game playing, as my article for the California District Attorneys' Association had suggested: use resistance as an excuse to get in expert testimony while its real purpose was a psychological one to challenge defense credibility in the jurors' minds. No more tricks; up front, I wanted expert testimony to support victim credibility.

Now I needed the case—and, as usual, the time to try it.

12

POWER IN A CORPORATION, I learned, flows along the windows and from corner to corner. In other words, executives are likely to have window offices and officers corner ones. When I apply this to the District Attorney, which certainly ranks as San Diego's largest legal corporation, I realize the accuracy of this observation: windows are coveted, corners rarely available.

Sometime in mid-1979 I was awarded a window. I assumed it was in acknowledgment of my work, seniority, acceptance, or maybe even as compensation for having spent the previous two years sharing a cramped, one-person inner office with a representative from the Attorney General's staff, whose six-month rotational term meant I had shown the ropes to at least four of them during that time. Anyway, with the addition of sunlight my natural color returned, I no longer read reports by fluorescence, and I could keep up with the comings and goings of planes, cruise ships, and fire engines.

There were rumblings that I might be promoted, which would make me the first woman to reach the administrative level in the San Diego County District Attorney's office. My grapevine reported strong feelings for and against such a move.

During the winter of 1979 I spent considerable time sitting at the feet of local political and legal gurus who supported my bid for an appointment as a Municipal Court judge. I was a complete novice to the world of politics and had much to learn. By early spring of 1980 my name had "come down," as we call it, from the governor's office for consideration.

On the crest of what appeared to be attainment of one or the other of the only two goals I had set for myself as my legal career matured, I was feeling better than ever before about my "place" in the criminal justice plan.

Either a promotion or an appointment to the Bench would reflect a supportive nod from the office. The first could mean a step closer to having a specialized unit handling sexual assault, domestic violence, and child abuse cases. The other, a vote of confidence in my loyalty and ability, both of which I had worked hard to prove.

I spent as little time as possible wondering what I might do if neither a promotion nor a judgeship was in my future. But I did think about it enough to know what failure to achieve one or the other would mean to my future as a prosecutor. While only the promotion was entirely within the office's control, the other was unattainable without my superiors' support. I'd been working among them for seven years and the time had come to see where I stood. I confided to a select few that if I was neither promoted nor appointed, I would probably leave the office. I tried to come up with a different solution whenever I could not force the subject from my thoughts, but none made sense.

There was little time, fortunately, to accommodate these darker concerns, and I realized in those months that I could never hope to be more satisfied in my work than I was right then. Looking back at my calendars (I saved them all for some reason), I can remember how good it felt to be on the leading edge of new fields. Although the subjects were grim, I took some measure of comfort in each hopeful resolution, and counted success in terms of future detection, prevention, and solutions, as well as convictions.

I argued that treatment for child molesters and spouse abusers was compatible with the goals of our assignment as public guardians, and that acknowledging these concepts was not tantamount to condonation.

I considered the need for simultaneous civil and criminal proceedings to solve the whole problem instead of treating it piecemeal, as with a battered woman in the process of divorce or the family with a sexually abused child in need of money compensation for counseling. When I rejected a rape case, or heard of one that had been rejected, I mentioned the possibility of a civil suit whenever I thought it was appropriate.

Within one three-month period, a nurse, a housewife, and a teenager were all rape victims in cases which, for one reason or another, did not enter the criminal justice system. In each case the attackers, a salesman for a name-brand vacuum cleaner company, a cable TV installer, and a delivery boy, respectively, were identified. All had jobs which gained them access to homes and neighborhoods under circumstances which left unsuspecting women and children easy prey to their attacks. Just as landlords owe tenants good security, business owners owe customers care in selecting those whom they send to do their bidding. I made these observations known and when two of the three cases resulted in civil settlements for the victims I was thrilled.

With child abuse homicide cases I was particularly resolute. Sometimes this determination was mistaken for that worst of all afflictions to befall a prosecutor, personal involvement. What I really accomplished for these victims was a balancing of the legal scales: since proving the crimes against them was so much more difficult, I had to put that much more effort into it. When a criminal cause of death could not be pinpointed, I decided to come at it from the other end: I succeeded in listing, and then eliminating, any and all other possible or probable legitimate causes of death, leaving as the only choice the defendant and his criminal act or omission. This took time, often occupying me for weeks before I walked into the courtroom, and for days after, once I got there.

Ideas came tumbling out during that time and I enjoyed filtering them through the clinical "laboratory" my job provided. I knew the "faculty" was somewhat hesitant about my "experiments," and I made every effort to keep the avenues of communication clear. It seemed, however, that these avenues always got a bit too crowded.

To be precise, it was the local press in our path which caused the congestion. The cases I handled, by their very nature, attracted attention, and once I started using my new ideas in court, reporters were often around.

I'd always *felt* I was speaking as a part of the District Attorney's team, but I often found out later that what I'd said was not what was heard, sometimes by the reporters, other times by the office. I had reached the point where my hands shook while I raced through a new article in the morning paper looking for something gone wrong, misquoted, left out, or overstated. Certainly, I liked being the one doing whatever it was they wanted to write about, but only in context with my job, and the office I represented, was it important.

When the promotions list came out, I was not on it. Of greater significance was Susan Christianson's transfer from felony trials to division supervisor. It was the first such assignment the office had ever given to a woman, and as with men before her in similar positions, it could be considered the first step up the management ladder.

As I was her predecessor by nearly three years, this double blow hit me very hard.

As in the grieving process, my emotions shifted daily. Disappointment, anger, hurt, frustration, but never, never resignation—either from the job or to some as yet undefined fate.

I threw myself into the political swirl and concentrated on a judicial appointment. I could accept the gap between us preventing a full partnership from flourishing, but I did not foresee a similar problem with the office in my bid for the Bench: as a *former* prosecutor I would be out from under foot, and as a former *prosecutor* I would bring to the Bench a set of legal experiences compatible with their own.

It was difficult to concentrate on work as I sweated out the background investigation undergone by all prospective judicial appointees. Questionnaires from judges, defense attorneys, and other prosecutors were being returned bearing their senders' conclusions on a wide assortment of personal qualifications, all really boiling down to two main things: legal experience and judicial temperament. The first was not a concern to me. The second was.

As the weeks passed and the final phase, a personal interview, drew near, a distant alarm sounded the approach of impending danger.

At first one always hopes the apprehension is merely envisioned and nothing more than anxious folly. But when uneasiness persists, as does the alarm, disquiet turns to dread and the peril can no longer be dismissed.

My early warnings came in the form of reminders of what had happened the first time I had sought an appointment to the Bench some three years before. I'd been considered too feminist, too controversial, not a "team player," too outspoken. Serious efforts on my behalf had failed to rally enough support, particularly from the District Attorney's office. Looking back, it was clear that I had not done much to cultivate that support. In fact, if anything, "antagonized" would probably be an apt description of the office's sentiment about me at the time.

Only months before my quest for the appointment that first time, an interview describing my feelings as a woman in the District Attorney's office appeared in one of the small weekly papers in the city's suburbs.

To say front-office reaction was "intense" would be an understatement. I felt discriminated against both in my assignments and in my treatment, and had said so. While today I can remember how angry and upset I felt when I said it, there is no doubt I would not have done it, as they say, if I had known then what I know now.

I realized it would take time to repair the damage, and was mindful of this episode when that promotion list came out. But three years of hard work had to have made a significant contribution to cementing some major cracks.

Word that the wounds were still open in some influential minds was my first, but by no means only, harbinger. There existed a significant number among the defense bar who feared that I would be a castrating judge, that I hated men and was in pursuit of a cause which would prevent me from remaining impartial.

I was powerless to combat these accusations. As a prosecutor, I had to represent the position of my office in public, although they frequently felt I did not. That I was in favor of diversion for batterers, treatment for molesters, training for defense lawyers to successfully defend their clients accused of murdering their husbands—all were beliefs I was not free to express.

Coupled with what I could not say was what I did say about rape and rapists. Taken together, conclusions were drawn about me that I was unsympathetic at best and lacked judicial temperament at worst, and it was the worst time for these misconceptions about my true attitudes to be broadcast by others.

Anger is primarily a disguise useful only when more relevant emotions fail us. Panic was the overriding emotion which swept past all the others that day. Unlike anger, which often lets us off too easily by consuming all other emotions, panic serves as a catalyst to open up a wide range of other emotions, all of which can survive simultaneously. In my case, among these reactions were fear that I might actually have to leave the office, depression over the prospect that, worse yet, I might have to stay because I wouldn't know what to do if I left, or frustration because I couldn't leave for financial reasons.

My personal interview was much as I'd expected, with heavy emphasis on judicial temperament. I left knowing I had not satisfied the concern which had been raised by the investigation. Three weeks later, a late-night phone call from one of my Sacramento contacts made it official: I had been found not qualified to sit as a Municipal Court judge.

That night anger consumed me, drowning out all other sensibilities under its weight. Anger and tears. My husband and I discussed how soon I could leave the office and decided it couldn't be yet. Going to work the next morning was probably the hardest part of all. The elevator, the hallways, the offices, all those intimately familiar places seemed so ambiguous and distant. I looked the same, everyone looked the same; but things would never *be* the same.

I made myself all sorts of promises. As long as I had to stay, I would, but I'd refuse any requests to take on extra assignments, I'd investigate my cases adequately but put in no overtime on either trial preparation or witness interviews, I'd decline to speak to community groups, and I'd be out the door at 5 P.M. Most of all, I'd object to handling any rape cases.

I don't remember how much time passed before I broke the first of these pledges, but within two months all but one had evaporated—and it was about to go. I was relieved that a level of apparent normalcy was reached without exacting yet another stiff emotional toll.

I was daydreaming, surveying the blend of diverse activities taking place on the other side of my window and, as I often did, thinking how I could see them all but they were oblivious to me and to each other. There were people on that plane settling on the runway, and others waiting for them inside the terminal. I could see the prisoners on this afternoon's calendar being unloaded seven floors below at the custody entrance to the courthouse; and slipping away at the far end of the harbor now was a carrier whose occupants didn't even know about the passengers or the prisoners—but I could see it all at once . . .

"Got a minute?" he began with the familiar chorus.

I welcomed this intrusion even less now than I had in the past, and I flashed him a quick look of irritation.

"Why, what is it?" I almost snapped in exasperation.

"Well, I've got a problem with this case. It's been around a while and now . . ."

"Whoa, Kent, whoa." I would be firm. "Before you get into this, I want you to know I don't have a lot of time, so try to ask what you need and get right to the point."

He was already on his way to a chair.

"Okay, I promise, only a couple of minutes. No more." He looked contrite and didn't sit.

"I assume it's a rape case?" I asked the question more for the information than out of curiosity.

"Yeah, it's a rape all right. A cop. Well, she wasn't a cop at the time, but she started at the academy right afterwards and is a rookie now. But she's really getting weird and I don't know if I can believe her anymore."

Kent Charles stood staring at me now like a kid who'd just turned around for a minute and when he looked back, whatever it was that had been there was gone. Actually, he always looked like a kid, with his baby face, short-cropped blond hair, and oversized glasses. Now he looked like a desperate kid.

I wasn't sure I'd heard him right.

"You mean she's become a police officer *since* the rape?" I asked.

"Yep, since the rape. But I don't think she's doing so well. The defense has subpoenaed all her records. The department keeps progress notes, reports, or something in the academy while they're rookies. Apparently she had some 'attitude adjustment' problems, whatever the hell that means. Anyway . . ."

"Well, how's all this relevant to the case?" I interrupted. I was slightly impatient with Kent, but mildly indignant about the subpoena too.

"I don't know yet." He shrugged. "But that's only one—I should say the newest—problem. Trial was set for May 8 and we were trailing till the sixteenth, but then sometime before that date she goes to New York."

"You mean she's gone?" I was getting confused in addition to impatient.

"No, I don't think so. The P.D. said it was a family emergency and told her to call me. She just did and says she doesn't know how long it will be before she can come back."

"Why?"

"It was a fatal accident—her brother or brother-in-law got killed. But even if she does come back, I don't know what kind of a witness she's going to make. I mean, she sounded real shaky even on the phone."

"Well, has she . . . sit *down* Kent, sit down . . ." I motioned him hurriedly to a chair, realizing it would no doubt be a mistake. "Has she been 'weird' all along or has she changed from right after the rape? When was the rape, by the way?"

"May of last year," he answered matter-of-factly.

"May of *last* year?" I repeated the words incredulously. "You mean the rape was nearly thirteen months ago and you're just getting around to trial? Why? What happened?"

"Mainly because of this police academy thing." His expression had taken on a slightly defensive air and he fidgeted in the chair. "Every time the T.D. would get close she'd beg me to be careful not to tell anyone at the academy why I was calling her, or try not to need her on certain days because she couldn't miss a particular class, or . . ."

"How many times *has* the case come up for trial?" I was meeting his defensive reaction with equally firm stares.

"Six. I counted this morning. She's got to stop stalling, or forget it."

"Six times!" I was disbelieving. "Six times you've been ready for trial and it still hasn't gone out because your victim wasn't ready?"

"More or less, yes."

"Then you should have already dismissed it if she's that unwilling to go to court and if you think it's getting worse."

"It isn't that she's unwilling . . . it's really the opposite—she's insisting we go to court and saying I'm the one who wants it dismissed."

"Oh . . . I see." I was beginning to see. "And are you the one who's dragging?"

"No, really it's her . . . mostly . . . until now. Now I'm not sure, like I said."

"Okay, Kent." I realized we weren't getting anywhere. "What exactly do you want from me?"

"Well, I know you took over a case from Jim Cross once when he and his victim weren't making it . . ."

"Oh, no"—I was shaking my head—"no way, Kent. That was different and . . . no, no way, sorry. You can ask me something specific and I'll try to give you an answer or recommendation, but no way will I take over."

I was emphatic. My eyes met his with cold resolution.

"Okay, Judy, okay. I thought I'd see." He was looking contrite again. "But you will help me out if something comes up, huh?"

"I'll try. No promises. That depends on what you mean by 'if something comes up.' I won't, I repeat, *won't* take over the case. You have to decide all by yourself, or between you and Daly, if it ought to be dismissed—and you can go back and tell him that."

I was proud of the way I was handling this. The key was not to know enough to want to know more. The need-to-know theory worked.

"Daly didn't send me, really, I just thought you might be interested . . ."

"Sorry, no." I smiled politely and shook my head. "Bye now," I encouraged. And to end on a light note: *"Do* come again . . ."

I delivered a sweeping gesture with my arm toward the door as he left.

Jim Cross had been gone just about a year now. I couldn't recall if Kent had been in felony trials back then, but even if he had, the chances of his remembering that I had taken over the case were slight. Besides, our cases could not be swapped back and forth like marbles and trading cards when we had too many of one kind or got tired of another.

I went back to the window. This time I examined the cluster of buildings which passed for San Diego skyscrapers. I wondered if I'd be out there soon, maybe looking over at the courthouse from a new office. But out there doing . . . what?

13

E X C E P T   F O R the pall of uncertainty, May came and went as May was supposed to. And June seemed to start out on a less demanding note; or maybe it was I who was less demanding. I had things other than cases on my mind.

In anticipation of leaving the office, I did more than just window-gaze. I knew I needed a way to keep up with the goings-on in the legal world once I was on the outside, especially if there was a gap between my leaving the office and finding another job.

I ran for a position on the board of directors of Lawyers Club of San Diego.

Lawyers Club had been formed in the early 1970s by women in the legal profession for the express purpose of addressing women's issues in their field, and in particular for promoting the passage of the equal rights amendment. But membership was not, and had never been, limited to women. We had been farsighted enough, even in the early 1970s, to realize that the exclusion of men was a perpetuation, only in reverse, of a concept we objected to in male-dominated organizations. On the more practical side, we knew we needed them to teach us the ropes.

I had been a "founding mother," as they called us, of Lawyers Club and had served briefly on the board in the mid-1970s. I'd resigned when I had been transferred, approximately two months after my election, to the northern part of the county and had found it extremely difficult to make it downtown for board meetings twice a month.

Many of my closest friends, those with whom I shared the growing pains of breaking new ground in the legal profession, had served on the board of Lawyers Club. The feeling of many was that the presidency of Lawyers Club provided a boost toward the Bench for a woman in San Diego, and for those who did not aspire to the judiciary, partnership in major firms or executive-level management positions seemed to come sooner to the organization's past officers.

What was more encouraging was that we appeared to have learned our lessons well from our male counterparts. During the four years before I ran for the board, there was a tremendous increase in the number of men seeking appointment to the Bench and other elective offices who joined just in time to garner support from Lawyers Club. This is not to imply that there aren't many dedicated men in the organization who belong because they believe in its purpose, but rather that we had become a force to be reckoned with. We had also learned that, while support from Lawyers Club carries weight, being identified as an active member is still undesirable for some purposes and at certain times. At least now we knew what and when.

I was one of four new members elected in 1980 and I immediately set about catching up on what had been happening during the last few years outside of my former safe haven in the halls of justice. Initially conversations often left me puzzled, since it was assumed everyone knew where the last episode in any story had left off. I hadn't realized how insulated I had become by working with the District Attorney.

A new generation of young women had joined up and I was amazed at how many of them there were. Amazed and impressed. Soon I began experiencing something I had previously only heard about: women who knew the rules of the corporate game and could play a pretty decent match. It did not take me long to feel at home.

I realized that, while I'd been around for its infancy, I'd been away for a number of the growing years and was returning to find the organization well past adolescence. I also recognized that I could not simply make a lateral transfer of "gamesmanship" know-how, because as a member of a neophyte class (women in a profession), I had remained just as isolated from the corporate mainstream inside the office as I had been isolated from its progress on the outside.

Within a month of my election to the board I was approached about teaching a course at one of the local law schools. New horizons began to appear. Up to this point in my legal career, it had not occurred to me that perhaps I knew something that others would benefit from learning. Most of the comments made throughout this book about the criminal justice system's rank and file needing to know more about the kind of work I was doing, were fleeting thoughts at the time I was actually in the midst of the fray. The rest has been a good deal of editorializing. It was only when I began to touch bases with sources outside the system that I began to see that my knowledge had its own "comparable worth." That it wasn't just a "feminist issue," or a "woman's issue," but rather a legal concern deserving the same attention accorded any new field of law, such as outer space, computers, or organized crime.

Now, teaching had never held even a remote interest for me in the past. I have enough trouble getting through homework at night with my two children. But the course that had been suggested to me was part of the law school's Women's Law Institute and I had been given free rein in putting it together, so long as its focus was on women.

I came up with a course entitled "Women in the Criminal Justice System," which would have speakers covering different themes each one of its seven weeks on subjects ranging from the roles of women who worked in the system (judge, attorney) and the special problems of women handled by the system (adult and juvenile offenders) to crimes affecting primarily women and girls (domestic violence, child abuse, sexual assault) and even discussions about offenses which are committed almost exclusively by women (prostitution, welfare fraud).

I wanted it to be a practical class combining an overview of the concerns of and for women in the criminal justice system with an introduction to community resources trying to deal with these concerns. Most of the graduates from this particular law school would be practicing locally and, I figured, should have an idea of what was out there.

Ideally I wanted to spark some interest in new legal issues for these future lawyers—specifically to nudge some toward helping other women and children, who, for centuries, have been dealing with a system designed to accommodate, treat, and understand men, whether working for it or being handled by it.

Back at my window one mid-June morning, reflections about life after leaving the District Attorney's office were becoming less ominous. Not easy to picture, but not altogether as frightening as it had been. It still didn't seem real, but I knew it was a matter of time—and money.

I supposed I should not have been surprised to see Kent Charles drift in and rest as much of himself as he could fit on the one unoccupied corner of my desk.

"I see you enjoy the view." His small talk was unconvincing. No doubt he figured I had lots of spare time to daydream since he always seemed to catch me doing it. This thought irritated me.

"To what do I owe the honor of this visit?" I was exercising restraint, and my tone was only moderately sarcastic.

"Well, I'm here for some help." He slapped his right hand down on my desk for emphasis.

"With . . . ?" I began the next sentence for him.

"With the Cole case, the one I talked to you about a few weeks ago, remember?"

"Oh, I remember. The victim-turned-police-officer case. Did she come back? If not, dismiss. See, wasn't that simple?" I was being glib. "Next problem."

His boyish face returned my feigned pleasure with no indication that he sensed the resentment smoldering so close to the surface.

"Actually it might be just that simple."

He paused to study my reaction.

I gave him none.

"Good. Thanks for telling me." I knew there was more. He was still poised on the corner of my desk.

"Except she did come back, and she still wants to go . . . but the P.D. has brought termination proceedings against her, and I may be called as a witness for the department."

"To say what?"

"It seems there was no emergency back home. She lied. While she was supposed to be grieving, a bunch of San Diego P.D.'s finest ran across her in Ensenada—with a guy." He was fiddling with a paper clip he'd picked off the desk, and being entirely too casual.

"So what can you say as a witness for the P.D.?"

"During that phone conversation with me she told me the same story—about the brother-in-law being killed and having to stay back East."

He saw the puzzled expression and anticipated my question.

"Oh, she went back East, but not for nearly a week after she told her lieutenant she was going. In fact, she had someone else call in for her to leave the original message."

"And there was no fatal accident?"

"No."

"My God, it sounds like you should dismiss this turkey. What other advice do you want—or need?"

Still he sat.

"I just came from Creelman's office. He agrees with me that there could be a conflict here for me and that I have to bow out."

"So dismiss it." I could see the punch line coming. There was nothing left.

"Well, the office wants this one treated with special care because she's a cop and the press is getting interested. She's fighting the termination and her lawyer is trying to stir up public support for her."

He stood up now.

"Creelman wants you to take it." He looked ready to run, like a child expecting a momentary whipping and watching for an opportunity to escape. If I hadn't been so furious I would have laughed.

"What do you mean he wants *me* to take it?" I was fuming. "Why me? Surely there's someone else capable of handling rape cases, even sensitive ones, besides me!"

I was nearly out the door. "I'll talk to him myself."

"Hold on, Judy." Kent touched my shoulder with his hand as I pushed by him. "Creelman figured you'd react like this, and he's not going to change his mind. But, he says, if after you've reviewed the file and talked to the victim, you think it should be dismissed, you have the authority to do it."

I stood staring at him, too outraged to reply, reduced to crude thoughts roaring through my head.

So it was the same old thing: get my blessing and then dump it.

"Okay," I said slowly, shaking my outstretched finger at him. "Okay, if that's what he wants, I'll read it first, talk to her, and get rid of it."

I sat down again and looked at him coldly.

"Where's the file? I want to write all this in the notes—now. I'm not even going to talk with Creelman, so you'd better be telling it like it is when you say I have authority to dismiss, because that's exactly what I'm going to do."

Damn them. Tears were so close I had to turn away. I pretended to look at my calendar.

"When's the trial, tomorrow?"

"July 16. Hey, this really isn't my fault, Judy. True, I don't want to try this case, but I didn't plan this."

I leaned back heavily in the chair. "Yeah, I know," I sighed. "It's not you." I had to calm down. "Please, get me the file," I repeated, more in control now.

"Sure. I'll have it back this afternoon and I'll leave it in your box. If you need anything, just ask."

He slid around the corner and I could hear his footsteps move quickly down the hall.

I reached for the phone.

I called my husband and told him I wanted to quit and then apologized for bothering him at the office. But I needed him to be thinking of every reason why I couldn't leave by the time I saw him that night, and they'd better be damned good reasons.

As I'd expected, they were, and then I cried. I warned him that the next time it wouldn't matter whether we could afford it or not.

The following day I called Jeremy Cole's attorney and informed him of the switch. I requested a continuance, which he agreed to without any argument, and trial was reset for shortly after Labor Day. I hadn't expected any trouble with a trial continuance. After all, he knew what was going on, and would like nothing better than to postpone his client's trial until after the victim's Police Department termination hearing.

Kent left the file in my box and I grabbed it along with the rest of my new assignments, dumping them on top of the "in" pile. I didn't touch it again until the first weekend in July. June was turning out to be as hassled as ever.

I put off tackling the file until the third and last afternoon of a beautiful, sun-drenched July 4 weekend, when I could think of no other way to give the defense attorney a decision by the next morning about what I was going to do with the Cole case.

As soon as I picked up the bulging brown envelope my mood darkened. The preliminary hearing transcript was heavy and in addition to it there were fifteen to twenty pages of police and follow-up reports to read and a tape recording to listen to.

A surge of resentment seized me. Except for direct confrontations like this, it was getting easier to keep that from happening as the days went on. I hated the knots of rage I could work into if I let myself, and I'd been intentionally sidestepping this job, knowing it would do this to me.

Even if I planned to get rid of this case, I had to read everything. Given my mood and what I already knew, there was little chance I would have any trouble justifying a dismissal. I'd certainly never tried harder from the outset to be so black about a case.

I organized all the reports in chronological order. First the one-page handwritten summary prepared by the beat officer sent to the scene.

"Officer Kelly and I responded to a 415 disturbance call . . . described also as an incomplete call for help."

Interesting, how a rape case can start out as a report of disturbing the peace. I wondered how that happened.

I didn't recognize the name of the officer at the bottom of the page. Probably new.

When they arrived they found the victim, Jill Bernadini, somewhat "disheveled and slightly disoriented," but insisting she didn't need assistance anymore since "her assailant had left." She wouldn't tell them anything, so after looking around and finding nothing extraordinary, they left.

They paused "outside the Bernadini door and as we did we heard Bernadini fall against the wall. We immediately re-entered the apartment and inquired about Bernadini's welfare." She continued to say she would be fine and they "again departed."

Hmm, she must have fainted and fallen, but where did they find her when they went back in? It struck me as worth putting in the report at least.

And the final paragraph.

"During the whole time we were with Bernadini she never indicated that she had been raped, or that she even needed our help."

Odd. It sounded almost defensive. I reread the last paragraph again. If they knew no more when they left than when they arrived, how come the report used words like "assailant" and "rape"?

I wondered how many times they'd had a woman faint and fall like this one who also appeared disheveled and disoriented. Did they ask if she wanted them to call someone for her, or take her somewhere? Did she look like she needed help? What did they ask to determine if she needed help? What had happened to her? Were they interested?

There was no follow-up report.

I asked all these rhetorical questions of myself in the time it took to read the report—maybe a minute and a half.

The neatly typed detective reports were twelve pages long. This time it wasn't Sografo. Too bad. I smiled to myself. He still wouldn't get a crack at being an expert. Even if I wanted to try the case.

"It's irrelevant evidence, you know," I said to no one except the dog lying at my feet.

Marge Lawrence hadn't been in sex crimes as long as Sografo, but she hadn't needed as much orientation time either. Her investigations were still a little rough around the edges, and she still needed to think through some of her answers on cross-examination just a little more carefully, but she was thorough.

Suspect: Jeremy Cole
            W/M 29
            6'3", 195 lbs. Brn/Blu

A big guy, this one. I searched the file for photos and found none.

"On May 10, 1979, the victim reported to the San Diego Police Department that she had been forcibly raped by the above-named suspect."

May 10, 1979!

"Today is July 6, 1980." I was scolding the dog again. "That's fourteen months and it's still two months to trial . . ." That is, it *would* be two months to trial, I corrected myself, if it were *going* to trial.

In less time than that, Sandy, Stacy, and Terri had all traveled from attack through verdict—Stacy twice—and except for Sandy, even that had been too prolonged.

Fourteen months. Enough to make anyone "weird." Even the D.A., I conceded.

Stop thinking, I chastised myself, *and just keep reading.*

Jill met Cole at a Recreation Expo held at the Anaheim Stadium, and had tried to sell him space in the upcoming San Diego boat show. He gave her a business card and appeared interested, telling her he would contact her next time he was in San Diego. She gave him both her home and work phone numbers.

When he did call several weeks later, they went out for a dinner, drinks, and dancing, returning to her apartment to talk for a while.

"He appeared to be getting ready to leave and all of a sudden he said, 'You were married before and your husband beat you.' I had mentioned to him during the evening I had been married before."

Uh-oh. Now *that* was weird.

"Then he said he wanted me to know what he had done. He told me that he had beaten a girl. He started to go into some of the details, but I can't recall exactly what he said. Primarily he was saying that he had beaten a girl badly."

I'd be getting *real* worried about now if I'd been in her place.

"I told him I thought it was about time for him to leave . . ."

That's an understatement.

". . . and it appeared again that he was going to go. Then he took me in his arms and said, 'I want to stay.' I told him that was impossible and pulled away from him. All of a sudden his entire demeanor changed."

Suddenly a different person, huh? Was it his eyes? Voice? Speech pattern?

"He began to drag me into the bedroom. At that point I didn't feel I had totally lost control. He was extremely strong but I thought I'd be able to talk him out of whatever he was planning on doing."

But she'd been wrong.

He took his clothes off, probably while holding her arm. She couldn't remember for sure. Then he took hers off and threw her on the bed. Every time she got up, he threw her down again.

"All this time I was thinking that I would find the time when I could run out of the house . . . I grabbed a T-shirt so that I would have it to put over me as I ran out."

I understood how she didn't really believe it was happening or would happen.

"He began to fondle me. I was crying and struggling but I didn't scream. The more I struggled, the more excited he became. He laid on top of me. First he put his fingers inside me. Then he had intercourse for a long time. He moved me around in different positions. He was talking to me but I must have been in shock because I can't quite recall what he said. He was extremely strong and extremely rough. I was in a lot of pain."

Even under a full summer sun, on a day as harmless as this, her words shifted easily to images for me.

"When he was getting ready to ejaculate he pulled his penis out of my vagina and ejaculated on my stomach. Then he began to eat the semen. After that he orally copulated me."

A frightening profile was evolving here, of violence, dominance, and deviance. Jill Bernadini may actually have been fortunate.

"At this point I didn't struggle anymore . . ."

And, she wisely observed, "he didn't make me do anything. He just used my body. Afterwards I was amazed because he seemed so calm. He acted as if nothing had happened."

He asked her for an alarm clock, told her to stop breathing so hard, and fell asleep on top of her. Then, when his breathing became rhythmical and she thought he was asleep, she slipped out from under him and quietly left the room.

"I called the operator and told her to give me the police, and she did. I gave my name and address. I couldn't bring myself to say that I had been raped. One reason was that I was afraid he would hear me and wake up. I couldn't think of any other word, like 'attack.' "

When the police dispatcher kept saying he couldn't hear her, she hung up in frustration. Within moments he called her back and the ringing phone woke her attacker.

This *had* to be a movie script.

"Then I couldn't say anything to the police. He was facing me. He took the phone from me and said he was my husband. He told the operator everything was okay. He gave me the telephone and told me to tell them I was okay. The dispatcher started yelling at me and asking how come I could talk loudly now but couldn't talk loudly before. I told him I was hurt. I was very upset."

Upset was the least of it. Terrified, panic-stricken, paralyzed with fear would be more descriptive terms in my opinion.

Could this dispatcher have really been so insensitive?

I fished the tape from the bottom of the file and dropped it into the recorder. I picked up a four-page transcript of the dialogue to follow along . . .

Two rings and a male voice:

D. "San Diego police, dispatcher 98."

In the very next instant I knew Jill Bernadini was not lying about what had happened to her that night.

The sound of breathing came in spasms, each one catching in the caller's throat. Then there were sounds which were obviously an unsuccessful attempt to form words.

D. "Hello, San Diego police."

More convulsive breathing.

B. ". . . send . . . somebody to 50 . . ."

D. "I can't hear you, ma'am."

B. ". . . will you . . . send somebody to . . . 5070 Caminito del Lago . . . number 221 . . ."

D. "What's the problem there?"

B. ". . . there's a . . . man here . . . that . . ."

D. "Ma'am, you'll have to speak up."

B. ". . . look . . . look . . . I don't . . . want . . . him to . . . wake up."

D. "What's that?"

Now only the drone of the dial tone answered him.

How do I evoke for the eyes words which for the ears require no explanation? Her voice reminded me of a child after a bout of hysterical crying and before the rhythm of breathing and speaking returned, when syllables are gulped or cut short in strange patterns.

And the dispatcher. What words would describe him?

"Give me the facts, ma'am, just the facts."

"At the tone the time will be . . ."

"All our lines are busy now . . ."

"At the sound of the beep . . ."

I rewound the tape and played the first part over again, then went on.

How could anyone miss what was happening here?

O. "Operator."

D. "What was her phone number?"

O. "555-9127."

D. "Oh—okay, I don't know what she's talking about but I'll find out. Thank you."

No change in tone, no urgency.

Now the phone was ringing. It must have shattered the silence, amplifying a thousand times in Jill's head.

Someone lifted the receiver but did not speak. The breathing began again.

D. "Hello, ma'am, this is San Diego police. What's the problem there?"

Only the arrhythmia of the breathing.

D. "Can you hear me?"

B. "Yeah."

D. "What's the problem there?"

B. ". . . can't you . . . just . . . send somebody . . . out?"

D. "Well, I'll be glad to, ma'am, but I have to know what I'm going for . . ."

Like hell he has to know! And *why* wasn't he trying to help her out? For instance: "Can't you talk? Is there someone there? Are you hurt? Are you sick? Do you need help? Are you in danger? Is someone armed? How many are there?" There were a thousand things he could do.

D. "What's the problem?"

B. "I can't . . . say . . . right now . . ."

D. "Why not?"

Why *not?* He's playing Twenty Questions. I couldn't believe this was for real.

There was another unsuccessful attempt at words but they were lost.

D. "I beg your pardon?"

B. ". . . could you just . . . send someone, somebody . . . over . . . ?"

There was a hint of desperation in the voice.

D. "You're at 5070 Caminito del Lago, number 221?"

B. "Yeah."

D. "Well, usually when I send a police officer somewhere, he has to know why."

The breathing grew more frantic and it sounded like a scuffle.

C. "Excuse me?"

It was a new voice, definitely male.

D. "Yes?"

C. "Yes, ah, everything is under control. She's getting . . . a little bit . . . hysterical here."

Was he nervous, or did I detect a slur?

D. "What's the problem?"

C. "Ah . . . to tell you the truth . . . I don't really know. She's just getting a little bit . . . out of hand, a little hysterical, and ah . . . I'm leaving. You know, like, I don't know what to tell you."

Definitely tinged with a slur.

D. "Do you live there?"

C. "Um-hum."

D. "Is this your wife?"
C. "Um-hum."
D. "Well, what do you think is wrong?"
This answer was garbled.
D. "And you're leaving, you say?"
C. "Um-hum."

I replayed those last four questions half a dozen times. The responsive sound all three times from the unknown male voice was identical. The "um-hum" to the first two was exactly the same as the answer to the last one, which was unmistakably an affirmative answer.

D. "Is that what she wants, or what?"
C. "Yeah."
D. "Okay, let me talk to her again, would you, please?"
I could hear breathing and muffled words escaping with a whooshing sound like a hand makes when it's over the receiver.
D. "Hello, ma'am."
Just the breathing again.
B. "Hello."
D. "He says he's leaving. What's the problem, just him being there?"
B. "I can't believe . . . you're doing this . . . to me. If you don't . . . send a . . . cop over right . . . now . . ."
I couldn't believe it either. Now the voice was a medley of emotions, with the strength of anger.
D. "How come you can talk so much better now than you could a minute ago? What's the problem, ma'am?"
His tone was insolent and condescending.
B. "My name is . . . Jill Bernadini. I gave . . . you my address . . . and you're . . . my number . . ."
D. "Yes, you sure did, but you didn't tell me what the problem is, ma'am. We don't just send police officers out because somebody calls in and says they want a policeman. We have to know why. You still haven't told me why you need a policeman."
B. "Because . . . he . . . hurt me."
A whisper again, and fear.
D. "He did what?"
B. "He . . . hurt me."
D. "He hurt you?"

B. "Yeah."

The way the dispatcher put it, it was not really a question, just a flat statement.

D. "Okay, and how do you spell your last name, ma'am?"

B. "Bernadini, what . . . is . . . your name?"

D. "How do you spell your last name, ma'am?"

B. "B-e-r-n-a-d-i-n-i."

D. "Okay, and you're in apartment 221?"

B. "I am."

D. "Okay, and your husband is leaving?"

Husband! Why, he never even asked her if he really was her husband. He simply took Cole's word for it.

B. "He is *not* . . . my . . . husband. I don't know . . . who he is."

Frustration and anger now, and near hysteria.

D. "Okay, we'll get somebody there, ma'am."

B. "Who . . . am I . . . speaking to?"

D. "You're talking to San Diego police dispatcher 98, ma'am."

B. "Are you dispatcher . . . 98?"

D. "Um-hum."

B. "Thank you."

D. "You have no idea who this man is? Hello?"

The breathing had stopped. The line was dead.

I played it through two more times, envisioning a jury listening. First, all the way through while the victim testified, next while I had dispatcher 98 on the stand—God, did I want dispatcher 98 on the stand—and at least one more time, probably during final argument.

I went back to the investigator's report. Jill said that after Cole handed the phone back to her he disappeared into the bedroom for several minutes. He came out just as the doorbell rang and even pushed the buzzer to admit the police to the building. Then he left.

"The police officers came to the door and asked if I was okay. I was near total collapse and I told them that the guy had gone and they might as well go away.

"They went into my bedroom and flashed the light around. I was amazed that they came back and asked if I was still okay. At the time I thought the bedroom was still in total disarray. When I'd left, the nightstand had been overturned, the mattress was askew, and my clothes were strewn all over the floor.

"It wasn't until later that I went into the bedroom and discovered that while he had been in there he had put the mattress back in place, the pillows on the bed, hung up my clothes, and totally cleaned the bedroom."

Marge's first report also mentioned that Cole had talked with Jill about a lawsuit he had against a police department in some town around L.A. for excessive force while he was at the jail, and that trial was set for June.

I wondered if violence was a way of life with this guy.

A lawsuit meant a transcript. If it had gone on schedule, the trial was over.

I learned from reading the follow-up report that it had taken a couple of weeks to track him down, using as a clue the business card Jill had been given by Cole at the Recreational Expo in Anaheim. After being shown the pictures from two different California driver's licenses, Jill identified Cole as her attacker in both photo lineups.

On the business card he had also written two phone numbers. One was identified as belonging to a "Mrs. Cole," the other to Cole's brother, Benjamin, who was also the owner of the business described on the card.

On Monday, June 11, 1979, Marge and her partner went to Fulmon, a small suburban community near Los Angeles, and found Jeremy Cole at his mother's, where he was living.

So the "Mrs. Cole" was his mother, not his wife. I looked for his DOB. 3/12/50. That's right, he'd been twenty-nine then. I'm certainly not suggesting that all, or even most, men who live with their mothers are rapists. But it was one of those peculiarities in rape cases which, over the years, seemed more than coincidental—like some of those repeated victim behavior patterns.

As Marge explained the circumstances of the arrest warrant to him, but before she had gotten to any mention of the offense, Cole "voluntarily made a statement."

"I know what this is about. That girl invited me down and let me into her house. I changed clothes and everything in her apartment. We went to dinner and she invited me back into her apartment. There's no such thing as a forcible intercourse."

He'd pushed the right button. I was interested.

On the drive back to San Diego, and after Cole was advised of his constitutional rights, Marge had an opportunity to do a lengthy interview.

Cole agreed that he and Jill had met at the Recreation Expo in Anaheim and that she was trying to sell space for the San Diego boat show.

"We talked for a while and then she left. She came back a little bit tipsy. I took her to a snack bar and bought her a hot dog and Coke. I asked if she wanted to stay the night. She said no because she had ridden up with someone else. I told her she'd better sober up a little bit before she went back."

How solicitous of him. But what difference would it make if she sobered up a little bit before she went back? She said she'd ridden up with someone else. I needed the person she'd ridden with.

"Later I called her and said I was going to be in San Diego and asked if she wanted to see me. I told her I'd take her out to dinner and call her. When I got down to San Diego I called and told her I was there. She said okay. I met her at her place. We had a glass of wine and went out to dinner. Afterwards we went dancing, talked, hugged, and touched."

Had she been this friendly? Did they talk business? Why was he in San Diego? Just to see her?

"After that we went back to her apartment. We sat on the couch and then we went into the bedroom. One thing led to another. After it was all over she said I raped her. I asked her what she meant. She kept saying that I had raped her. I said, 'You're telling me you didn't enjoy it?' She got hysterical.

"I got up and put on my pants. She said she was going to call the police. I didn't really think she was going to. She made a call and I said, 'Let me see the phone.' She gave me the phone and the guy said it was the police. He asked me some questions. Then he said something and I gave her back the phone. She talked to him and demanded that they come over. I couldn't believe it. I said, 'You've got to be kidding.' "

The rush-hour traffic syndrome was back: what "thing" led to "another"? Was "it" and being "all over" the way he always described making love? Had she no trouble repeatedly using the word "rape" with him, but had been unable to say it even once on the phone? I'd bet money he asked her if she was enjoying "it" all right—probably all the time he was doing "it."

He'd mentioned nothing about the phone ringing and what exactly were the questions the police asked. And why had he said he was her husband?

"I was going to hang around until the police came, but she kept saying she wanted me to leave. I said I didn't want to leave until the police got there, that they might come after me, and she said she wouldn't tell them anything and to please leave. I thought she would calm down, so I left."

Methinks thou protesteth too much, or he certainly could have waited outside the apartment if he had been so concerned.

When Cole had finished his explanation Marge began to press him for details.

"I asked him if he pushed the button to let the police in. He said he had not. I asked him if he had gone to sleep. He said he had not. He said he had been sitting on the edge of the bed while Jill was calling the police. He said he did not think that she would really call the police."

I played the tape over in my head.

B. ". . . there's a . . . man here . . . that . . ."

D. "Ma'am, you'll have to speak up."

B. ". . . look . . . look . . . I don't . . . want . . . him to . . . wake up."

Sure, he was sitting on the edge of the bed, with all the lights on, too, no doubt.

Marge asked Cole to go into more detail about how they got from the living room to the bedroom, and how he got her clothes off.

"We were in the living room and we were . . . I think I was fondling her breasts. I said, 'Why don't we go into the bedroom?' There was a smooth transaction until she blew up. . . .

"I don't recall, I think I unzipped her dress, or she pulled it off or I pulled it off. Not wanting to be disgusting but the only thing I can remember her saying was when we were having intercourse she said, 'Oh, your cock feels so good inside me.'"

Hello? Who asked for that? The clue was a good one, though. Probably the gist of what he was asking Jill all during the attack while she'd been too shocked to hear his words: how much she really was enjoying what was happening, and really wanted him to make love to her.

But when Marge asked him questions about the possibly deviant and questionably acceptable sexual behavior, he was equivocal and denying.

"I asked Cole if he had orally copulated her. He said, 'I don't think so.' I asked if he had withdrawn his penis from her vagina and ejaculated on her stomach and licked it off. He said, 'I ejaculated inside her. I know I didn't ejaculate on her stomach and lick it off.'"

Giving this accusation the truth test weighed heavily in Jill's favor. The alternative was to believe she had taken the time to embellish her rape with a very bizarre addendum.

Why, Marge wondered, would Jill claim he had raped her? He didn't know. And had she told him anything about her background? She hadn't, he replied.

Was he drunk?

"I was high. We drank at dinner and while we were dancing."

"High" was usually reserved for something else; drugs was what I had in mind.

Marge seemed to be reading my mind, or I hers. "I asked him if he was so drunk that he didn't know what was happening. He said, 'No, I was not that drunk.' I asked if he had anything to drink when they returned to Jill's apartment after dinner. He said, 'I don't recall.' I asked if he had any drugs. He said, 'I smoked a joint on the way to dinner.' I asked if Jill had smoked any of the marijuana. He said, 'Not as far as I know.'"

At first glance, it would appear that admitting to smoking grass and denying Jill's participation made Cole look like an honest man. In truth, it was very self-serving. It certainly was a lot better to take a rap on a misdemeanor marijuana charge than to go down for rape.

When he was questioned about whether Jill was drunk, or if he felt he was in complete control of his faculties, he answered, "I don't recall," to both.

He hadn't straightened up the bedroom because it wasn't messed up.

Was there any reason, Marge asked, why his prints would be on the nightstand, or why the nightstand might have been overturned?

"Maybe I touched it, since it was next to the bed," but, no, it had not been knocked over as far as he could recall.

"I asked," Marge wrote, "is there any reason your prints would be on the bottom or near the area where you would have touched it if you'd picked it up after it had been knocked over?"

Oh, you sneaky devil, Marge. I smiled. We already had the print report back and none could be identified.

He took the bait. "My prints might be there."

She let out some more line. "I asked if the victim had put up any type of resistance. I indicated that all women say no at some time or another, and Cole replied, 'She might have been a little resistant. I did pick her up and carry her partway into the bedroom.' "

But, he insisted, he only "laid" her on the bed. He did not throw her.

So, maybe she *was* just a tiny bit resistant? His charms alone won her over quickly, of course.

When Marge inquired, out of context, about the location of the phone, "he told me it was in the front room."

That must have been some reach—from the end of the bed.

Marge's partner, Stu Rand, asked the next and, as it turned out, last set of questions.

Q. "What positions were you in?"

A. "The position changed. We were side by side, and then I was on top of her."

Q. "Was she fondling your penis?"

A. "Yes. She stroked it."

Q. "Did she put her mouth on your penis?"

A. "I don't recall."

Q. "Did she help you put your penis in her vagina?"

A. "She enjoyed it. I think it got inside by itself. She was wet, she definitely wasn't dry. She was enjoying it."

Where had I heard that same language before? Or, I suppose, the question should be: when hadn't I heard it?

Q. "Did she ask you to orally copulate her?"

A. "Not that I recall."

Q. "Did she put on a T-shirt or anything?"

A. "I think she put on a T-shirt or bathrobe afterwards."

That was four times now, when not asked even once, that Cole's opinion about Jill's enjoyment had been volunteered.

Cole decided at that point, the report concluded, that Marge was writing down only the things she wanted to. She offered to read everything back for him, and when she did he caught the slip-up about the possibility of his prints being found on the bottom of the nightstand.

"I don't know if the nightstand got knocked over or not," he added at that point.

This was the only correction he made.

I read it all again. It just didn't *feel* like a dismissal—not yet, at any rate.

Mark Fisher, the defense attorney, was disappointed the next afternoon when I broke the news, but took things in stride.

"My client would have been pleased, but I prepared him for you."

"Did you, now?" I played along amiably.

"Yep. I told him you were known around. J. R. Superstar, isn't it?" he quipped.

"Ah, gee, Mark," I purred. "It's nothin', really. By the way, did Cole go to trial in Fulmon last month?"

"You mean that P.I. case he had against the Fulmon P.D.?"

"Unless there's more, that's the one I mean."

"Yeah, well, I think he did and now he wants to appeal. The court threw it out, but he says it wasn't fair. Anyway, that's all I know."

"That's enough," I replied as I jotted myself a note to write up an investigator's service request for the transcript. "Oh, and, Mark, are there any more cases?"

"If there are, he hasn't told me. Talk to you later."

Mark Fisher was one of those defense attorneys with whom I had to take care to sidestep the prod, to avoid taking the bait. He was clever, bright, and experienced. His body language, including his walk, mirrored his personality: sort of quick, and flip. It's interesting how people's personalities match their body language. Just as slow talkers and thinkers often have movements to match, Mark Fisher's were quick and flippant.

I was not close enough to taking the Cole case to trial to play mental gymnastics with his attorney. I hadn't even seen the victim yet. And there was the small matter of her Police Department termination proceedings—for lying. While the California Evidence Code does not allow many "character traits" to be used to impeach a witness in court, a person's reputation in the community for "truth and veracity" is one of the specific exceptions to that rule.

I cleared an entire afternoon and scheduled a meeting between us.

Jill's voice on the tape, and in our two or three brief phone conversations, left me with certain impressions about her personality. Shy, retiring, maybe even mousy. I was in for a shock.

It hadn't occurred to me that since she was a police officer, Jill's arrival wouldn't need to be announced.

"Are you Judy?"

I recognized the voice but couldn't immediately place it.

I looked up to see as much of a pair of shapely, slender legs as short-shorts would permit.

"Yes, I'm Judy," I answered with only brief hesitation. "You're . . . ?"

"Jill Bernadini," she finished the sentence. She stood uneasily in the doorway.

"Please, have a seat." I pointed to the chair nearest her. She sat down cautiously.

I must have been imagining her eyes when I was listening to that tape, I said to myself. They were the only feature which contained the vulnerability that I had heard. Hazel like mine, they had the benefit of long, dark Italian lashes and shoulder-length blond hair. Even though it was obviously bleached, from the bottle and by the sun, it looked great.

The rest of her facial features were small and, except for the moderate Brooklyn accent each time she spoke, her manner was refined.

She wore a halter top which did for her above the waist what the shorts accomplished below. In between was a midriff without a trace of fat.

A tan like that would have to be painted on me, I observed somewhat enviously.

But I did not envy her. Over all the head-turning good looks, she wore an unmistakable mantle of sadness. At different times during the afternoon she was up and down, sometimes approaching a nearly cheerful smile, occasionally plummeting toward anguish. But never was she free of this pervasive sadness.

I started out by giving Jill the same speech Terri had gotten when I took over her case. I couldn't emphasize enough that nothing would be worse than finding out the truth only after we got into court.

"Jill, are you still interested in going through with this?" I addressed her with steady eyes, but held my breath. If she said no, maybe I wouldn't be foolish enough to persuade her to reconsider.

"Yes, I am." Her eyes met mine with conviction. "I never have said otherwise. Only Mr. Charles acted as if I didn't, like he didn't believe me. Really, I know he doesn't believe me."

"Okay, we're going to have to start at the beginning and go all the way through. I know you've already gone over it countless times, Jill, and I'm sorry, but you've never done it for me."

She nodded and even her nod was sad.

Actually, she probably never had gone through the whole thing the way I was about to do it.

14

ONE OF THE FIRST THINGS I discovered about Jill Bernadini
—besides her stunning physical appearance—was that she had anything but a shy and retiring nature.

Her real personality, the sum total of the first twenty-seven years of
her life up until May 10, 1979, was of a pretty much all-together, self-
assured, and self-sufficient woman who had not yet discovered exactly
what she wanted to do with her life, but was not letting any grass grow
under her feet in the meantime.

The difference between the person she revealed herself to have been
and the one I saw sitting in my office was so striking as to suggest that
she had undergone an upheaval in her life of great proportions. Unless
it turned out to be due to something about which I was yet to learn—
and that was certainly not beyond the realm of possibility—I would
assume her life had been shattered by Jeremy Cole.

Jill had been raised in New York City, primarily Brooklyn, in a fairly
close-knit Italian-American family. She graduated from high school at
age sixteen, and neither she nor her two sisters and one brother had
gone on to college.

"My parents thought college was a waste of time, especially for girls.
Boys should get a job if possible, and we should get husbands, right? So
I did."

At eighteen Jill married a high school friend. But it was a stormy
relationship almost from the beginning. She discovered her husband
was a petty thief by profession, not believing in more conventional
ways of earning a living, and he spent several extended periods of time
in jail. He was also violent, and if she protested or argued with him
about his criminal lifestyle, he beat her.

"It was worse if I resisted or tried to fight back, so I usually didn't," she said, adding as she touched her cheek, "especially after he broke my nose."

During the three years they were married, Jill and her husband lived together only six months. Just before their final break she became pregnant, but, knowing she was about to divorce, she had an abortion.

"It was no way to bring a child into the world."

After the divorce, she decided she wanted to get out from under the close and constant watch of her parents, and to put some distance between herself and her "old life," as she referred to it. When her new boyfriend asked if she wanted to go to California with him, she accepted, and at age twenty-one, made the trek West with little money and no friends.

"I figured out that college was the route for me, and everyone said California was the place for a low-cost university education."

She settled in San Diego almost right away, found work easily, and began to wait the necessary year to establish residency before entering the public university system.

"But you know how it is, once you have the job and the income, it's hard to draw the curtain."

I could relate to *that* all right.

Jill worked nearly four years for a group of plastic surgeons as a salesperson. From what I could understand, she sold people on the idea of plastic surgery.

Soon after starting this job she broke off with the man who brought her to California and began dating an attorney ten years her senior who had decided to give up the practice of law for the practice of law enforcement.

Alan Eubanks had been a police officer for about three years now, and for the most part had been assigned to the academy as an instructor, which was what he liked to do best.

"Alan was the first man I ever met, I ever went with who wanted more out of life than a woman to hang on his arm and a beer to hold in his hand."

Like so many intelligent women I had met, Jill was all-together except when it came to her love life.

Had she ever made it to college?

"No, not quite. I got close, though. I even quit my job with the plastic surgeons right after New Year's of 1979. I figured I'd take five or six months off and start college in the summer, or fall at the latest. But things didn't work out that way. Maybe someone up there is trying to tell me the halls of learning are not for me."

She smiled the sad smile.

If not through formal learning, where had she gotten her gift for language?

"I read everything. Sort of a vicarious education, you can say."

Three months into her "vacation," Jill felt the pinch of the absent paycheck and looked around for short-term employment.

"It had to be a job I already knew something about because I was also Alan's campaign treasurer. He ran for a seat on the City Council last year, along with everyone else."

Oh, *that* Alan Eubanks. I knew the name sounded familiar, but I thought it might have been because he had the same last name as someone I had seen on television. But now that Jill mentioned it, I remembered. It had been a highly publicized election to fill a vacancy and twelve or so candidates had gotten a lot of press.

". . . so I took a sales job again, but just for one thing—to sell space for the boat show."

The job paid a low salary, but the commission potential attracted Jill, and this kind of work came easily for her. It meant an occasional trip as far away as Las Vegas or Sacramento to solicit exhibitors who would pay a hefty sum to show their wares.

"But mainly it meant lots of phone time contacting local boat dealers and short hops up the coast as far as L.A. We'd go in groups for the day and work other expos, you know, playing up the show and giving all the reasons why everyone should come to San Diego."

"Do you remember the Anaheim show?"

"Oh, I remember it, all right. I'll always remember the Anaheim show. I don't think I'll ever go to Disneyland again either!"

I hadn't thought of that. Disneyland was right across the street from the convention center where the show had been held.

Jill rode up with another salesman, Paul Murdock. They seemed to draw many of the same weekend duty days and took turns driving. Paul was married and Jill was going with Alan, so it was a comfortable arrangement for everyone.

I told Jill what Cole had said about their meeting that day.

"I *never* drink when I'm working, ever, unless it's a social setting like dinner or cocktails. And he never bought me anything to eat either, and he certainly didn't invite me to stay overnight."

Their contact had been friendly but strictly business, she said, and as a matter of fact, he had let her believe that *he*, rather than his brother, was the owner of the business. He also let her believe that he made regular business trips to San Diego and said that he wanted to discuss purchasing some space in the boat show the next time he was in town.

"If I'd known his brother owned the business I would have tried to sell space to him, not to Jeremy."

She had more or less forgotten about Cole when he called a couple of weeks later and suggested dinner while they discussed business.

Did she tell Alan?

"Of course I told him. He knew how and where we'd met too. I even told him I thought I'd make a sale."

I noticed Jill had a tendency at times to tip her chin down slightly and peer at me almost through her lashes. It was definitely a flirtatious mannerism. She admitted she had been told this before. Since I knew she wasn't flirting with me, it was simply a part of her communicative style; but it was one she had to be aware of for court purposes. I'd seen many women, and men too, do the same thing—particularly with each other.

Cole's description of the evening was accurate, Jill acknowledged after I had summarized it for her, except for the touchy-feely.

"I realized during dinner that I'd been wrong about his interest in buying space for the boat show. I figured that we could still enjoy the evening. I mean, it would have been real tacky to say, 'Okay, take me home if you're not going to buy anything.' But there was no come-on by him. Then I *would* have asked him to take me home."

He offered her a hit on his joint in the car, but she told him she didn't do any drugs. In addition to the wine at her apartment, he had several cocktails before dinner and bought a bottle of wine with dinner. She had one cocktail before and one glass of wine from the bottle. She rarely got drunk. Alan could tell me that too.

Their conversation was social small talk and, as best she could recall, some trading of personal background information. She told him, for instance, about her marriage and being hit by her husband. He told her about the injustice of his arrest by the Fulmon Police Department and his suit against them. But he remained the perfect gentleman.

When they returned to her apartment, it was after midnight, but he seemed to want to keep talking, so she offered him a cup of coffee before his drive back north. Instead, he asked for a drink, which he fixed himself. She drank the coffee.

"There was sort of a pause in the conversation when I thought he was about to leave. Then all of a sudden, out of nowhere, he started talking about my husband having hit me and how he had beaten a woman too."

What was she thinking then?

"Well, that it was a bit odd, but I figured if I stood up and made like it was time to call it a night, that would be it. I told him something like that, but he just took hold of me, pulled me near him, and said he wanted to stay."

And what did she think of that?

"Not much, I guess, only a little uneasy. I said no, or that he couldn't do that."

How did he change?

"Mostly in his voice; it got slow and deeper. And in his eyes. They were sort of glazed-looking and faraway, but he was staring right at me, describing how he had hurt this woman, a girlfriend, I think."

Jill had put up with more than words in her time, and was sure enough of herself to think she still controlled the situation. It was not like it had been with Terri Richardson, who had frozen at O'Conner's first touch. But when Cole began to drag her to the bedroom, her reserve did begin to slip.

"I thought he might try to beat me at first, but if I kept talking I'd get a chance at some point to pull away. Being raped didn't even occur to me. Not until he started taking off my clothes."

Her sense of control dissolved completely when she realized Cole intended to rape, rather than beat, her. And, as with her husband, the more she struggled, the more violent he got.

What was going through her mind now?

"Fear, pure fear. I started thinking that maybe he was going to kill me; he got so excited when I struggled. Then I cried. I remember thinking I couldn't believe this was happening to me."

But it was happening and experience warned her not to go on struggling. She remembered everything he did to her, but not what he said, except general things, and there seemed to be a lot of questions. She remembered feeling sick when he ejaculated on her stomach and licked it off.

"When he was through with me, he was like he had been before."

She was hysterical, but tried to obey his order to quiet down. She could see the front door from where they lay on the bed. When he fell asleep it was with one arm and a leg on top of her. She slipped out, holding her breath, and tiptoed very softly to the living room.

She decided against unlocking the door. He could easily see her standing there and the noise might wake him up before she could get out.

Cautiously she turned off the light, trying to avoid a click. He would stay asleep better in the dark, she reasoned. She stood for a long time waiting for any movement from the bedroom. Every breath escaped with a sudden spasm from her chest and felt like thunder, loud enough to wake the neighbors. But no one came.

Slowly, she took the phone in her hands and lifted it from the side table. Even more slowly, she crouched down behind the large wing-backed chair which hid her from the bedroom's view. Her whole body shaking, she was naked and cold, and stricken with terror. Her head throbbed from the effort to hold back her sobs.

Thank God, she remembered thinking, the buttons were silent as she called the police number which was on the small sticker attached to the receiver. Alan had put it there last year.

When the dispatcher answered, she knew what she wanted to say, but no words came out. She feared she would scream if she pushed any harder; and then the dispatcher claimed he couldn't hear her.

"Even when I could finally say something, the word 'rape' just wouldn't come out. The voice on the phone was not what I'd expected and I just knew I would wake Cole up if I kept talking, so I hung up."

What was she thinking, crouched naked behind that chair in the darkened room, her assailant asleep a few yards away?

"I don't know. Mostly that I was ready to die any minute. I had no more plans, no more thoughts, really."

And when the phone rang?

"I picked up the receiver from force of habit, I suppose. I knew I was dead. Nothing could save me. I can still hear the ringing. The same man began talking to me but I couldn't say things any better."

Within seconds she was aware of Cole standing over her, but she kept talking.

I have relived these descriptive moments many times in the years since Jill and I talked that first afternoon. Even now it occasionally crosses my thoughts when a phone rings in a darkened room—particularly if I'm alone.

Despite her fear and sense of imminent death, Jill's inner strength—something cultivated through a lifetime of personal experiences—rallied frustration and anger at her treatment by dispatcher 98.

"Knowing Alan had done a lot to change my attitudes about the police. With him I had met cops who didn't fit my image of them as bullies and powermongers. And then when I really needed one . . ."

It hadn't occurred to me that Jill generally distrusted the police.

"I grew up in Brooklyn, remember? Cops weren't exactly your Boy Scouts next door. And being married to Dennis and having that kind of contact with them didn't help either. Alan and I almost broke up when he first went to the academy. I felt very uncomfortable socializing with cops."

How, then, had she ever reached the decision to become one herself?

"I still wonder some about that, but it has to be because of the way I was treated. I didn't want other women to go through what I'd been through. I hoped I could make a difference."

Whew. I knew many rape victims ended up volunteering at rape crisis centers as a way of working through their emotional struggles, but becoming a cop? That was impact—and tough-minded determination. And maybe a mistake.

It hadn't only been dispatcher 98, I discovered, who shook her newfound trust in the police. The two responding officers had contributed as well.

"The older cop, he did all the talking. He was big and seemed very . . . well, agitated. Nervous. He almost yelled at me and was very annoyed when I couldn't bring myself to answer questions. The younger one looked like he really wanted to help me, to say something, but didn't dare. He just looked around the apartment."

Jill had been too drained, too exhausted to relate the humiliating circumstances and terrible details of her ordeal to this bully who only increased her own anxieties.

"I must have fainted after they left. I remember standing up one minute and then being on the floor by the closet the next. Even then I couldn't tell them. I wanted them to protect me, to stay with me and to help me, but they didn't."

It seemed too much for one person to bear. Only her shock and terror kept Jill from being as angry at the time as she was later. And then she made the ultimate statement to the ultimate violation—she became a cop.

When these officers were gone, Jill called Alan and the sound of her voice alone had him there in ten minutes. It took another ten or fifteen minutes of comforting and gentle questioning before she could tell him what had happened. Alan angrily reported the attack himself and demanded an investigation. It was then the two officers returned, along with their supervisor, and wrote that defensively worded report I had questioned.

By now it was 4 A.M.

Jill spent the next three hours making a report to the police and then was assigned an officer to take her to the hospital for a physical evidence exam.

I pulled out the report. It was a two-page form supplied by the police. The bottom half of the first page had been, as minimally as possible, filled in by some attending physician whose name I could not read. I jotted myself a note to subpoena the records in order to identify the doctor so I could get him to court.

There was that perceptive diagnosis again: "W♀ in no acute distress"—white female in no acute distress. Was that physical distress? Mental distress? How had he determined this? What did he observe?

"What was really depressing about the hospital thing," Jill volunteered as I studied the scanty medical report, "was the cop."

The cop? How so?

"On the way home he asked if I'd like to go to lunch with him. Or maybe he could call me sometime?"

"He asked you for a *date?* Did he know what had happened to you?" I was dumbstruck.

"He took me to a hospital from the station," Jill answered. "He knew."

I looked at the report again. Of course he knew. The top half of the medical exam form had been filled in and signed by this officer: Craig

Nelson, ID 728. I would have a talk with him—and then maybe his supervisors.

Jill's description of all these events was given calmly and retrospectively. There was no anger in her voice, no tears in her eyes. Just sadness. Yet I was sure she had not resolved the emotional impact of this trauma in her life. Nothing she had told me so far had seemed to suggest that she had.

And small wonder. The criminal justice system not only had done nothing to settle the turmoil, but continued actively to thwart attempts at this objective. Quite aside from law enforcement and medical insensitivities, the prosecution had repeatedly delayed trial, causing subpoenas to go out no less than six times over a ten-month period, disrupting Jill's life and reopening old wounds each time.

"Jill." I needed to get back on track. "How is your relationship with Alan now, and since the assault?"

"We broke up about four months later, right after I started at the academy."

I learned that she had slept with no one but Alan for well over a year before the rape, but had not been able to have satisfactory intercourse with him, or anyone else, since. She never attempted it again in her own apartment, and at his place she had cried the two or three times they had gotten close to making love; so they stopped trying, and their relationship had deteriorated through the summer.

"Alan was kind to me, but I couldn't let him back in, emotionally or physically."

I would have a long talk with Alan. Ideas were spinning. Maybe I had *the* case here.

"Has there been any enjoyable sexual relationship for you, Jill, since the assault?"

"Not until, would you believe, the last ten days. I finally met someone I can get close to again. I didn't think it would ever happen."

"Okay, but are there any other men," I wanted to know, "who would be able, with your permission of course, to tell me what happened in a physical relationship with you since this happened?"

Jill's face expressed alarm. "Do you have to bring other men into this? I thought that wasn't allowed anymore."

I was ready to take the plunge.

"Jill, have you ever heard of the rape trauma syndrome?"

"No." She twisted nervously in her chair, still waiting for an answer to her last question.

"Look, you're right. Past sexual history isn't allowed as evidence anymore, but before I answer your question I want to tell you about the rape trauma syndrome and what I have in mind, okay?"

I gave her a brief outline of how the rape trauma syndrome had been discovered and how I'd found out about it. I explained the two stages and described some details about Sandy and Terri. I did not discuss the symptoms, since I hadn't really gathered that information from her yet and didn't want to be accused later of suggestive interviewing.

"Now, I don't know enough at this point to decide if we'll actually go the expert route," I finished, wondering just how I'd do it even if I decided to, "but please, Jill, trust my judgment for now. I believe *you,* try to believe in me."

Her nod gave me the permission I needed, but the eyes did not agree. I realized my responsibility not to make things worse for her than they already were.

We eased back into the subject of dating and Jill disclosed, with obvious embarrassment, that one of the reasons she and Alan had split was her desire to go out with other men.

"Or maybe it was the other way around," I reflected. "Because you were drifting apart, you began to think of others."

"I hadn't thought of it that way." She sat back in her chair for the first time, as if she might just stay for a while. "No, I'd never looked at it that way."

"When did you start going out?" I sure hoped it wasn't the first week.

"Oh, I remember exactly. It was two nights before I was starting at the academy. It was in September. Alan was really distant around that time and I told him I was tired and was just going to bed. But instead I went across the street from my apartment to a bar for a drink." She was leaning forward again, her signal of tension. "And, I think, to see who I might meet."

"And did you?" I was feeling tense too.

"Yes, I did." She was really squirming.

"I not only met someone, he ended up coming home with me."

Great. A jury would love *that.*

"I have never, ever done that before—taken someone home from a bar, much less the first time I met him," she stressed.

"And what happened?" I would keep an open mind and look for the silver lining. "Did you tell him what had happened to you?"

"I wasn't planning to tell him, but as soon as he began to touch me . . . well, up until that point, I really felt like making love with him, but then it was as if the whole thing was happening again. I fought it, but . . . all of a sudden I started to cry. You can imagine his reaction. I had to tell him. He was wonderful. We talked a long time and then he left."

"Do you know how to reach him, or remember his name?" I sat poised with pen in hand.

"He's waiting for me at the reception desk."

I felt like dispatcher 98 should have felt. But I was also confused.

"Jill, I'm sorry if I sounded like he was a one-night stand. But I'm not sure I understand."

"His name is Bretton Walker, and he's been one of the reasons I haven't gone completely crackers."

She was sitting back again, now shaking her head. "He kept calling and I kept trying. But after three or four more times with the same results, we decided to just be friends. We both ended up crying the last time."

"Will he talk to me, Jill?" I was trying not to be ghoulish and impatient. This was not hypothetical, this was real, even though it was taking on the movie-script feeling.

"Sure. Bret wants to do anything that will help, but let me talk to him first."

Before Jill left she introduced me to Bret and we set up a time to talk. He looked like he adored her, and I figured he was hoping if he waited long enough something would change.

It must have been very hard on him.

When we got together for our interview, he confessed to being in love with Jill but realized he'd come along at the wrong time in her life for her to reciprocate.

"I'm willing to just hold her when she needs it. We hold each other a lot, in place of making love, and it's okay. We can be friends."

Bret was willing to describe for a jury the problems he'd witnessed with Jill's sexual dysfunction.

"Were there any others, Jill?"

"Not after what happened with Bret. I went out with my girlfriends or over to the bar every once in a while, but it was worse. Sometimes I'd get a panicky feeling just walking into the place."

"Okay, so there was Alan, Bret, and now someone you don't get that feeling with, is that right?" All I needed was for the defense to dig up someone else after she had testified to only Alan and Bret.

"Yeah, that's right, nobody else, besides Todd Bishop . . . but you meant before Todd, right?"

"Yes, before the last week or so."

"Right. That's all, then."

This whole conversation sounded like we were notching a belt full of conquests. But I knew precisely what I would do with this evidence: it was the most dramatic example of sexual dysfunction I'd yet discovered, and I knew its persuasive value in front of a jury could be of enormous benefit to Jill's credibility.

Before I let the horse take the bit and run, however, I would have some very serious thinking to do about what I might be unleashing if I "opened the door" with testimony about Jill's sexual history. I needed time to play my own devil's advocate. I certainly would need a judge with the best reputation for legal skills. If he followed the law, and limited any defense probing to impeachment of Jill's claim to virtual celibacy, then I'd be home free—unless she was lying to me. But if I got a judge who would allow a rush for that open door when sexual history had been introduced for any purpose, it would sink our ship faster than a torpedo could.

"Did Alan know what was going on between you and Bret?"

"He doesn't know that it started while we were still seeing each other. Obviously he knew things had changed. I mean, we'd been talking about marriage the night before the . . . rape, and within a couple of months afterwards we'd go for days without even talking on the phone."

"Do you still see Alan?" I sure hoped she did. We needed him.

"We're still friends, yes. I haven't seen him for a few months now, but we're still friends."

She gave me Alan's home phone number and his number at the police academy. When I called to set up the appointment, I found him willing to talk with me once I'd explained the purpose. He asked about

Jill and seemed concerned. I felt sorry for him too. Like the ripple effect of a stone hurled into the water, how many lives had been affected by this one act of violence and terror.

In addition to the sexual dysfunction, Jill suffered from nightmares and insomnia. She was afraid to go out alone or try new places, although this was improving. She had no appetite for weeks after the rape and was anxious sometimes for no apparent reason.

At work her sales dropped off for the boat show and she felt disorganized much of the time. She managed to finish assisting Alan in his campaign, which helped her keep her mind off the rape.

But it was the subpoenas which triggered the most acute reactions, especially after she was at the police academy. Each time she got one, the intensity of her anxieties increased.

"I felt as if I would explode sometimes. I was afraid I'd be booted from the program if administration found out I'd been raped, and I was paranoid about having my classmates, all those men, know."

"You never told the Police Department you'd been raped?" I wondered how in the world she thought she could keep such a secret indefinitely if she was training with the same agency which was handling the investigation of her case.

"No, I didn't. I was afraid I wouldn't get in if they knew."

She was no doubt on target about that.

"And I was right. When they did find out, I was fired."

We hadn't yet talked about the termination hearings.

"I have to understand what happened in the academy and what has happened since."

"There hasn't been any 'since.' It was the first day of my first assignment when I didn't . . . report. And I'd been really looking forward to it."

"What went wrong?"

"I don't know exactly. I just felt like I was having a nervous breakdown. Although I'm not sure exactly what that would feel like. It started when Kent Charles called me on May 6 to say we were trailing. Then on the ninth he called to say it had been continued again, this time until July. I went to pieces. I had counted on the whole thing being over when I reported for my first duty assignment as a police officer on May 17. A new beginning, you know."

I knew better than she realized. Now Jill would have to worry about supervisors and beat partners finding out about the rape if she were subpoenaed at work.

"By May 14 I was a basket case. I wouldn't leave the apartment. I wasn't eating, and I cried at everything, even TV commercials."

Then, on Thursday, the night before she was supposed to report for duty, Bret and her best friend, Peggy Murray, came by to see how she was. They found her shaking uncontrollably and unable to sleep or eat.

"They told me I had to tell the department what was going on, or at least call in sick, because I was in no condition to work."

Jill remembered sitting on the end of her bed while Bret and Peggy talked over what she needed to do. She heard their words but was not able to participate or do anything about her situation. It felt like she was in a trance, she said.

"Peggy and Bret realized I was a zombie and they decided to take things into their own hands . . . and I let them."

They concluded that Peggy would call Jill's supervisor and tell him there had been an emergency in the family, a death or something if he asked, and that she had already taken a plane back East, that she wasn't sure how long it would be before Officer Bernadini would be back.

"They were going to see how long it was before I looked normal, I guess. They're both so sweet."

Jill put up no resistance to the idea even though it made her more nervous. Peggy managed to pull it off.

"And I was relieved somewhat after that. By Saturday afternoon I was feeling much better and Bret suggested we go for a drive. We did —to Ensenada."

"Did you intend to go home?"

"Yes, absolutely. I needed to see my parents, to be with my family. In fact, Peggy tried to get me a flight out on Thursday, but in order to get the economy fare, which is all I could afford, we needed seven days' advance reservation. So she booked a flight for me on the twenty-third and told me to lay low in the meantime."

She had been anything but successful on that score.

Unbeknownst to Jill and Bret, the annual Tecate-to-Ensenada bicycle race took place the same Saturday they took their drive. A rather large contingent of San Diego's finest had ridden the grueling seventy-mile course and participated in the celebrating all over Ensenada that night. Jill and Bret were out strolling when they literally walked into four or five San Diego police officers, one of whom knew her.

"There was no way to avoid them. Even if I'd turned and run, he had already seen me. I was literally sick to my stomach, and I don't think it was the food. God, I even get queasy thinking about it now." She held her abdomen and grimaced.

She and Bret came back from Ensenada that night and waited for the ax to fall. It almost didn't. Jill learned later that the officer in the Ensenada group who knew her happened to notice her name on the sick list for the day he'd seen her in Baja. He mentioned this to Jill's supervisor a day or two later when he ran into him, and then the ball was rolling.

"I flew to New York on the twenty-third and learned we'd been found out a few days later. At first I thought about not coming back, but decided I had to finally face it and tell them the truth about the rape."

By the time she got back, the department was already talking about termination.

"I went in for the hearing and laid it all out—just like I'm doing for you. I was sworn in and there was a court reporter taking everything down. I felt like a criminal."

When Jill finished her explanation she was asked to wait outside while the report from the rape was located and reviewed. When that had been done, she was called back.

"Do you know what the lieutenant *said* to me? He said I hadn't behaved like a police officer should at the time of the rape, that I hadn't lived up to their standards."

"You mean"—I was dumbstruck again—"you should have known how to react like you would now?"

"That's what they said, and that because of the way I acted I couldn't be trusted as a partner. I mean, now the guy wouldn't have gotten me past the first armhold. Now I know what to do. I play it over and over in my head—just how I'd have handled it if I'd known then what I know now."

"Were these comments on the record?" I could see why she had an attorney who was fighting the termination.

"No, they weren't. The reporter wasn't told to come in when I went back. I tried to get the lieutenant to repeat them later for my attorney and when a reporter was there, but he wouldn't come right out and admit to having said it. The official reasons are being given as failure to obey an order to return to work and lying."

"So what's happening now?"

"Well, the review board has decided to give me a rehearing. I think it's all the publicity Bob Butler—he's my attorney—has generated that made them grant it."

"Jill, I suppose the next question is: do you still really want to be a police officer if they decide to let you stay?"

"I don't know. I think I'd like to try, to see if I want to be one. I don't know—but," she stressed with certainty, "I want the choice to be mine."

It occurred to me Jill may have become a police officer for all the wrong, though admirable, reasons. To make a success of it would require more than the usual amount of luck and dedication. To start out with a cloud this big over her head might be too much.

She told me she had some trouble in the academy—primarily in passing the physical requirements, which included beating a dummy with a baton; she found this idea so repulsive she had refused for a long time to comply, but had ultimately overcome her block and had completed the course successfully.

Jill had also been recommended for a psychological workup by the Police Department medical staff because a preliminary interviewer had some question about her suitability for police work.

"I went, was accepted into the academy, and never heard about the results." She shrugged. "I guess they were all right."

I had Jill sign another release form and sent for the report.

When Jill left I called her attorney and agreed to a meeting. Three days later the newspapers were full of the rehearing news, but no outcome was expected for some time. The chief of police was to make the final decision.

When I did get a copy of the termination proceedings file, the most poignant and revealing part was a two-page handwritten letter of support and explanation from Peggy Murray. It read in part: "Approximately one year ago, Jill was the victim of a rape. I will not expound on the devastating effects such an experience would have on any woman. I will assume a degree of compassion and understanding on the part of the reader."

It went on to chronicle Jill's strength in completing the course at the academy and her FTO (field training officer) program while waiting, sometimes on telephone standby, to be called to court. When in May 1980 her case appeared almost certain to go to trial, Jill was "looking forward to the prospect of starting fresh.

"But instead," the letter went on, "she received word that she would be placed back on telephone standby. This development upset her greatly, and when I met Jill late on the afternoon of May 16, 1980, she was distraught. She was fearful of the effects of the upcoming trial on her life and her job, she was apprehensive and had a feeling of hopelessness."

The letter concluded with Peggy's admission to being the instigator of the fabricated emergency, but explained she had done it for Jill's health and sanity when it was obvious that Jill could not make any decisions for herself.

Peggy Murray was the kind of friend everyone needed. It was a good thing Jill had her—and Bret too. They would both impress a jury.

During the first interview with Jill I had almost tripled my witness list and then had sent a pack of follow-up work orders out to investigations. By the end of July most had trickled back, and each one read like a new episode in a small-claims court soap opera.

Both officers who had responded to Jill's call for help were interviewed. Each described Jill as being distraught, sobbing periodically, and unwilling to reveal any details of what had been the cause of her obvious trauma.

The older one, the "bully" as Jill described him, had the impression that Jill did not know "whether to be most upset with herself, the man, or the two officers." I thought this an insightful observation, not in keeping at all with his otherwise unresponsive and callous behavior that evening with Jill. I subpoenaed him for the trial and all hell broke loose.

It seems that this officer had been granted a psychiatric disability leave shortly after Jill's rape. His psychiatrist had diagnosed him as severely depressed and suicidal, and warned that a trip to the witness stand could put him over the edge.

How comforting it was to know that Jill had been ministered to by a mentally ill police officer—and she had sensed it. My investigator described this officer as highly agitated during their interview, pacing back and forth, and almost yelling his responses to questions at times.

I decided to press for this officer's testimony and forced the psychiatrist to take the stand and testify that his patient's appearance might jeopardize his life. I felt the jury needed to see for itself that Jill was giving an accurate, and not exaggerated, description of the police response that she encountered.

The young officer, the one who looked like he wanted to help her, admitted his partner had been very gruff with Jill, had been under a lot of personal stress, and hadn't been himself lately. Yes, he had almost broken in to ease the tension between the two, but, being a rookie, he decided not to.

If this, along with dispatcher 98, wasn't bad enough for the Police Department, what I learned next would top everything. I was reading the paper one morning in late July when a headline caught my eye. A San Diego police officer had been arrested the night before and charged with a series of burglaries which had been plaguing an area of the city for some time. The officer's name was Craig Nelson. It rang a bell and sounded familiar, but it was not until almost halfway through the day that I realized it was the officer who had transported Jill to and from the hospital for an examination. The one who had asked her for a date! I decided against telling Jill, at least then.

That was another one down. I knew dozens of cops who were dedicated, ethical, and experienced. Jill had sure drawn a whole crop of losers.

I heard through the grapevine that dispatcher 98 had received his subpoena with great trepidation, since he also got word I was after his scalp. Being contrite was not enough, but it was a good start.

Another investigative report came back bearing the results of an interview with Jill's co-worker—Paul Murdock, with whom she shared a ride to the Anaheim Recreation Expo. He remembered driving with Jill to and from Anaheim. He had not then, or ever, seen Jill drunk, intoxicated, or unable to drive because of alcohol consumption.

Murdock said that when he and Jill attended any boat show it was strictly to pursue sales, that there was very little or virtually no drinking done during working hours. After the Anaheim show they had returned directly to San Diego.

Of all my known witnesses, Alan Eubanks remained the only one to be interviewed, but I was already certain I had the right case to try for the expert again. This time it would be much more sophisticated.

Alan Eubanks was tall, over six feet, slim, and neatly dressed in a coat and tie. He was formal-looking even when I later saw him wearing slacks and a T-shirt. And his glasses gave him an even more serious appearance. I had seen a side of Jill which would not have set well with Alan at all: her spontaneity and her humor. Alan did not strike me as having a humorous bone in his body. But he was very understanding.

He described Jill as very withdrawn, depressed, and in shock when he got to her apartment the night of the attack. I had asked the investigator to find out if Eubanks had seen Jill's reactions to fear in the past. He said that she usually became withdrawn and quiet when either frightened or hurt—the way he had found her that night.

I had also asked the investigator to find out if Eubanks had ever seen Jill drunk. The report indicated that he had on occasion, but that she wasn't drunk or intoxicated the night of the attack. And yes, she had told him about the meeting and dinner with Cole.

Now, in my office, I needed to talk about much more intimate things than drinking.

"Mr. Eubanks"—he looked like a Mr. Eubanks—"have you . . . ?"

"Please call me Alan, all right?"

"Okay, Alan. Have you ever heard of the rape trauma syndrome?"

He nodded his head. "I've heard about it a little bit."

I realized he, too, looked sad.

I went through the now familiar briefing about the rape trauma syndrome, zeroing in on the sexual dysfunctioning aspect.

He knew what I was after.

"Jill wanted me with her a lot after the rape, but not to make love—just to be there. Sometimes she woke up crying at night and a couple of times I had to wake her up because she was having a frightening dream."

"Did this go on until you broke up?"

"Well, it became less frequent, but what did go on was her waking up in the middle of the night and not being able to get back to sleep. I'd find her sitting in a chair or on the couch in the dark, or standing by the window just looking out."

"Did you understand her withdrawal from you?" I asked, feeling a little like a Peeping Tom.

"We talked about it several times and I told her I understood. But no matter what I did, she found reasons to fight, and then began doing things she'd never done before."

"Such as?" My interest was sparked anew.

"Such as not telling me her plans in the evening and then being upset when I asked her where she'd been, or getting home at two or three in the morning. And a couple of times not showing up to meet me when we'd made plans ahead of time."

"Were all of these behaviors ones that you saw only after the rape?" I was taking notes at a furious rate.

"Only after the rape, yes."

Jill seemed to be sabotaging the relationship intentionally, but no doubt subconsciously, since she saw things somewhat differently. She had described Alan as a real "mother hen" after the rape, always "checking up on her." She wanted Alan to be the one to end things, however, since it would be much easier on her that way.

"Alan"—this was going to be risky—"did you wonder if Jill was seeing anyone else besides you for the year before her rape?"

"No, I didn't. But I think she probably was after the rape before we split. I don't know who, though."

That saved me from asking the next question. I was relieved.

He didn't ask if I knew who and I didn't tell him. What I needed was his testimony about the relationship before the rape, their plans for marriage before the rape, their satisfaction with each other before the rape—and the disintegration of all that after the events of one specific night. In fact, I would use all the witnesses to show this night to have been pivotal in Jill's life.

Alan Eubanks would be a marvelous witness and expressed a desire to help Jill any way he could.

"You already have, Alan, you already have. I only wish it hadn't been at the expense of your future together."

That August was a dull month, not because there wasn't enough work to do, but because it was, and had been traditionally, a month for the lawyers to either take vacations or handle only easy matters in court. Excitement was usually nil. Mine should only have fit the norm.

Jill's termination hearing was back in the news the third week in August, because the police chief had asked for further investigation.

There were also some comments from Cole's attorney in the articles about the District Attorney's new tactic and the expert stuff.

He especially made sure the paper got wind of the sexual dysfunction idea and surmised what I was going to try to prove with it.

Very clever. That would surely extend time for jury selection.

Someone had brought the morning paper to my office (I never got around to it until after dinner, homework, and the kids' bedtimes had passed) and I sat musing over what kind of trial it would be with an attorney who was more aggressive than those I had dealt with in the past on the Harter and O'Conner cases.

The ringing of my phone, as usual, disrupted my thoughts just as I got going.

"Is this Judith Rowland?" the unfamiliar male voice inquired.

"Yes, it is. May I help you?"

"Maybe I can help you," came the reply. "Or maybe I can't, but I wanted to call you rather than the defense attorney."

"Which defense attorney?" It sounded as if this conversation had started in the middle.

"Well, I just read the article in this morning's paper about the case with Jill Bernadini, the rape victim. If there hadn't been a picture of her I never would have remembered her by the name alone."

I was beginning to get a very bad feeling.

"I don't live in San Diego anymore, but my parents still do and I come to visit them a few times a year. I just got in last night, and opened up the paper this morning over a cup of coffee and saw the article."

"What can you tell me about the case?"

I was certain that I didn't want to hear whatever it was he had to say. My heart was pounding.

"I slept with Jill Bernadini after she broke up with that boyfriend." The torpedo had hit.

My voice was remarkably calm—it even surprised me—while I questioned this saboteur about his relationship with Jill.

"I couldn't forget anyone as attractive as this lady," Lyle Daniels summed up when I wondered if he was certain we were talking about the same person. "She was alone at the Carousel bar and we must have talked for a couple of hours."

He seemed reliable and able to remember everything about his brief encounter with Jill Bernadini.

Maybe he was a defense plant, I hoped silently. *Stop it, Rowland,* I cautioned myself.

They had then gone back to Jill's apartment, Daniels went on, and had spent the night there. His account certainly sounded familiar.

But how could Jill have done this to me? My anger was fueled by a sense of betrayal more than anything else—loss of face, or the case, certainly, ranked up there too, but betrayal was paramount.

I knew I should wait to call Jill until I calmed down, but my fingers seemed to gravitate toward her phone number the instant I put the receiver down.

When I heard the sound of Jill's voice on the other end of the line, I didn't know what to say first. None of it was printable, little was coherent—in my head, anyway.

I was once again surprised to hear how calmly the words came together.

"Jill, it's Judy. We've got a problem." I wasn't yelling, but I gave her no time to talk. "Do you know a man by the name of Lyle Daniels?"

"Lyle Daniels?" She sounded appropriately nervous. My tone obviously didn't disguise everything. "Lyle Daniels? . . . No . . . I don't recognize it . . . I don't . . . think so. Why?"

"Well, my dear"—I was trying hard not to lose control—"he says he slept with you last year, after the rape. Do you have a car?"

"He says he slept with me?"

I hadn't heard her voice sound this way since the phone conversation with dispatcher 98. It made me feel a sharp twinge of guilt for condemning before I'd heard her side.

"That's what he says, Jill. Look, do you have a way to get down here? We need to talk."

"Uh, yeah . . . yeah. I'll have Todd bring me. But tell me, what . . . ?"

"Jill, let's wait until you're here, okay," I cut in, anticipating her question. "I'd rather do this face to face. How long will it take you?"

"Uh, probably, uh . . ." She was sounding more like the tape every second. "Probably no more than . . . thirty, forty minutes."

"Okay, I'll see you then . . . bye."

I let the receiver fall heavily in its cradle, feeling certain I should hear from somewhere off behind me a voice pipe up, "Okay, cut, print. It's a take!" But it didn't.

I had visions of how I'd tell Mark Fisher, and tried not to think about what he'd say to me. And Daly: he'd be the restrained captain, stalwart and strong, maybe letting me off with only an observation or two. And Kent, and the press . . .

In less than twenty-five minutes Jill stood in my doorway, looking much like she did the first time I'd seen her, only more frightened. I looked at her eyes. Eyes always carried more weight with me than anything else.

Hmm. The eyes aren't lying, I said to myself as I motioned Jill to a chair without a word.

We sat looking at each other for what seemed like a very long time.

"I *must* know what happened." My words shattered the fragile silence which, from the expression on her face, seemed to be all that was keeping Jill from physical pain.

I quickly told her the details Lyle Daniels had given me. Still, the expression did not change.

"I swear to you," she began when I finally gave her the opportunity. "When you called I did not remember this man."

"But you do now?" I was not being kind.

"Yes, I think I do. But if it's him, then . . . then he was right . . . I did *sleep* with him . . . but we never made love." Her panicked eyes still revealed no deception. "We had no sex, no intercourse."

It's amazing how quickly a lawyer can shift mental gears. I was confused, but already churning through ways to salvage the case.

"I met a man, this Lyle Daniels, I guess, in the Carousel bar one evening during that same time when I met Bret—after Bret, but I don't know exactly how long after. We talked for a few hours . . . and then . . . I invited him to the apartment. Well . . . actually, the same thing happened with him that happened with Bret."

"You mean"—the wheels still turning for a way to make this all sound plausible—"that you cried when he tried to make love to you?"

"Yes." Her voice was softer now, almost a whisper. "Yes. I cried. And told him some story about just breaking up with a boyfriend . . ."

"You didn't tell him about the rape?" This was like feeding information to a computer and then having it spit out logical, understandable results on the screen.

"No . . . I didn't . . . it's so hazy . . . but I'm sure I remember not wanting to just keep telling people about the rape whenever I cried, or couldn't have sex. Anyway, we talked and then we slept for a few hours."

Jill then told me she'd never seen the man again.

"And you forgot all about him?" I didn't know what to believe, but if Daniels confirmed this version I could see some hope.

"Yes, I forgot all about him. It was almost a year ago and so much has happened. Does that seem so improbable?" She looked at me this time with no flirtation in her eyes.

Well . . . improbable? . . . Really, it didn't, I supposed. Between September of 1979 and August of 1980, Jill had ended a four-year relationship with a man she had been close to marrying, had gone through the police academy and her field training program, and had been subpoenaed six times to testify at her own rape trial—something she was also trying to keep anyone from knowing about.

I picked up the phone and dialed the number Daniels had left me.

"Mr. Daniels, this is Judy Rowland from the District Attorney's office. Could you please tell me *exactly* what you meant when you said you 'slept' with Jill Bernadini?"

I was watching Jill's face—still no change.

"Well . . ." He seemed not to be sure of my question, but I didn't want to put words in his mouth—no, damn it, I couldn't bring myself to ask if they'd made love because I dreaded the answer. "If you mean was there more than sleep, the answer is yes, but we didn't have intercourse, because she said she couldn't, that something had happened recently and she couldn't."

"What do you mean there was more than sleep?"

"I mean, we . . . she seemed to *plan* to make love, but after we had our clothes off and . . . well . . . after the foreplay, she just froze up."

"Froze up?" I was writing down every word I could get. "What exactly did she do?"

"It's what she didn't do. She stopped kissing me and went stiff . . . and . . . well, didn't respond."

"Did she cry?"

"Cry? Ah, I remember . . . what do you *want* me to remember?"

"Mr. Daniels, I realize you called me because you wanted to help Jill . . ."

"And I sure as hell don't want to help defend a rapist," he interrupted.

"Yes, I understand that too, but it's what you really remember that I want to know. Do you remember if she cried?"

"Not really. She was very depressed and apologized, but I don't remember if she cried."

"Do you recall what explanation she gave you about her behavior?" I was beginning to see the answer to this crisis appear on that screen.

"Yeah, she said it had to do with a recent relationship she'd had and asked if I'd mind just staying with her for a while."

And then, as if the thought had just struck him: "God, now I realize it was the rape. Jesus Christ! I hope you hang this Cole guy."

When I hung up I told Jill what I'd learned. I couldn't decide whether my behavior pegged me for an S.O.B., a hypocrite, or a justifiably righteous attorney. I concluded that I had jumped on her too soon, but as time went on and I rehashed the whole thing over a few more times, I also concluded that, even for a person of my persuasions on the subject of rape, this had been an unfair test.

I asked Jill to spend some serious time trying to remember if there were any other similar situations. Then I called Mark Fisher and told him I just hammered another nail into his client's coffin.

Hmm, from my torpedo to his coffin nail in a little over two hours. Not bad for an afternoon's work.

15

THE BERNADINI RAPE CASE could be called a true rags-to-riches story.

Within days of our brush with disaster, I sat at my desk with a half-inch stack of police arrest reports on Jeremy Cole which spanned more than a decade of clashes he'd had with the law starting at age fourteen.

A week later I was immersed in a 500-page transcript from the trial of his lost civil suit against the Fulmon Police Department for alleged police brutality during an arrest for drunk driving.

What I learned about this man frightened me beyond words, confirmed once and for all the course I knew I wanted my future to take, and had there been any lingering doubts about Jeremy Cole's guilt in the case I was considering taking to court, they were gone forever.

In 1972 there was a conviction for being under the influence of drugs, and an arrest on suspicion of armed robbery (of drugs from a pharmacy). His vehicle was identified as the getaway car, but apparently there wasn't enough evidence for a case against him.

He had no convictions in 1973, but there were three arrests for possession of marijuana—on three consecutive days in September. And an arrest for burglary. I could find no disposition for the latter case, but the police reported positive identification by a witness that Cole was the man seen attempting to break into a business next to his residence —a business that had suffered a burglary at the identical point of entry three weeks earlier.

Then in 1974 came his first conviction for driving under the influence of alcohol, although his first arrest for this offense occurred in 1971. In 1974 he was also convicted of another trespass offense which started out as a burglary.

There appeared to be a two-year hiatus for 1975 and 1976, as there was a complete absence of documented criminal activity for those years.

In 1977 he was back, and my reports showed four separate arrests between January 8 and June 30 for driving under the influence of alcohol, with at least one conviction.

Once again Cole seemed to disappear, leaving no trail of criminal activity for the remainder of 1977 until early 1979 with the arrest in Fulmon which led to his suit against that city's Police Department.

There were some vaguely disturbing reminiscent observations in the myriad of police reports which I had in my possession: Cole had been unemployed at the time of every arrest except once, when he listed bartending as his occupation; his addresses were always different and several times he appeared to be living with "new girlfriends." His emergency reference was always his mother; he mentioned at least twice, once as early as mid-1973 and again in 1979, that he was taking medication and was under a psychiatrist's care.

Yet there were no direct signs in any of his files that Jeremy Cole was violent or might be a rapist—until I read the transcript from the civil suit.

Now, most D.A.'s will never have access to the expansive personal information I was afforded in the Cole case. But positive confirmation of what aroused my suspicions in the first place about Cole's "profile," for lack of a better word, was a clear indication that more can and should be known by the criminal justice system about accused rapists' backgrounds and behavior.

By the time I had finished the case, I was a walking encyclopedia. But I'm getting ahead of myself again, if only a little.

The trial transcript filled in the two voids of absent criminal behavior in Cole's arrest record. In 1975 he enlisted in the Army and in late 1976 he received a medical discharge—based on psychiatric problems.

It was the 1977–78 time period which really confirmed all my suspicions. During this time he had wandered about on the east coast living hand to mouth, at least for some months, with a woman in a small Connecticut town.

Then he was hospitalized twice for serious psychiatric disorders, being diagnosed first as a paranoid and then as a psychotic. The latter hospitalization resulted from a display of violent behavior in front of a major military hospital on the east coast. Upon admission, Cole complained of hearing voices, of being followed by people out to get him, and of having severely beaten a woman with whom he had recently lived.

Cross-examination of Cole in the civil case revealed the name of the woman with whom he had lived in Connecticut, although he denied ever having beaten her.

I wondered if I could find her. I put out an investigative service request suggesting a phone call to every number in this small town assigned to someone with this woman's last name. It was worth a try. I didn't have long to wait.

"Judy," he began as soon as I picked up the phone, "I can't believe it myself, but I think I found your lady last night."

"No kidding!" I was even more surprised than he.

"Well, actually I found her father, who was adamant about not wanting to get his daughter involved with this fellow again. He says she is newly married, and that she's expecting a child. He was frantic. I think I calmed him down, but you need to call."

I didn't know where to start. "Did he tell you about the beating?"

"Only by inference. That the guy seemed nice enough, they gave him some odd jobs, carpentry and repair work around the house, and then—wham . . . he nearly . . . and he didn't finish. I think he'll listen to you about conveying some message to his daughter. I tried to convince him that she should make the decision, not him. Do you want the number?"

My hand was shaking as I wrote it down. I felt like Perry Mason, Ellery Queen, Sherlock Holmes—all rolled into one! I was shaking even more as I dialed.

The phone rang once . . . twice . . . then the recording: "The number you have reached is no longer in service and there is no new number . . ."

I should have known. I dialed again just to be sure. No mistake, it had been disconnected. A quick check showed a new, unlisted number had been issued.

I felt like jumping on the next plane and taking a regiment of police with me. I was so close, so close . . .

"I'd have done the same for my daughter," I said to myself calmly. "I know I would have."

It wasn't fair of me to rekindle this family's memories of horror so suddenly without provocation. Unfair maybe, but how about necessary? I spent a couple of days debating with myself and finally decided not to persist. There are some boundaries to the pursuit of justice—some convictions command too high a price, as do many defenses. If this one turned on the absence of testimony from this lady, so be it.

The trial transcript did provide me with a variety of usable information. I learned that Cole had suffered from a variety of mental problems for years and that he came from a broken home in which his father had been distant and cold while his mother had been protective and totally suffocating.

His only permanent address for his entire life was his mother's— where he had been when arrested on the rape charges.

I had absolutely no idea how I was going to get any of this extraordinary information into the courtroom, but I was certain by now I was not prosecuting an innocent man.

I also realized with a sudden chill that Jill had indeed been extremely fortunate. I think she believed me, at least a little, after I told her everything I had learned about her attacker.

It occurred to me that sixteen months—the time since the rape— was too long for Cole to have had only one arrest, especially for something as minor as drunk driving, considering the violence which had surrounded it. I again sent out my investigative tentacles.

Within twenty-four hours of my request for outstanding police reports on cases which were pending, I had a fourteen-page file on my desk accompanied by a criminal complaint for burglary against Jeremy Cole in the city of Weston, a suburb of Los Angeles.

But this one was different. Very different. And very frightening.

A ten-year-old girl had heard noises outside her family residence at about 8:30 on the evening of January 14, 1980. When she had gone to investigate, she noticed the outline of a male figure at the window. She moved quickly down the hall to her bedroom, but the noises also moved closer, and when she peeked around the corner of her bedroom, she could see the outline of the male figure again, this time at the bathroom window.

Frightened, the girl ran to the den at the back of the house and told her father what she had seen. Upon investigating, he too could see the male figure at the bathroom window, and could hear him fooling with the screen.

After calling the police, the girl's father went outside, and the figure moved quickly away, across the street and through a neighbor's yard. Within minutes the police arrived, were filled in on what the witnesses had seen, and launched a foot pursuit.

At least five police officers spent upwards of twenty minutes pursuing the shadowy figure through the adjoining residential streets before capturing Cole. The shoes he was wearing had sole prints matching those found under both windows of the girl's residence where she and her father had seen and heard the male figure. A search of Cole's clothing revealed a screen latch and an examination of the bathroom window area found a latchless screen.

By this point in the report I already had chills. And the most frightening part was yet to come.

At first Cole gave a false name, but after some initial questioning he admitted his true identity and began to talk to one of the police officers. He told him that he had been looking in the windows at "that house" in order to get a better view of a young female who had been standing at a bedroom window massaging her breasts!

At this point Cole was advised of his constitutional rights and chose to continue with his story. He told the detective that he lived in the neighborhood with a woman and that while walking home he passed that house and noticed a young female standing in the window, with her blouse up, massaging her breasts. He stood watching for several minutes and then moved up to the window to get a better look. Twice she repeated this behavior, stopping for a couple of minutes in between, and each time Cole watched, he reported.

Then, he went on, he figured she would be going to the bathroom to get ready for bed, so he went to that window and removed the screen. He professed a desire only to look into the bathroom, not to enter.

When interviewed, the ten-year-old girl told the police that she had been watching television when she heard the noises and that she never rearranged or changed clothing during the episode.

Scary stuff, real scary. Not only was Cole awaiting trial on a felony charge of rape, but he was stalking ten-year-old girls and acting on fantasies.

I needed help, lots of high-powered help. I was determined to stop this man.

This, of course, translated into dollars and cents.

After a short briefing with Daly, during which I artfully stated my intent in question form, I took everything I had on the Cole case and stormed Ronald Creelman's office. This time he sat trapped behind his desk at 11:30 in the morning, unprotected by the 5 P.M. bell. An hour later, I left with permission to hire experts, thanks to a combination of Creelman's outrage at what I'd shown him about Jeremy Cole and his belief that I just might have come up with the right legal approach to the use of the rape expert: to bolster the victim's credibility.

I promised him an outline of my trial brief. I hated writing briefs, especially before they were due, but it was part of the bargain.

Fortunately for me, no dollar limit was imposed on me and this trial brief ended up costing its weight in gold—not because of my excesses, but rather because of its newness and experimental nature. Now, such preparation can be, and usually is, moderately priced. At that time, however, I didn't want to take *any* chances. I called Ann Burgess in Boston and we began a running dialogue about my plans. Through late summer and into early fall we exchanged ideas, with me even tracking her down late one night at her summer home after bribing her son into giving me the number. She never objected and was always a most enthusiastic supporter.

It was nearly impossible for me to give her a definite date as to when I would need her to come to the west coast to testify, and it was causing escalating anxiety on my part that she might not be available at the fateful moment.

During one of our many phone discussions, I happened to mention to Ann what I had learned about Jeremy Cole's background.

Her response was immediate. "You should be talking with Nick Groth. He's the leading expert in this country on rapist behavior."

"Expert?" I was startled. "There's an *expert* on rapist behavior and I can't even get to first base with victim behavior?"

"Well," she quickly added, "those of us in the field realize this expertise, but only one court has recognized it—and it was federal."

"Nick Groth . . . Nick Groth." The name did have a familiar ring. Later I found I had it among some notes I had made almost two years before during a discussion with another of the leading researchers in the field of rape victim behavior.

Dr. Pauline Bart, a psychologist in Chicago, had been one of my earliest mentors. She had been doing research on rape victims longer than just about anyone else and had encouraged my efforts with Harter and O'Conner. She and her study results were where I often turned when I needed support for a position I had taken on some aspect of rape victimology.

Pauline had even been responsible for modifying my position on victim resistance in the face of rape. My experience and research had led me to believe that resistance was a last resort and not an advisable coping strategy under most circumstances. When a local college professor began to make the news by advocating that women who fight back are more successful in escaping the attack, I angrily called Pauline, expecting her to support me in my public statement to the contrary.

"As a matter of fact," she replied instead, "I have just completed a study that suggests your professor may be right."

She went on to tell me that, as a result of a national magazine survey she had conducted for a research project the year before, she had, quite coincidentally, received thirteen replies from women who had each been both a victim of a rape and an avoider of a rape attack on separate occasions during their adult lives. She had decided to do a follow-up study on just these women.

"The common denominator, or difference," she concluded, "for these women the time they avoided rape seemed to be their resistance."

She had been somewhat surprised herself, but other researchers also seemed to be coming up with similar results.

"It's the surprise of the attacker at the victim's anger and her immediate resistance rather than the trembling and fear he had expected to encounter."

We had both agreed that women still should be aware that risk of injury could increase as risk of rape decreased.

I emerged from the experience with the attitude I still advocate today: there is no one right or wrong way to respond to a rapist's attack. The best preparation is for women to be aware of *all* their options and possible coping strategies, and equally important, to know as much about *rapists'* behavior as is available. With this knowledge, the best decisions can be made under the particular circumstances.

Anyway, if this Nick Groth was good enough for Pauline Bart and Ann Burgess, he certainly had potential for the Cole case. Before I called him, though, I decided to read his book. I had to make a special trip to an L.A. bookstore to find a copy. No one carried it, at that time at least, in San Diego.

"Men Who Rape: Psychology of the Offender, by A. Nicholas Groth, with H. Jean Birnbaum." I said the title aloud, and turned to the last page. Two hundred twenty-three pages of information on a rapist?

I next looked at the back flap to see what I could learn about the author. Groth had a Ph.D. and was director of the sex offender program at the Connecticut correctional institution in Somers, Connecticut. He was also a clinical psychologist and a graduate of Boston University. Now I knew the connection between Nick Groth and Ann Burgess. He specialized in the area of sexual assault and worked with both offenders and victims in institutional community-based settings. He held several teaching positions in colleges in the northeastern United States and conducted workshops on rape and child molestation with the Massachusetts Criminal Justice Training Council in Boston and for the FBI training academy in Quantico, Virginia. He was also a consultant for the sexual trauma treatment program of the state of Connecticut's Department of Children and Youth Services. I noticed that he had lectured and published extensively and was known both nationally and internationally.

I knew I had found the person I had been looking for.

There was a dedication to Ann Burgess and a table of contents with chapters addressing "Clinical Aspects of Rape," "Patterns of Rape," and "Guidelines for Assessment and Treatment"—all directed to the *offender.*

The chapter which really attracted my attention, however, was entitled "Psychodynamics of Rape"—in other words, why do men rape? It contained, I noticed, excerpts from an article which Groth had co-authored with Burgess and Holmstrom for the November 1977 issue of the *American Journal of Psychiatry.*

I already knew that rape was primarily a violent rather than a sexually motivated act, but why did some men hurl their violence at women through sexual acts? As in my first reading of Burgess and Holmstrom's articles on victims in 1978, the revelations I found here about rapists were awesome and had a profound effect in completing my total education about this area which had so captivated my efforts and attempts to understand it as a lifelong work.

I have done extensive quoting of the chapter entitled "Psychodynamics of Rape" from Nick Groth's work in this section of my book because there is no way I could have said it better than it has already been said.

"One of the most basic observations one can make regarding men who rape is that not all such offenders are alike. They do not do the very same thing in the very same way or for the very same reasons. In some cases, similar acts occur for different reasons, and in other cases, different acts serve similar purposes. From our clinical experience with convicted offenders and with victims of reported sexual assault, we find that in *all* cases of forcible rape, three components are present: power, anger, and sexuality. The hierarchy and interrelationships among these three factors, together with the relative intensity with which each is experienced and the variety of ways in which each is expressed, vary from one offender to another. Nevertheless, there seems to be sufficient clustering within the broad spectrum of sexual assault so that distinguishable patterns of rape can be differentiated based on the descriptive characteristics of the assault and the dynamic characteristics of the offender.

"Rape is always and foremost an aggressive act. In some offenses, the assault appears to constitute a discharge of anger; it becomes evident that the rape is the way the offender expresses and discharges a mood state of intense anger, frustration, resentment, and rage. In other offenses, the aggression seems to be reactive; that is, when the victim resists the advances of her assailant, he retaliates by striking, hitting, or hurting her in some way. Hostility appears to be quickly triggered or released, sometimes in a clear, consciously experienced state of anger, or, in other cases, in what appears to be a panic state. In still other offenses, the aggression becomes expressed less as an anger motive and more as a means of dominating, controlling, and being in charge of the situation—an expression of mastery and conquest. And in a fourth vicissitude, the aggression itself becomes eroticized, so that the offender derives pleasure from both controlling his victim and hurting her/him—an intense sense of excitement and pleasure being experienced in this context whether or not actual sexual contact is made. These variations on the theme of aggression are not mutually exclusive, and, in any given instance of rape, multiple meanings may be expressed in regard to both sexual and aggressive behaviors.

"In every act of rape, both aggression and sexuality are involved, but it is clear that sexuality becomes the means of expressing the aggressive needs and feelings that operate in the offender and underlie his assaults. Three basic patterns of rape can be distinguished in this regard: (1) the *anger rape*, in which sexuality becomes a hostile act; (2) the *power rape*, in which sexuality becomes an expression of conquest; and (3) the *sadistic rape*, in which anger and power become eroticized.

"Rape is complex and multi-determined. It serves a number of psychological aims and purposes. Whatever other needs and factors operate in the commission of such an offense, however, we have found the components of anger, power, and sexuality always present and prominent. Moreover, in our experience, we find that either anger or power is the dominant component and that rape, rather than being primarily an expression of sexual desire, is, in fact, the use of sexuality to express these issues of power in rape. Rape, then, is a pseudosexual act, a pattern of sexual behavior that is concerned much more with status, hostility, control, and dominance than the sensual pleasure of sexual satisfaction. It is sexual behavior in the primary service of non-sexual need."

So it was anger and power expressed as sexual behavior that I had been seeing but had been unable to put my finger on. First Burgess and Holmstrom had focused the victim for me. Now Groth had accomplished the same with the offender. I was breathless with anticipation. I was not to be disappointed.

"In some cases of sexual assault, it is very apparent that sexuality becomes a means of expressing and discharging feelings of pent-up anger and rage. The assault is characterized by physical brutality. Far more actual force is used in the commission of the offense than would be necessary if the intent were simply to overpower the victim and achieve sexual penetration. Instead, this type of offender *attacks* his victim, grabbing her, striking her, knocking her to the ground, beating her, tearing her clothes, and raping her. He may use a blitz style of attack, a violent surprise offensive in which the victim is caught completely off guard. Or he may use a confidence-style approach to gain access to the victim and then launch a sudden, overpowering attack. In the former situation, the offender approaches the victim directly by hitting her. In the latter situation, victims often relate that at first the assailant seemed pleasant enough, but that at some point he changed. Suddenly and without warning he became mean and angry."

Clearly the "blitz" style is what most people think of as "real rape": the victim is knocked down, dragged into the bushes, clothes torn off, and then sexually assaulted.

"The rape experience for this type of offender is one of conscious anger and rage, and he expresses his fury both physically and verbally. His aim is to hurt and debase his victim, and he expresses his contempt for her through abusive and profane language. If his primary motive is one of anger, and if he is not sexually motivated, why doesn't this offender contain his assault to a battering of the victim? Why does he also rape her? The answer seems to be that such a man considers rape the ultimate offense he can commit against another person. Sex becomes his weapon, and rape constitutes the ultimate expression of his anger. Often this type of offender forces the victim to submit to or to perform additional sexual acts that he may regard as particularly degrading, such as sodomy or fellatio. In some cases, contempt for the victim is expressed by urinating or by masturbating and ejaculating onto her."

Was I reading about Jeremy Cole? I later learned that there were gray areas in categorizing anger and power rapists and that Cole exhibited characteristics of each and possibly bordered on the sadistic as well. As I read on, I began to identify behaviors, language, and events which had characterized Harter, O'Conner, and many of the other offenders whose cases I had handled or reviewed over the years.

"Characteristically, this type of offender does not report being in a state of sexual excitement or arousal. In fact, he may be initially impotent during the assault and able to achieve an erection only by masturbating himself or having the victim perform oral sex on him. Sexuality itself is typically regarded by this type of offender as something basically 'dirty' and offensive at some level of subjective experience, and, therefore, it becomes a weapon, a means by which he can defile, degrade, and humiliate his victim.

"Typically, such an offender reports that he did not anticipate committing a rape. It was not something he fantasized or thought about beforehand—it was, instead, something that happened on the spur of the moment. Sometimes he will say that he felt 'something was going to happen' but could not identify or anticipate what course of action his feelings would lead to. Even during the offense itself the offender may psychologically disassociate himself from the assault as if he were in a trance or more an observer than a participant; the event is experienced as unreal, and the offender may not fully appreciate the extent of his aggression.

"Relatively speaking, such attacks tend to be of short duration. The offender strikes, assaults, and flees. Such assaults appear to be more impulsive or spontaneous than premeditated, and the offender finds it difficult to account for his assault, when he cannot deny it, except to rationalize that he was intoxicated or on drugs, or that he just 'flipped out.'

"In describing the evolution of the assault, the offender typically reports being in an upset and distressed frame of mind, at the time of the offense. His predominant mood state appears to be a combination of anger, distress, frustration, and depression and the offense itself is typically preceded by some upsetting event, often, but not invariably, involving some significant woman in the offender's life. The assault is in response to some identifiable precipitating stress. For example, some offenders reported a serious dispute with their wives prior to the offense. These arguments revolved around a number of marital issues, such as the wife's threatening to or, in fact, leaving him, arguments over his drinking, complaints about her housekeeping skills, suspicions of infidelity, and the like. Others felt aggravated with their parents for imposing unfair restrictions on their activities or unjust punishments for their misbehavior. Some of the offenders cited conflicts with their girlfriends, such as being stood up, rejected, taunted, or sexually frustrated. Others reported feeling upset over such things as being rejected from military service, being fired, being burdened by financial debts, or being harassed in some fashion by other people. The common theme appeared to be one in which the offender felt that he had been wronged, hurt, put down, or treated unjustly in some fashion by some individual, situation, or event. Rape served to discharge the resulting anger, resentment, and frustration. In this fashion, the anger rapist revenges himself from what he perceives to be wrongs done him by others, especially women.

"The anger rapist's relationships with important persons in his life are frequently fraught with conflict, irritation, and aggravation. The anger, resentment, hostility, and frustration engendered in these relationships are often displaced onto other individuals and, therefore, the victim may be a complete stranger to the offender, someone who has been unfortunate enough to be in his presence at the moment at which his controls begin to fail and his rage erupts. Although she has done nothing to warrant it, she becomes the target of his revenge—not revenge in a calculating, planned fashion but, instead, the recipient of an impulsive reaction precipitated by a situation she has had no part in.

"In some cases, the victim of the anger rapist is the actual person toward whom the offender harbors such anger, but in other cases, she is simply a substitute person, a symbolic and available 'object' against whom the assailant discharges his wrath and fury.

"The anger rapist strikes sporadically and infrequently, because his assault does not serve to discharge his anger, and it then takes time for his frustrations and aggravations to reach a volatile point again. His intent, then, is to hurt and degrade his victim. His weapon is sex, and his motive is revenge."

There then followed a section concerning victim impact following an attack by an anger rapist.

"Although all rapes involve anger, power, and sexuality and impact on the victim to disrupt her physical, behavioral, social, and sexual lifestyle, depending on the type of rape the victim is a victim of, certain issues may be more prominent or take on an added significance in the recovery process.

"The medical examination of the victims of an anger rape generally reveal considerable physical trauma to all areas of the body, often requiring X-rays and consultation of other medical specialists. Victims report experiencing the rape as a life-threatening situation. Although the anger rape is a physically brutal and violent assault, the victim may have less long-lasting traumatic effects from the attack, relatively speaking, for a number of reasons. First, she is visibly injured, and there is much concrete evidence (as bruises and torn clothing) to support the fact that she is a victim of rape. There is less suspicion of either false accusation or victim participation. She may receive much more comforting and support from those who subsequently come into contact with her (police, hospital personnel, family and friends), and there may be less of an accusatory undertone to their questions and comments. Also, psychologically the aim of this victim is to survive the assault, since she has suddenly and without warning become the target of an excessively brutal and uncontrolled rage on the part of the assailant which has placed her life in jeopardy. She hopes to live through the attack and she does. So her primary aim or objective is accomplished. Perhaps the most salient issue, then, is one of her vulnerability and her increased awareness of being at risk. Awareness of life-threatening dangers, the realistic assessment of high-risk situations, and the devising of strategies that will serve to protect her better and make her less accessible and vulnerable are key issues for this type of victim. Safety becomes a principal issue. The aggression is far more blatant than the sexuality, and if the victim has been a significantly older or even elderly woman this may serve to help reduce the sexual overtones of such offenses. However, since the physical effects of such an assault are highly visible, the victim has less choice in keeping her victimization secret.

"Another key issue in working with a victim of an anger rape may be to help her appreciate the dynamics of such an assault. The victim will want some understanding of why this has happened to her and what has prompted the offender to behave in such an apparently irrational manner. When something is understood, it is less threatening and disturbing than something which appears mysterious, or bizarre, or unexplainable. The victim's sense of intimidation may be partly relieved by being able to make some sense out of what initially appears incomprehensible. The victim may also fear that she continues to be at risk of further assaults from her offender. In fact, this is not at all likely. Frequently, anger rapists report that they had no idea who their victim was or what she looked like. Many have said that even when they saw the victim again in court, they were unable to recognize her. It appears that at the time of the assault they were 'blind with rage,' so to speak. Even if not apprehended, the offender is unlikely to assault the same victim again simply because women are objects to him, and objects are interchangeable. They are symbols that have no meaning in and of themselves to him. Therefore, when the offender again reaches that point where his anger is erupting and his controls are failing, he does not seek out a specific victim, but, instead, discharges his anger into someone who is immediately available."

It certainly was not difficult to see why victims of anger rapists were the ones most sought after by the criminal justice system. For all the reasons that Groth and Burgess and Holmstrom had determined in their research, the victim of the anger rapist was certainly the most desirable for convincing a jury in a courtroom, beyond a reasonable doubt, that she had truly been a victim of rape. Here there was no time for an assailant to discover personal and detailed information about his victim, there was less question of her participation in, and her culpability for, the attack.

While I was reading this chapter in Groth's book, I had to take frequent breaks to sort out my thoughts as they raced backward over facts of old cases I'd tried in the past and then jumped ahead to what I was hoping to do in the future with this wealth of newfound knowledge.

The next section dealt with the identification of the power rapist.

"In another pattern of rape, power appears to be the dominant factor motivating the offender. In these assaults, it is not the offender's desire to harm his victim but to possess her sexually. Sexuality becomes a means of compensating for underlying feelings of inadequacy and serves to express issues of mastery, strength, control, authority, identity, and capability. His goal is sexual conquest, and he uses only the amount of force necessary to accomplish his objective. His aim is to capture and control his victim. He may accomplish this through verbal threat ('Do what I say and you won't get hurt!'), or intimidation with a weapon ('I told her to undress, and when she refused I struck her across the face to show her I meant business'). Physical aggression is used to overpower and subdue the victim, and its use is directed toward achieving sexual submission. The intent of the offender usually is to achieve sexual intercourse with his victim as evidence of conquest, and to accomplish this, he resorts to whatever force he finds necessary to overcome his victim's resistance and to render her helpless. Very often, the victim is kidnapped or held captive in some fashion, and she may be subjected to repeated assaults over an extended period of time.

"Such offenders entertain obsessional thoughts and masturbatory fantasies about sexual conquest and rape. The characteristic scenario is one in which the victim initially resists the sexual advances of her assailant; he overpowers her and achieves sexual penetration; in spite of herself, the victim cannot resist her assailant's sexual prowess and becomes sexually aroused and receptive to his embrace."

So, the power rapist has fantasies that the victim is enjoying herself, wants the sex, clearly was a participant in what he knows to be a pleasurable experience because of his prowess: the language that Cole used; the observations of both Harter and O'Conner that the victim really "wanted" sex because she was either wet or aroused or "enjoying it." Albert Drake clearly fit the pattern of a power rapist, as he drove his victim around the county over an extended period of time as if she were a captive.

"Since it constitutes a test of his competency, the rape experience for this type of an offender is a mixture of excitement, anxiety, anticipated pleasure, and fear. In reality, the offender tends to find little sexual satisfaction in the rape. The assault is disappointing, or it never lives up to his fantasy.

"Whatever he may tell himself to explain the situation, at some level of experience he senses that he has not found what he is looking for in the offense—something he cannot clearly identify or define is missing or lacking. He does not feel reassured by either his own performance or his victim's response to the assault, and therefore, he must go out and find another victim, this time 'the right one.' His offenses become repetitive and compulsive, and he may commit a whole series of rapes over a relatively short period of time.

"The amount of force used in the assaults may vary depending in part on situational factors, but there may be an increase in aggression over time as the offender becomes more desperate to achieve that indefinable experience that continues to elude him.

"The offenses themselves are either premeditated (the offender goes out in search of a victim with the clear intent of sexual assault) or opportunistic (the situation presents itself in which the offender unexpectedly finds that he has access to a victim and this access activates his propensity for sexual assault).

"The victim of the power rapist may be of any age but generally tends to be within the same age range as the offender or younger. The choice of the victim is predominantly determined by availability, accessibility, and vulnerability.

"Although the power rapist may report that his offense was prompted by a desire for sexual gratification, careful examination of his behavior typically reveals that efforts to negotiate the sexual encounter or to determine the woman's receptiveness to a sexual approach are noticeably absent, as are any attempts at lovemaking or foreplay. Instead, the aim of the offender is to capture, conquer, and control his victim. Sexual desire, in and of itself, is not the primary or paramount issue operating in this assailant. If it were, there are a number of opportunities available in our society for consensual sex. In fact, sexual assaults always coexist with consenting sexual relations in the life of the offender. In no case have we ever found that rape was the first or only sexual experience in the offender's sexual history, or that he had no other alternatives or outlets for his sexual desires. To the question 'If what you wanted was sex, why didn't you just go to a prostitute?' the power rapist is likely to reply, 'A real man never pays for it,' revealing that one of the dynamics in the assault is reaffirmation of his manhood. Such offenders feel insecure about their masculinity or conflicted about their identity. For this reason they find homosexual activity particularly disturbing or frightening and often adopt antagonistic attitudes in this regard.

"Rape, then, becomes a way of putting such fears to rest, of asserting one's heterosexuality, and of preserving one's sense of manhood. The power rapist frequently reports becoming preoccupied with and troubled by homosexual thoughts at some point in the evolution of his offense.

"Sometimes clinicians tend to misinterpret such thoughts as latent wishes or unadmitted desires on the part of the offender, but, in fact, they seem to be more a reflection of his insecurity and personal discomfort in regard to human sexuality in general. Even heterosexual acts other than genital intercourse may be regarded as 'perverted,' and masturbation, likewise, may be thought of as abnormal. Although such rapists may engage in homosexual activities with the same frequency as normal males, they are not comfortable with such encounters. In fact, they experience all types of sexuality as threatening, and their heterosexual pursuits have a driven, compulsive, counter-phobic quality. Their anxieties may be converted into a tough, assertive, macho stance, or they may be reflected in a rather curious demand for validation and reassurance in regard to their victims.

"This offender tends to engage in conversation of a sexual nature with his victim but is both assertive (giving the victim instructions, orders, commands) and inquisitive (questioning her about her sexual interests or asking her to evaluate his sexual skills), reflecting both power issues and reassurance needs."

Both Sandy Adkins and Terri Richardson had been commanded by their assailants, Harter and O'Conner, respectively, to follow orders. In addition, each had been asked by their attackers if they were enjoying the sexual maneuvers being performed upon their bodies by their assailants, and when finally arrested, they spoke as if they knew that the victims had been willing participants in the sexual acts. And all the questions that Jill vaguely recalled having been asked of her during the shock of her attack, no doubt these, too, were the inquisitive questions needed by a power rapist to give him the satisfaction of both power and reassurance.

"The quest for power, mastery, and control appears to be an unresolved life issue operating in this offender that he acts out in his sexual assaults.

"Not only may the victim symbolize everything the offender dislikes about himself (being weak, powerless, effeminate, and the like) but his desperate need to reassure himself of his virility and sexual competency often results in his attributing his own wishes to his victim, distorting his perception of her and misinterpreting her behavior. Frequently, the power rapist denies that the sexual encounter was forcible. He *needs* to believe the victim wanted and enjoyed it. Following the assault, he may insist on buying the victim a drink or dinner and express a wish to see her again. In some cases, this may be understood as a way of 'cooling the mark,' that is, a gesture of friendliness and 'no hard feelings,' or a way of discrediting any subsequent report of rape by her; but in other cases, it reflects his fantasy expectation that sexual conquest has created a desire for him on the part of the victim. Even when entrapped and apprehended in this fashion (that is, the victim may agree to a 'rendezvous' at an appointed time and place which the police stake out), the offender cannot accept that the victim was not attracted to him but rationalizes that she had to allege rape to protect her reputation.

"The assault may be triggered by what the offender experiences to be a challenge by a female or a threat from a male, something which undermines his sense of competency and self-esteem and activates unresolved underlying feelings of inadequacy, insecurity, and vulnerability. He attempts to restore his sense of power, control, identity, and worth through his sexual offense. When one feels there are no other avenues of expression left, there are always the physical resources: strength and sexuality. The relative importance of power needs over sexual needs with this type of offender is reflected in some cases by the offender's keeping his victim captive, that is, in his control, for an extended period of time beyond the sexual activity. In other cases, the offender may be deterred from an intended offense when his victim addresses the power need in some fashion. For example, one offender who had raped six women reported being deterred on one occasion: he spotted his potential victim while riding on a subway and decided that if she got off alone at her stop, he would rape her. She did exit alone in a rather remote area of town, but as the offender followed her, she turned to him and explained that because it was so late at night she didn't feel safe walking home alone and asked him if he would be kind enough to accompany her until she reached her house. He did so and never touched her, puzzled that his wish to rape her had suddenly disappeared."

I wondered, as I read this description of how one woman had avoided being raped, if this had not indeed been a very successful and brave coping strategy on her part. I know that if I had been that lady walking home at night alone I would have realized that there was a man behind me and that he perhaps had something in mind besides accompanying me to my front door. It was fascinating to read what was on the rapist's mind rather than on the victim's.

"Power rapists often experience a sense of omnipotence through their assault and may express this by identifying themselves to their victims, by offering to drive them to the police station, or by some other such defiant act.

"Unfortunately, such offenders can and do frequently get away with their crimes, which only further increases their sense of power and control.

"The intent of the power rapist, then, is to assert his competency and validate his masculinity. Sexuality is the test and his motive is conquest."

As interesting and revealing as the information was in this chapter up to this point, it was the section on victim impact of the power rapist that really held the most valuable information in terms of the criminal justice system's approach to prosecution of this type of rape. It was here that I found some answers to what appeared to be the difficult hurdles faced by the system when trying to understand a victim of power rape.

"The victim of the power rapist is typically within the same age group as her offender, or she may be younger. Hospital examination may show minimal or inconclusive evidence of physical trauma. Although she may have come out of the assault relatively uninjured physically, the response of others to her plight may be less supportive. Hospital personnel, police, family, friends, and the like may be more accusatory in their questioning. They are dubious about her efforts to resist assault and they tend to feel that she deliberately or inadvertently invited or encouraged the assault—participation is misinterpreted as provocation and cooperation as consent.

"As noted above, in power assaults the language of the offender is typically instructional and sexually inquisitive. He may ask his victim if she enjoyed the sexual encounter, and if she would like to see him again, if before they part she will give him a kiss, etc. Many times, the victim plays along with the offender, reassures him that he is sexually impressive, tells him that she really did enjoy the sexual encounter, kisses him—in other words, cooperates in the service of survival. However, should she go to court, these coping strategies may be used to impeach her credibility about her resistance and lack of consent.

"Following the assault, the power rapist may not immediately release his victim. He may, for example, drive around town with her in his car. He may stop for gas or go into a fast-food stand to get himself and his victim something to eat."

Had Groth read about Drake and O'Conner?

"People find it difficult to understand why the victim does not call out for help to the gas station attendant or make good her escape when her offender goes into the fast-food shop. To understand this, one must realize that the victim feels powerless. She hopes that if she cooperates, her assailant will ultimately release her. She does not want to chance doing anything that might antagonize him. She is fearful that if she attempts to escape, he will hurt her. And where can she run to? Her home? Her job? At some point prior to, during, or after the assault, the offender usually questions the victim and learns where she lives and where she works. He may also have gone through her purse and found some identification. He knows where to find her if he wants to. This knowledge extends the sense of power and control, and the victim cooperates in the hope of not alienating him and of reducing the risk of further victimization.

"In the course of such assaults, when the offender does learn the victim's identity, she becomes fearful that he will return. Typically, the offender may make such threats as a continuation of his power and control over the victim. In fact, however, the likelihood of his actually carrying out such threats appears minimal. In our professional experience with over two hundred and fifty rape offenders, we have yet to find a single instance where this actually did occur, although it is a very common threat.

"Whereas for the victim of an anger rape her vulnerability becomes a prominent issue, for the victim of the power rape it is her helplessness. It is important, therefore, to respond to such victims in ways that serve to undo their feelings of powerlessness and re-establish a sense of personal control and self-determination. Their cooperation and permission should be requested in regard to examination and investigative procedures. Consent, choice, and decision making on their part must be respected—they should not be pressured into agreeing to something they are undecided about or opposed to.

"One of the key issues in working with victims of power rapes is their anger at themselves and self-blame for being victimized and not being able to escape the assault. It is important to help them realize that no strategy would necessarily have been more effective than the one they tried. What deters one assailant only encourages another, but frequently the victim feels that if she had said or done something different, she would have discouraged the assault. And it is this feeling of not having achieved her primary goal—that of escaping the offender —that affects the victim and retards the recovery from the trauma of sexual assault."

Both Stacy Billings and Terri Richardson had experienced captivity the way Nick Groth had described it. Each had been driven for prolonged periods around San Diego County and each had had what many felt were several opportunities to escape. Each had expressed, when asked why they had not availed themselves of these "opportunities," the feeling that they really didn't know why they hadn't run. Groth had just explained it.

Inadequacy of the medical exam on victims of power rapists was also explained in this part of Groth's book. The fact that those with whom the victims come in contact feel less than sure about her complaint of rape, when there are little or no physical signs of attack, certainly must be reflected in the quality of the examination. The last section in the chapter about profiles of the rapist, dealt with the sadistic rapist, and was not an unfamiliar scenario.

"In the third pattern of rape, both sexuality and aggression become fused into a single psychological experience known as sadism. There is a sexual transformation of anger and power so that the aggression itself becomes eroticized. This offender finds the intentional maltreatment of his victim intensely gratifying and takes pleasure in her torment, anguish, distress, helplessness, and suffering. The assault usually involves bondage and torture and frequently has a bizarre or ritualistic quality to it. The offender may subject his victim to curious actions, such as clipping her hair, washing or cleansing her body, or forcing her to dress in some specific fashion or behave in some specific way. Such indignities are accompanied by explicitly abusive acts such as biting, burning the victim with cigarettes, and flagellation. Sexual areas of the victim's body (her breasts, genitals, and buttocks) become a specific focus of injury and abuse. In some cases the rape may not involve the offender's sexual organs. Instead, he may use some type of instrument or foreign object, such as a stick or bottle, with which to penetrate his victim sexually.

"In extreme cases—those involving sexual homicide—there may be grotesque acts, such as the sexual mutilation of the victim's body or sexual intercourse with her corpse. One infamous sex killer committed four grisly murders in the span of one summer. As described in the pathologist's report, each victim had been dismembered into five parts. The skin was peeled off the breasts and vagina. On the legs and buttocks, there were multiple stab wounds and punctures. Stab wounds were also present in the interior chest well. Sperm were found in both the vagina and the rectum of the body, and findings were consistent with its having been deposited post-mortem.

"Prostitutes, or women whom the offender regards as promiscuous, may be particular targets of the sadistic rapist. Usually, his victims are strangers who share some common characteristics, such as age, appearance, or occupation. They are symbols of something he wants to punish or destroy. The assault is deliberate, calculated, and preplanned. The offender takes precautions against discovery, such as wearing a disguise or blindfolding his victim. The victim is stalked, abducted, abused, and sometimes murdered.

"In contrast to the anger rapist, the sexual sadist's offenses are fully premeditated. He is not suddenly exploding in a rage. Usually, he captures his victim, then works himself into a frenzy as he assaults her. The rape experience for the sexual sadist is one of intense and mounting excitement. Excitement is associated with the inflicting of pain upon his victim. Such abuse is usually a combination of the physical and psychological. Hatred and control are eroticized, so that he finds satisfaction in abusing, degrading, humiliating, and, in some cases, destroying his captive.

"For some sadistic rapists, the infliction of pain itself provides gratification; for others, it is a necessary preliminary to other forms of aggression. The more aggressive they are, the more powerful they feel; and, in turn, the more powerful they feel, the more excited they become. This self-perpetuating and self-increasing cycle results, in extreme cases, in the offender working himself into a frenzy in which he commits a lust murder. The sadistic rapist may report feeling aroused by his victim's futile resistance. He may find her struggling with him an exciting and erotic experience. He may initially be impotent until his victim physically resists him, or he may experience a spontaneous ejaculation during his assault without intromission.

"Because of the ritualistic and potentially lethal nature of his offenses, the sadistic rapist is often believed to be blatantly psychotic, but, in fact, he is usually able to conceal these darker impulses from others. There is a hidden side to his personality which harbors these forbidden wishes. One of the disconcerting features of such offenders is that they are often quite personable, an impression in sharp contrast to the expected stereotype of the vicious 'sex fiend' and a quality that they capitalize on to gain access to unsuspecting victims.

"The morbid, the occult, the violent, and the bizarre may preoccupy the sadistic rapist, and sadistic themes are the focus of his masturbatory fantasies. He is interested in sadomasochistic pornography and may have a collection of souvenirs and mementos of his victims, such as photographs and articles of clothing. His sadistic attacks are repetitive and interspersed with other less dramatic offenses as well as consenting sexual encounters. However, there may be a progression over time in regard to his offenses, with each new assault showing an increase in aggression over the prior one.

"His sadistic impulses may also be apparent both in the context of his consenting sexual encounters, as, for example, in his marital relationships, and in activities that are not explicitly sexual, such as cruelty to animals and fighting."

For me, as for others, I am certain, identification of the sadistic rapist is by far the easiest. Jack the Ripper and the Boston Strangler were the first cases which came to mind as I read this part of the chapter. Theodore Bundy and the infamous Hillside Strangler were two others.

"Victim impact is particularly horrible in this type of rape; even though she may have physical evidence of having been raped, the horror is so great that recovery is particularly difficult.

"The victim of the sadistic rapist may not survive the assault. For some such offenders, the ultimate satisfaction is the murdering of their victim, not only to eliminate the witness to the crime and thus avoid detection, but also because such killing is intrinsically pleasurable to them—'better than an orgasm,' as one offender put it. An autopsy will identify sexual homicides by evidence of rape in some cases, of bondage and mutilation in other instances, and by 'overkill' in still others.

"When the victim survives the assault, her treatment needs extend beyond crisis-intervention counseling and usually require protracted and expert psychiatric care. The terror and horror of the assault may have been so overwhelming that the victim wished to die rather than endure it any longer. Frequently, such victims express the fear that they will 'lose their minds' or never fully recover from the impact of such an assault. Sometimes, the victim experiences a severe depression as an aftermath to the assault, and there may be the risk of suicide. If the victim has sustained permanent injury from the assault, this will continue to remind her of her nightmare experience. Some victims may adopt ritualistic behavior patterns in an effort to undo the trauma. For example, one victim who was run off the road, abducted from her car, sadistically assaulted, and left for dead, found that she felt compelled to retrace the route she had been driving at the time over and over again."

While symptoms described by Groth as affecting the victim of a sadistic rapist might be most pronounced in a victim of that type of rape, I had found that victims of both power and anger rapists also experienced a feeling that they might "lose their minds" or became severely depressed or adopted certain behavior patterns which they had previously not experienced. Clearly, there is no black and white, and much gray, in categorizing either victim or rapist behavior patterns, but there appear to be norms by which women who might find themselves in a position of imminent sexual attack can judge the behavior characteristics of their potential attackers and react accordingly.

I was particularly interested in Groth's statistics concerning the various types of rape, that is, anger, power, and sadistic.

"In examining the incidence of these three primary patterns of rape, we find that power rapes constitute the most prominent pattern. More than half (55 percent) of these cases referred to us were primarily power rapes. Approximately 40 percent were anger rapes, and about five percent were sadistic rapes. However, since we were seeing primarily convicted offenders, this may very well be an inflated estimate in regard to the anger rapist and an underestimate in regard to the power rapist. Since there is characteristically more physical abuse in anger rapes than in power rapes, there is, relatively speaking, more corroborating evidence of assault and a greater probability of conviction in cases of anger rapes. It is our opinion, then, that power rapes, in fact, far outnumber anger rapes in our culture. The relatively low incidence of sadistic rapes is in sharp contrast to the amount of attention paid to such assaults in the news media. From Jack the Ripper to the west coast Hillside Strangler, the sadistic rapist appears to capture the interest and fascination of the general public. Probably, the very fact that such cases are rare and atypical explains the inordinate amount of attention they receive. However, it may be that the projective figure in regard to the incidence of sadistic rapes is an underestimate, since the sexual components in some murders may go undetected and the crime is not identified as a sexual homicide. Another possibility, that such offenders may not be convicted because psychiatric examination did not find them to be either competent to stand trial or criminally responsible for their actions at the time of the offense, was ruled out by a study of the types of sexual offenders committed to a hospital for the criminally insane. The types of rapists found in this setting corresponded to the distribution among types found both in prison and in a security treatment center designed especially for dangerous sexual offenders."

Indeed, when I had made Nick Groth's acquaintance, and we had worked together for a while, my questioning of statistics in regard to anger and power rapists became a frequent topic of conversation. Since I first met Nick Groth, it has become clear that the percentage of power rapes could be as high as 75 to 80 percent, and anger rapes as low as 15 to 20 percent, while the sadistic rape statistic appears to be probably accurate. I know that in my experience, not only with the cases I have tried but also with those I have reviewed and rejected, the vast majority of victims had been attacked by power rapists, and consequently had very little in the way of evidence to corroborate their testimony for the purposes of criminal trial.

Groth next went on to discuss what he had learned about resistance and deterrence on the part of the victim.

"One of the most frequently asked questions is: What should a victim do to deter an offender? Should she scream? Should she fight? Should she try to talk her way out of it? Should she carry a whistle or a weapon? It is not a question that can be easily answered. First of all, in many cases the victim may have no opportunity to attempt a defense strategy or maneuver. She may be attacked without warning. She may be at home, in bed, sleeping, or she may be knocked unconscious. And although many offenders do report having been deterred from some of their intended assaults, there is a wide variety of individual differences among men who rape, and what serves to deter one assailant may only encourage another. For example, one offender said, 'When my victim screamed I ran like hell.' But another stated, 'When my victim screamed, I cut her throat.' In discussing the issue of deterrence with convicted offenders, three common qualities emerged in those cases in which the victim had an opportunity to confront her assailant and to resist the assault successfully. First, she managed to keep self-control and refused to be intimidated. Second, she did not counter-attack; she was assertive without being aggressive. And third, she said or did something that registered with the offender and communicated to him that she was a real person and not just an object.

"Most offenders advised trying to talk the assailant out of the assault on the premise that even if the strategy does not succeed it does not create further jeopardy for the victim. They suggested that the victim capitalize on the offender's underlying sense of ambivalence toward the assault—something to the effect that 'you know what you are doing is wrong, and it's not too late to stop'—rather than humoring him or being condescending. Obviously, what options are available to the victim are in part determined by the offender she is faced with, the situation she finds herself in, and her own physical and mental resources. Most offenders advised against the victim's carrying a weapon unless she is capable of using it and intends to do so.

"Confronting the assailant with the enormity of what he is doing (asking him how he would feel if someone attempted to sexually assault his mother, his sister, or his wife) and the futility of his efforts (rape is not going to provide a solution to his troubles, nor will it be a satisfying sexual experience), as well as encouraging him to verbalize his feelings, may help to lessen his tendency to attack.

"However, not all offenders can be talked out of an assault. In the last analysis, there is no one defense strategy that will work successfully for all victims, against all offenders, in all situations, and the goal of survival is more important than the goal of escape. It is for this reason that submission may be an adapted coping strategy in some cases. Unfortunately, just as the victim is often blamed for precipitating her assault, she is also frequently faulted for not successfully deterring her assailant. Every strategy that has been used to deter an offender has succeeded in some cases and has failed in others. It is important to recognize that the victim did the best she could in the situation, and she should not be faulted for not having successfully resisted. There is no guaranty that any other strategy would have been any more effective in averting the assault, and it could have proved even more disastrous for her."

I could see the work of Burgess and Holmstrom in all of the analysis respecting the victim. These three made quite a team.

"Regardless of the pattern of the assault, rape is a complex act that serves a number of retaliatory and compensatory aims in the psychological functioning of the offender. It is an effort to discharge his anger, contempt, and hostility toward women—to hurt, degrade, and humiliate. It is an effort to counteract feelings of vulnerability and inadequacy in himself and to assert his strength and power—to control and exploit. It is an effort to deny sexual anxieties and doubts and reaffirms his identity, competency, and manhood. It is an effort to retain status (in gang rape) among male peers, and it is an effort to achieve sexual gratification. Rape is equivalent to symptom formation in that it serves to defend against anxiety, to express a conflict, and to gratify an impulse. It is symptomatic of personality dysfunction, associated more with conflict and stress than with pleasure and satisfaction. Sexuality is not the only—nor the primary—motive underlying *rape*. It is, however, the means through which conflicts surrounding issues of anger and power become discharged. Rape is always a combination of anger, power, and sexuality, and each of these components must be examined in evaluating the offender and in assessing the impact of the assault on the victim and the nature of her trauma.

"Sexual assault represents a crisis for both the offender and the victim. For the assailant, it may result from a sudden and unexpected inability to negotiate life demands adaptively or from the progressive and increasing sense of failure in this regard. It may be symptomatic of transient and extraordinary life stresses that temporarily overwhelm the individual's ability to manage his life, which, under ordinary circumstances, is usually adequate, or it may result from a more indigenous state of affairs in which the offender's psychological resources are developmentally insufficient to cope with the successive and increasing demands and stresses of life. A crisis is precipitated when that individual begins to experience the biological, psychological, and social impact of adolescence or when he is confronted with the responsibilities and life demands of adulthood. His sexual assault is symptomatic of an internal or a developmental crisis in the offender which, in turn, precipitates an external crisis for the victim. The assault triggers an acute disruption of the victim's psychological, physiological, and social lifestyle as evidenced by somatic problems, disturbances in sleeping and eating patterns, and the development of minor mood swings and fears specific to the circumstances of the assault. The sexual offense, from this standpoint, constitutes a situational crisis imposed on the victim, and the impact of the assault may disrupt the biopsycho-social functioning of the victim for an indefinite period of time. Tragically, the victimization often does not end with the assault."

I found this last sentence to be a true understatement. Ironically, in my work I have found that the actual act of the rape itself was only the beginning of the rape victim's trauma. The psychological aftermath was by far the most devastating and long-lasting.

"Rape is a crisis both for the offender and for his victim. Both are in a state of crisis in responding to stress. In examining the crisis aspects, we find the offender responding to an internal condition (failure in psychological control) and his victim reacting to an external event (loss of self-determination). The offender asserts control and expresses hostility through his assault. The offense impacts on his victim in two basic ways: powerlessness and vulnerability. Persons who subsequently come into contact with the victim must be particularly careful not to compound the core issues underlying the trauma of being raped. It is crucial that the individuals (police officers, examining physician, family members, etc.) not be angry with the victim for having been victimized, that is, not blame her for the assault. It is equally important that she be permitted to have as much opportunity as possible to be self-determining again and to have some say in the subsequent series of events, activities, and decision-making processes that come into play following the attack. By capitalizing on these opportunities, much can be accomplished in helping the victim to restore her sense of competency, adequacy, and self-worth. Failure in this regard will not only retard recovery from the psychic injury done the victim but will also compound or perpetuate her victimization more seriously.

"In dealing with a rape victim cues can be derived from the type of rape assault that has occurred, which should help the counselor to ascertain the most immediate, the most pressing, and the most disturbing aspects of victimization. It can help guide the counselor into focusing on these target issues in working with victims. Some basic clinical knowledge about the men who rape may prove helpful in this respect. Just as it is important to dispel myths and stereotypes about victims, it is equally important—especially for the victim—to dispel myths and stereotypes about the offender, since such misinformation and impressions may reinforce fear and continue her sense of intimidation and victimization."

Everything that the authors found important in terms of identification and treatment of victims, and offenders, for purposes of counseling and recovery, could be applied with equal success by providers within the criminal justice system. In plainer terms, prosecutors of this country would do well to understand the dynamics of both victim and offender behavior, and would feel far less anxiety, and contribute less to the victim's, if they were able to key their case analysis, preparation and presentation to the dynamics which have been proven, rather than the myths which have been disproven.

I feel that I have been an example of how successful this approach can be, albeit I did it as the blind lead the blind, and with only an intuition of some sort that I was approaching it from the right perspective. I now find that rather than intuition, my gender most likely provided the perspective which allowed me to see beyond the traditional criminal complaint and the elements that must be proved and to reach the human factor.

I went on to read the discussion of the various characteristics which seemed to be most common and exhibited most frequently by rapists. Not one of the four or five most significant of these symptoms was new to me, but it was very gratifying and certainly educational for me to realize that what I had seen was, indeed, fact and not a product of my imagination—something that I was reading into the case because I wanted it to be there.

First there was the symptom of sexual dysfunction of the rapist during the course of an attack. Sexual dysfunction basically means an inability to have an erection. How many cases I had handled, including several of the ones in which I had used the expert, when the victim reported that she was ordered to orally copulate her attacker, because he was not erect. It was interesting that in each case the assailant had denied this accusation.

"It is commonly—and mistakenly—assumed that men who rape do so either because they are sexually aroused or because they are sexually frustrated, or both. In fact, as we have seen, the motives underlying such assaults have more to do with issues of anger and power than with pleasure and desire. Rape is a pseudosexual act, a distortion of human sexuality, symptomatic of personality dysfunction in the offender, rather than a sexually gratifying experience.

"This conceptualization is supported by an examination of the offender's physiological functioning during his sexual assault. If rape is symptomatic of psychological conflict and anxiety, it would be expected that offenders would evidence more sexual dysfunction in their assaultive sexual acts than in their consenting sexual acts. They in fact do. In our clinical work with identified rapists, we found that one of every three offenders recorded experiencing some sexual dysfunction during their offense, and we believe this to be a conservative estimate."

If sexual dysfunction is that common in rape, what is the effect of the physical exam on the victim which shows no sperm present? Groth addressed this also.

"Medical legal aspects of a physician's role in the treatment of the rape victim has been receiving increasing attention in literature as there is more focus on sexual violence in our society. The medical record can play a crucial part in the criminal justice process, and thus there is a need for precise and objective recording of laboratory findings. From such data, interpretations are made to support and test the allegation of rape. It is important to recognize, therefore, that in a large number of cases, sperm may not be present because of the high incidence of sexual dysfunction exhibited by rapists during the assault period. Careful interviewing of the victim might explain the absence on this basis. The absence of sperm, in and of itself, does not contradict sexual penetration. We need to appreciate what happens physiologically in fact during rape to interpret more clearly what the results of a physical examination of a victim indicates—specifically, that negative findings do not counter-indicate sexual assault and penetration—and to clarify the interpretation of negative findings in the prosecution of such offenses."

And, I might add, the same is true when a physician is examining a victim of rape for symptoms of rape trauma syndrome. There are many behavioral characteristics which I have discussed throughout the book that would be observable to a trained eye, and who could we count on more to record the symptoms than the physician whom the victim often sees right after the attack?

Intoxication was the next symptom discussed, and one which I had found repeatedly in my cases.

"Over 40 percent of the rapists we worked with had a history of chronic drinking, usually dating back to their early adolescence. About one-third of them were steady but moderate drinkers, and one out of four reported only minor occasional alcohol abuse. As a group, then, these men tended to be relatively heavy drinkers, and in 50 percent of the cases, they had in fact been drinking and/or using other drugs (usually marijuana) immediately prior to their assaults. It was typical for many of these offenders to attribute their offenses to the influence of alcohol.

"However, careful examination of these instances in which alcohol and/or drugs were associated with the commission of rape revealed that the amount of drinking and/or drug use engaged in by the offender at the time of the offense did not constitute a significant departure from his customary drinking or drug habits.

"The use of alcohol, in and of itself, is insufficient to account for the offense. Although some offenders were to some extent intoxicated at the time they committed their assaults, these same men were more often not sexually assaultive when intoxicated. Our data suggest then that alcohol may at most serve as a releaser only when an individual has already reached a frame of mind in which he has planned to rape.

"In examining the relationship between alcohol/drug abuse and rape, we found no significant difference between the offender's characteristic pattern of drinking and his use of alcohol/drugs at the time of his crime. Although as a group identified rapists tended to be relatively heavy drinkers, this can be understood as an independent and parallel symptom of their psychosocial dysfunction. Some rapists are also alcoholics, but they do not commit their offenses only when intoxicated or always when intoxicated. For other offenders, the effect of alcohol may be to disinhibit underlying assaultive impulses. It gives them the courage to act. At most, however, alcohol and/or drug abuse plays a contributing role, not a causative one, in the commission of the sexual offense. It may diminish the offender's control but never his responsibility for his actions."

For me, understanding the degree of sexual dysfunction and intoxication in the scenario of rape was just one more affirmation on my part that I was on the right track in my desire to present the whole picture of both victim response and rapist behavior to a jury in a rape trial. Many, if not all, of the cases I had tried had included either one or both of these symptoms. How much clearer it would be both to the criminal justice system and to members of the jury to understand all of the components which go into the entire picture when they are called upon to make a determination of the ultimate issue—credibility.

It was a third symptom that Groth discussed in the section on clinical aspects of rape that proved to be the most startling to me. It is something that I had never considered when I attempted to understand the behavior patterns of men who rape.

"One of the intriguing aspects about forcible sexual assault is the question of symptom choice. Why does sexuality become the mode of expressing power and anger and of discharging tension and frustration?

"What developmental factors or experiences play a part in the etiology of this form of sexual psychopathy?

"Symptom formation is complexly determined and may involve such factors as genetic defects, constitutional vulnerabilities, parental deprivations, pathogenic family patterns, social pathology, and developmental traumas. In this section, the latter factor is addressed. Specifically to what extent do sexual aggressors (rapists and child molesters) have a history of sexual trauma during their formative years?

"Sexual trauma is defined as any sexual activity witnessed and/or experienced that is emotionally upsetting or disturbing. Evidence of some form of sexual trauma was found in the life histories of about one-third of the offenders we worked with. This statistic appears significant in comparison with the finding that only one-tenth of adult males (non-offenders) report similar victimization in their lives. The incidence of sexual trauma appears to be consistent for both rapists and child molesters.

"A little less than half (45 percent) of those offenders who experienced a sexual trauma during their formative years described being the victim of a sexual assault.

"About one-fifth (18 percent) of the victimized subjects were pressured into sexual activity by an adult; that is, the adult occupied a position of dominance and authority in regard to the child and enticed or misled the child into the sexual activity. For example, one subject who raped an elderly victim reported that he was introduced into sexuality by his mother at about age 8. She would take him into her bed and have him perform oral sex on her. This involvement continued until he was 16 years old."

I read this sentence over several times. Even I, who had been in the criminal justice system now for nearly eight years, had not considered the possibility of a large number of male children being the subjects of molestation by their mothers. I think in the entire time that I'd been in the District Attorney's office I had seen one, perhaps two, such cases. Our concern and our efforts are almost exclusively directed to victimization of female children. As I read on, and for many months thereafter, this figure and this information haunted me—especially in light of what I knew about Jeremy Cole.

Groth then discussed some differences which emerged between the pattern of victimization of men who sexually assaulted adults compared to those who sexually assaulted children.

"The most prominent type of traumatic event for the rapist appears to be a sex-pressure/sex-stress situation, whereas for the child molester it was a forcible sexual assault. More rapists reported witnessing disturbing sexual activity on the part of their parents than did child offenders. Although for both groups their assailants were mostly familiar persons, for the rapists they were predominantly family members, whereas for the child offenders they were not. The character of the rapist's early sexual victimization, then, was much more incestuous in nature, and females outnumbered males as their assailants."

In discussing his findings about sexual traumatization and the developmental histories of repetitive sexual aggressors, Groth observed that one-third may be a conservative estimate, since such data was not retrievable from some 12 percent of the rapists.

"Furthermore, when asked if they were ever the victim of a sexual assault as a child, a number of subjects gave the curious response, 'It might have happened, but if it did I don't know it.' They were unable to elaborate or explain why they felt this was a possibility. Also, since many of the subjects were undergoing evaluation for disposition of their cases, a number of them may simply have denied victimization out of concern about how such information might be viewed. In any case, for one offender out of every three, there appears to be a high instance of sexual victimization, especially when compared to a non-offender peer group. Although obviously not the only factor that may play a part in the determination of symptom choice, its significance should not be overlooked."

Groth's conclusion that "since rapists were victimized more by females than by males, this may in part explain the selection of women as targets of their hostile sexual offenses," seems certainly to be a logical one. His further observation that "the results of this study would suggest that the incidence of sexual offenses against children perpetrated by adult women is much greater than would be expected from the rare instances reported in crime statistics," is also worthy of much greater attention. It is clearly not a macho or desired male attribute to confess to being the victim of molest by one's mother, whereas for a girl who has been raised as the receiver rather than the provider of care, it is more acceptable.

"Finally, in regard to the treatment of sexual aggressors and the prevention of sexual aggression, it may be that for identified offenders, one facet of their treatment-rehabilitation that needs to be taken into consideration is the assessment and treatment of unresolved sexual trauma. There is also, then, a need to train providers of social services to identify symptoms of sexual trauma and to develop and support victim service programs to provide therapeutic intervention in such cases.

"Although the complex social problem of sexual assault cannot be reduced summarily to the results and perpetuation of early sexual trauma, the sexual assault of children and adolescents poses an issue that should not be ignored and underscores the need of intervention services to prevent any long-range aftereffects, whether these be sexual dysfunction, sexual aversion, sexual aggression, or other non-sexual problems."

While this understanding of offender behavior did not dissuade me from championing the cause of rape victims, it did give me a new and at first somewhat confusing perspective about the rapist whom I was then prosecuting. In the future I hope we are able to address the needs of male children who might be victims of undetected sexual trauma at the hands of adult females, and I would certainly be among the first to aid in this endeavor. However, this developmental trauma cannot be used as an excuse, as intoxication cannot, to shield a rapist. While I have more empathy than I had before, it is still to the victim's plight that I address this book.

Within days of reading his work, I was in telephone contact with Nick Groth, and an oversized envelope containing all the information I had concerning Jeremy Cole was winging its way to Connecticut.

16

EVIDENCE AGAINST JEREMY COLE seemed to snowball during the last two weeks of August, and as the Labor Day weekend approached I was close to being buried under the avalanche.

The conclusions reached by Nick Groth, describing Cole as a power rapist with certain overlapping anger and unsettling sadistic undertones, did not come as a surprise. He even found significance in the newest case involving the ten-year-old girl, and identified this conduct as an indication that, rather than progressing to violent and aggressive behavior against adult female victims, Cole had taken the other common path of some power rapists over a period of time: turning to children as a means of more easily assuring themselves the fulfillment of power and dominance over their younger victims.

Nick and I discussed at length the federal case in which he had testified as a government witness concerning the offender profile. The rape had taken place on a large military base (which was why the case had been tried in a federal court) and had been against a young woman with a reputation for "sleeping around." Nick was qualified as an expert and analyzed the victim's account of how the rape had unfolded, including language used and the timing of the assailant, along with the defendant's statements concerning how and what he thought had occurred. His conclusion was that the defendant was a classic power rapist, and the military court convicted.

I next spoke to the military lawyer who had used Nick in his case.

"Without Groth's testimony," he summed up matter-of-factly, "there would have been no conviction. He literally provided the victim her credibility in the eyes of the tribunal. Her story seemed implausible until it was given direction by Nick."

Ann Burgess and I weighed the possible approaches to the use of her testimony at trial, since neither of us was aware of a precedent anywhere in the United States in which information in her field had been allowed as evidence in a criminal trial.

"I've testified in some civil suits, though," she volunteered.

"And with what kind of results?"

"Well, the object was money damages for the victim, so I suppose seven hundred fifty thousand dollars is a solid victory."

"Seven hundred fifty thousand!" I marveled. "I'm in the wrong end of the business!"

The suit had been brought against the owner of a building in which the two elderly victims owned a retirement condo. There had been repeated requests for improvement in building security, all to no avail. The assailant gained access through a faulty stairwell door with minimum locks, and raped both women.

In addition to proving inadequate and negligent attention to building security, the plaintiffs' attorney called Ann to testify about the long-term psychological effects the elderly victims would suffer due to the attack. The argument was that the owner was responsible, along with the actual assailant, for this damage, since victim access was due to his negligence in failing to adequately secure the building. The legal theory is known as an action in tort, or a wrong done against another person, specifically in this case negligent infliction of emotional distress attributable to the landlord's act of omission, and intentional infliction of emotional distress attributable to the assailant's act of commission.

Ann discussed the two phases of the rape trauma syndrome in general, and outlined more specifically the symptoms which the elderly victim might encounter.

"Read the section in Nick's book about impact on the elderly victim," Ann advised me, "and imagine two ladies in their late sixties and early seventies sitting in front of twelve jurors listening to me describe what this attack had done to their lives."

I did.

"Age is no defense against rape. Even women of advanced years are vulnerable to sexual assault. Moreover, from our data it appears that when they are sexual victims, they are the targets of particularly brutal assaults. The older woman appears to symbolize an authority figure over whom the offender wants control and/or an actual woman against whom he wants to retaliate or revenge himself. Sexuality becomes the means through which anger and power are expressed and the means by which he can hurt, humiliate, and degrade his victim. The sexual assault of the older victim clearly reveals rape to be a distortion of human sexuality. It is sexual behavior serving non-sexual needs and motives. The majority of victims were assaulted on their own premises by complete strangers. In many cases, their advanced age and related life situation (for example, living alone) made them particularly vulnerable, and vulnerability and accessibility play a more significant role in determining victim selection than does physical attractiveness or alleged provocativeness. Rape is far more an issue of hostility than of sexual desire.

"A number of issues may complicate the recovery from sexual assault when the rape victim is an elderly person. The biopsycho-social impact of rape may be aggravated by the diminished physical, social, and economic resources that often accompany aging. The elderly victim may be more susceptible to physical trauma from the assault. There may be fewer available friends or associates to turn to for support and comforting in this time of distress. The social values of the generation may compound the psychological impact of the offense; for example, she may see it as a shame or disgrace that she has been sexually victimized and may find it especially embarrassing to relate the sexual details of the assault. She may feel too humiliated to report having had to perform sexual acts that she regards as perverted. Her sense of increasing helplessness and mortality may be activated by the experience of the assault. In cases where she is also robbed, she may lose possessions that symbolize important aspects of her life. The theft of money may further jeopardize someone who must manage on a fixed income, and financial considerations may limit her alternatives for coping with the trauma. For example, moving from her living quarters, when this has been the site of her assault, to a new residence may not be feasible. If the victim reports the offense, the effect of aging on her cognizant and perceptual faculties may hinder her assistance in regard to the investigation and the apprehension of the suspect. Finally, if the elderly victim decides to prosecute, she may have particular difficulty in understanding the confusing and frequently frustrating procedures of the criminal justice system.

"Rape is underreported in general, and apprehension and conviction are more unlikely than probable. This may be especially so in regard to cases involving elderly victims. The small incidence of such victimization reported in the literature clearly does not accurately reflect the reality and the magnitude of this disturbing social problem, nor the special importance and particular seriousness of the sexual victimization of this target population."

I could well imagine the juror impact when testimony by an elderly victim, and her friends, followed this kind of information. In a civil case, there would be a double purpose: empathy for the finding of increased damages and credibility for purposes of believing her in the first place.

But there was certainly going to be a difference between using Ann's testimony in a civil suit, where the standard of proof is a preponderance of the evidence and the agreement of only nine of twelve jurors is sufficient for a judgment to be reached, and its use in a criminal case, where the standard of proof is "beyond a reasonable doubt" and the unanimous agreement of all twelve jurors is required for conviction. And the rules for admissibility of evidence in a criminal case are so much more confining than those in a civil case.

I went to the library and began to pull out everything I could on the use of experts. I took a giant step forward when I discovered the briefs from the Inez Garcia trial. I remembered the case from the huge media attention it had received. Inez Garcia had been raped by two men who had broken into her home. Before they left, they threatened her, and one of them promised he'd be back for more later.

After they had gone, Garcia took a rifle, loaded it, and went out in search of her assailants. When she found them, she shot and killed one (the one who had promised to return), and was promptly arrested and charged with murder, even though she stated she feared for her life because of her attackers' statements.

Inez Garcia was convicted of murder and an outraged feminist community came to her aid. A brilliant San Francisco attorney, a woman, appealed her case and won a retrial. This time, utilizing the new perspective she brought to the case, she focused on the introduction of expert testimony about the behavior of rape victims, particularly their fear of death and the reasonableness of Garcia's reaction in killing her assailant. Her legal theory was one of self-defense in the face of a life-threatening danger which she perceived as a result of having been raped.

This theory of self-defense was an innovative departure from the traditional approach used at the first trial, and commonly employed when women are accused of committing homicide: that of impaired mental state, relying on the age-old belief that women who kill are disturbed.

In addition to this new legal approach, Garcia's attorney also modified jury instructions which referred to "he" or "him" and substituted "she" and "her," argued a standard of self-defense based on the "reasonable woman" theory rather than a "reasonable man," and convinced the Court to allow her great latitude in jury selection by questioning prospective jurors about their beliefs on a wide range of subjects which could unjustly affect victim credibility.

This time, Inez Garcia was acquitted.

Although Garcia was technically a *defendant* for committing a homicide, she was just as surely a *defendant* for being a rape victim, I reasoned, and the evidence which a jury needed to understand in order to assess her credibility as a defendant was just as critical in assessing her credibility as a rape victim. I could see a trial brief shaping up.

Next I discovered that a self-defense theory based on the battered woman syndrome was being used with moderate success to help women accused of murdering their husbands. This theory proposed that a woman who had lived for years in a battering relationship and was familiar with the cycle of violence (explosion, forgiveness, escalation, and then a repeat of the same) reached a point where she reasonably believed that if she did not kill him, he would kill her, and she therefore responded by pulling the trigger.

It was here that I found the legal standard I felt would satisfy the need to qualify both an expert and a field of expertise which would withstand the tests of appeal.

Simply stated, to qualify as a field of expertise, three criteria must be met: (1) the scientific methodology used in the field must be generally accepted; (2) the person called as a witness in the field must qualify as an expert (there are specific guidelines in both state and federal codes to make this determination); and (3) the subject matter of the field must be beyond the ken of the average juror.

The case I used as a model, *Ibn-Tamas* v. *United States*, involved a woman who had shot and killed her physician husband. The defense called Dr. Lenore Walker, a psychologist and one of the country's leading authorities on the battered woman syndrome as well as author of a comprehensive book on the subject. The trial court did not allow

Dr. Walker to testify, saying only that her opinions usurped the job of the jury, that is, whether the defendant was telling the truth. The appellate court sent the case back for the first and second criteria of the test to be determined, and commented at length on the third:

"Another way for an expert to preempt the jury's function is to speak to matters in which the jury is just as competent as the expert to consider and weigh the evidence and draw the necessary conclusions. This is the substantive element of the three-part test we expressed in *Dyas*. It means that Dr. Walker's testimony, to be admissible, must provide a relevant insight which the jury otherwise could not gain in evaluating the defendant's self-defense testimony about her relationship with her husband. More specifically, the expert must purport to shed light on a relevant aspect of their relationship which a lay person, without expert assistance, would not perceive from the evidence itself.

"On cross-examination of the defendant, the government attempted to discredit her testimony by suggesting that her account of her relationship with her husband had been greatly overdrawn and that her testimony about perceiving herself in imminent danger was therefore implausible. For example, the government implied that the logical reaction of a woman who was truly frightened by her husband (let alone regularly brutalized by him) would have been to call the police from time to time or leave.

"In an effort to rebuff this line of attack by the government, the defense proffered Dr. Walker's testimony to (1) inform the jury that there is an identifiable class of persons who can be characterized as 'battered women'; (2) explain why the mentality and behavior of such women are at variance with the ordinary lay perception of how someone would be likely to react to a spouse who is a batterer; and thus (3) provide a basis on which the jury could understand why Mrs. Ibn-Tamas perceived herself in imminent danger at the time of the shooting.

"More specifically, Dr. Walker told the trial court, out of the presence of the jury, that she had studied 110 women who had been beaten by their husbands. Her studies revealed three consecutive phases in the relationships: 'tension building,' when there are small instances of battering; 'acute battering incident,' when beatings are severe; and 'love contrite,' when the husband becomes very sorry and caring. Dr. Walker then testified that women in this situation typically are low in self-esteem, feel powerless, and have few close friends, since their husbands commonly 'accuse them of all kinds of things with friends, and they are embarrassed. They don't want to cause their friends problems, too.' Because there are periods of harmony, battered women tend to believe their husbands are basically loving, caring men; the women assume that they themselves are somehow responsible for their husbands' violent behavior. They also believe, however, that their husbands are capable of killing them, and they feel there is no escape. Unless a shelter is available, these women stay with their husbands, not only because they typically lack a means of self-support, but also because they fear that if they leave they will be found and hurt even more. Dr. Walker stressed that wife batterers come from all racial, social, and economic groups (including professionals), and that batterers commonly 'escalate their abusiveness' when their wives are pregnant. She added that battered women are very reluctant to tell anyone that their husbands beat them. Of those studied, 60 percent had never done so before (Dr. Walker typically found them in hospitals), 40 percent had told a friend, and only 10 percent had called the police.

"When asked about appellant, whom she had interviewed, Dr. Walker replied Mrs. Ibn-Tamas was a 'classic case' of the battered wife. Dr. Walker added her belief that on the day of the killing, when Dr. Ibn-Tamas had been beating his wife despite her protests that she was pregnant, Mrs. Ibn-Tamas' pregnancy had had a 'major impact on the situation . . . [that is, a particularly crucial time].' Dr. Walker's testimony, therefore, arguably would have served at least two basic functions: (1) it would have enhanced Mrs. Ibn-Tamas' general credibility in responding to cross-examination designed to show that her testimony about the relationship with her husband was implausible; and (2) it would have supported her testimony that on the day of the shooting her husband's actions had provoked a state of fear which led her to believe she was in imminent danger ('I just knew he was going to kill me'), and thus responded in self-defense. Dr. Walker's contribution, accordingly, would have been akin to the psychiatric testimony admitted in the case of Patricia Hearst 'to explain the effects that kidnapping, prolonged incarceration, and psychological and physical abuse may have had on the defendant's mental state at the time of the robbery, and insofar as such mental state is relevant to the asserted events of coercion or duress.' *Hearst* 1, at 890. Dr. Walker's testimony would have supplied an interpretation of the facts which differed from the ordinary lay perception ('she could have gotten out, you know') advocated by the government. The substantive element of the *Dyas* test—'beyond the ken of the average layman'—is accordingly met here.

"We conclude therefore that as to either substantive basis for ruling that Dr. Walker's testimony would 'invade the province of the jury'— either the 'ultimate issue' or the 'beyond the ken' basis—the trial court erred as a matter of law. *Ibn-Tamas* v. *United States* (1979)."

The court felt that, as a matter of law, the expert offered by the defense could not be disqualified and that her background and credentials supported the second *Dyas* criterion—sufficient skill, knowledge, or experience in the expert's field.

Finally, as to the third prong, the court stated:

"The third *Dyas* criterion is whether the state of the pertinent art or scientific knowledge is sufficient to permit an expert opinion. The government argues that the 'battered woman' concept is not sufficiently developed, as a matter of commonly accepted scientific knowledge, to warrant testimony under the guise of expertise. But the third criterion of *Dyas* focuses on the general acceptance of a particular methodology in the field, not on the subject matter studied. It deals with a 'state of the art' of inquiry, not with the quantity of substantive knowledge. Thus satisfaction of this criterion begins and ends with the determination of whether there is general acceptance of a particular scientific methodology—not an acceptance, beyond that, of particular study results based on the methodology. On this record, we cannot say as a matter of law that Dr. Walker's methodology falls short."

Once again this theory of self-defense was being used for the benefit of a *defendant*, but the analogy between the rape trauma syndrome and the battered woman syndrome for purposes of victim credibility seemed clear: each could result in juror acceptance of new knowledge with which to evaluate a woman's credibility.

Whether the woman happened to be a defendant or a victim in this scenario should not have been of concern—but I was not that naïve: the door was always wide open to legal theories for the benefit of America's criminally accused, but barely ajar for her victims of crime. I intended to push a new wedge through the crack.

I was stuck in rush-hour traffic again! I could see a brief in which I substituted the words "rape trauma syndrome" for "battered woman syndrome." It was getting clearer.

I'd use more than one expert, however, just to be safe. First a psychiatrist—preferably white and male, or white and female, I was told—to examine Jill. I would have preferred Ann Burgess or a psychologist, not only because of the bad feelings so many have about psychiatrists in the courtroom these days, but also because rape victims usually represent a small segment of the psychiatrist's patient population, as opposed to both rape counselors/sociologists and psychologists, who more frequently specialize.

Next, I'd go right to the top and have the Lenore Walker of rape trauma syndrome—Ann Burgess, of course—and for the offender profile, who else but Nick Groth? I wasn't really sure I'd try to introduce evidence of offender behavior, which might give an appellate court too many ways to skirt the main question (the use of expert rape testimony) and reverse without ever addressing this issue. I'd decide that later.

Now I had to come up with a real expert to examine Jill—no more Anne Kennedy. It took two weeks and phone calls across the continent to get a name on the west coast—we couldn't be sending for experts from Boston or New York every time an expert was needed for a rape case. Dr. Joshua Golden, an M.D. and professor of psychiatry, was, and is still at the time of this writing, director of the Human Sexuality Program at UCLA's Neuro-Psychiatric Institute. I drove up one day in early August to see if there was anything more to him than all the big titles. I was curious about a man's interest, to the point of expertise, in rape victims at a time when it was certainly not "in vogue." His reasons seemed sound. His background, he related, was in human sexuality. In the early seventies he had been asked to head a new center on violence within the Department of Psychiatry at UCLA. Although it never really got off the ground, his year or so of preparatory study on different areas of violence, coupled with his background in human sexuality, led him to develop a particular interest in rape victimology, and he had kept up with the fledgling research, watching it mushroom over the next several years.

I explained to him about the Harter, O'Conner, and Drake cases, and the bad precedent I had to overcome before he would even get a shot at the jury.

"I have to distinguish my own earlier cases from what I'll be trying to do now in *Cole.* I have no difficulty seeing the differences, but it will take a strong judge to agree with me. They are very skittish about bouncing a case back to their own appellate court on the same subject that has already been ruled on, only dressed differently."

That was sure to be my toughest test: getting a San Diego Superior Court judge (who had no doubt never heard of rape trauma syndrome anyway) to see the distinction between what I'd first done (using an expert to address the element of resistance) and what I now wanted to do (use an expert to bolster victim credibility). I knew I would have to finesse my way into the right courtroom—and I had a candidate in mind.

Jill spent a morning with Joshua Golden three days after my visit with him, and he had no difficulty in diagnosing her as suffering from rape trauma syndrome. To assist him in familiarizing himself with the case, I had provided him with everything in my file, including the police psychologist's report on Jill at the time she had applied to the police academy. In part, the following observations had been made by that psychologist:

"The validity of this patient's test results have been impaired by a strong tendency to deny problems and to present herself in a favorable light. The pattern is less deviant when it appears in a relatively well-educated and sophisticated individual who is accustomed to maintaining a good social appearance, although it does suggest guardedness and perhaps an overcompensation for feelings of inadequacy. In individuals of less social attainment, the pattern may represent an extreme defensiveness and unwillingness to examine herself objectively. This may be accompanied as well by concealed feelings of inferiority and insecurity. In either case, such a pronounced denial of emotional problems is likely to cause difficulty in establishing and maintaining a therapeutic relationship. This patient has difficulties with impulse control; although her anger may sometimes be directly expressed in temper outbursts, she is more likely to repress her hostility and to experience vague physical complaints. She is somewhat depressed and may be irritable, tense and suspicious, as well. This person is characterized by denial of anxiety or worry; she expresses self-confidence, affability and self-acceptance.

"The patient is an attractive, but seductive-appearing young woman of apparent stated age. She relates in a bright but demonstratively guarded fashion. Although she is spontaneously productive, she portrays herself as entirely normal, with no difficulties whatsoever. She portrays her family as completely healthy and normal and represents herself as being the 'all-round all-American girl.' "

When Dr. Golden and I got together in a phone conversation after his examination, he had some specific observations about that previous report.

"Judy, you should subpoena the psychologist who prepared that report," he urged. "His findings only strengthen your position that Jill was suffering the effects of rape trauma syndrome: denial, anger, hiding something. He was absolutely right—but for the wrong reasons, since he didn't know about the rape."

I put out the subpoena as soon as we hung up and met resistance from the moment it was received, which bothered me not in the least. When this psychologist was called to testify at the trial, he admitted that the rape could account for his findings, and that now, knowing of such a trauma, his examination results were most probably invalid as an assessment of her potential success on the police force.

I also figured out, and Dr. Golden added his confirmation, that Jill's sudden interest in seeking out other men after the rape and taking them home with her was part of the denial phase: she was telling herself that everything was fine, that she was fine and she would prove it. Of course, everything wasn't fine, as the psychological examination, administered during the same period Jill was trying to date, proved.

Just to be extra sure that my trial judge would accept rape victimology as a field of expertise, I decided to throw in a bonus.

During the various lectures and workshops I had given, I'd met Marianne Felice, a physician who had come to San Diego to take a position as Chief of Adolescent Medicine at the UC-San Diego School of Medicine. Before that, she had spent several years at the University of Maryland School of Medicine in Baltimore, where, quite by accident, she had made some significant discoveries about rape of teenagers.

Dr. Felice worked extensively in the adolescent outpatient clinic of the University of Maryland Hospital, and would frequently see patient files with a large letter "R" written in red in one corner. Unable to determine the significance of this designation, she finally asked, and was told that the "R" meant the patient had been a rape victim.

Paralleling her ignorance concerning the letter "R" on certain files,

Dr. Felice had noticed that many of her teenage patients presented complaints and symptoms for which she could not define a cause: cramps with no corresponding cycle dates, headaches with no immediate stress, or depression with no obvious cause.

Once Dr. Felice learned about the "R" files, as she now referred to them, she went back and reviewed her notes on these patients: she found that many were the cases which had been so hard to diagnose: vague, psychosomatic complaints of undetermined origin. Dr. Felice was aware of Burgess and Holmstrom's work and of the rape trauma syndrome, and was immediately curious to know if there might not also be a teenage rape trauma syndrome.

From March 1, 1975, through February 29, 1976, she, and several colleagues, offered a follow-up program to all adolescent girls initially seen in the emergency room with the chief complaint of rape. At year's end, the results clearly demonstrated a pattern much like the adult rape trauma syndrome, but with symptoms different enough to warrant the separate title. The results of her study were published in the April 1978 issue of *Clinical Pediatrics*.

In teenage rape trauma syndrome, fears and phobias are among symptoms of the initial phase, followed later by denial of problems and finally the emergence of psychosomatic complaints (this is where Dr. Felice had first come in). Because of their emerging sexuality, adolescents had manifestations of symptoms which differed somewhat from the adults'; after having been raped, for instance, many teens would try to hide their sexuality by dressing in baggy clothing, to disguise their sexuality.

Knowing what to look for, Dr. Felice was able to ask questions which addressed present, but seemingly unexplainable, complaints in her patients who did not offer the information about their rape.

What I wanted to point out to my trial judge was the historical context of this research: with the emergence of women in all disciplines, bringing with them the unique perspective of their gender, new fields were developing all around us. I would point out that Marianne Felice, Ann Burgess, and Judith Rowland were all witnessing things during the same years that we knew had a significance beyond our initial abilities to understand. It was precisely because the fields could not emerge until women, in their respective professions, were there to "birth" them that they were all relatively young. And as the court in

Ibn-Tamas had pointed out, quality, not quantity, was the test. So it should be with the rape trauma syndrome.

I prepared Marianne to testify during the pre-trial phase of the case and told her to give the same talk for the judge that she had made the time we both appeared at a California Medical Association conference.

"People v. *Jeremy Cole."*

It was Thursday, August 28, 1980, the date set for trial, and Mark Fisher and I stood when the case was called.

"Ready for the defense, your honor," my opponent announced much too blithely.

"Ready for the People, your honor," I lied convincingly.

I was taking a calculated risk. A few phone calls during the week had revealed a serious backlog in trailing cases due to the large number of vacationing judges. Those who remained—my chief target for the Cole case included—were accepting new assignments from Presiding as soon as they began jury instructions on the old ones. A call to Presiding on Wednesday, just before I left the office for the night, assured me I was safe for Thursday, since no courts were open. It was unlikely, according to the court clerk, that anything would get out until after the Labor Day weekend.

I knew, as I stood with such false but masterful confidence, that Cole would take precedence over just about anything else on the calendar, for a number of reasons: the seriousness of the charges, the age of the case, and because I had expressed my exasperation at the numerous delays.

I sat tensely while the Presiding judge went through the rest of the calendar. My anxieties reached fever pitch when it became obvious that if there was but a single courtroom available, the Cole case would be assigned to it! Briefly I considered doing something rash, like throwing up or getting cramps.

"Ladies and gentlemen, there are no courtrooms for you this morning." The Presiding judge surveyed his subjects. "But would counsel on Cole, Reedy, Portsky, and Mynor please be on telephone standby with my clerk. For the remainder of the cases on calendar, let's start looking for some new trial dates, shall we?"

My stomach began settling down with each step I put between myself and the Presiding department. After a few words with Mark

Fisher, assuring him he would have my brief by trial day, I headed toward Department 27.

Judge Walter Lusk was one of, if not the, best-respected jurists sitting on the Superior Court Bench—certainly this was true in San Diego and, from what I had heard, elsewhere as well. He had spent the first half of his career in the same District Attorney's office which I was now serving and, at the time of his appointment to the Bench, had risen to the position of Assistant District Attorney.

On the Bench, Lusk had quickly proved himself to be a fair and impartial judge, and demonstrated a thorough mastery of legal principles and the law, was known to be a good listener, and, most importantly, was seldom reversed. The appellate court had come to respect his opinions and did not overturn his well-thought-out legal decisions with any more frequency than lawyers took exception to them.

I had given a lot of thought to the choice of judges for the Cole case, and from every aspect—distinguishing the old theory from the new, accepting the field of expertise, qualifying the expert, latitude in jury selection, chance of reversal—Lusk was the one. He had presided over a six-week trial of mine some three years before in a very complicated child abuse homicide, and had demonstrated all the qualities then which I sought out now. We had made new law together that time too.

I slipped into the courtroom and purposely, but quietly, made my way to the clerk's desk. Lusk was intensely, but without expression (as always), listening to a sentencing argument.

"Gene," I whispered, crouching nearly to desk level, "what kind of case have you got going?"

"A robbery with two defendants," he whispered back without looking up.

"When's it going out?"

"It's hard to say, Judy. You know how lawyers are." He smiled at me from the corner of his mouth. "You want in here badly, huh?"

"Yeah, Gene, I do. How about an educated guess?"

"Umm, not before next Wednesday, maybe even the following Monday. The judge has to be out of town for some meetings on Thursday. Look, call back this afternoon. I ought to have a better idea."

I returned Lusk's nod as he caught our sotto voce conversation, and slipped out. At 4:30 Gene calculated another week before an opening.

Since new cases were rarely assigned on Friday, I was safe until Tuesday.

Over the Labor Day weekend I finally sat down to organize the massive amounts of material I had accumulated in order to prepare a "Trial Memorandum and Points and Authorities in Support of the Presentation of Expert Testimony on the Subject of Rape." By Monday evening I had it piled in the order I planned to use it, but had not yet put pen to paper. I had never done anything like this before.

"I'm not sure I can now," I lamented to the same dog at my feet. "God, I hate writing!"

But since I've always enjoyed reading what I've written, I kept that in mind as I headed back toward Presiding on Tuesday morning. I assured Mark Fisher once again that he was about to have an awesome trial brief laid upon his legal shoulders, and looked skyward as the Presiding judge announced no new openings for cases for at least one more day. There was a repeat Wednesday.

By Thursday, Gene was able to tell me his judge's court would probably be ready to accept a new case the following Wednesday, September 10. On Friday, Presiding notified me that Cole would definitely be assigned on Monday morning to one of two available courtrooms.

I was too close to accept defeat—so I did something I had not done since my kids had been babies and the housekeeper had failed to come back on Sunday night: I got the Monday-morning flu. In this case, it extended through Tuesday.

When Daly called late Tuesday afternoon with the news that Lusk would be open the next morning, I was appropriately excited.

"Grab him for me, Daly. Tell Presiding I'll crawl in if I have to."

I felt only slightly guilty, more pleased actually, with my deception. Could I help it if there weren't more judges who were as fair-minded as Lusk?

The brief I handed to Judge Lusk and Mark Fisher on Wednesday morning was forty-two typed pages, followed by three pages of bibliography. I was prouder of it than anything I had ever written—before this book, of course. It was a clear and thorough presentation of rape from its historical origins through the rape trauma syndrome, of lay and juror myths and misconceptions, of offender profiles, of case precedent and legal and evidentiary relevance.

Both Lusk and Fisher asked for the rest of the morning to study it and we agreed to begin pre-trial hearings on admissibility of the expert at 1:30. I had given Nick Groth the go-ahead right after I hung up with Daly the day before and he was to arrive by noon. We had decided he would testify about both the rape trauma syndrome and the psychology of the offender at the pre-trial stage, and I would not bring Ann Burgess out until I was ready for her to take the stand. Besides, her schedule was looking worse and worse. I hoped that, between them, Groth and Golden could do the job if she couldn't come.

Jill and I had discussed what should happen to the case if Lusk denied my motion for use of the expert. I had been firm.

"I won't tell the defense ahead of time, but if we don't get the expert in, I'm going to dismiss the case. We can't win without it."

I planned to introduce evidence of prior sexual history and admissions of lying, in addition to dealing with the usual hurdles inherent in a power rape case. It was essential to juror understanding and victim credibility that the expert weave everything into context. Jill understood and agreed.

I needn't have worried about Groth and Golden. They were magnificent. Both proved to be able scholars as well as competent clinicians on the rape trauma syndrome, and each covered his own area of expertise flawlessly—offender psychology for the former and victim examination for the latter.

At the end of nearly two full, exhausting days of testimony, and almost three hours of intense argument, Judge Lusk denied the motion for use of the expert. He was unable to separate the precedent I felt I had set from what I now insisted I wanted to do.

Disheartened is much too mild a word to describe my mood as I sat at my desk watching the evening lights across the city below. It was 8:15, and I had not yet reached Jill. I was too depressed to cry. I'd been so close—there was no one from whom I could get the appropriate solace. I called my parents and they were disappointed for me—especially my father. He so enjoyed my victories and suffered my defeats.

At 8:30 Jill answered the phone and I gave her the news.

"I haven't let on to the defense yet."

The least Cole could do was sweat another night. "I'll make the motion in the morning, Jill. You're still in agreement with this decision, aren't you?"

"Yes," she whispered, but the whisper was stronger than it had been four months before. "You've saved my life, Judy Rowland. I'll do whatever you think is best."

I slept fitfully through the night, arguing repeatedly, differently, sometimes more forcefully, at other times more calmly—but I never came out the winner.

At 9:55 the next morning I leaned heavily on the door of Department 27, carrying only the skeletal file, and found Mark Fisher already perched on the edge of the clerk's desk.

"Oh, there you are, counsel," Gene acknowledged when I was only halfway in the door. "The judge would like to see you both in chambers before he calls the jury panel."

"Okay, Gene, thanks," I sighed. But hold the jury panel, I thought as we were ushered into Lusk's office. I was in a fog.

"Good morning, your honor," Mark Fisher offered in what was obviously the tone of a victory in the air.

I nodded.

"Good morning, counsel. Please . . . sit down." His mood was very somber. "I spent a very restless night, Ms. Rowland." He looked directly at me.

Then his eyes moved on to Mark. "And, Mr. Fisher, I came to the conclusion that I made a mistake yesterday."

I wasn't keeping up with him yet.

"I have reviewed all the evidence and, frankly, I think Ms. Rowland has distinguished *Harter* from what she intends to do here. There is a difference in legal theory and its application between victim credibility and the use of an expert to prove cessation of resistance."

I was just beginning to hear him, but I still wasn't able to speak—an unusual situation for me. Fisher argued gallantly for several minutes, but I could see I was in little danger of Lusk's changing his mind.

I didn't know of a previous occasion when he had ever reversed a ruling he had made from the bench—and after telling and retelling this episode in the months and years to come, no one else had either.

I just listened, and began to feel life pulse through my limbs again.

"Judy," I heard Lusk call me from somewhere, "are you ready to pick a jury?"

"Ah, yes . . . but"—I shook off the last of the fog—"do I understand you are also allowing me the latitude I requested in jury selection?"

"Well, up to a point. We'll play it by ear and see what happens." He smiled. "I'll stop you if you go wild."

"Thank you, your honor."

Elated would be too mild a word to describe my mood as I floated out of the judge's chambers and into the courtroom. At noon I called Jill Bernadini and she in turn alerted the others.

For three days jury selection went on. I used the same method I had started to develop in *Harter*, more refined now, and added the Inez Garcia list as well. When we agreed to a panel the following Tuesday afternoon, I realized the case had already been won or lost, the ultimate decision resting on my ability to have weeded out the critical prejudices.

As for Judge Lusk: "I've never been a party to such blatant jury preinstruction to an attorney's point of view as I witnessed here, Ms. Rowland," he joked with a feigned solemnity.

"Then why did you let me do it?" I rebounded in like spirit.

"Because"—he threw up his hands—"you did it according to the rules. I couldn't find a reason to stop you."

He still mentions that jury selection to me when I stop by to see him from time to time.

Due to another out-of-town conference, Judge Lusk was not ready for opening statements until Thursday morning. Following my usual rule—to keep promises of evidence to a minimum in opening statements—I made my opening brief, and Jill spent the remainder of the day on the witness stand. We were slow and deliberate about everything, leaving out nothing, providing no opening for the defense to crawl through. Her inner strength, those twenty-seven years before May 10, 1979, served Jill well.

When we recessed for the weekend, I noticed several jurors shake their heads as they filed past us, their eyes full of empathy and disbelief that she had endured as she had, and made it.

Yes, she had made it—she could sense it too.

Monday morning, September 22, found Jill still undergoing intense cross-examination about her sex life all the way from the day of the rape through the day of the trial. Mark Fisher was employing psychological warfare, and had subpoenaed every man she had ever known to court at the same time. On each break she had to see them all sitting in the hallway.

By noon her testimony was over, and we headed for my office for a little counseling session.

"Okay, Jill, you know what he's trying to do to you. Don't let him. You were great, and now it's finished."

"I'm trying not to, but, God, it's hard. I'm so sorry about involving these innocent people in this horrible thing, just because they know me. I mean, he's interviewed them all, he knows what they're going to say. Why . . . ?"

"To get you, and it worked, right? So let's not show him we care." I stood up. "Do you want something to eat?" I asked as I grabbed my wallet. "I'm going down to the machines on the fourth floor."

"No, no, thanks, I couldn't."

"I'll be back in a couple of minutes. Meanwhile take some deep breaths and relax."

As I turned down the hall I heard my phone ring, and decided to ignore it, but the switchboard operator caught me before I could completely escape.

"Judy, it's your mother." Joyce had such a great English accent. "Shall I take a message?"

"No, Joyce, thanks. My mother I'll talk to." She didn't call often. My father—that was different. I might have let her take a message from him.

"I didn't get far, did I?" I smiled at Jill as I slid around the desk and into my chair.

I picked up the receiver. "Hi, Mom, how are you? You just caught me on the way to the yummy sandwich machine."

"Judy, I didn't want to call," she began after the characteristic pause, "but Vivian Walters said if I didn't, she would . . . Your father died this morning."

Her words didn't sink in. "*Whose* father died this morning?" I repeated. I felt something strange, but not definable. Jill sat up straighter in her chair.

"Your father died this morning," she repeated calmly. "I heard him get up about six-thirty, go to the bathroom, and get back into bed . . . When he wasn't up by eight-thirty I went in . . . and he had died."

I heard her this time, but I still felt I was discussing someone else's father.

"*My* father died? Dad died? . . . Are you okay? You mean he died before eight-thirty and you didn't call?" I was thinking about what I'd been doing at eight-thirty and all morning while my father was dead. It wasn't real yet.

"I knew you had this important rape trial, sweetie, and there was nothing you could do." She sounded so much in control, but maybe I detected a catch in her voice now and then.

"Look, I'll be there in forty-five minutes. Long . . ."

"No." She was firm. "I'll meet you at home this evening. We'll be together then."

"You're sure?"

"I'm sure."

"Okay, Mom, but you call if you need me."

"I will."

We sat looking at each other, Jill and I.

"Shall I leave?" she asked softly.

"No." I didn't feel anything—yet. I wondered when I would. Shouldn't something be happening? But the case. There was Jill to think about. We had to finish this trial before Lusk went off to the annual judges' conference next week.

"No," I repeated. "I'm okay."

I wasn't hungry, so we talked about my father. "It's the first time I've lost a member of my family," I told her.

I sent Jill on ahead of me to court and stopped to tell Susan.

"Look, kid, you can't go back to court this afternoon. How are you going to concentrate? What in the world are you thinking of?"

"I think I can concentrate." I felt okay.

Post-traumatic stress disorder. The words came to me as I stepped into the empty elevator. I pushed "3."

The next thing I knew, the doors opened and I was in the lobby. I don't remember the doors opening on "3." They must have, though. I just don't remember.

Maybe I would take the afternoon off. I told Lusk and Mark Fisher of my father's death, and we recessed for the day. Still I felt okay. When would it hit me? What would it be? Late that night I realized I'd never have anyone again who believed in me the way he had. I was sad, but it would be two years before the void inside cried out—exactly six months after my mother died of cancer.

17

BETWEEN TUESDAY MORNING and Thursday afternoon I introduced Jill's supporting witnesses to the jury—her best girlfriend, her former fiancé, her male companions, her co-workers. I challenged dispatcher 98 (who openly conceded he had been insensitive and too hasty in concluding Jill's call was the result of a family disturbance) and played the infamous tape—twice. I questioned the police detectives and physician. I made sure the jury was aware of one officer's psychiatric problem and the other's criminal behavior.

In the middle, I called Joshua Golden, who, because of the numerous delays and because I felt he was capable, testified without Burgess or Groth (the former was completely booked on the east coast and the latter would have cost a small fortune to keep on the west coast for ten days between the pre-trial hearing and his actual trial testimony).

We both felt the significance as he was sworn in: that more than likely we were the first to be doing this in a rape trial.

God, I loved those highs!

Q. "Dr. Golden, what is your occupation?"

A. "I am a psychiatrist."

Q. "And where are you presently employed?"

A. "UCLA School of Medicine."

We covered his educational background, his professional affiliations, his previous work, his publications, his research, and all the other foundational information necessary for a court and a jury to pay attention to an expert witness.

He chronicled the development of his interest in rape, starting with the 1973 request that he head the sexual violence section of a center for the study of violence.

Q. "All right. You indicated back in 1973 that when you were requested to participate in this violence center at UCLA, you spent the next six months of that particular year gathering and assessing the information and literature which were available at that time on the subject. Have you since that time kept abreast of the literature in the area of rape?"

A. "Yes."

Q. "Can you tell us, in 1973 and 1974, back in that period of time, what did you find available on the subject?"

A. "Well, there was a surprisingly small amount of information available. There was a very scant literature on rape. There had been very, very little in the way of any kind of systematic scientific study of rape as a phenomenon, or of rapists. There were some articles by psychiatrists and psychoanalysts and a few psychologists, particularly, who had speculated on the causes of rape and the motivation of rapists, but no systematic collection of data."

Q. "How about on the victim? Anything on the victim back in that period of time?"

A. "No, I think, surprisingly enough, there was nothing really much about victims at all. And certainly nothing that would qualify as sound scientific study."

Q. "Did that change?"

A. "Yes, since 1973, and really I would say particularly since 1975 and 1976 and up to the present, there has been a real explosion of interest, I think, in large part as a result of the funding and the establishment of a National Rape Center in the Department of Health, Education, and Welfare. There is now a very extensive literature on rape."

Q. "And directing your attention particularly to what has been done in the area of victim study and the impact of rape on the victim, can you tell us how that area developed?"

A. "Well, the civil rights movement, generally in the sixties, had led, in my view, to a certain establishment of civil rights for other groups, including women, and there was a very active and vigorous women's movement, and one of the major concerns of the so-called women's movement was the concern of victims of crimes like rape. A series of rape crisis centers were set up in the country in the mid-seventies and late seventies, generally staffed by people who were not always professionals, but with a liberal mixture of professionals working in them.

"Many of these women had themselves been the victims of rape and were eager to then do something about the problem, and they, among other things, attempted to provide psychological support and counseling for victims of rape. They were very effective in the establishment of the National Rape Center with federal funding, and their activities and interests, I think, spawned a series of research projects.

"The best-known study of victims of rape has been by two investigators from Boston, a sociologist and a nurse, Lynda Holmstrom and Ann Burgess, and they have done, at least up to this time, the most extensive studies, although there have been a number of other studies of the victims of rape attempting to show generally what the natural history, if you will, of psychological and other consequences of rape may be."

Q. "Was the purpose of these women who set up the rape crisis centers, and those who initiated the studies of the victims, to better aid the victim of a rape in her recovery?"

A. "Yes, not only to better aid the victim, but also a very major reason for the work and for the publication of the work was that the reactions of rape victims were generally not recognized by either the public or the professional community. People were, I think, extraordinarily naïve about what the normal psychological consequences of being a victim of rape were like; so their interests were not only in trying to make a somewhat more effective treatment available, but also to help people understand the reactions of those who were victims of rape."

Q. "Out of the studies that you have mentioned so far, did there come a name for what the researchers found in regard to the emotional reactions of the victim, a rape victim?"

A. "Yes, they called it the rape trauma syndrome; it was Burgess and Holmstrom's designation."

Q. "Okay. Following Burgess and Holmstrom, has there been a body of literature which has followed behind them and which has either supported or negated the concepts?"

A. "There has indeed been a body of literature, other studies which have supported the notion that there is a fairly predictable series of responses and reactions to the kind of stress that rape represents."

Q. "Now, can you tell the jury how that first study was done and basically if the studies which followed have used the same method?"

A. "Yes. The first study was done at Boston City Hospital, which is a large city and county hospital in the Boston community, and, in essence, what they did was to request that they be called to the hospital at the time that any rape victim would appear, and either Lynda Holmstrom or Ann Burgess, or both, would come at whatever hour of the day or night the women were brought to the emergency room and identified as victims of rape. I think there were some one hundred and forty or so who were brought in during the course of the study, which went on over a year's time.

"They then selected from that hundred and forty some ninety-two people who represented a span in age of approximately seventeen years to about seventy-two years of age, who came from a variety of different socioeconomic backgrounds, racial and ethnic backgrounds, and were the victims of either completed or attempted rape. They saw those people in the hospital emergency room and contacted them afterward for follow-up, interviewed them over a period of several months and even beyond the year of the study. There has now been a five-year follow-up of that initial study group."

Q. "The results of that five-year follow-up have also been published, is that correct?"

A. "They have."

Q. "Go ahead."

A. "And on the basis of that experience of talking to many women who were representative of rape victims, coming from all walks of life, age, racial, ethnic, and socioeconomic background, they then attempted to describe their findings in terms of what the reactions were of that group."

Q. "Who were considered the other authorities in that area, if you are familiar with them, back in that period of time?"

A. "Well, there are a number of other people who have worked in the area of rape."

Q. "Particularly with the victim, and have identified symptoms similar to Burgess and Holmstrom's rape trauma syndrome?"

A. "There are other investigators, Sutherland and Sheryl, and Hayman and Lonza, and there is another extensive study that was done by Judith Becker, who is now at Columbia but was then, I believe, at Missouri.

"There are no others that I can recall immediately who were working in the area of victimization at that time. There are others who have subsequently worked in the area of victimization. Diana Russel in Oakland and Pauline Bart have just recently published a study in Chicago, University of Illinois. There has been fairly extensive research activity in other areas but mostly, I think, those are the major victimization studies."

Q. "In terms of the rape crisis centers that now have sprung up all over the United States, have they followed the methods, the original methods, of Burgess and Holmstrom in interviewing and aiding the rape victims, if you are familiar with these methods?"

A. "Yes. I am familiar with them. I think that Burgess and Holmstrom's methods were essentially designed to gather data as well as to be helpful to the victims, while, in a sense, the order in purpose is probably reversed when used by rape crisis centers, but the methods are similar.

"I think that the major point of treatment that is advocated by not only the rape crisis centers but all people who are knowledgeable in an attempt to provide victims with some social support is to make them understand what they can expect to happen in the days, weeks, and months following the rape."

Q. "In other words, what I am saying, Dr. Golden, is that, knowing what many, many others have experienced in the past, they can tell or explain to the victims who come to the rape crisis centers what types of symptoms and what types of behavior patterns they may experience, is that correct?"

A. "That is correct. I think it is a crucial concern that most people do not understand what it is like to be raped. There are a number of myths about what causes people to rape and what role victims may have in perhaps coming to be victims of rape. Those myths are not accurate. It is difficult for people who are the victims of rape to have to deal with other people who don't know what it is like. It is greatly beneficial to the victim to have the experience of working with other victims and professionals who do understand what it is like to be a victim of rape."

Q. "Now, I take it, then, that the development of this area is not something new, but rather it is just something newly researched?"

A. "That is correct."

I had now covered the basic method or state of the art of the field of study known as rape victimization. I next turned to the specific science from which the symptomatology had evolved.

Q. "Is there something specifically within the medical field of psychiatry to which the reactions of rape victims and their responses and behaviors can be directly related?"

A. "Yes, what is known as the rape trauma syndrome is really very much a part of a class of psychiatric disorders which are responses to traumatic events."

Q. "And this is classified as one of them, is that correct?"

A. "Yes, the trauma is of a sort which is generally perceived by people to be a particularly distressing, particularly severe, potentially life-threatening kind of trauma; this has been recognized in psychiatry over a relatively long period of time. For example, during World War I, it was referred to as 'war neurosis' or 'traumatic neurosis,' and the same kind of predictable psychological reactions occur in response to a variety of other events, such as to those who have survived earthquakes, fires, natural disasters, or automobile accidents in which people have died or have been badly injured, witnessed airplane crashes, been prisoners of war, and, most recently, rape victims. In other words, they have been experiences of violence and death."

Q. "In other words, all of these things that you have mentioned as being examples are instances of trauma which, potentially life-threatening or not, may be closely related to the death of someone else?"

A. "It may or may not be close to the death of someone else. The major point is, that the person who *experiences* the reaction *perceives* it as being a major, massive stress to their well-being or to their integrity, or perhaps to their life. They see it as potentially life-threatening, although it may not actually be."

Q. "Is there an accepted medical diagnosis for this particular area?"

A. "Yes, there is."

Q. "And what is it?"

A. "It is a traumatic stress reaction, and its official classification is the 'post-traumatic stress disorder.' "

Q. "Where is it recognized?"

A. "There is a publication every ten years by the American Psychiatric Association, which is the major professional psychiatric body in the United States, that is known as the Diagnostic and Statistical Manual of the American Psychiatric Association, known throughout the profession as the DSM. In January of this year, 1980, the most recent revision came out and it is officially known as the Diagnostic and Statistical

Manual Number 3, or DSM-3, and the post-traumatic stress disorder now officially recognizes as a subcategory of that diagnosis the rape trauma syndrome."

Q. "So this is the instrument that is used nationally by psychiatrists and psychologists when they are, say, writing reports, so that others, when they read them, will know when they use this particular term or that particular number, it is an accepted and known term or number in the field and that they can then look at this manual and understand the symptoms which have been described by the diagnosis?"

A. "Yes, it is certainly one of the major, if not the major system of diagnosing and categorizing psychiatric disorders. There are others, as well, such as an international classification of diseases, and so on, which is essentially parallel. They use somewhat different terminology, but they describe the same circumstances, the same diseases, and the same reactions."

Q. "Could you tell us, Doctor, could you explain to us, please, the post-traumatic stress disorder, how it manifests itself in the first place, in general terms, and then we will get into rape in particular."

A. "The syndrome is the sort of thing which may affect anyone. Obviously, if you are a person who is vulnerable to psychological stress or psychological disorders, then the same event may have a more profound effect on you who are more vulnerable than somebody else, but it is the sort of thing which could, conceivably, happen to anyone, and you do not have to be psychiatrically abnormal in order to experience it.

"Following the exposure to the initial event, perhaps something like being in a battle of war or being in an accident or in an earthquake or fire or being the victim of violence of one sort or another, there is an initial stage of disorganization that varies somewhat according to the individual. A person may tend to be very fearful, to be very apprehensive, not to be able to think, to feel upset and be emotional. That initial psychological disorganization may last for moments or hours or up to two or three weeks and even more. Sometimes it is manifested by a superficial kind of calm and composure, but underneath the people may be just as upset and distressed and frightened, and, obviously, stressed as is the first category.

"Following that initial period, then there is a second phase, somewhat like a gradual reorganization that may go on for months and in some cases even years. That is characterized by a more or less kind of superficial calm and return to what may have been the pre-existing psychological state, at least superficially; but people tend to be troubled by events which remind them in one way or another of the initial traumatic event or which occur more or less spontaneously. They frequently have reactions of fear, they are frightened by things that are reminiscent of events, so that they may, for example, be fearful about driving in an automobile if the original precipitating event was an automobile accident; if the experience was something that occurred outside in a particular area, they may be fearful of that area and avoid the area. They are commonly affected by disturbances in their sleeping patterns, they may be unable to get to sleep, or if they do get to sleep, they may awaken early and not be able to go back to sleep.

"Characteristic features that are common, but not always present, are disturbing dreams and nightmares that are either similar to the events or actually do depict events. People frequently do things to more or less guard themselves against exposure to the event. They will move away from an area, avoid certain activities or other things that may be, as I said earlier, reminiscent of the event, and if they are exposed to something that reminds them of the circumstance, they will very frequently then manifest more obviously the original reaction to some degree."

Q. "Okay, now let's talk particularly about the rape experience and how it fits in. Can you tell us how the rape trauma syndrome, if it does, has phases, how they are broken down, and if it is any different from or quite similar to the general symptoms of post-traumatic stress disorder?"

A. "It is really quite similar. In this instance, the experience of rape is the precipitating event, stress format, that is perceived by the victim as overwhelming and threatening."

Q. "Now is it perceived by victims, generally, as a life-threatening event?"

A. "Yes."

Q. "Although we know that in the vast majority of cases it doesn't end in death?"

A. "That is correct."

Q. "But in the vast majority of cases it is perceived as a life-threatening event?"

A. "That is correct."

Q. "Go on."

A. "The reactions tend to be, at least as described by Burgess and Holmstrom and certainly consistent with my experience, they tend to be of two general sorts in the immediate aftermath of the experience of rape. People are frightened, very apprehensive, fearful, frequently tearful, terribly upset. Victims characteristically, whether it is a rape or any other kind of post-traumatic stress, often feel guilty and ask themselves such questions as 'What have I done to deserve this?' 'Why did this happen to me?' They frequently will search through the events that have taken place to ask themselves whether they had done anything to contribute to it. This is particularly true in rape, because the attitudes of society are such that people often believe that anybody who is a victim of rape might tend somehow rather to have provoked it by their behavior, their attitudes, and the notion that women are somehow rather inclined to be seductive in the sense that they contribute to rape.

"They not infrequently will experience difficulties with eating and sleeping; some people are superficially calm, and characteristically people who are victims of rape are fearful of being in the neighborhood or in the area where the event has occurred and will not uncommonly move or make efforts to put locks on the doors or find some degree of protection for themselves, and very commonly and characteristically will seek out sources of emotional support. They will go visit their parents, frequently move away, if their parents are away, and will see them. That is the initial phase. The initial experiences of feeling defiled and violated and dirty are very characteristic of people who are victims of rape, and it tends for most rape victims to be a particular problem in the area of their sexual relating, because the context of a rape occurs in that domain, and so frequently any kind of sexual experience will be the sort of event which reminds them of the initial trauma. Women frequently have difficulty in being able to participate in sex, tending to feel at the time or in anticipation of that experience some of the same degree of anxiety and apprehension and depression and preoccupation which is associated with the original event."

Q. "Is there a second phase to the rape trauma syndrome?"

A. "Well, characteristically the second period, after the initial disorganizing phase, is one in which people frequently will attempt to behave as though everything is fine and, in essence, try to deal with the whole thing by pushing it out of their awareness. In that sense, they tend to deny to themselves that it existed, that it really happened, or that it was in any way significant to their lives. The persistence of these reactions, the tendency of these reactions, seems to be evoked by events that remind the person of the original trauma and is a situation that may persist over a long period of time, try as they might to deny its existence."

Q. "If they are reminded in some way over a long period of time, it will again evoke the same types of disorganization reactions?"

A. "Yes. Usually to a lesser degree."

Q. "Is there a natural cycle that would normally take place, if not reminded of the event over and over, which will allow the victim to work through this pattern over a period of time?"

A. "Yes, it is true that for most people, over more or less a predictable period of months or so, they gradually get over it."

Q. "Now, with rape in particular, has it been found that the event has a significance on its victims in terms of their work, job, or career orientation?"

A. "Well, I really wouldn't be able to say that it changes their careers all that often. I think that events of this sort frequently will lead people to change the way that they operate. I think that the establishment of rape crisis centers, which was motivated by and supported by women who themselves had been victims of rape, is one indication of the sort of thing that you are suggesting, that people who have suffered through that experience often become highly motivated to do something about it and to try to change the likelihood that other women will experience the same things."

Q. "That is what I was trying to ask, Doctor. Was that something you've just found with rape victims?"

A. "That it is quite common, yes, not in all rape victims, of course. I think most people still tend to respond to rape as a sort of embarrassment and shame at being a victim of rape, who is generally, in the minds of most people, someone who is looked upon as at fault and somehow or other embarrassed; there is a percentage, a smaller percentage certainly, of rape victims who very actively attempt to do something about it and to change the situation."

Q. "Might the decision to do something about it be activated more or less by the individual rape experience too? In other words, how the system and those around the victim have reacted?"

A. "That is certainly possible."

Q. "All right, Doctor, is there anything else in terms of the general nature of the rape trauma syndrome that we have not covered up to this point?"

A. "No, nothing I can think of at this moment."

Q. "You indicated that there had been a follow-up study, one done by Burgess and Holmstrom. Has there been anything found recently about symptoms over an extended period of time?"

A. "Yes, there has been. In particular, Burgess and Holmstrom noted what they have called an anniversary reaction. It is characteristic for a variety of psychologically stressful events, such as on the anniversary of when the trauma had occurred, that people will reexperience to some degree the feelings associated with the original event. It is very commonly seen in, let's say, the death of someone whom we have come to love and care for, or a parent, or a spouse, or whatever, and on the anniversary of that death they frequently experience again the same kinds of feelings. It is certainly characteristic of other psychological reactions as well which are stressing and stressful, including rape, which is what Burgess and Holmstrom found. A number of rapes have occurred to people that are not reported and are not acknowledged, and, obviously, if somebody has had the experience of rape or some other experience of a traumatic event, something which will evoke it again or be similar to the initial reaction can produce the reactivation of symptoms, and not be recognized as such because the victim has not reported previously."

Q. "That brings up another point, that failure to report. Now, in your work, do you look for certain types of things, even if, say, a woman comes to see you and she doesn't report she has been a rape victim, but are there characteristic things that you might look for to indicate to you that somewhere in that background there was a precipitating event about which you do not know but for which you need to look because the problems that the person presents do not seem to be explainable in the context of what she tells you is going on presently in her life?"

A. "Well, yes, I think there are certain things that one would look for that would suggest the possibility that rape had occurred, and those would be changes, specifically characteristic and dramatic changes, in some areas of behavior or attitudes that would be likely to be associated with rape. For example, if somebody had been doing quite well in an area and then at some point began to have difficulty, one would naturally reasonably wonder what happened at that period of time to bring about that change. If a particular patient presents certain psychosomatic symptoms—that means aches and pains—which I cannot explain in the context of what she's telling me presently, I would perhaps dig deeper and look for something more serious in her background to explain these symptoms."

I think I had covered the history and content of the rape trauma syndrome thoroughly enough. I noticed that the jurors, who had previously been paying rapt attention, were beginning to fidget. So I moved on to Jill in particular.

Q. "Now, Doctor, did you, at my request, examine a young lady by the name of Jill Bernadini?"

A. "Yes, I did."

Q. "Did I ask you particularly after the examination if you could render an opinion as to whether or not Ms. Bernadini suffered from the rape trauma syndrome?"

A. "Yes."

I noticed the jurors sit up and listen once more.

Q. "And did you, at the conclusion of your interview and examination, and after reviewing the materials I provided you, come to a conclusion, and can you render an opinion on that subject?"

A. "Yes, I did come to a conclusion and in my opinion her behavior was consistent with and characteristic of someone who has been the victim of rape."

Q. "Consistent with the rape trauma syndrome?"

A. "Yes."

Q. "Could you tell us, please, on what you base your findings?"

A. "Yes, I can. Initially, Ms. Bernadini presented herself as a pleasant, composed young woman who was straightforward and cooperative. We talked for an hour or so, generally about the circumstances of her present life, her past life, and then we moved on to the circumstances of the rape.

"At times, particularly in talking with her about the circumstances of the rape and in talking to her about some details of her past and present life after the rape, but particularly those that had to do with her attempts to establish sexual relationships with boyfriends that she had had, her attitude and her behavior changed, and she became obviously anxious and even tearful as we discussed the actual moments of the attack, and she had difficulty in speaking and was visibly upset."

Q. "At those times in particular?"

A. "At those times in particular and not at other times.

"In talking with her about the things that had happened to her after the time of the alleged rape and trying to make an assessment of how she had behaved and why she had behaved as she did, it seemed to me to be perfectly consistent with the kinds of psychological reactions which are associated with rape. For example, in the initial period following the alleged rape, she felt very overwhelmed, frightened, guilty, questioned herself with thoughts of what she had done to contribute to this difficulty, anticipated that people would judge her harshly and find her at fault because of what had occurred.

"She expressed a great fear of, and difficulty in, sleeping. She had no appetite and didn't eat anything for the first day or so after the alleged event. She made an effort to contact her family and went back, as many victims do, to visit the family and to be with them, seeking out emotional support. She did this with others as well. Others who were particularly close to her.

"Following the initial reaction, her behavior was to attempt to deny that anything was wrong and to go about her life pretty much in the sense that she had spent it before. This is evidenced by the psychological report that was prepared in conjunction with her application to become a police officer. She didn't have recurrent nightmares, but she claimed her sleep had been disturbed in a way that was not characteristic before the event, and that she had difficulty going to sleep and would awaken early. Frequently, she would awaken tearfully and crying without any recollection of what had gone on, and she also mentioned to me that it was not characteristic of her that she ever recalls or remembers the contents of dreams, so she did remember dreaming, but found it was very unusual or uncharacteristic for her to awaken from sleep crying.

"Particularly in the area of her sexual conduct, she had previously been normal sexually, that is, responsive and able to enjoy that aspect of relating to her partners. Following the alleged events of the rape, she found herself much more averse to the idea of engaging in sexual activity, and when she did, she was unable to respond generally, and up until a time close to when I saw her, she had avoided sexual contact altogether, although it was more than a year after the alleged rape had occurred."

Q. "And during that period of time, were you told that she had made a career choice that was somewhat different from the direction she had been taking?"

A. "Yes, I was told she had attempted to join the Police Department and had gone through the training and had begun to work as a police officer."

Q. "Did she tell you about that at the time you interviewed her?"

A. "We discussed it somewhat, not at great length."

Q. "Was she able to tell you why she wanted to be a police officer?"

A. "Not specifically or with any great conviction. She did say, in general terms, I believe—if I might refer to my notes—that her own experiences with the assault and its aftermath were so profoundly troubling that she formed a need to provide effective safety in the form of a police officer for others who might suffer in similar ways."

Q. "You discussed that?"

A. "Yes."

Q. "She expressed those thoughts to you?"

A. "Yes."

We then covered the effect of the long delay between the time of the rape and the actual trial date, emphasizing the consequences to recovery of repeated incident-related anxieties each time a subpoena was received. He told the jury that Jill's crisis in May 1980 had been compounded by the anniversary reaction, even though she did not realize it, and that her inability to handle the already stressed emotional buildup reached overload as the anniversary of the attack approached.

So far, so good. I made a check mark by each subject that we covered as we did it. Next on the list was the psychological examination done by the Police Department.

Q. "Now, Doctor, I believe you are aware that in September of 1979, Ms. Bernadini was attempting to enter the police academy, and that as part of the entrance requirement she underwent a psychological examination. Do you recall that?"

A. "Yes."

Q. "And you had an opportunity to review that psychological examination, is that correct?"

A. "Yes."

Q. "Is there anything in the psychological evaluation that aids you in the larger picture of rendering your opinion, that is, coming to a conclusion, that Ms. Bernadini suffered from the rape trauma syndrome?"

A. "Well, in the sense that her reaction, as I judge it, was one generally of trying to deny that it had had much of an effect upon her, yes."

Q. "Is that how you perceived it, in your professional opinion?"

A. "I'm not quite sure if you're asking that question in the affirmative or in the negative, but no, in my professional judgment, it indeed had a very significant effect on her, but I perceived that her effort was to deny that it was a meaningful thing. For example, she was advised on various occasions, as I understand it, to seek some help and some counseling from competent people and has, to the best of my knowledge, not done so. The report of the psychologist who saw her and the report of the psychological test that he asked her to take were consistent with somebody who is attempting to vigorously deny the presence of something which was at least suggested in the psychological testing to be distressing or bothering her."

Q. "Did you know that she had not told that particular person that she had been a rape victim, so that these symptoms were apparently coming through even though she hadn't told him?"

A. "Yes, I was aware she had not told him."

I now wanted to talk about subject areas in anticipation of defense issues before Fisher had a chance to cross-examine Jill.

Q. "Doctor, were you aware that Ms. Bernadini had been married to a person who had beaten her?"

A. "That is what she told me, yes."

Q. "Assuming that is so and that these beatings occurred some seven years ago, is there anything about these beatings or that particular portion of her life that suggests to you that the symptoms that she had had after May 10, 1979, were a result of those beatings or something that reminded her of the beatings?"

A. "Well, there is no indication that she was able to provide me in discussing her past history from the time of the beatings until the time of the alleged rape to suggest that she was experiencing the kinds of reactions before the rape that she has experienced since, so I would conclude that although the beatings that she described were distressing to her and that they had undoubtedly left some mark, they had not produced the kinds of symptoms that have occurred subsequent to the alleged rape."

Q. "Dr. Golden, you are aware, are you not, that Ms. Bernadini has had two abortions in the past?"

A. "Yes, I am."

Q. "And you are aware that one of those abortions occurred just before she left the man, her husband, the one who beat her in New York, and the other occurred here in California since she has lived in San Diego?"

A. "Yes, that is my understanding of the sequence."

Q. "Is there any significance to you, knowing these facts in this case?"

A. "Yes, I think that abortion ordinarily represents a fairly substantial and significant stress to women. I think it would represent such a stress to some extent to Ms. Bernadini, because although she was not raised in a religious home particularly, she was raised as a Catholic, and apparently her first abortion was not the profoundly disturbing one, but rather a second abortion, which she had experienced in California, that had caused a certain amount of distress. As she tells me, she did seek some counseling for that one."

Q. "In your opinion, do you feel that that particular event, something that occurred on the night of May 10, caused her, after whatever number of years it was, to exhibit all the symptoms that she has caused by either the first or the second abortion?"

A. "No."

Q. "Why?"

A. "Well, there is no record of her having similar symptoms at all following the first abortion, and although I'm not exactly aware of the circumstances or her condition at the time that she had the second abortion, she gave me no description of having experienced anything like the things she experienced following this alleged incident on May 10, 1979."

Q. "What about the fact that she did seek counseling at the time something was distressing her following the second abortion?"

A. "That would suggest that she felt much less guilty and ashamed, embarrassed, personally responsible for her reactions to the abortion than she may have felt toward the rape."

Q. "What I'm really asking, Doctor, is there anything at all that you found or that you now know that would suggest to you any other cause for the variety and number of symptoms that Ms. Bernadini exhibited from May 10 and thereafter, anything other than that of an event that occurred at that time, namely, the rape in her life?"

A. "Nothing that I found."

Q. "Or that you now know?"

A. "Or that I now know."

We took two hours to complete direct examination.

Mark Fisher's cross-examination was brief, but, as I had anticipated, better than in any of the previous cases. When it was again my turn for redirect, I went straight through the list of defense-perceived weaknesses which Mark Fisher had grilled Golden about.

Perhaps, the defense suggested, any number of other traumas in Jill's life could have produced the reactions the good doctor attributed to the rape. The first, of course, were the abortions. I touched on that issue only briefly since we had covered it so thoroughly in direct. A second area had been that Jill's symptoms were not rape-specific but could have been the result of any of a number of other stressful traumas or ones perceived as life-threatening.

Q. "In regard to one of the last questions that were asked of you by Mr. Fisher in terms of dealing with a particular trauma, do you find, when you interview rape victims, that there are certain significant things that are not associated with other types of life-threatening traumas, such as accidents, dismemberment, surgery, and so on, that they are more reluctant to talk about that particular type of trauma?"

A. "Yes, that certainly is true of rape. Somebody who has been the victim of an automobile accident is much more likely to be able to discuss that freely without feeling as though they were going to be judged harshly or without the likelihood that people will feel that they have done something wrong in particular to contribute to their being the victim of such an accident. In the case of rape, the attitudes generally tend to be that if rape occurs, the victim had probably done something to produce it, and victims, as representatives of the general society, tend to share those opinions."

Q. "After you were asked, in regard to the trauma of rape in general, if there is a continuum of reaction from either very little or none all the way to extremes of crying and inability to function to the blatantly psychotic, you said that somewhere in this wide spectrum one might tend to find the—I hate to say it—'average' rape victim? Is that correct?"

A. "That is correct."

Q. "Are there any specific things about a particular rape instance which might give you a clue and might affect where a rape victim will fall in that spectrum?"

A. "Well, it really does depend upon the individual and the rape. However, there are certain factors which can be considered important with regard to the rape itself which would tend to determine that. Factors such as the amount of force used, the brutality, threats of force and brutality, and the degree to which the person who was the victim of the rape was forced to do things which may be degrading to them, such as to perform certain sexual acts like orally copulating or being the victim of anal penetration or whatever."

Q. "Are you saying that those reactions or those events, those behaviors, affect the victim so as to make the rape more traumatic and the recovery more difficult?"

A. "The reaction of the victim is a more profound and severe reaction if there has been force used, or the threat of force has been used, or if they have been forced to do humiliating and degrading things."

Q. "And after you were asked several questions in regard to the psychological examination which was administered by the San Diego Police Department psychologist in conjunction with Ms. Bernadini's application to become a police officer, I believe that counsel asked you a question along the lines of: if the story of rape were not true and then several months later Ms. Bernadini had a psychological evaluation which showed that, for some reason, although not reported to the person doing the interview that she was a rape victim, she manifested symptoms of denial and repression, that it was not because she was raped but because she told a false story that she was raped?"

A. "No. Just telling someone else a false story, a lie, would not be likely to cause somebody to manifest repression and denial as symptomology in a subsequent psychological examination. The manifestation of repression and denial are probably typical of her general personality and would certainly be influenced by a wish to present herself in the most favorable possible light, which is a somewhat naïve way of presenting oneself, because people normally have some troubles in their lives."

Q. "In other words, what you are saying is that if she were calculating this particular event to be another step in the process of fabricating a good solid story of a false rape, she would have thought of being more sophisticated at this point in time as well, in the sense that she would have said there was something wrong with her and not have just been the good old American girl—I think is the way they put it—with no problems?"

A. "If she was as good a liar as that question suggests and had made her story a false story up to the point of the psychological examination, I certainly think she would have been able to carry it through the psychological examination as well."

The process of trying to pass information of such a complex nature to a lay jury, in such a way that they would understand it, had left me physically and mentally exhausted. I was not certain I had accomplished what I'd set out to do, but I felt reasonably sure that the jurors were still with me, since they were still listening.

I had continued to debate all the while I was putting on my case whether I should be brave enough to use the offender profile evidence. I figured at some point the right decision would come to me—and it did. As Joshua Golden was excused, I had no doubt an appellate court had more than enough material for some heavy review with only the rape trauma syndrome to consider. I wasn't going to make it easy for them to ignore this issue by providing them some alternative ones.

Try as I might, I knew I would be unable to complete my case before we were up against a week-long break caused by the annual legal and judicial state conferences. Judge Lusk was an officer and was obliged to attend, as he had informed us when we first started.

I had my suspicions that Mark Fisher planned his case to force a jury hiatus. In any event, when we reconvened two weekends and five days later, only one half day of testimony remained for the defense before the case was ready for argument to the jury. Such a hiatus is always bad, as it clearly causes the jury to peak far too soon.

I was about halfway through my closing argument when I suddenly and surely knew I was going to lose: the reason was juror number eight, sitting directly in front of me. There were several things which made me sure: how he shook or nodded his head as Fisher and I spoke, the timing of his note taking, little things I now sifted out from the past weeks having watched him sit in court. But above all I saw for the first time that he physically resembled Jeremy Cole. He had the same build —height and weight—and was good-looking and single.

"How *could* I have missed such a thing?" I lamented over and over while I waited for the jury to deliberate. "How? How? He's *got* to identify with the defendant. I mean, he probably has no idea what it feels like to be overpowered. How did I let it happen? He'll probably be the foreman."

And he was. And the jury hung ten-two for "guilty," the foreman being the only consistent "not guilty" vote throughout the deliberations, joined off and on by an indecisive woman who admitted she had trouble judging someone else's behavior (she, of course, denied this was a problem for her during the jury selection process, but that's what we need to be able to recognize in spite of them).

I was, of course, disappointed. I had wanted so much to take the case all the way to the California Supreme Court—and beyond if necessary. But I felt no sense of loss on the other hand. Quite the contrary, I felt wonderful, exhilarated at having convinced a judge and ten strangers beyond a reasonable doubt.

And what had this vote of confidence done for Jill?

"Ten people out there, who never knew me, believed me—that I wasn't lying. And you believed me, and Dr. Golden. I can never thank you enough. I really don't feel like we lost."

The jurors themselves were my greatest triumph. All ten who voted for "guilty" asked if they could appear at Jill's termination hearing to urge that she be given another chance as a police officer!

Despite our combined efforts, Jill was terminated from the San Diego Police Department for the reasons originally charged. She chose not to fight, perhaps realizing she had made the wrong choice, perhaps because it was time to move on. We stayed in touch for the next couple of years and her life slowly came back together. Then she moved back East and in 1983 was remarried.

And Jeremy Cole. The office would not permit a retrial, nor would I have forced one on Jill. All charges were dismissed against him and he left a free man to live among us.

As for me, well, the time had come to leave. During our week-long break I had been informed that, once finished with the case, I would be receiving a new assignment. I was being sent to El Cajon, an eastern suburb, there to try petty thefts, drunk driving, traffic tickets, and fish and game code violations.

Besides, there was no longer a doubt about the direction I was headed in the future. Sandy Adkins, Stacy Billings, Terri Richardson, and Jill Bernadini were only the tip of that proverbial iceberg. It would take some time to explain this to everyone who needed to know—probably a lifetime.

EPILOGUE

THERE HAS BEEN much activity surrounding the use of expert testimony and the rape trauma syndrome since 1980 within the legal profession—too much to cover here and quite enough for the next book.

A brief update, however, at this point would be helpful.

In civil cases, the use of expert testimony is receiving favorable results. In the spring of 1983 a Seattle victim was awarded several hundred thousand dollars using this theory, and filings nationwide for damages based on this type of evidence have increased markedly.

In criminal cases, the results have not been so good. Between 1980 and mid-1984, five states have heard the issue of expert testimony on rape trauma syndrome at the highest state level, usually the supreme court. Only one state, Kansas, has upheld its use. Four others—Minnesota, Missouri, Oregon, and most recently California—have banned it to victims and prosecutors.

Typical of the reasoning to deny evidence of the rape trauma syndrome in criminal prosecutions of consent defense rape, is that used by California Supreme Court Associate Justice Otto Kaus in his opinion on the case:

> Because the literature does not even purport to claim that the syndrome is a scientifically reliable means of proving that a rape occurred, we conclude that it may not be used for that purpose in a criminal trial.
>
> Unlike fingerprints, blood tests, lie-detector tests, voiceprints or the battered child syndrome, rape trauma syndrome was not devised to determine the "truth" or "accuracy" of the particular past event . . . [but] was developed by professional rape counselors as a therapeutic tool, to help identify, predict and treat emotional problems experienced by the counselors' clients or patients.
>
> . . . permitting a person in the role of an expert to suggest that because the complainant [victim] exhibits some of the symptoms of rape

trauma syndrome, the victim was therefore raped, unfairly prejudices the appellant [defendant] by creating an aura of special reliability and trustworthiness.

Such reasoning brings immediately to mind some puzzling questions. If information designed for one purpose has no place being used for another—in this case a diagnostic or therapeutic tool crossing the line into a courtroom—how can insanity, diminished capacity, or, more recently, the battered woman syndrome, be justified when introduced on behalf of a defendant who stands accused of a violent crime? Is our criminal justice system saying that "an aura of special reliability and trustworthiness" can be justified only when it is created for protection of the accused—but not when it would benefit victims? Is the credibility of one more important than the other in arriving at the truth?

In an interesting aside, the California Supreme Court did not reverse the conviction, saying once again the use of the testimony was "harmless error," since the prosecution case was so strong without the evidence that it was "not reasonably probable that the erroneous admission of the expert testimony affected the judgment."

We have, to paraphrase a great American poet, so much left to do— and miles to go before we sleep.

INDEX

72, 73, 100, 104, 105,
106, 140, 144, 159, 178,
200–3
Stack, Kelly (witness), 11, 97–
100, 104, 112, 116

Teenage victims, 321–22
Torture, 297
Trials
rules of, 25–26
scheduling of, 30–31
See also specific cases

Verdicts, 109–12, 130, 203–4,
349–50
Victims
abortions, 22, 66, 81, 86, 88,
346–47
activism by, 340–41
of anger rapes, 288–90
backgrounds of, 9–10, 121–22,
144, 251–53
and battered woman
syndrome, 315–18
birth control use, 18, 81
characteristic changes in, 341–
42
communication with
prosecutors, 133–35, 147–
48
consideration of rape prior to
attack, 17–18, 20, 82–83,
145
credibility of, 218
crisis of rape, 303–4
crying during trial, 8, 74–75,
77
depression in, 299

descriptions of, 3–4
elderly, 312–14
flirtatious mannerisms of, 254
friends, support from, 264–67
generalization by, 155–57,
166–67
hysteria after rape, 45–46
injuries to, 26, 91–92, 96–97,
141–42, 297
killing of offenders by, 314–15
lifestyles of, 61–66
medical examinations of, 96–
97, 142, 258, 288, 296
motivations in bringing
charges, 85–88
nightmares of, 91–92, 146
offenders, familiarity with, 80–
81, 134, 147–50, 253–54
physical appearance in court,
71
positive identification of
offender, 14–15, 44
of power rape, 291, 294–96
prosecutor's perspective of,
143
psychological examinations of,
320–21, 344–45
relationships of, 16–17, 142–
43, 146, 259, 260–62,
269–70, 271–75
reporting rapes, 238–43
repression and denial by, 348–
49
retrials, concerns re, 120–21
of sadistic rapes, 299
sexual dysfunction in, 261–64,
269, 271–75, 343–44
sexual habits of, 63–66

A WORD TO OUR READERS

More information on the long- and short-term effects of sexual assault on victims is desperately needed. Your help is valuable, whether or not you yourself have ever been a victim of such an attack.

Ms. Rowland is currently conducting a study of such effects, as well as on the effect of *The Ultimate Violation* on your life and experiences, and needs your help. Would you please send a card to the following address, giving us your name and address, so that we may send you a survey? All information on the survey will be held in complete confidence, and will be used only for research and educational purposes.

Please send your name and address to:

The California Center on Victimology
2441 "E" Street
San Diego, California 92102

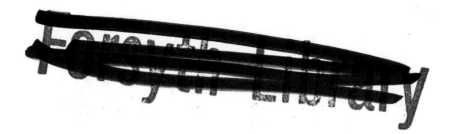